A Cultural History of Underdevelopment

NEW WORLD STUDIES

J. Michael Dash, *Editor*

Frank Moya Pons and
Sandra Pouchet Paquet,
Associate Editors

A Cultural History of Underdevelopment

LATIN AMERICA IN THE U.S. IMAGINATION

John Patrick Leary

University of Virginia Press

Charlottesville and London

ML | the
modern language
initiative

THIS BOOK IS MADE POSSIBLE BY A COLLABORATIVE GRANT FROM
THE ANDREW W. MELLON FOUNDATION.

University of Virginia Press
Printed in the United States of America on acid-free paper

First published 2016

9 8 7 6 5 4 3 2 1

Library of Congress Cataloging-in-Publication Data

Names: Leary, John Patrick, 1979– author.
Title: A cultural history of underdevelopment : Latin America in the
    U.S. imagination / John Patrick Leary.
Description: Charlottesville : University of Virginia Press, 2016. | Series:
    New world studies | Includes bibliographical references and index.
Identifiers: LCCN 2016002825 | ISBN 9780813939155 (cloth : alk. paper) |
    ISBN 9780813939162 (pbk. : alk. paper) | ISBN 9780813939179 (e-book)
Subjects: LCSH: United States—Relations—Latin America. | Latin
    America—Relations—United States. | Latin AmericaForeign public opinion,
    American—History. | Public opinion—United States—History.
Classification: LCC F1418 .L43 2016 | DDC 327.7308—dc23
LC record available at http://lccn.loc.gov/2016002825

Cover art: "Landing U.S. Marines in Cuba," *New York World,* May 15,
1898. (Courtesy of the David M. Rubenstein Rare Book & Manuscript
Library, Duke University)

Prospero, you are a great illusionist:
You know all about lies.
And you lied to me so much,
lied about the world, lied about yourself
that you have ended by imposing on me
an image of myself.
underdeveloped, in your words,
incompetent,
that's how you forced me to see myself.
And I hate that image! And it is false!
But now I know you, you old cancer,
and I also know myself!

—Aimé Césaire, Une Tempête (1968)

Contents

Illustrations

Acknowledgments

I AM IN the debt of many people whose labor, brilliance, and friendship have shaped this project. This book began in graduate school, where Ana Dopico was an inspiring teacher, a brilliant mentor, and a good friend. It was in her courses that I first encountered the critical histories of uneven development, dependency, and revolution that guide this book. Besides her fierce intelligence, her humor and generosity as a teacher and a critic have always stood out in a profession that rarely values these enough. When I first met Ana as a nervous prospective graduate student at NYU, she told me, warmly and reassuringly, "Well, it sounds like we'll have a lot to talk about." Happily, that has never ceased to be the case. Kristin Ross has pushed this book in new theoretical and geographic directions, and I have always been grateful for her spirit of solidarity, her humor, and her immense critical energy. Gerard Aching and Ada Ferrer have been rigorous and generous readers since this project was in its infancy, and I have found myself returning repeatedly to the lessons I learned (and many of the friends I learned them with) in Philip Brian Harper's seminar on Marxist literary theory.

I am grateful to many librarians and archivists who helped me during the years of primary research for this book, especially those at New York University's Bobst Library, the Detroit Public Library, the New York Public Library, the Duke University Library, the University of Chicago library, the University of Florida Library, and the American Antiquarian Society (AAS). The AAS granted a Petersen Fellowship for research on its Latin American collections, and I am thankful for the help of many brilliant people there, especially Andrew Borque, Ashley Cataldo, Paul Erickson, and Jaclyn Penny. Elizabeth Dunn and the David M. Rubenstein Rare Book & Manuscript Library at Duke University made available an unmatched treasure of "yellow press" newspapers in their original print form. A travel grant from the University of Florida's Latin American Studies Library facilitated research on the Cuba annexation movement. Finally, the American Council of Learned Societies supported this project with an Andrew Mellon Dissertation Completion Fellowship.

This book reflects the arguments, criticisms, and insights of many friends and colleagues at NYU, Wayne State University, and beyond. My thanks especially to many friends who have read and critiqued drafts of what eventually became this book: Diego Benegas Loyo, Kate Benward, Roosbelinda Cárdenas, Jennifer Cayer, Ipek Celik, Sarika Chandra, Maggie Clinton, Sasha Day, Jennifer Duffy, Jonathan Flatley, Nattie Golubov, Greg Grandin, Miles Grier, Rob Jansen, Walter Johnson, Bill Johnson González, Leigh Claire La Berge, Kathryne Lindberg, Aaron Love, Michael Palm, Hugo Pezzini, Elizabeth Reich, Naomi Schiller, Ramón Suárez, Quinn Slobodian, Smita Tripathi, and Dillon Vrana. Paul Kershaw and Tracy Neumann read many early drafts, and their critiques, encouragement, and friendship have been essential. The inimitable Jon Miller has been a great and inspiring friend during some difficult passages in and out of Detroit. Jordi Carbonell at Café con Leche in Southwest Detroit provided space, nourishment, and translation assistance. I am grateful to the anonymous readers whose feedback improved the book considerably. Finally, my deep thanks to Eric Brandt, Cathie Brettschneider, and Anna Kariel at the University of Virginia Press for all of their expertise and hard work.

Although I am often skeptical about some of the practices of solidarity I consider in this book, the desire for community and shared struggle across artificial boundaries, whether national, disciplinary, professional, or otherwise, is something very dear to me. It is through my own experience of this political desire, and with it my own misunderstandings and misplaced assumptions, that I became interested in Latin America in the first place. Solidarity was often on my mind as I began the work of this book, both as a research topic and a practice of being in the world and in the academy. In all these senses, I am particularly grateful to everyone who played a part in building the Graduate Student Organizing Committee and UAW Local 2110 over the years. Without them, graduate school would not have been possible nor nearly as rewarding.

Lara Langer Cohen was present at this project's inception and has believed in its worth when I often did not. The skepticism of her powerful intellect is matched by her capacious imagination and peerless generosity as a reader and critic. Her influence is on every page. I have learned more from my older brother Charley Leary than I am sure he realizes or would ever admit. As I followed his lead to Chicago, to New York, and then to academia, he has been a mentor, co-conspirator, and friend. Finally, this book is a product of all the debates that started around my parents' dinner table. Most of what I know about the power of ideas and argument I learned there from my mother, father, and brother, often (though I would still insist not always) in a losing effort. This is dedicated with gratitude to them.

I AM THANKFUL to the editors of the journals in which chapters 3 and 5 appeared in earlier form. Chapter 3 appeared as "America's Other Half: New York Slum Journalism and the War of 1898" in the *Journal of Transnational American Studies* 1 (2009), and chapter 5 appeared as "Havana Reads the Harlem Renaissance: Langston Hughes, Nicolás Guillén, and the Dialectics of Transnational American Literature" in *Comparative Literature Studies* 47 (2010).

All translations, unless otherwise noted, are my own.

A Cultural History of Underdevelopment

Introduction

Latin America and the Meanings of "Underdevelopment" in the United States

The country that is more developed industrially only shows the less developed [*entwickelten*] the image of its own future.

—Karl Marx, *Capital*

The power and authority wielded by macropolitics are not lodged in abstract institutions but in their management of meanings, their construction of social categories, and their microsites of rule.

—Ann Laura Stoler, "Tense and Tender Ties:
The Politics of Comparison in North American
History and (Post) Colonial Studies"

Mr. Polly felt himself the faintest underdeveloped simulacrum of man that had ever hovered on the verge of non-existence.

—H. G. Wells, *The History of Mr. Polly*

THE DANGER of falling behind has haunted the United States at every stage of its existence: in a country that belongs so self-consciously to the future, the fight against national obsolescence is one of the enduring conflicts of U.S. cultural politics. Long before the emergence in the mid-twentieth century of the "third world" as a political category, many in the United States sought to distinguish their republic's uniqueness in temporal and cultural terms from the nations around it. The United States was "advanced" when others were "backward," had subdued a wilderness that triumphed elsewhere, became modern when others languished in "tradition," and by the middle of the twentieth century, had "developed" itself while others stagnated in a condition that came to be called "underdevelopment."

"Underdevelopment," of course, is a concept that most readers will associate with the Cold War–era social sciences. I will show, however, that it is also, even primarily, a cultural category that helps us understand the history of American exceptionalism, the conviction that the United States belongs, alone, to the future. Development discourse has been shaped by so many global precursors—anticolonial struggles in Asia and Africa, these countries' postcolonial relations with the former European imperial powers and with the United States and U.S.S.R., and so on—that it would be fruitless to make a claim for any one region or culture's exceptional primacy over all others in the history of underdevelopment. What a broadly hemispheric Americanist perspective on underdevelopment and its nineteenth-century genealogy shows, however, is how imbricated it has been in the tangled history of the United States in Latin America, which has always been marked both by a claim of shared origins by the hemisphere's revolutionary republics, on the one hand, and by an Anglo-American assertion of imperial power and providential leadership, on the other. This complex history of mutual recognition belies the cultural hierarchies and national time scales assumed, and often made explicit, in historical uses of the term "underdeveloped." In this book, I argue that what came to be called Latin American "underdevelopment" is best understood as the ideological projection abroad of the United States' own internal uneven development. Because U.S. intellectuals could only define it in comparative terms, the Latin American condition of underdevelopment was inevitably a reflection of the United States' spatial and political inequalities, from the sprawling urban slums of the coasts to the rural poverty in the south and west. Viewed comparatively and ideologically, underdevelopment is an ideology that alleviates American fears of falling behind.

Why is Latin America especially important to this history of U.S. modernity? At a general level, a hemispheric approach centers what Aníbal Quijano and Immanuel Wallerstein call "Americanity," the historical importance of the "New World" in shaping the categories that would come to mark difference in the "modern" world: coloniality, ethnicity, race, even "the concept of newness itself."[1] In the case of the United States, the answer has to do with the complexities of "empire" in U.S. history and culture. As American exceptionalism assumes its modern forms, it emerges from what Greg Grandin has described as an ideological contest with Latin America, one which distinguishes inter-American relations from the north-south conflict between Europe and its African and Asian colonies. Iberian America was not an "an epistemic 'other,'" writes Grandin, but a competitor in the fight to define republicanism, democracy, and "above all the very idea of America."[2] Indeed, it was John O'Sullivan, an ardent Cuba annexationist, who coined the phrase "manifest destiny" and called the United States the "great nation of futurity" to agitate for war with Mexico. Yet his notion of the United States' futurity reflected a complex nationalism that defined itself both with and against Latin American examples, simultaneously embracing and disavowing the hemispheric meaning of "America." Mexico, in his view, was racially incompatible with the United States and a vestige of the "Old World" persisting in the New. By contrast, O'Sullivan saw Cuba as a white, Christian country, a natural and necessary part of the United States' modern future. These contradictory discourses of difference and desire have produced a durable fiction of Latin America as either an incorrigibly backwards other or as an aspirant, but not yet arrived, partner. Latin America has been a good neighbor and a revolutionary threat, an image of the possible future and a relic of the superseded past. Rather than a straightforwardly foreign or exotic specter, as some scholars have suggested, Latin America in the U.S. imagination has been a kind of vanity mirror, with its best features in flattering reflection, but also a place where U.S. writers have seen their own country staring back at them.[3]

This paradox is the ironic product of the "singular intimacy" of the nations of the Americas. I take this term from William McKinley, who used it to describe the United States' relationship with Cuba after the U.S. invasion and occupation of the island in 1898. "The new Cuba yet to arise from the ashes of the past," he said, "must needs be bound to us by ties of singular intimacy and strength if its enduring welfare is to be assured."[4] It is important to take McKinley seriously here, even though his defense of the U.S. invasion as a "humanitarian" crusade has been convincingly debunked by generations of Cuban and U.S. scholars. He echoed U.S. politicians, travel writers, businessmen, and landowners who saw in Cuba a "primitive" or Edenic country, as well as others who observed that its economy and infrastructure resembled and in some cases surpassed that of much of the United States. These shifts resemble the swings of a pendulum, in which Cuba, in a pattern repeated elsewhere in Latin America, moves from confederate to adversary and back again. This book examines the complex terrain of U.S.–Latin American cultural relations, in which enmity joins hands with imitation, divergence with resemblance, and comparison with competition. The result is a combination of imperialist condescension and sympathetic collaboration, of fear and solidarity, of the colonial "backwardness" that writes the global South out of conscious history, and the postwar promise of a global modernity that would erase that "backwardness" from our maps and from our vocabularies. Besides the proximity of Latin America and the contingent nature of inter-American borders, "intimacy" can refer to an affective relationship, of contempt or of love, of resentment and hostility, and of political and personal longings.[5] In an argument about the unrecognized contributions of Caribbean intellectuals in U.S. culture, Jeff Karem borrows an evocative metaphor from Edgar Allan Poe to describe "purloined" islands, "appropriated and nationalized by U.S. culture, hidden in plain sight."[6] The combination of obscurity and disclosure that Karem points to means that the cultural politics of inter-American "intimacy" must be seen as the product, not just of political dominance and xenophobic aggression, but of anxious, often panicked competition. "Intimacy," as I use the term, reflects this dynamic of proximity and unfamiliarity, celebration and exploitation, affection and contempt, that has characterized the United States' ideological contest with Latin America. What this means is that the U.S. fantasy of exceptional development is an expression, not of security from one's peripheries, but of the periphery's constant, intimate presence.[7]

Before proceeding, a clarification of terms: following the geographer Neil Smith's usage, I use "uneven development" in this book to refer to a *process* of reproducing inequality under capitalism within and between regions, cities, and nations. "Underdevelopment," by contrast, is the inequality produced at whatever scale—most often the nation—by this process of capitalist uneven development.[8] Development and underdevelopment are also ideological categories whose political force has come from their marshaling of nationalism and the seemingly apolitical force of *techne*. As for geographical terminology: when describing a person or idea originating from the United States, I prefer when syntactically possible to use the adjectival "U.S," in light of the contested meanings of "América" and "America," especially during the period under consideration here.

A Brief Semantic History of Underdevelopment

The debt owed by "development" and "underdevelopment" to biological notions of organic growth and idealist models of historical progress, with their origins in the nineteenth century, helps explain the terms' obstinate necessity and seeming naturalness. The intellectual historian Robert Nisbet complained in 1969 about development's epistemological debt to biological metaphors that project onto a society the life-cycle of an organism.[9] And it is hard for a writer to avoid using "development" to describe any process that takes place over time. What other word seems so naturally suited to describe the "growth" of an idea, the "transformation" of an institution, the "evolution" of a writer's work, or any generally positive change that takes place over a measurable period of time?

When I ask undergraduate students, most of whom were born in the mid-1990s, to define "underdevelopment," a word whose use peaked in the Cold War, they recognize it instantly, with unusual consistency. Whether they are sitting in an underfunded public university in the center of one of America's poorest cities or a pastoral private campus in a wealthy eastern suburb, they invariably define "underdevelopment" by referring to late-night infomercials for NGOs like Save the Children: the ads that solicit, for "just pennies a day," the sympathy of a northern insomniac for some unfortunate child elsewhere. The appeal comes from an older white man in a tropical shantytown on behalf of a child of color. ("He's always got a beard! *Always,*" said one student of mine, emphatically, observing the same biological metaphor of growth and maturity that Nisbet noted.)

The most common modern meaning of "underdevelopment" comes, of course, from international economics, where it has been used to describe material deprivation on a global scale. Most scholars date this usage to a 1942 article by a British economist, Wilfrid Benson. Benson's piece, "The Economic Advancement of Under-developed Areas," was included in the proceedings of a colonial planning meeting devoted, as he put it, to the "development of 'backward' areas.'" We can see "underdevelopment's" geographic specificity: its use, in the so-called first world, for clearly defined "areas" abroad, either colonial territories and, later, nations. Benson used "under-developed" to argue for a more robust version of colonial trusteeship. The "poverty" of "under-developed areas," he wrote, "was not only relative to Western European or North American standards of decency: it was absolute as a negation of the material standards which, rightly or wrongly, our civilization regards as a minimum for strength of the body or health of the soul."[10] His conflation of the two terms "underdeveloped" and "backward" shows the two siblings' common parentage and their slow estrangement.

In his 1957 book *Rich Lands and Poor: The Road to World Prosperity,* the diplomat and author Gunnar Myrdal was careful to distinguish "underdeveloped" from the "'the backward countries,'" which it replaced. "We have all come to refer to this majority of very poor countries as 'the underdeveloped countries,'" Myrdal wrote.[11] "Backward" implies cultural stagnation, he argued, while "underdevelopment" is dynamic and thus comparatively egalitarian, foregrounding a capacity for change appropriate to the age of decolonization. Yet both imply a hierarchy, with an implied temporal progression of "backward" to "advanced" and a spatial progression of "under" and "above." The direction of "advancement" is onward in time, upward in space to the United States and Western

Europe, and outward in economic growth. For these reasons, many readers might now have a harder time seeing the significant difference that Myrdal does between the two terms. Indeed, "underdeveloped" is now often replaced in professional literature and foreign-policy journalism by the unbounded gerundive construction "developing," which emphasizes the dynamism that Myrdal liked in "underdevelopment" without specifying the direction in which a country is "developing." "Underdevelopment" has experienced a steady, gradual decline since a high point in 1982, according to Google's Ngram database, which tracks the appearance of terms in books archived in the company's archive of scanned texts. Yet it has never disappeared. Professional economists who focus on global poverty and the third world still use it, as we shall see. On the right, it is still regularly invoked to describe a nation or a region's cultural or environmental resistance to progress, lending a scientific sheen to cultural and racial generalizations. And on the left, "underdevelopment" was retained precisely to underscore the intractable global inequality that its use by Myrdal aimed optimistically to overcome.[12] What has been mostly consistent is the seemingly obvious meaning the word's syntax suggests: underdevelopment is the absence of development. Marxist dependency theorists in the 1960s and 1970s took aim at this formulation by framing "underdevelopment" not as a lack of capitalist development, but as its logical product; underdevelopment separated the global "core" from the "periphery" and transferred the wealth of the latter to the former. The Guyanese historian Walter Rodney argued in *How Europe Underdeveloped Africa* that underdevelopment was not a preliminary stage of capitalist modernity, but the consequence of global patterns of capital accumulation whose origins lay in colonial resource extraction. The resultant poverty was a consequence, in Andre Gunder Frank's memorable phrase, of "the development of underdevelopment."[13] Despite the shortcomings that its critics have criticized in dependency theory—its generalizations, its assumption of the integrity and development of the "core" nations—*dependentistas* raised two central questions: Are "develop" and the neologistic "underdevelop" transitive or intransitive verbs? Consequently, is underdevelopment a historical process or a political practice?[14]

The economic historian H. W. Arndt offers an etymology of development that runs from Marx's use of the term to the twentieth-century Austrian economist Joseph Schumpeter and the British colonial officer Lord Milner, the last of whom urged that "the economic resources of the Empire should be developed to the utmost." For Marx and for Schumpeter, economic development was "a historical process," Arndt writes, the consequence of a nation's productive capacities, rather than the will of an individual or a bureaucracy. For Milner and other colonial policy-makers, by contrast, development was an activity pursued by governments. Arndt summarizes the profound shift encoded in these changes of syntax: "In Marx's sense, it is a society or an economic system that 'develops'; in Milner's sense, it is natural resources that are 'developed.' Economic development in Marx's sense derives from the intransitive verb, in Milner's sense from the transitive verb." This critical contradiction comes to a head in the postcolonial era, where the transitive exploitation of natural resources (as in "to develop Venezuela's oil fields") must be linked to the intransitive improvement of a people's welfare (that is, "the development of Honduras' secondary education system"). These are understood in the colonial era as separate questions: development is a strictly transitive economic concern, while "welfare" refers to the intransitive improvement of the living standards of the "natives."[15] As Benson's article shows, early postwar uses of "underdevelopment" only begin to trouble this economic and social distinction. Gradually, the transitive exploitation of the economic resources of a country comes to be seen as an impetus for the intransitive "development" of its people's welfare. The latter kind of "development" can be "developed," a tautology that underscores the concept's imprecise meanings, its air of historical destiny, and thus its inescapable ideological power—it is a tautological circle from which there is no escape, and it is also the direction in which we are all inexorably moving.

While Benson is credited with coining "underdevelopment," Harry Truman popularized it in his 1949 inaugural address. Truman called in that speech for "a bold new program for making the benefits of our scientific advances and industrial progress available for the improvement and growth of underdeveloped areas."[16] As María Josefina Saldaña Portillo has argued, Truman's appeal relied on both the transformative possibilities of science and the desire on the part of the underdeveloped to be improved. "We are aided," the president declared, "by all who desire self-government and a voice in deciding their own affairs." Technical changes implied cultural ones, however. In fact, they required them. The best-selling policy intellectual and popularizer of midcentury modernization theory, Walter Rostow, explained development as a measurable process of transformation to modernity from the "traditional society," which he defined by the "pre-Newtonian" persistence of superstition, rural modes of production, and stasis. His 1960 bestseller, *The Stages of Economic Growth: A Non-Communist Manifesto,* reframed a Marxian model of historical stages as a liberal capitalist thesis of progress toward modernity.[17] This historical movement requires a transformation of what Rostow calls a people's "effective attitudes": a society must adjust its attitudes "toward fundamental and applied science; toward the initiation of change in productive technique; and toward the taking of risk; and toward the conditions and methods of work."[18] Rostow's metaphor for the moment when a society moves from traditional to modern society was the "take-off," a term that captures both the progressive certainty of his theory and the technological utopianism of the space age. The metaphor is an ambiguous combination of the transitive and intransitive meanings of "develop": on the one hand, "taking off" can be considered a conscious choice, the result of the deliberative decisions Rostow thought underdeveloped societies must make. On the other, it is a historical transformation, a stage societies reach in the course of history. And as Molly Geidel has observed about a different Rostow text, for all his economic training and apparent empiricism, development for Rostow was a cultural practice. It was, Geidel writes, "a foreign policy imaginary whose central goal is emotional and psychological transformation."[19] Rostow and Truman introduce what Saldaña Portillo calls "the desiring subject of development" that emerges from the contradiction between the ideal of capitalist modernization and the civilizational discourse of colonialism. The third-world subject (in the sovereign sense of this word), still needing the "improvement" of the West, is now a free subject (in the grammatical sense) who chooses his own improvement.[20] Marking as it does a shift in the agency ascribed to postcolonial peoples, this is a significant change, even if it is a discursive one—one reason to doubt some development critics on the left, like Gilbert Rist, who argue that the age of development is merely a postcolonial mirage offering an "illusion of change" that recapitulates the earlier imperialism.[21] The deracialization of cultural difference changed the "othering" of the global South, mostly doing away with the language of "advancement" and "backwardness." No longer condemned by cultural inferiority or their languorous climate, the peoples of underdeveloped areas could now be identified as late arrivals to a worldly pageant, rather than "primitives" written off the invitation list altogether.

At stake in the syntax of the verbs "to develop" and "to underdevelop" are three main questions: *agency,* or who is doing the developing or, as Rodney saw it, the "underdeveloping"; *direction,* or where the developing is headed; and *national differentiation,* how this work of developing distinguishes the United States, which was for Rostow and others the implied endpoint of the process. The regular conflation of development's transitive and intransitive meanings—as economic investment (or for critics on the left, exploitation), on the one hand, and as improvement of the general welfare, on the other—makes it difficult to answer the first two questions, as Cowen and Shenton argue. They point to a deeper tautology in the use of the concept, in which development as a process is regularly confused with development as the end point of the process—a nation undergoes development in order to achieve development.[22] James Ferguson also notes the word's common, careless usage as both a historical process of industrialization, on the one hand, and a moral imperative to reduce misery, on the other, goals clearly not identical or even necessarily compatible.[23]

In U.S. popular media, the term "underdeveloped" is most often used to refer to unfriendly foreign powers like China or Venezuela, summoning the Manichean comforts of the Cold War and the iconography or style of the anticolonial third world (the government of Hugo Chávez, for example, with his long speeches, anti-imperialist rhetoric, and occasional military dress, often earned the sobriquet).[24] Yet its power as a concept that expresses national difference is most clear, ironically, on the rare occasions when it is applied to U.S. citizens. In the best known recent example, "underdeveloped"—and associated terms like "third world" and "refugee"—was used to describe the devastated city of New Orleans and its displaced, mostly African American residents after Hurricane Katrina. In one televised report, CBS reporter Nancy Giles exclaimed, "We have American citizens, not refugees from an underdeveloped country, waiting for food, water, shelter and electricity for four, five, six days."[25] Giles's comparison denounces the effectively second-class U.S. citizenship of the mostly Black Louisianans suffering these hardships. Yet this comparison also implies another: the U.S. government was treating its citizens with an indignity usually reserved for foreigners. The controversy that resulted from these comparisons of the Gulf Coast and the "underdeveloped" world proved that while the United States may possibly be unevenly developed, the weight of the term "underdeveloped"—its temporal and cultural meanings, its colonialist genealogy—falls on the global South and the racialized populations identified with it.

Underdevelopment's project of national differentiation is internally contradictory and deeply dysfunctional at the level of meaning. The concept's susceptibility to tautology, interpretive circles that bind their object, suggests that it is more successful as an ideological framework than an empirical description. In any case, "development" and "underdevelopment" are terms deeply resistant to anything we might call "clarity." (That they are syntactically dysfunctional does not mean, of course, that they are not symbolically functional.) As the sociologist Dean Tipps wrote in a 1973 account of "modernization," imprecision has always been part of its appeal. While "modernization" may have its own rigor, he writes, its popularity and communicability, both within and outside the scholarly and policy precincts where it has circulated, has to do with more insubstantial and inchoate meanings, longings, fears, and resentments attached to it.[26] Underdevelopment, modernization's object and its opposite, does something similar: it mobilizes what Hsuan Hsu calls "spatial feelings": sentiments like nostalgia, patriotism, or love that ground people's experiences and attachments to home and the globe. Hsu argues that spatial scales index our subjective impressions, longings, fantasies, and feelings about the world we inhabit, and how the nation, region, or city we know and love (or hate, as the case may often be) fits into that wider world.[27] Our modern terms, "development" and "underdevelopment," are as imprecise as what Hsu calls "longings"; in this respect they are like the other, more archaic terms by which those of us in the "first world" have understood the lands outside "our" borders.

"Like civilization in the nineteenth century," Ferguson writes, development is the name for an "interpretive grid through which the impoverished regions of the world are known to us."[28] Development organizes our frames of international geographical reference. Ferguson's argument gives development a colonial ancestry, but his term also shows the combination of the subjective, interpretive faculty of seeing underdevelopment and the modern pretense to geographical and technical precision in measuring it that are both involved in its use. His case study is the development apparatus in Lesotho, but U.S. thinkers have long conceptualized their nation's relationship to the rest of the Americas, and consequently its own privileged modernity, through this interpretive grid and its colonial antecedents. Given their elusive incoherence, this book does not aspire to a more satisfying definition of what development and underdevelopment mean, since their use varies so much even among those who think they mean anything. Rather, accepting their dysfunctional imprecision and tautological circularity as part of their power, I will concentrate on what these terms have done.

Marking Time and Making Space in Underdevelopment's *Longue Durée*

While the structures of capital that drive economic development have always been global, we speak of development and underdevelopment, rather improbably, as national traits—there are "developed" countries and "underdeveloped" ones, and the latter aspires to become the former. The adjective "underdeveloped" is rarely used for anything but national and international categories: rare is the "underdeveloped" city, state, or province, a consequence of development studies' nation-based administrative and research apparatuses and historically Eurocentric approach.[29] The United States, in spite of its inequality and stark regional disparities, is a "developed" nation, all the way from west Baltimore to the Arizona borderlands. In addition to its national framework, the word "development" plots difference along a historical trajectory. As such, it is wedded to nineteenth-century notions of time as linear and progressive, and to geographical space as a metaphor for the inexorable movement of history.[30]

Latin America has played a foundational role in defining, for Anglo-Americans, these twinned notions of historical progress and decline from which the national fantasy of U.S. development derives. Even those without firsthand experience of Hegel's "geographical basis of history," as Kerwin Klein argues, adopted a sense of history in North America as the inevitable realization of a destiny written in the topography of the continent.[31] It is a familiar convention of Anglo-American writing on Latin America to identify it with the past, either with antiquity or with supposedly vestigial forms of social and political life surpassed in the United States: the repression of women, plantation slavery, indigeneity, and Catholic "superstition." Eliot Durand put it bluntly in his 1891 travel narrative, *A Week in Cuba:* "Everything is done backward in Cuba, from an American standpoint."[32] In 1888, William McElroy Curtis, a former diplomat in Mexico, made the point with a gruesome metaphor: "It wounds the pride of the Yankee tourist," he lamented, "to discover that so little of our boasted influence has lapped over the border, and that the historic halls of the Montezumas are only spattered with the modern ideas we exemplify." Imagining U.S. influence as fluid and implicitly modernizing, Curtis is disappointed by its thin coverage of Mexico: "lapping" over the border and merely "spattered" in the capital, it hardly seems worth the cost of the American blood spilled there in 1848. "Besides the most novel and recent product of modern science," says Curtis, "one finds in use the crudest, rudest implement of antiquity. Types of four centuries can be seen in a single group in any of the plazas."[33] Signs of uneven development are treated as persistent remnants of the past, rather than constitutive parts of the present.

This treatment of Latin America as an anachronism has proven durable in the twentieth and twenty-first centuries. The reframing of the retrograde as revivifying can take surprising forms. As Ana Dopico has argued, Wim

Wenders's 1999 documentary about post-Soviet Cuba, *Buena Vista Social Club,* fashions an anachronistic Cuba out of the island's post-Soviet landscape. In Havana, the ruins of one progressive social project (socialism) are reconfigured as the nostalgic, Technicolor kitsch of that project's erstwhile enemy.[34] Beyond the literature of cultural tourism, "underdevelopment" persists in economic and political literature as a deracialized marker of national belatedness. Witness the recent flood of popular economic-history books with titles like *The Wealth and Poverty of Nations: Why Some Are So Rich and Some So Poor; Collapse: How Societies Choose to Fail or Succeed; The Mystery of Capital: Why Capitalism Triumphs in the West and Fails Everywhere Else; The Bottom Billion: Why the Poorest Countries Are Failing and What Can Be Done About It;* and Daron Acemoglu and James A. Robinson's best-selling *Why Nations Fail: The Origins of Power, Prosperity, and Poverty.* These books are described (without apparent irony) by the *Economist* as the "'how to help the world's poorest' genre," an implicit if unwitting acknowledgment that, despite the grandiose ambitions displayed by these titles, the genre's reproduction of itself may be its most lasting accomplishment.[35] These glibly declarative titles promise answers to an ancient, intractable question scaled to global proportions: Shall the "poor nations," like "the poor" in general, always be with us? Acemoglu and Robinson frame their *Why Nations Fail,* one of the most successful of the genre, with a comparison between the border towns of Nogales, Sonora, and Nogales, Arizona. Writing of an Arizona city in which 30 percent of the population lives below the U.S. federal poverty line—a fact they omit—the authors write that residents there "can go about their daily activities without fear for life and safety and not constantly afraid of theft, expropriation, or other things that might jeopardize their investments in their businesses and houses." (Perhaps there's not enough left to expropriate?) Economic security is a function, moreover, of political security: "Democracy is second nature to them," the authors conclude about these residents of a country whose national voter participation runs roughly equivalent to Mexico's in an average national election year.[36] Denied the privileges of political and economic security, Mexican Nogaleses, the authors conclude, "live in a different world shaped by different institutions."[37] For Acemoglu and Robinson, the geography of underdevelopment is defined by such clear spatial and temporal breaks—breaks manifested, to be sure, not by cultural deficits, but technical, "institutional" ones.

    Underdevelopment here is what Arturo Escobar, borrowing Edward Said's term, calls an "imaginative geography": a means of delimiting the space that is "ours" from that which is "theirs," and relatedly, of producing forms of knowledge that enforce the relations between the one and the other.[38] Acemoglu and Robinson's argument rests on the absurd premise that the Arizona borderlands are a place of clearly demarcated difference between two nations, rather than exactly the opposite, as cultural theorists from the Latino studies and postcolonial traditions have long argued. At the "center of the periphery," as José David Saldívar has called the U.S.-Mexico borderlands, the macroconflict between the U.S. "core" and Latin "periphery" is a dialectical, not a static contradiction, one that creates more centers within those peripheral spaces, and multiplies peripheral spaces within those imperial centers.[39] Saldívar presumes that since capitalism reproduces itself unevenly, underdevelopment is not a national condition but rather a local circumstance that reproduces itself within and across the borders of North and Latin America. In Acemoglu and Robinson's model of the two Nogaleses, by contrast, the lines marking the "imaginative geography" of underdevelopment are clear. Thus, the residents of Nogales, Sonora, can be thought to live "in another world," spatially proximate but culturally and institutionally remote from their Arizona neighbors.

Acemoglu and Robinson's conclusions reveal less about Nogales, Mexico, as it is, and more about the industrialized, democratic, rationally organized place they imagine Nogales, Arizona, and therefore the United States, to be. In this respect, they work in a long tradition of imagining development as a mirror of American self-regard. As scholars like Escobar, Alyosha Goldstein, Saldaña-Portillo, and Saldívar, among others, have pointed out, the changes promised by modernization held out the possibility of a universal equality while still reasoning from the provincial perspective of the United States: the world of the future looked a lot like the America of the moment. "Modernization is even because it holds within itself a theory of spatial and temporal convergence," writes Kristin Ross: "all societies will come to look like us, all will arrive eventually at the same stage or level, all the possibilities of the future are being lived now, at least for the West: there they are, arrayed before us, a changeless world functioning smoothly under the sign of technique."[40] "Technique," not politics, is the engine of transformation. According to Nils Gilman, "development" in the United States did not outline a historical process so much as it captured a conviction and a desire that the social, cultural, and economic aspects of the premodern could be transformed by technical means. The postwar school of liberal social scientific thought known as modernization theory, he writes, was intellectually committed to the division of the world between "traditional" and "modern" societies, as well as the possibility of transforming the one into the other. To be modern meant to possess an industrialized, democratic, egalitarian capitalist welfare state, which was governed by a technocratic elite responsible for up-to-date infrastructural, agricultural, and communications technologies. Modernity defined in this fashion carried an implicit irony: it was placeless and universal, yet it was also, Gilman argues, an "abstract version of what postwar U.S. liberals wished their country to be."[41]

Given the durability of underdevelopment's imaginative geography, it can therefore be surprising to find that a reason Latin America became a useful laboratory for studying third world underdevelopment was not because it was emphatically different, but because it was not. In her history of the academic discipline of Latin American studies in the United States, Helen Delpar argues that it was the political exigencies of the Cold War that reframed Latin America as "non-Western," repudiating a longer legacy of Pan-American unity that had claimed a shared history for North and South America.[42] Goldstein's account of Peace Corps training in impoverished communities in the United States is a fascinating example of Delpar's broader point. As Goldstein explains, the Corps was a project of cultural diplomacy that formed one part of John F. Kennedy's Alliance for Progress, the developmentalist initiative begun in 1961 to counter the socialist example of development offered by revolutionary Cuba. To train some of the first Peace Corps volunteers, the program focused on what it called "culture shock," a term that referred as much to language and mores as to poverty itself. As Goldstein explains, by the early 1960s, poverty was what made Latin America "foreign." Yet the training sites for acclimating to this foreign condition were domestic: southern New Mexico and Latino Manhattan. In Goldstein's account, the Corps' training program constructed an underdeveloped Other, the recipient of U.S. aid, sympathy, and expertise, who was at once dramatically foreign yet uncannily familiar. New Mexico was chosen for what its governor called "its islands of primitive peoples and underdeveloped communities," with an indigenous population that would apparently help acclimate volunteers bound for Central American and Andean countries. Meanwhile, trainees bound for a more urbanized Colombia were sent to the Puerto Rican neighborhoods of Spanish Harlem and Chelsea in New York City.[43] The author of a *New York Times* report on the New York training sessions sheepishly acknowledged that it was "somewhat ironic" that "the world's richest city . . . has become a laboratory and classroom for these students of deprivation and backwardness" (note the persistence of the latter term). Yet it was the availability of "foreign" poverty at home that would make possible its alleviation abroad through the work of the Corps.[44] Here is a clear example of the reconstruction of the United States' own underdevelopment as a putatively foreign condition.[45] Approaching "underdevelopment" as a reflection of U.S. fears of inequality and obsolescence allows us to peel back its hardened empirical shell to examine the rather thin flesh beneath and to reconsider, as well, the value of this enduring economic concept to the work of hemispheric cultural studies.

Underdevelopment and Hemispheric American Studies

In tracing the long history of Latin America in the U.S. imagination, this book also explores how both dominant and radical notions of the hemisphere (or, to use a more modern coinage, the "transnational") have evolved. A cultural history of underdevelopment is a history, as well, of hemispheric thinking in the United States, of the reactionary, liberal, and revolutionary forms it has taken. Like underdevelopment itself, "the hemisphere" is a constructed artifice, institutionalized in official bodies like the Pan American Union or the Organization of American States that mostly bureaucratically pantomime the internationalist ideals they espouse. As Stephen Park puts it, they "naturalize the power dynamics of the hemisphere by draping them in the logic of international cooperation."[46] Yet the hemisphere, like underdevelopment, also represents a set of unrealized desires, for the kind of universal modernity that midcentury modernization theory imagined or, from another point of view, the international socialism to which Cuban development aspired. It is these meanings of the hemispheric—as an institutional fiction and a political desire—that a critical approach to the history of "underdevelopment" can help us unpack.

Informed by postcolonial studies and a return to "empire" as a category of U.S. political history, the hemispheric or transnational turn (the terms are used interchangeably) in American studies has compelled scholars to reconsider how the cultural geography of the Americas resists the national boundaries of our conventional maps. Yet as a set of skeptical transnationalists have shown, this hemispheric framework has always been dogged by persistent challenges to its coherence as a field and a project. One skeptical position views the hemispheric as an invitation to philologically reckless comparison, as Vera Kutzinski has recently claimed, or as a stalking horse for an imperial expansion into Latin American studies.[47] Others critique the field's utopianism, both in its political aspirations (internationalist, typically antinationalist, but often U.S.-centric) and at the level of its vast archive, as Kimberly O'Neill and Paul Giles have argued. Ralph Bauer notes that given the subfield's origins in Anglo-American postcolonialist and multiculturalist paradigms, the United States—and the twentieth century—is often at the center of much critical work here. Ironically, this U.S.-centrism manifests itself partly in the field's antinationalism, since nationalism in Latin America and the Caribbean does not necessarily connote an ethnocentric or conservative politics, as it typically does in the United States.[48] Rodrigo Lazo has inveighed against the field's repetitive geographic reframing of a place called "America," suggesting that much hemispheric work reframes old questions. When, for example, O'Neill observes generously in a review essay that a new book "constellates subjects who transcend national and racial boundaries and ultimately expose the limits of those categories," one cannot help feeling that this is a point made so regularly in this field that it can hardly qualify as an "exposure." Such repetitions are a product, writes Lazo, of an "impossible epistemology."[49] The hemisphere is so vast, its archives so dispersed, and its national traditions so varied that it remains impossibly elusive: there is no "hemispheric America," simply a series of arguments about it. Instead of seeking to discover the hemisphere once again, Lazo argues, the hemispheric field itself—its assumptions and archives, its political desires and limitations, its debts to other comparative discourses—should be the object of criticism and of study.[50] In this book, admittedly, the United States is very much at the center; I am investigating underdevelopment's representation in the place where it is said not to exist, the United States. *A Cultural History of Underdevelopment* thus redefines this ostensibly empirical economic category as a comparative concept, the product of a century of inter-American cultural contact that defies the easy distinctions we still make between the "developed" north and the "underdeveloped" south, and between nationalism and transnationalism.[51] For this reason, development's *longue durée,* and its historical embeddedness in discourses of both imperialism and international fraternity, helps to situate the contemporary transnational critical impulse in a historical context of both U.S. empire *and* anti-imperialism.

Transnationality, I want to emphasize, is both an institutional fiction and a political *desire* of long standing in the hemisphere, one that is only occasionally *internationalist.* At the same time, reading Latin America in U.S. cultural history also compels us to rethink not only the politics and archive of the transnational but its periodization as well. Underdevelopment is a concept that implies both a spatial and temporal direction of movement, after all; it also combines both a hemispheric spatial scale and an implied national timescale. As Raphael Dalleo argues, this means that periodization is itself inseparable from a developmentalist and therefore Eurocentric myth of progress. Periodizing development, given the developmentalist logic of periodization, can feel like a kind of impossible riddle, a tautological dead end. In the Caribbean, Dalleo writes, it is "almost impossible to draw distinct lines between these different periods; the real topic of periodization is the lines themselves."[52] His point about the impossibility of periodization recalls Lazo's claim about the spatial framework of the field: given this "impossible epistemology," it is the transnational archive that should be examined.

In calling the United States the "great nation of futurity," O'Sullivan described the country as more than a cultural unit or a territory, but "a magnificent domain of space and time."[53] Raúl Coronado and Matthew Pratt Guterl have asked scholars to pay closer attention to the latter, given the national teleologies to which many such transnational histories are yoked, even if skeptically. Coronado's work, on the age of revolution in Texas before and after the Mexican-American War, asks us to pay closer attention to "worlds not to come," the political movements and national visions in Texas that failed to take shape within what eventually became Mexico and the United States. And as Guterl has pointed out, transnational histories offer new spatial frameworks—remappings of "America," reconfigurations of the Atlantic or the South—but rarely new temporal ones. So while the Age of Development, the Cold War, or slave emancipation may be internationalized, the periodizations themselves remain intact.[54] As a result, the transnationalist project is "haunted by the present," as Russ Castronovo has argued, hard-pressed to articulate historical argument and contemporary critique.[55] This book, therefore, proposes a diachronic reading of the term "underdevelopment" as one that belongs to both the United States and to the present historical moment. Hence this book's long historical sweep and broad geographical range, from the mid-nineteenth century to the present day, and across nations, like Cuba and Mexico, with different historical experiences of U.S. empire.

In another sense, transnational American studies is "haunted by the present," since the field is motivated, more than many others, by an activist political sensibility. The specter of the imperial present can sometimes lead transnationalists to project present-day dynamics onto the past moments that they study in ways that can obscure the dynamics of competition as well as comparison—fear and desire—that have shaped the cultural history of underdevelopment in the Americas. For example, McKinley's invocation of the "singular intimacy" of the United States and Cuba should remind contemporary scholars of liberal defenses of humanitarian intervention in Iraq. Reading the imperialist literature of 1898 as a prelude to that of 2004, as Caroline Levander does in her essay "Confederate Cuba," underlines the connections to our own period of alternately jingoistic and humanitarian nationalism in illuminating ways. Yet drawing this connection too closely causes us to miss our predecessors' obsessions with their own country's uneven development. Quoting one of the triumphalist postwar almanacs published after the war, which routinely declared Cuba's resemblance to the United States, Levander reads these declarations of international fraternity as dissimulations that "worked to sanitize U.S. imperial designs on Cuba."[56] Yet what if we consider the observations of U.S. similarity as also sincere, rather than only "sanitizing"—and the professions of similarity therefore disruptive, rather than only compensatory? In the effort to undermine their integrity, reasoning from the Manichean distinctions of the Cold War naturalizes them as themselves cohesive and permanent, as if the United States' position in the hemisphere was always assured. We are back, again, to the "dysfunction" of developmental narratives. What is surprising today, and therefore easy to overlook, is how anxiously competitive U.S. accounts of Latin America have always been. This underscores their most powerful and necessary ideological work: negotiating the reality of uneven development at home, without ever acknowledging its existence as such.

The Chapters

Mindful of Lazo's cautions about the "impossible archive" of hemispheric American studies, I have not organized this book around traditional literary forms. The order of these chapters is dictated by a rough chronology, but in order to challenge conventional periodizations of the United States in Latin America, it is not a linear narrative history. In each instance, the seemingly clear distinctions between our global categories of differentiation are troubled by the fact that in looking at Latin Americans, Americans are routinely looking at themselves—either the history they think they have surpassed, or their desires for the future. Nor does it attempt a comprehensive account of development theory, with continental coverage; this is not, in other words, *the* cultural history of underdevelopment. Focusing on Mexico and Cuba, and to a lesser degree on Venezuela, Nicaragua, and Puerto Rico, the book is organized around six dominant conventions by which U.S. writers, photographers, and filmmakers have represented Latin America in comparison to the United States. Each chapter takes on one of these conventions as they have appeared from the imperial era of the mid-nineteenth century through the Cold War. These are: Latin America as historical anachronism; as "tropical" nature; as a warzone; as a place of cultural vitality and (for U.S. Americans) revitalization; as a space of revolution; and as an object of solidarity.

Marx's line from the preface to *Capital*—the "country that is more developed industrially only shows the less developed [*entwickelten*] the image of its own future"—draws upon a common nineteenth-century meaning of "underdeveloped" that does not fit into the economic and colonial etymology sketched above. The word's earliest use in English was neither economic nor historical, but instead described a photographic plate's underexposure to light.[57] In one of the first literary uses of the term, which applies it metaphorically to social and historical questions, H. G. Wells describes the hapless protagonist of *The History of Mr. Polly* as an "under-developed simulacrum" of a man, a metaphor that describes Mr. Polly's provincial invisibility and irrelevance. Having not yet emerged into full being, Polly remains merely an image of what he could become. This book's epigraph is taken from Aimé Cesaire's *Une Tempête,* a postcolonialist restaging of Shakespeare's play about the power of images and language to fabricate worlds. In one sequence in the play, Prospero has conquered Caliban's island and imposed upon him what Caliban calls "an image of myself." The "image" of "the underdeveloped" is Prospero's greatest weapon: it becomes "the way you have forced me to see myself," says his rebellious subject.[58] If "underdevelopment" retains its early metaphorical association with light, vision, and sensation—and my students' recourse to the late-night infomercial suggests that it does—we can appreciate the importance of subjective impressions, "spatial longings," and frustrated desires in the making of Latin America in the U.S. imagination. The reliance on metaphors of vision and media technologies to render visible global economic processes was not limited to "underdevelopment." Quinn Slobodian traces a shift in central European economic writing on the novel concept of the "world economy," from metaphors of the "panoramic"—which depicted "the market" laterally, emphasizing territorial expansion—to the photographic, which underscored its local manifestations and the precise verisimilitude with which it could be isolated and measured by some particular datum. Schumpeter made use of metaphors of the camera and precinematic moving pictures in describing what he called "snapshots" of the "world economy" in the study of price changes, a local example that could illuminate the global. Like a zoetrope or the magic lantern, "snapshots" of the global economy could be animated to simulate a fluid movement in time. These various photographic metaphors underline, firstly, the importance of representation in the making of economic common sense. The photographic roots of "the world economy" also emphasize that, like "underdevelopment," its evolution as a concept has not been as fluid as it may seem. "The vision of a natural planet overlaid by manmade infrastructure and transformed into a 'world economy' is as much an inheritance of the 19th century," Slobodian writes, "as the categories of nation and empire. We see the world economy today, in part, through lenses prepared over a century ago."[59]

The origins of the word "underdevelopment" in visual media, and its reproduction as a political, economic, and cultural category through film, photography, and assorted print genres, dictates the archive of this book. The first three chapters offer examples of the contested, unsettled meaning of "the foreign" in late nineteenth-century America. I begin in the 1850s when, as Amy Kaplan as shown, the domestic definitions of "home"—as family and nation—were forged in "a crucible of foreign relations."[60] Chapter 1, on Latin America as anachronism, focuses on the movement for Cuban annexation before the Civil War. I explore the island's dynamic, shifting place in U.S. popular consciousness, where it represented a "backward" anachronism and an untouched Eden for some, and a would-be modern republic for others. Cuban annexation was also the co-creation of white Cuban exiles who forged an alliance with U.S. expansionists to chart a future for republicanism and for slavery. I focus on this alliance through a reading of the bilingual New York newspaper *La Verdad* (The Truth), organ of the annexationist movement. To read the poems, novels, and polemics that made up the literature of annexation is to encounter visions of a future we can scarcely recognize, with chattel slavery on California's coast or a Havana congressional delegation. What can these unrealized visions of the continent's future tell us about the countries that created them? Chapter 2, on Latin America as "nature," explores how Anglo-American travel writers framed "the tropics" as an ecological and cultural category in the era before mass tourism. Travel writers in these decades around the turn of the century represented the southern American hemisphere as a place of fecund beauty and unmanaged excess. At a moment when "development" still carried its colonial meaning, a moral geography of climate aimed to account for Latin American poverty scientifically, as a function of the intemperate environment of the tropics. The scientific critique of racial explanations for colonial "backwardness" was, on the one hand, a thin new veneer on an old piece of furniture, but it anticipates the later developmentalist celebration of *techne* over culture. Chapter 3, on journalistic representations of Cuba during the War of 1898, examines contemporary U.S. notions of Latin America at war: as a place of violence, disorder, suffering, and finally, though the aid of the United States, salvation. This chapter emphasizes two related aspects of the nascent discourse of underdevelopment at the beginning of the "American Century": a rhetoric of sympathy *for* and an anxious sense of competition *with* the Latin American other. New York's "yellow press" combined eyewitness reporting with bold graphic design to make the Caribbean and the Lower East Side newly legible to readers; I focus on the comparisons that war correspondents like Stephen Crane made between Cubans and poor New Yorkers, as they interpreted the suffering and resentment of Cuban civilians and soldiers by analogy to the tenement dwellers of New York's "other half." As I argue, Jacob Riis's domestic "other half" was displaced by a Latin "other America" in need of rescue.

The book's final three chapters examine how U.S. writers and film-makers have treated Latin America less as an example of "the foreign" than as a return of the repressed. Chapter 4 explores the cultural politics of "latinophilia," my term for the twentieth-century enthusiasm for Latin America as a source of revitalizing energy for an apparently declining United States. In the period between the end of Mexican revolutionary war in 1920 and the Cuban Revolution in 1959, folklorists, modernists, bohemians, political radicals, and tourists "discovered" Latin America. Where an earlier generation had identified Latin America's impoverish-ment negatively as a function of its climate and a sign of "backwardness," interwar bohemians valorized uneven development as the sign of cultural vitality. The "intimacy" of Mexico and the United States could thus be a source of common strength, but latinophilia was also predicated on myths about indigeneity and cultural stasis in the underdeveloped world that undermined the solidarity it sometimes promised. Chapters 5 and 6 consider the politics of representing Latin American radicalism, which has been an object of both admiration and fear in the United States. Intimacy, once again, is both an ideology of inter-American cooperation that often denies the power dynamics that divide the hemisphere, but which also draws upon unspoken, suppressed, or misremembered his-torical entanglements of race and nation. Chapter 5, on the cultural poli-tics of inter-American racial solidarity, focuses on links between Black modernist movements in interwar Harlem and Havana. This chapter explores the complex relationship between the Harlem Renaissance and the Afro-Cuban revival, through the personal and professional relationship of Langston Hughes and Nicolás Guillén. While their friendship and collaboration is often treated as a triumphant example of literary internationalism, mistranslations and misreadings of Cuban cultural politics by Hughes's biographers have caused Americanists to overlook Guillén's suspicions of both Hughes and the Harlem Renaissance. This chapter foregrounds Afro-Cuban responses to the Renaissance as both a U.S. movement—which Cubans were often inclined to resist—as well as a diasporic one. I highlight the dysfunction I emphasized above as a central part of hemispheric thinking: here we encounter not only solidarity and communication across borders but also the misapprehensions that produce diaspora culture. Chapter 6 turns to the erotics of the male revolutionary hero in U.S. mass culture. From the Augusto Sandino and Pancho Villa surrogates that have swaggered across U.S. film screens, to the images of Che Guevara and Fidel Castro that have circulated in the United States and around the world since the revolutionary 1960s, Latin American revolutionaries are alternately represented as dangerous threats, romantic rebels, comic charlatans, and salutary heirs to U.S. revolutionary traditions. Consistently, though, Latin American revolutions have been imagined as the result of embodied political passions that are restrained in the developed, bureaucratic politics of the United States. The eroticization of the revolutionary, which closely dovetails with the figure of the Latin lover in U.S. cinema, is a means of depoliticization—instead of making the personal political, the political becomes purely personal in these stories, and ever-more distant from the horizon of U.S. life. Here is the paradox of intimacy: when Latin America is most familiar and even seductive to Anglo-Americans, it is also irretrievably foreign.

The cultural history of the United States' relationship with Latin America shows that "underdevelopment" haunts the United States with an uncanny familiarity. The labor of the global South has built much of the wealth of the United States, as the most rudimentary historian and casual consumer knows. The labor of that world also shapes the songs U.S. Americans sing, the books they read, and the national myths they cherish. One of the most cherished of those tautological myths—that the United States was developed because it was free, and free in part because it was so developed—has been one of Latin America's most undervalued exports.

1 Latin America as Anachronism

The Cuban Campaign for Annexation and a Future Safe for Slavery, 1848–1856

In Cincinnati in 1851, an Ohioan named William Bland penned a memoir of the last expedition of Narciso López, the Venezuelan-born, self-styled liberator of Cuba who twice tried and failed to forcibly annex the island to the United States. Bland's sensational book, entitled *The Awful Doom of the Traitor; or the Terrible Fate of the Deluded and Guilty*, was a record of the defeat and betrayal of López's U.S. volunteers, supposedly penned by one of their surviving number.

Bland was spared execution under an amnesty issued by the Spanish government to surrendering "filibusters," as the U.S.-based, proslavery, privately organized militia expeditions to Latin America were called in the United States (though the Spanish newspaper *Diario de la Marina* simply called López's men "pirates").[1] The most successful filibuster was the diminutive Tennessean William Walker, whose army briefly occupied Nicaragua in 1856 and 1857, reinstituting slavery and establishing English as the official language. Until he was deposed by a united Central American force, Walker stood, as Brady Harrison writes, "a five-foot-five colossus across the isthmus."[2] López shared Walker's grand ambitions but never achieved even his modest success. His final expedition ended with the 1851 execution recounted in Bland's book. In one of its most implausible episodes—the book was printed by a publisher of sensational literature, and it meets many of the genre's conventions—the Ohioan watches López's garroting through his prison bars from a point of view high in Havana's Morro fortress. From this vantage point, Bland sees all. Far below in the city streets, López's effigy is beaten by angry crowds before the general himself is led to the gallows. Like the public ritual of effigy burning, the execution as described by Bland is an elaborate ritual, redolent of the Catholic superstition and excess that he associates with

Cuba. As the crowd looks on, López's Spanish jailers seal their conquest with the garrote, the execution machine favored by Spain:

> López came forth with a firm and steady step, but a pallid face and ascended the platform. His person was enveloped in a white shroud—the executioner then removed the shroud—and there stood the general, in his full military uniform, before the assembled multitude; his appearance was calm, dignified, and heroic, not a muscle quivered. He looked upon the preparation for death unmoved; his countenance remained unchanged, and his whole bearing was firm and manly. The executioner now removed his embroidered coat, his sash, cravat, and all the insignia of his military rank, as a token of his disgrace.

The executioner turns the garrote's screw, crushing his victim's throat, and López's head drops, heavy with symbolism, upon a crucifix held by a priest. "There sat the body," Bland concludes, "which a moment before was alive, but now a ghastly and inanimate corpse!"[3] Just as López's inanimate head rests in a priest's hands, so is "the benighting influence of priestcraft resting, like a dark spell of sorcery, upon the whole island."

An illustration of López's execution shows an audience of faintly sketched figures watching the proceedings as a soldier on horseback looms in the background. Meanwhile, on the scaffold, the focal point of the image is the seated general framed by two ominous figures. A Black executioner busies himself with the garrote and a fat priest in dark robes sanctifies the entire proceedings, completing the image's three-part indictment of Cuban society. For Anglo-Americans who supported its annexation, Cuba had long been perceived as a white republic-in-waiting suffering under an ancient European despotism, which offered men like Bland the historic (and lucrative) opportunity to fulfill the United States' providential mission to free the hemisphere.[4] Now, that dream was an "inanimate corpse" resting on a priest's crucifix. Before this pathetic end, López had been feted by crowds in New York City and courted as a statesman by southern expansionists like Mississippi's governor, John Quitman. As a postmortem analysis of López's doomed filibuster and of Cuba itself, Bland's tale is revealing for reframing as a space of barbarism what had been, mere months before, one of heroic republicanism.

A little-known episode from a failed antebellum imperial adventure is perhaps an unlikely place to begin a cultural history, not only of underdevelopment but of Latin America's circulation in U.S. culture, given the multitude of successful imperial adventures the continent has suffered. Yet the annexationist episode is exemplary, not only because it shows such an ambitious vision of Anglo-American imperial "futurity," but also

"There sat the body which a moment before was alive, but now a ghastly and inanimate corpse!—P. 14.

Narciso López at his execution. From William Bland, *The Awful Doom of the Traitor*, 1852. (Courtesy of the American Antiquarian Society)

because it demonstrates this vision's failure. The era of U.S. filibustering and expansion is a historical origin point for the very notion of "Latin America," a terminology that first emerged at this time as a counterpoint to the militarism of what U.S. expansionists called "Anglo-Saxon" culture. The mid-nineteenth century was a formative moment in the modern geography of the Americas, but the imaginative coordinates of a "modern" North America and a belated Latin America were not yet fixed, as we can see from a careful reading of annexationist discourse. Visions of Cuba as anachronistic competed in this moment with a conviction that the path to North America's future passed through Havana.

The imaginative coordinates of northern modernity and southern belatedness that buttress the modern ideology of underdevelopment were as unfixed in this moment as the hemisphere's political boundaries. Indeed, the conventional use of "expansion" to describe the United States' mid-nineteenth-century conquests of territory in the Caribbean and the west suggests that the country merely grew to its natural size, like a balloon inflated to its logical limits.[5] This "fetishized image of national coherence," as Mark Rifkin calls the familiar U.S. map, with its coastal boundaries to the east and west, river border to the south in Texas, and straight lines on the Canadian frontier to the north, overwrites indigenous and Mexican geographies and histories and encourages us to think of the nation's present-day borders as inevitable.[6] D. W. Meinig's multivolume work on the historical geography of the United States, particularly his study of western expansion and filibustering, helps us unthink this geographic destiny. As Meinig points out, there were many possible futures for the hemisphere in the 1840s and 1850s: a "lesser" United States extending to the Mississippi River, with a vast Indian territory across the Rocky Mountains and a Californian Republic in the west, or various versions of a "greater United States" encompassing Cuba, the Yucatán Peninsula, Baja California, Mexican territory south of the Rio Grande River, and parts of present-day Canada.[7]

Revisiting the notable failures of U.S. "expansion" also indicates the surprising leadership role played by Cuban émigrés in the fabrication of American exceptionalism, which guided Cuban annexation and obviously survived it. For most of the nineteenth century, in fact, white Cubans and Anglo-Americans described Cuba as racially, culturally, and geographically linked to the United States, in ways that have shaped the discourse of inter-American "intimacy." Cuba has, of course, also played the role of the picturesque exotic and passive beneficiary of U.S. modernity. But in the 1840s and 1850s, Cuba was still widely regarded as what John Quincy Adams, writing in 1823, called a "natural appendage" to the United States. Adams said of Cuba that the United States "cannot cast her off from its bosom . . . looking forward to the probable course of events for the short period of half a century, it is scarcely possible to resist the conviction that the annexation of Cuba to our federal republic will be indispensable to the continuance and integrity of the Union itself."[8] The midcentury "Young American" expansionist John O'Sullivan saw Mexico, by contrast, as a passively foundational player in the formation of the "great nation of futurity" at midcentury, a vestige of the Old World to be displaced. Cuba, however, was different. In 1852, O'Sullivan's *Democratic Review* published an essay on "The Cuban Debate" that presented Cuba as a modern, white country ready to join the Union: "Cuba contains half a million of whites, and is in a perfectly organized state, with her material and other interests, her civil and religious institutions, her manners and customs, her roads and bridges, her schools and churches, her fields of plenty and her climate as matchless as the ground is fertile."[9] Cuban and Anglo-American annexationists insisted alike that Cuba was the path to the future, a conviction that only magnified Bland's disappointment. Cuba was supposed to be the place where the European 1848 might come to pass in the Western Hemisphere, a place to "carve out fame and fortune with the sword of Liberty," as another of López's U.S. volunteers recalled his earlier enthusiasm. Such an opportunity, wrote Richardson Hardy, had not existed "since the Age of Chivalry."[10] Those who opposed annexation, O'Sullivan insisted, were "old fogies" stuck in a rapidly disappearing past. "They are about to disappear before the flood of progress and improvement," he stormed, "which they do not understand and cannot resist."[11] The island thus summoned a set of unstable temporal and cultural associations in the United States of mid-century: both white and Black, 1848 and "the Age of Chivalry," the advance guard of history and its priest-ridden junk heap. It is an ideal place, therefore, to begin to explore the singular intimacy of the Americas.

Annexation, *La Verdad,* and Slavery's Futures Past

The movement to annex Cuba was at its height between 1848 and the beginning of the United States' Civil War. For this reason, as Tom Chaffin and Robert May have argued, it has mostly been read as an antebellum curiosity, rarely treated by Americanist scholars outside of the provincial lens of U.S. sectionalism in the run-up to the Civil War—an eccentric project of the Old South.[12] Annexation, however, was not merely a regional but also a national and international enterprise, with support from across the United States, especially in centers of Cuban immigration and exile like New York and New Orleans. Determined that Cuba take its place among the revolutionary nations of 1848, Cuba's annexationists pitted the autocracy of the Spanish colony against the progressive republic to their north. The most prominent annexationist publication, the New York–based *La Verdad,* spoke on behalf of Cubans and in defense of a flexible vision of "republicanism."

La Verdad was published in New York every two weeks in Spanish and English between 1848 and 1856, and then briefly in New Orleans before folding. The paper was founded by Gaspar Betancourt Cisneros, an exiled Puerto Príncipe planter and essayist who served as the paper's principal editor; O'Sullivan of the *Democratic Review;* Moses Yale Beach, publisher of the *New York Sun;* and Jane McManus Storm Cazneau, a key ideologue in the antebellum world of proslavery imperialists working to secure a long future and a broad geographic girth for slavery. Cazneau was a former Texas settler, a *Sun* correspondent in Cuba, *Democratic Review* editor, and then after the Civil War, a leading advocate of Dominican Republic annexation.[13] Under her pen name, Cora Montgomery, she bylined most of the paper's editorial articles, in both languages. She likely only wrote the English-language section, however, leaving the Spanish articles to her (mostly uncredited) Cuban colleagues.[14] Betancourt Cisneros and Montgomery were joined on the *La Verdad* staff by Pedro

Santacilia, a Cuban exile who later became a high-ranking official in the liberal Juárez government in Mexico, and Miguel Teurbe Tolón, a poet and member of the student-oriented Junta Cubana Anexionista in New York.[15] Narciso López's former secretary, a young writer named Cirilo Villaverde, would later become *La Verdad*'s editor-in-chief and one of Cuba's most celebrated novelists. After Betancourt Cisneros's exile in 1837, he adopted for himself the pen name "El Lugareño," a colloquial term used to describe a provincial local of some rural place. It was a picturesque and self-effacing nickname for a politically ambitious plantation owner, which captures the Cuban annexationist movement's embrace of an agrarian patriotism connected symbolically to the Cuban soil. Adopted in exile to establish his local belonging, the nickname calibrates two widely different scales: the global sphere of annexationist politics, and the regional sphere of its imagined Cuba. This was a contradiction that *La Verdad* tried to manage: to rhetorically align local Cuban desires for "freedom" with the global designs of an expansionist United States.

The newspaper's purpose was to agitate in the United States, and through illegal circulation in Cuba, for the United States' annexation of the Spanish colony. If Cuba failed to join the United States, *La Verdad* suggested, it would mean that Hispanophobes like Bland were right: Cuba might really be condemned to permanent feudal status, languishing in the shadow of its advanced neighbor. One 1852 editorial argued, in English: "If we, Hispanic-Americans, continue under military and theocratic governments, if we do not shake off the aristocratic customs which retain the people in ignorance, in misery . . . this will be precisely to admit of a Providence, preordained and inflexible, that decreed that the United States of America and the American people must be the only great Republic, the only great nation that in the world of Columbus merits the sympathy, recognition, and the respect of all peoples and nations of the civilized world."[16] In placing Cuba, and more broadly, "Hispanic America," at this historical crossroads, *La Verdad* challenged its readers to ensure that Spanish America not be left behind by the United States.

In his classic essays "Brazilian Culture: Nationalism by Elimination" and "Misplaced Ideas," the Brazilian literary historian Roberto Schwarz writes of the anxious self-consciousness of nineteenth-century Latin American elites who measured their nations' modernity and originality by their adherence to foreign, metropolitan models. Latin America was an "anachronism," a temporal framework used to compare Latin American social forms unfavorably to the modern nation of "futurity," as the *La Verdad* editors do above. Schwarz points out that "anachronism" is based on a false notion of history as a continuity, and of progress as spatially autonomous: spreading, that is, from advanced to backward nations along a timeline that the latter must follow to catch up to the former.[17] Dividing the globe into vestigial or progressive, imitative and original, "anachronism" offers a false distinction between capitalist modernity and forms of feudal life, such as theocracy or slavery, that allegedly cannot coexist. As many scholars have argued, such "feudal" barbarities as Caribbean and North American slavery were in fact intrinsic to the formation of the modern world, not exceptional to it. C. L. R. James made this point in *Black Jacobins,* where he argued that the slaves of Saint Domingue labored under a regime that in its structure and patterns of authority was a *"modern* system," in which slaves lived what was "in its essence a modern life." Schwarz argues against what Sybille Fischer calls the fallacy of "'pure' cases," the modern standard of a modern, evenly developed England, France, or the United States, from which other places deviate or behind which they stumble.[18] Schwarz emphasizes the ideological effects of this fallacy, what we might consider the structure of feeling it creates. The juxtaposition in slaveholding Brazil of "modern" (that is, European) liberal ideas with colonial institutions, most especially slavery, *does* produce a "sense," a "feeling" of what he calls an "off-centre" intellectual life, the "ideological comedy" in which the lofty rhetoric of the "rights of man" coexists more or less functionally with its most blatant, brute contradictions.[19] I would argue that the same ideological comedy existed in the United States and Cuba, which we can see in the pages of *La Verdad.* Cuban annexationists proclaimed their loyalty to both slavery and republicanism, and their metropolitan model, the "pure case" to which they aspired, was itself a slaveholding "anachronism" of its own. *La Verdad* proclaimed that as U.S. citizens, Cubans would no longer be (metaphorical) "slaves" of Spain, yet the editors defended chattel slavery as an institution that would be saved by the United States. Annexation's U.S. allies likewise saw Cuba as a valuable addition to a future republic where slavery would grow and thrive. This chapter examines this ideological comedy, one that unites Cuba and the United States, the humiliated colony and the modern republic, deeply entangled as they were by their shared commitments to the future of a barbaric, modern institution.

What did *La Verdad*'s Cuban editors want from annexation? The paper addressed white Cuban creoles in New York and on the island, where the newspaper reputedly had an illegal circulation, according to the Cuban historian Ramiro Guerrez y Sánchez.[20] It invoked liberal principles of self-government, republican notions of egalitarianism, and white fears of absorption by the Black majority in agitating for attachment to the United States as a slave state. Of all these seemingly contradictory motivations, the most urgent argument appears to have been white racial self-preservation. Betancourt Cisneros wrote to his political rival, the antiannexationist exile José Antonio Saco, "I want for Cuba the advantages and the protection of the United States, of the Colossus, of the American Briareus with its twenty millions of strong and robust arms."[21] The danger from which Cuba needed protection was racial. If Cuba were to remain under Spanish domination, went one Spanish-language editorial, "and if it does not seek its salvation in the wise, strong, and benevolent North American Confederation," it would be destroyed either by slave revolt, as in French Saint Domingue or, in the best case, by the "Africanization" wrought by British emancipation. Another article in the same issue invoked the category of "slaves" (*esclavos*) to describe free white Cubans without political and property rights, for whom "nationality" is a superficial "outer garment" rather than an animating passion: "Peoples that do not have political rights, and that must suffer even the most sacred or natural of them to be usurped and restricted, are slaves: Slaves have no nationality. They wear the outer garments of such a spirit, and this can inspire no such noble sentiment."[22] As a defender of what David Luis-Brown calls an "imperialist anticolonialism," *La Verdad* accepted the legitimacy of chattel slavery, while comparing the campaign for annexation in 1848 to the liberation struggles of Poland, Hungary, and Ireland that year.[23] Antiannexationists often ridiculed their opponents on cultural nationalist grounds, warning of the loss of Spanish language and culture that would come with mass emigration from the United States.[24] But how could annexationists justify vindicating Cuban "nationality" by submitting to the rule of the United States? Critics have offered a few answers. Herminio Portell Vilá, author of one of the first historical accounts of the Cuban movement, distinguished between "annexationists for economic reasons"—free-traders opposed to Spanish taxation and mercantile restrictions—and "annexationists for patriotic reasons," which would presumably refer to liberal intellectuals like Villaverde, Tolón, and Betancourt Cisneros.[25] However, in reading the paper this distinction begins quickly to dissolve. "Slavery," in annexationist usage, was both a patriotic metaphor and the social institution that underlay the nation the annexationists envisioned. In this respect, slavery was both an economic and a patriotic institution.[26] For annexationists, separation from Spanish colonialism could not be contemplated without securing the future of slavery under the protection of the United States. Even José Antonio Saco, a determined antiannexationist, agreed that there could be no free men in Cuba without disciplined slaves.

Given the nation-within-a-nation the Cuban annexationists hoped for, we ought not read *La Verdad* only as a "protonational discourse about Cuba," as Rodrigo Lazo calls it. For one, this conclusion rests on the teleological assumption that the eventual Cuban independence movement—that is, a "national" discourse that eventually takes the form of independence—was the inevitable result of the political ferment of the nineteenth century. Secondly, it presumes that the annexationists' loyalties were primarily "national," with the combination of cultural, political, and affective ties this suggests, rather than racial, political, or economic.[27] Annexationists in both countries were interested in imagining the future, not just of a "free" Cuba or an expansive U.S. republic, but of slavery for both.[28] Instead of the future that eventually came to pass, what of the alternative, failed futures that Cuban annexationists, their allies, and opponents hoped to bring about? The stakes of assessing annexation's historical failures, rather than its eventual victories, become clearer if we consider Raúl Coronado's discussion of the unrealized futures of Latino print culture in Texas in the 1840s and 1850s. Coronado cites Foucault's concept of a historical genealogy, which in challenging a view of history as a continuity, foregrounds instead "the errors, the false appraisals, and the faulty calculations that gave birth to those things that continue to exist and have value to us."[29] A genealogical perspective on these productive failures, Coronado writes, "will allow us to produce a history that is not teleological, one that does not assume that previous generations consciously sought to arrive precisely at the world we inhabit today."[30] To borrow Coronado's grammatical formulation, we must think of the annexationist project in Cuba—and in the United States—in terms of the spaces that "would become" each, rather than the inevitability of the nation-states that "became" what we know now. Coronado's verb tense is meaningful here: "the future-in-past tense of the auxiliary 'would' and inchoative aspect of 'become,' rather than the past tense proper." As he argues, "the future-in-past tense draws out, unfolds, and lengthens the process of 'becoming,' which itself denotes the *processes* entailed in any radical shift in thought."[31] In the case of Cuban annexation, so many midcentury predictions for what Providence had in store for the United States and Cuba—what each "would become"—have proven profoundly wrong. What seems more improbable now than a Cuban state in the Union? And while contemporary Anglo-American conservatives fret about "border insecurity," the 1850s were a time of border invisibility: O'Sullivan thundered about American "futurity" as a national ideology of progress not to insulate the country *against* its "outside," but precisely because there was no coherent "outside" yet. And yet there is something uncannily familiar about annexationist rhetoric: its embrace of American exceptionalism; its throaty cheering for empire; its opportunistic celebration of *some* Latin Americans, especially white Cubans, and its dismissal or contempt for others; and its worries about the decline sure to come if the "fogies" get their way in charting a weak, ineffectual foreign course. The alternative American hemisphere the annexationists and *anexionistas* imagined seeds the history of inter-American abolition and imperialism with the unmade maps of futures past that remind us, as well, of the histories we have inherited. "Development," as I wrote in the Introduction, is a descendant of the nineteenth-century spatialization of time. As the postcolonial theorist and anthropologist Johannes Fabian has argued, "Geopolitics has its ideological origins in chronopolitics"; that is, the political organization and imagining of national and global space originates from the political organization of time.[32] The era of Mexican and Cuban annexation is critical in the fabrication of a chronopolitics of progress and futurity that has endured to the present day. What the Cuban case emphasizes, though, is how so much of that enduring chronopolitics of futurity was based on a future that never came. One of the many ironies of American exceptionalism is that it is the product, in so small part, of two things it would seem now to exclude: Cubans and failure.

This speculative vision of Cuba appeared in the context of an American hemisphere in flux. The temporal categories of progress and anachronism that mapped onto hemispheric spatial coordinates of north and south corresponded, as well, with racial designations like "Anglo-Saxon" and later "Latin American." In an exhaustive study of the term's history, Arturo Ardao attributed the first use of "América latina" to the Colombian poet José María Torres Caicedo, who used it in a poem entitled "Las dos Américas." As Ardao explains, the name was coined in response to U.S. predations in Central America and Mexico. Caicedo's poem describes:

La raza de la América latina,
Al frente tiene la sajona raza,
Enemiga mortal que ya amenaza
Su libertad destruir y su pendón.

[The race of Latin America,
Is confronted by the Saxon race,

Mortal enemy that now threatens
To destroy its liberty and its banner.][33]

Caicedo's use of "race" to describe Latin America in clear opposition to the "Saxon race" underscores Mónica Quijada's argument that the nascent concept of "América latina" was not just a political concept of unity among Spanish-American peoples, like Bolívar's Gran Colombia, but a racial concept as well, formed in response to the aggressive territorialization of the racial category "Anglo-Saxon."[34] The annexationists of *La Verdad* accordingly couched their struggle as both racial and hemispheric, although they avoided either the terms "Anglo-Saxon" or "Latin American," which would have suggested a racial rivalry the editors intended to discourage. The paper instead described a population racially compatible with the United States, framing their struggle as a battle to save a white, Christian island from perdition, with the protection of the United States.

If Cuban dissidents understood annexation as the pursuit of white republican nationalism, what did their Anglo-American allies want from the island? The economic advantages were obvious. The island's lucrative sugar crop, the bustling port of Havana, and the island's location near Atlantic shipping lanes made it "the key" to the Gulf of Mexico, to use a common metaphor in proannexation circles. Access to Cuba would secure control of the Central American isthmus and the canal then being considered. New York's *Hunt's Merchant's Magazine,* in a common assertion, argued in 1849 that if annexed to the United States ("if her ports were free") Cuba would command the Gulf of Mexico, furnish a warehouse for products on the Mississippi, harvest trade from Latin America, and speed emigration west to the Pacific. As the key to the Gulf, Cuba would unlock both oceans, driving U.S. commerce and the settlement of the North American continent.[35] More imaginatively, for annexationists in the United States Cuba helped draw the unwritten map of the proslavery future. "Looking into the possibilities of the future," wrote the Virginian Edward Pollard, "regarding the magnificent country of tropical America, which lies in path of our own destiny, we may see an empire as powerful and gorgeous as ever was pictured in our dreams of history."[36] Cuba in particular belonged to a white "American Mediterranean," as Matthew Pratt Guterl has called it, in which New Orleans was the "keystone city of the 'great nation of futurity.'"[37] The Spanish colony seemed to collapse time and space, synchronizing the scale of the continent to the progressive history of the United States. Of course, the Civil War rendered these dreams impossible. In its failure, however, annexationism offers an example of what Rafael Pérez Torres, writing on the much different context of the borderlands in Chicano literature, has called the "discontinuities of history and power" that Latino literature uncovers.[38] One of these "discontinuities" lies in the term itself: Coronado uses "Latino" as a term of identity that "refers less to a subject position than it does to a literary and intellectual culture that emerges in the interstices between the United States and Spanish America," decentering the nation as a unit of historical analysis. *La Verdad,* which worked to balance the interests of Cuban creole patriotism and U.S. Anglo-Saxon expansionists, offers an example of such an "interstitial" consciousness.

The instability of the boundaries between the nations to which *La Verdad* appealed comes out clearly in its *prospecto,* or statement of principles, in its first issue, attached to the January 9, 1848, edition of the *Sun.* The English and Spanish versions both cultivate a Pan-Americanist theme of the "unity" of the American republics, but are otherwise dramatically different. Written under Cora Montgomery's byline, the English statement of principles makes no reference to Cuba or Spain. Translating the paper's name for its readers, the English editorial declares its mission and its audience to be as vast as the continent: "We firmly declare we but seek the mutual advantage of those who publish and those who read the Truth. Acting upon this clear idea, and animated by strong hopes of success, we offer to the public LA VERDAD twice a month, and in two languages. Truth twice a month, and in the two languages which divide between them this continent. What more can be asked in a corrupt world in which we scarcely catch the echo of her footsteps?" Montgomery goes on to say that the editors "flatter ourselves that close communications with redeemed and tranquilised Mexico will induce such intimate attachments and family relations as will make her noble language almost a common property." A lengthy bilingual report of the U.S. Army's march to Mexico City appears opposite the column, recasting that conquest in the terms of domestic "intimacy" and, strikingly, Spanish-English bilingualism.[39]

La Verdad's Spanish *prospecto* uses the word "American" to describe both a political unit defined by Hispanic colonial legacies—what it calls elsewhere in the article the "Colonias y Republicas del Sur"—and as a geographical location that includes the United States. It did not attempt to justify the newspaper's English text, and it is sufficiently different from that version that it cannot be considered a translation.[40] *La Verdad* instead identified itself as an organ of the progressive virtues of the day: "las ideas del orden, de la justicia de la paz y de la union" ("the ideas of order, of justice, of peace, and of union"). Speaking on behalf of a hemispheric "gran familia Americana," the paper sounds a note of hemispheric cooperation and unity. The author (again identified as Montgomery) writes that the only inspiration to what she calls "nuestro pueblo" (our people) is "el deseo de aumentar y estrechar sus relaciones con los otros pueblos del Continente y de las islas vecinas" (the desire to increase and strengthen its ties with the other peoples of the Continent and the neighboring islands). The editorial leaves the identity of "our people" ambiguous, attributing the origin of the paper's progressive ideas to "the thinking men of the Union." Especially given Montgomery/Cazneau's authorial voice here, the United States seems to be the "people" in question, the protagonist of the great work of the paper. If we presume that the Spanish-language piece was likely written by Betancourt Cisneros or another of the paper's Cuban leaders, though, this conclusion is less clear.[41] The ambiguity here is quite politic and presumably strategic. The *prospecto* continues:

> Persuadidos, pues, del grande interes que tiene la América, y en particular el pueblo de los E.U. en la adopcion de un sistema jeneral, de un principio unico, y de una política enteramente distinta de la política de Europa, nos ha parecido que el mayor servicio que puedieramos hacer a esta causa, es encargarnos de la redacción de un periodico, que solo tenga por objeto ajitar sus principios, descubrir sus míras y despejar la opinión de aquellos pueblos que, por sus circunstancias particulares, se han rezagado del curso jeneral de las ideas en América.

> [Thus persuaded of the great interest that América, and in the particular the people of the U.S., have in the adoption of a general system, under a single principle, and of a politics entirely distinct from the politics of Europe, it has seemed to us that the greatest service we could render this cause would be to charge ourselves with the task of editing a periodical, that has as its only object to agitate for these principles, to enlighten the vision and awaken the opinion of those peoples who have, until now, been left behind in the course of ideas in América.]

The *prospecto*'s Spanish text laments that Cuba is being "left behind," while the English boasts of familial intimacy between Cuba and the United States. In referring to the United States, *La Verdad* adopted a Cuban voice, using "América" to refer to a hemisphere divided between a progressive United States and those peoples "left behind in the course of ideas." Meanwhile, in its English section, the paper's editorials adopt the point of view of an Anglo-American annexationist, using "American" (in the *estadounidense* sense) in the third person, celebrating the Mexican conquest as a redemption, and identifying the Spanish language as the language of nearly all of the "civilized inhabitants of this New World," along with "our own."[42]

For its Anglo-American readers, the map of the "New World" was divided not so much between the United States and "Latin America" as it was between white and nonwhite worlds. For Spanish-language readers, the newspaper holds out the prospect of temporal unity, of a "general American system" that would synchronize all of Spanish America with the United States. In its pages, *La Verdad* aimed to negotiate this double posture: to justify U.S. annexation to its Cuban readers as an expression of liberatory republicanism, and to justify Cuba's whiteness to its U.S. readers. To address the former problem, the editors declared that if Cuba were allowed to sink further into poverty, autocracy, and even slave rebellion, then the uneven development of the American hemisphere, with the United States as the only model democracy, might in fact come permanently to pass. To address the latter problem, *La Verdad* wrote of "volcanic fires" spreading from Haiti across the Caribbean. The threat of a Caribbean-wide slave revolt, Montgomery wrote, was "the *most urgent cause,* if not the *principal,* which compels the Cubans to shake off the Spanish yoke, and place themselves under the protection of the United States, where the negroes *are not* an obstacle to the liberty or the political rights of the majority; where the negroes *are not* an instrument in the hands of the government to terrify and subjugate its citizens."[43] Even among Northerners opposed to the spread of slavery in the United States, Cuba could help solve the United States' most pressing political and geographic dilemma. New York's Richard Kimball, for example, maintained that annexing Cuba would calm U.S. sectional tension, guaranteeing the "permanent equilibrium of the Republic" while preventing unpleasant upheaval on the island itself.[44]

Not all Cuban dissidents were swayed by this appeal, and the antiannexationist Saco offered an alternative interpretation of the future annexationists dreamed of under U.S. rule. From his Parisian exile, Saco denounced annexation in a series of spirited polemics with Betancourt Cisneros and the *Verdad* editors. Saco opposed annexation on cultural nationalist grounds—annexation would be "Anglicization," he wrote— and out of a conviction that any U.S. attempt to annex the island would itself set off a slave uprising, not prevent one. Emancipation, he added, was in fact most likely a Spanish tactic to forestall any annexation by the United States. Saco asked his annexationist compatriots how they could be certain that slavery would survive "even in the event that we unite peacefully with the North American Confederacy? It seems that the future is not quite so brilliant nor so certain as is generally believed," he wrote."[45] To her Anglo-American readers in *La Verdad,* Montgomery downplayed the threat posed by Cuban slaves, reassuring creole planters and others that annexation posed no threat to slave property. In one early editorial, Montgomery expresses in the most succinct way the annexationist thesis of Cuban nationalism as an ideology of white citizenship in the American empire for liberty: "We consider a Cuban every person born in Cuba; and what we wish is, that white people be born by thousands, every hour."[46]

The history and rhetoric of U.S. designs on Cuba, and Cuban creole interest in annexation, in the 1840s and 1850s was so vexed that it frustrates any single reading of the annexation campaigns as an adjunct to U.S. sectionalist debates, a Southern fantasy, an episode of "manifest destiny," or a cynical ploy of the Cuban creole elite to advance their economic fortunes. The various ways in which Cuba is metaphorically domesticated, infantilized, Orientalized, and eroticized, in one instance praised as a splendorous, untouched Eden, then denounced as a decadent, Catholic, Africanized barbarism, then celebrated as a modern, would-be republic groaning under Spanish tyranny, with its annexation to the United States rendered in the loftiest democratic rhetoric, show how dynamic were the cultural boundaries between Anglo-America and Spain's richest colony in the Americas.[47] For many, the eventual attachment of Cuba to the United States simply seemed inevitable, the result of historical and Providential forces written on the map of the hemisphere. Hueston, for example, claimed, "We are borne onward by a force which seems hastening some great consummation."[48] A similar sense of destiny comes from James Buchanan, the future president and the coauthor of the 1854 Ostend Manifesto, a declaration by U.S. diplomats, later repudiated, that called for Cuban annexation by purchase. As Polk's secretary of state, Buchanan wrote in 1849, "Cuba is already ours. I can feel it in my finger ends."[49] Cuba's certain place in the United States' future competed, however, with representations of it as anachronistically out of date; for some U.S. writers, Cuba's "Edenic" tropicality complemented, rather than contradicted, the economic appeal to its futurity. For *La Verdad's* Cuban editors, by contrast, Cuba's backwardness was political—the "slavery" in which it was kept by Spain. The *Boston Post* described Cuba as a hemispheric anachronism in 1850, due to "the languor that characterizes the people of tropical regions."[50] In his convalescents' travel book *Gan-Eden; or, Pictures of Cuba,* William Henry Hurlbut wrote, "The name of Cuba leaves a ring of doubloons on the ear, a flavor of guava on the lips. Within three days' sail of our southern ports lie scenes than which India itself offers nothing more thoroughly strange to our eyes." The *New York Sun* called Cuba "the garden of the world," and many Southerners also described the colony as a paradise barely touched by civilization—this during a decade of boom times in the industrialized Cuban sugar trade.[51] Such appeals to Cuba's appealing richness competed with the primary problem facing Southern militarists, Cuban annexationists, and Democratic expansionists: unlike the biblical garden to which it was often compared, Cuba was full of people, many of them Black. For this reason, advocates of annexation were emphatic in defending Cuba's whiteness and, therefore, its assimilability to the United States.[52] "This continent," the *Democratic Review* argued, "is for white people, and not only the continent, but the islands adjacent, and the negro must be kept in slavery at Cuba and Hayti, under white republican masters."[53]

Spain's unwillingness to part with one of its last colonies made peaceful annexation a political nonstarter in the end. In 1860, John Abbott traveled to Cuba and pronounced the political and military obstacles to annexation too great to be overcome: "We cannot seize Cuba. We cannot buy. We shall continue to look wistfully at it. That is all."[54] By 1859, the annexationist dream was practically all but dead, although it faded slowly. Richard Henry Dana, the Boston lawyer, former sailor, and maritime author, wrote in his 1859 travelogue *To Cuba and Back* of the irredeemable "Africanization" of Cuba. His book included a sustained argument against annexation, suggesting that the issue was still alive and controversial then, by which time López was dead, *La Verdad* had folded, and the organized annexationist movement had all but disappeared. Cuba's racial and religious difference made it too remote from the United States to ever be a part of the Union, Dana contended.[55] In the next section, which considers the work of the most ambitious English-language antiannexationist, we will see how brittle were the foundations upon which this cultural and political antinomy rested.

Brushing History against the Grain: The Revolutionary Anachronism of *Blake, or the Huts of America*

"You, Placido, are the man for the times!"
—Martin Delany, *Blake, or the Huts of America*

La Verdad's attempt to rhetorically reconcile revolutionary republican progress and slavery ultimately failed in its most important mission: to encourage Cuba's entry into the United States. Yet this was not necessarily because the gross theoretical contradiction constituted a practical problem. The *discursive* inadequacy of universal political rights in a society ruled by slavery did not at all trouble Cuban thinkers like Saco, who settled the problem of republican slavery by declaring, much as the U.S. Supreme Court did around the same time, that one part of the island's population did not have rights that the most powerful were bound to respect. (Saco proposed to count free people of color as citizens in the Spanish census, to increase Cuba's seats in the Cortes, but to deny them the franchise.)[56] For Cazneau, Betancourt Cisneros, Tolón, and even Saco, slavery and liberal institutions could coexist in a future Cuba, for Saco in a sovereign slaveholding democracy within the Spanish empire, and for the annexationists, inside the slaveholding democracy of the southern United States.

For Cuban and Anglo-American annexationists, this possibility rested on Cuba's exceptional status within the nation of futurity—a status guaranteed by its supposed Christianity and whiteness. As Martin Delany observed, this mutual identification concealed the terror under which defenders of slavery lived in either country. An abolitionist journalist, editor, and novelist, Delany was one of the most vehement and vocal opponents of the annexation of Cuba. In an 1849 article in the *North Star,* the newspaper he coedited with Frederick Douglass, Delany excoriated annexationists by pointing out the central issue that, he argues, motivated all their plottings: fear. "Few people in the world lead such a life as the white inhabitants of Cuba, and those of the South now comprising the 'Southern Confederacy of America,'" Delany wrote. "A dreamy existence of the most fearful apprehensions, of dread, horror and dismay; suspicion and distrust, jealousy and envy continually pervade the community; and Havana, New Orleans, Charleston or Richmond may be thrown into consternation by an idle expression of the most trifling or ordinary ignorant black."[57] His 1859 novel *Blake, or the Huts of America* dramatizes these fears by resuscitating a defeated conspirator from the recent past. Serialized in 1859 in *The Anglo-African Magazine* and again in 1861 in *The Weekly Anglo-African, Blake* seems to be set in 1852, just after the passage of the Fugitive Slave Act and the election of proannexation New Hampshire Democrat Franklin Pierce. The Fugitive Slave Act, which compelled Northern states to enforce the "property rights" of Southern slaveholders, proved to abolitionists like Delany that the federal government and the Northern states were in league with slavery, rather than pursuing its extinction. If the United States were united in support of human bondage, Delany's *Blake* imagines a rebellion that would unite slaves across the Caribbean to destroy it.

Delany restages in the present of his writing a Cuban slave revolt loosely based on the failed 1844 Escalera, or "Ladder," conspiracy, a purported plot organized by rebellious slaves on sugar plantations that year. Scholars have pointed to the *Escalera* plot (so called for the method of torture by which Spanish authorities beat suspects bound to a ladder) as a major, if not the principal motivation for annexation advocates on and off the island, because the terrifying prospect of slave revolt mobilized planter support and Spanish repression. Robert Paquette, the leading historian of the *Escalera* episode, concludes that the available evidence confirms the existence of a conspiracy of some size on Cuban plantations in 1843 and 1844. As he argues, the events of 1844 and the repression that followed provided the greatest arguments for annexation. López developed his plans for a filibuster of the island in the "Year of the Lash" that came after the discovery of the plot, when Spanish authorities pursued a widespread crackdown on Cuban reformers and free people of color. Meanwhile, Southern expansionists and Cuban annexationists found common cause in their mutual fear of a slave uprising on the largest island in the Caribbean.[58] Delany's novel, therefore, does for the recent past what Coronado suggests that contemporary historians do: it considers the futures envisioned and conditioned by past failures. One of the most famous victims of the Spanish repression that followed the conspiracy was the poet Plácido, a free-born mulatto who was executed by Spanish authorities for his alleged participation in the conspiracy. Plácido's death and legacy were fought over long after his execution: even *La Verdad* reprinted his poetry, laying claim to him as a Cuban nationalist martyr against Spanish repression. The U.S. abolitionist William Wells Brown eulogized Plácido as "the slave's poet of freedom" in his 1863 historical encyclopedia, *The Black Man, His Antecedents, His Genius, and His Achievements*: "His songs are still sung in the bondman's hut, and his name is a household word to all," he wrote. "As the 'Marseillaise' was sung by the revolutionists of France, and inspired the people with a hatred to oppressors, so will the slaves of Cuba, at a future day, sing the songs of their poet-martyr, and their cry will be, 'Placido and Liberty.'"[59] Delany's story speculates on that "future day" with its title character of Henry Blake, the free-born son of a Cuban mulatto landowner captured by American slave traders while working at sea. Like *Uncle Tom's Cabin* and other abolitionist novels it parodies, *Blake* is structured around a domestic tragedy: when Henry's wife Maggie is sold onto a New England judge's Cuban sugar plantation, his quest to locate and rescue her takes him across the United States and eventually to Cuba. In *Blake,* however, domestic reunification becomes an occasion for revolutionary mobilization. Along with Maggie, Henry meets up with his cousin Plácido, who in this novel was never executed in 1844. Henry and his fictionalized cousin begin organizing a rebellion of enslaved Cubans that, the novel suggests—though it ends before its realization—will spread to the U.S. South from a free Cuba.

Blake's use of a dead historical figure to restage the "would-have-been" of a past Cuban revolt is itself anachronistic. Rather than invoking anachronism to serve a cultural hierarchy topped by a modern Anglo-America, though, Delany imagines the vestigial past as a liberatory resurrection. Delany references an older failed revolution to revive its spirit in the near future. In this respect, Delany is playing on the two temporal citations of Cuba we have seen in annexation discourse above: Cuba is at once a site of belatedness, cut off from the path of "progress," but it is also the key to unlocking progress' future. When read against annexationist literature, Delany's out-of-date use of Plácido reads almost like a parody of the fraudulent temporal hierarchies of "advanced" nations and vestigial ones that O'Sullivan and *La Verdad* used. For one, the representatives of progress are in this novel brutes and hypocrites, and annexation is a reactionary effort to forestall emancipatory progress. More complex is Delany's manipulation of the historical figure of Plácido: his appearance in a novel set in 1852 is a rather disorienting assault on fictional verisimilitude that captures the sense of historical uncertainty of this period in Cuban history, where the recent memories of failed rebellions weighed heavily on the brains of the living. By reviving this famously dead historical figure as Henry Blake's comrade, Delany emphasizes something deceptively simple. Not only does the Cuban past live on in its present, but Cuba and the United States inhabit the same temporality, one defined by a hemispheric economy based on slavery. With its suggestion that Cuba and the United States belong to the same time, Delany's novel sets up an alternate geography of the "misplaced ideas" of republican freedom, coming to deliver the huts of all the Americas from their self-styled republican oppressors. In Delany's vision, neither the South or Cuba is more "advanced" than the other, nor can either lay a greater claim on the "backwardness" of chattel slavery.

The novel opens with a Baltimore meeting of annexationists, including Henry and Maggie Blake's owner, Colonel Franks. When the scene shifts to Franks's Mississippi plantation, Delany introduces the colonel's friend,

Judge Ballard, "an eminent jurist of one of the Northern States." Ballard, we learn, is also the absentee owner of a slave plantation in Cuba, where he sends Henry's wife after purchasing her from the colonel. Ballard, an enthusiastic supporter of the Fugitive Slave Act, tells his Southern hosts his legal opinion on the Missouri Compromise of 1850, repeating the famous words of the majority opinion in the Dred Scott decision that ruled it unconstitutional—a decision only rendered in 1857, five years after *Blake* is set but two years before the novel appeared in *The Weekly Anglo-African*. Ballard tells his hosts that overturning the decision "was a just decision of the Supreme Court—though I was in advance of it by action—that persons of African descent have no rights that white men are bound to respect!"[60] Ballard's thesis of rights under slavery is an example of the tortured logic of liberalism "misplaced," in Schwarz's term, in slaveholding societies like the United States, Brazil, and Cuba, where the reactionary institution of slavery cohabits with the progressive discourse of rights. As Walter Johnson writes, one site of this dissonance is the slave body itself: "The abstract value that underwrote the southern economy could only be made material in human shape—frail, sentient, and resistant," he writes. "And thus the contradiction was daily played out in a contest over meaning."[61] In the quotidian world of slaveholding society, this "contest over meaning" was also played out in the maintenance of an artificial moral and ideological distinction between slavery and the market, which asserted a special distinction between the commodity-form to which enslaved people were reduced and the commodities their labor produced.

Delany's novel is preoccupied by the fraudulence of such a distinction. In one passage, he sketches the connections between slave-owner morality, annexationist politics, and the material economy of the plantation through a conversation between Judge Ballard and Colonel Franks. Recently returned from Havana, the judge tells his friend of his distaste for Cuba's racial mores, a common complaint among white visitors from the United States. "'I cannot for a moment tolerate it!" announces the judge. "One of the hateful customs of the place is that you must exchange civilities with whomsoever solicits it, consequently, the most stupid and ugly Negro you meet in the street may ask for a 'light' from your cigar.'" Colonel Franks tells his friend that he is far too "fastidious" on racial matters. Does he not realize that the very cigar he holds in his hand is certainly rolled, and his tobacco likely picked, by Black fingers? "Does that surprise you, Judge? I'm sure the victuals you eat is cooked by black hands, the bread kneaded and made by black hands, and the sugar and molasses you use, all pass through black hands, or rather the hands of Negroes pass through them; at least you could not refrain from thinking so, had you seen them as I have frequently, with arms full length immersed in molasses."[62] "The hands of Negroes pass through them": for Franks, that labor is more obviously a commodity secondary to the others that passive Black hands "pass through." For Delany's purposes, the Southern slave-owner's proximity to slave labor redresses the Northerner's self-satisfied ignorance of the labor that sustains him.

As Walter Benjamin suggests in "Theses on the Philosophy of History," the aesthetic of "historicism"—the passive desire to see the past "as it really was"—empathizes with history's victors. Blake's use of Plácido, by contrast, imagines one of history's recent "losers" in resplendent triumph.[63] In this context—in which John O'Sullivan has proclaimed the United States an empire of futurity, Cuba is a partner in a slave republic to come, and yet also an anachronistic vestige of the European empires that have been—Henry's quotation resounds most strikingly. "You, Plácido, are the man for the times!" says the Mississippi fugitive, looking to Cuba as the instrument of the future his oppressors fear most. The novel ends abruptly with the public garroting of Narciso López, which augurs a fierce Spanish surveillance of Plácido and Henry.[64] Delany thus ends his novel where Blunt began his sensational memoir: Narciso López is dead, and Cuba, once a bulwark in the imaginative geography of American whiteness, is now a crack in its edifice. For Delany, this is only the beginning of the story: out of the ashes of proslavery annexation's failure a more democratic future might rise. Annexationists were intent on emphasizing Cuba and the United States' shared interests, so *Blake* emphasizes all that the ruling classes of Cuba and the United States had in common—their hypocrisy and their fear, their contradictory conflation of republican principles and slave-owners' privilege. His novel, which reanimates the recent past by brushing it against the grain, gestures to but does not complete its ending. It was a history, Delany hoped, still in the making.

2 Latin America as Nature

U.S. Travel Writing and the Invention of Tropical Underdevelopment

The ill-smelling rum of the country is cheap and plentiful, tobacco grows everywhere, but these men neither drank nor smoked, nor swore—triple vices to be taught them by the first rush of Anglo-Saxon emigration, if there ever is one, for these people, when they live away from towns, seem quite free from grossness, both in customs and manner. Perhaps they were influenced by the knowledge that three strangers were within ear-shot; perhaps their simple lives, spent with nature in her loveliest and most majestic forms, gave the bent towards romance and sentiment.

—S. Desmond Segur, "On a Venezuelan Coffee Plantation" (1895)

Life in poor climes, then, is precarious, depressed, brutish. The mistakes of man, however well intentioned, aggravate the cruelties of nature.

—David Landes, *The Wealth and Poverty of Nations: Why Some Are So Rich and Some So Poor* (1998)

IN THE AUGUST 11, 1895, issue of the *Los Angeles Times,* S. Desmond Segur offered readers a study of "the pessimism that hovers, black-winged, over countless wretched little towns lying stagnant on the surface of our planet, and to one of which I propose to conduct my readers for the benefit of contrast," with the United States, of course. Unlike the dynamic United States, the "wretched little town" of Cariaquito, on a remote peninsula on the Caribbean coast of eastern Venezuela, is "stagnant"; in contrast to their optimistic neighbors to the north, its people are trapped by a "pessimism" that Segur links metaphorically with one of the "black-winged" insects of tropic swamps. This stagnant pessimism, however, allows Segur to appreciate the majestic nature he finds there. Cariaquito's people are gentle and innocent, he writes, and live in close contact with their beautiful natural environment. Ironically, though, the "romance" of that environment is lost on the people most familiar with it. Cariaquiteños lack the ability to appreciate the landscape aesthetically. What's more, its pristine beauty is passing. "So the little town lies," Segur writes, "hopelessly unchanging, while people are born, grow old and die there, and the busy thousands abroad, down whose throats it yearly pours such a stream of coffee and chocolate, know nothing about it."[1]

Segur's combination of sad, aesthetic reverence and moralistic contempt for the culture wrought by the "tropics" is one of the more enduring conventions of Latin Americanist writing in the United States, both for travel writers like him and professional students of the region's ecology and economy. In his 1915 study *Civilization and Climate,* Yale University's Ellsworth Huntington, a pioneer in what was then the new field of human geography, made a scientific study of the poverty of the tropics. Dispensing with the aestheticism of travel writers taken by the tropics' natural beauty, Huntington interpreted the poverty of the global South as a consequence, not of its racial inferiority, but of its climate. A century later, David Landes's best-selling *The Wealth and Poverty of Nations: Why Some Are So Rich and Some So Poor* began to answer its subtitle's question in much the same way. Huntington reframed familiar racist claims about "indolence" and "industry" as scientific consequences of climatic factors. Positioning himself against the pseudo-scientific geographic tradition established by Huntington, much as Huntington distinguished himself from the racial thinking of his own predecessors, Landes argues that "the law of heat exhaustion" applies to all. Landes's opening chapter, "Nature's Inequalities," is at pains to frame his argument as one about "inequality," not "incapacity," and he is quick to disavow the racism of geographers who have found in climate a "natural" explanation for underdevelopment—but then again, so was Huntington. The second chapter of *Civilization and Climate,* after all, was called "Race or Place." Its primary objective, Huntington wrote, was to minimize the effects of the former by concentrating on the greater power of the latter, "to separate the effects of race from those of place, heredity from environment."[2] Andrew Kamarck's *The Tropics and Economic Underdevelopment,* a 1977 World Bank study on the connection between poverty and climate, also makes a point to distinguish its empirical analysis of tropical soil, rainfall, and the agricultural technologies employed in the South from the legacy of geographers like Huntington. "Tropical climate is not *temperate* in its essential sense of moderation," writes Kamarck, committing the same confirmation bias as predecessors who defined "moderation" in terms of temperate seasonal patterns—rather than, say, a relatively constant year-round temperature—and thus defined "tropical" as a deviation from these normative standards. The empirical and the moral meanings of "moderation" and "temperate" are not so easily separated; indeed, they are hopelessly confused. The empiricism of development and climate science too often simply recapitulates the cultural assumptions at work.[3]

This chapter considers Latin American travel writing from the last decades of the nineteenth century until the dawn of the modern tourist industry in the early twentieth, when U.S. writers charted national difference in the Americas by a moral geography of climate. The most successful industry in the tropics, most of these writers agreed, belonged to Mother Nature. "South," at the global scale, came to mean two distinct but related things: it was both a spatial and environmental category, and a temporal and historical one, belonging to a place beneath and behind the temperate zone. Furthermore, both of these global meanings became gradually disentangled from the "south" as an underdeveloped region of the United States. The "tropics" to the south of the United States were identified with "indolence" and "lethargy," two common terms that had both moral and ecological meanings, referring both to widespread cultural habits and the weather that encouraged them. Latin American nations became the "south of the south," to borrow a phrase from Melvin Dixon—more than just the geographic neighbor of the southern U.S. states, but a belated counterpart of a U.S. South emerging from its own obsolescence.[4] The past became a foreign country, as belated forms of social life and economy were mapped onto a Latin American topography where they were naturalized as part of the landscape. This was often a deeply contradictory, even dysfunctional combination. To begin with, treating the tropics as a naturally belated region raised the troublesome problem of where, exactly, to draw their northern boundary. And if the weather put Euro-American "development" largely out of reach, what was the point of building the sewers and draining the "fever swamps" that would mollify the climate's dangerous effects for U.S. soldiers, investors, and settlers? These contradictions are in many ways endemic to the travel-writing genre, which relies on both the exotic power of difference and the explanatory power of analogy—a negotiation, that is, of difference and recognition. This negotiation exemplifies two of the fundamental points made in the Introduction about "development" and "underdevelopment": their indebtedness, firstly, to colonial tropes of geographic difference that predate them, and secondly, their tautological interdependence, underdevelopment's reliance on comparison to underline its difference. As Neil Smith observes, hemispheric geographical scales like "the tropics" are ways of mapping spatial organization under capitalism, and they are also ideological mystifications of those relationships. The moral discourse of the "tropics" suggested both discrete national differences, but the reality it described was much more volatile and proceeded at much more local scales than the terminology of "the tropics" and "the temperate zone" would suggest. The problem raised by this era of travel writing is how to reconcile the United States' increasingly planetary consciousness with its own recent history of regional conflict and dissension, which was not exceptional at all in the postcolonial Americas.

Segur's account of tropical premodernity in Venezuela conforms to a pattern that has been described in American studies scholarship, environmental history, and travel literature criticism alike. His preemptive nostalgia for the landscape's destruction by the "machine in the garden"—embodied here by the gluttonous U.S. coffee and chocolate consumer, whose throat lays open to receive the region's bounty—resembles the pattern famously outlined by Leo Marx. Segur's understanding of tropical nature in its pristine state as abundant, fertile, and intensely beautiful also works within a tradition made famous by German naturalist Alexander von Humboldt's encyclopedic accounts decades earlier. "If America occupies no important place in the history of mankind, and of the ancient revolutions which have agitated the human race," Humboldt wrote in 1814, "it offers an ample field to the labours of the naturalist. On no other part of the Globe is he called upon more powerfully by nature, to raise himself to general ideas on the cause of the phaenomena, and their general connection."[5] Nancy Stepan outlines the major characteristics of Humboldt's account of tropical nature: first, tropical nature could be framed aesthetically, in terms of "views" of a landscape that could be organized for the European or Anglo-American spectator, as in a painting. Second, "the tropics" were primarily vegetative, that is, defined by plant life as opposed to animal or human life. Finally, the tropics' extraordinary fertility is what most distinguished this region from the so-called temperate zone. The tropics' beauty comes from this combination of natural creativity and beauty, as well the naturalist's ability to appreciate it, as Segur does when he assesses Cariaquito's pleasing "forms."[6]

Frederick E. Church's *The Heart of the Andes,* a large painting first displayed in New York in 1859, is a case in point that underscores the moral content of this aesthetic framing of tropical ecology. Church, a landscape painter of the Hudson River School and an admirer of Humboldt, composed the work after a trip to Ecuador.[7] *The Heart of the Andes* became "a touchstone," art historian Katherine Manthorne writes, "of the North American pictorial consciousness of Latin America."[8] When it was first unveiled in New York, the painting attracted huge crowds of visitors who lined up for a glimpse of the canvas, which was displayed in a darkened room lit by gas jets. The painting depicts a lush mountain valley in the middle ground; looming in the background is a forbidding snow-covered peak. In the foreground, a river tumbles over a waterfall into a broad pool. Off to one side, framed by two deciduous trees—one of them dying, the other looming, its roots exposed, over the pool—is a mountain path on which we can see two small figures in indigenous dress, praying before a cross. In an 1859 review, *Cosmopolitan Art Journal* described the scene as a "boundlessly rich . . . South American tropical valley forest," and celebrated the painting for capturing an "unmixed grandeur, modified by the sweetness of the purely beautiful."[9] Other critics read the Andean landscape as an untouched, even "pre-Adamic" wilderness.[10] Yet far from depicting a "boundless" tropical wilderness, Church's painting is actually a pastoral mountain landscape, with a village in the middle distance and a man and woman in the foreground, with a tree fern the only clear sign of tropical vegetation.[11] Many contemporary critics overlooked this human content entirely.

Church's friend Theodore Winthrop described the tree fern as a botanically correct adjustment for the highland climate—a claim that was unusual for Anglo-American critics in its appreciation of the distinction between "the Andes" and "the tropics." This was a distinction that also held deep moral significance. The tree fern is an aesthetically complex and energetic plant: it "surpasses even the palm in refinement," Winthrop wrote, and is a hardier tree better suited than the palm for cooler climes "where the latter would chill and wither."[12] The *Cosmopolitan Art Journal,* for all its convictions about "tropical" flora, did note the painting's resemblance to Church's New York work. But where his painting *Niagara* was merely an impressive reproduction of the great falls, "the Niagara daguerreotyped," *The Heart of the Andes* was a work of sublime imagination, reaching "into realms of ideality" as yet untouched by his North American landscapes.[13] Winthrop's exhibition pamphlet observed that in the cooler temperatures of the Andean highlands, "vegetation assimilates to that of the temperate zones," and "can develop its life without harsh discipline of frost, and grow without need of frantic impulse after long lethargy. Hence," he concluded, "we are at home and yet strangers in these woods."[14] The geographical liminality of Church's painting, both wild and pastoral, neither the fertile "tropics" nor the frigid mountains, midway between torrid and temperate, both "at home" and exotic to the North American viewer, suggests that this iconic Latin American image was uncanny in its resemblance to the United States—a familiarity belied by the moral and ecological strangeness that tropicality otherwise connoted to the Anglo-American viewer. Latin American nature, at least at these spiritual and literal heights, is not an exotic deviation, but an ideal form of the familiar North American wilderness.

Winthrop's lengthy, detailed guide only once mentions in passing what he calls "the natives" in the foreground.[15] This elision of the human transformation of the ostensibly "natural" world is in keeping with what William Denevan has called the "Pristine Myth" of America as a pre-contact wilderness.[16] This treatment of nature as a sublime Eden or a primeval wilderness lent Latin American travel writing in this period much of its sense of moral purpose. In the latter half of the century, Mary Suzanne Shriber writes, travel was "an imperative that bordered on the religious," an exercise of leisure as much as duty. Travel was "an excursion into history, into the linear progression from which the role of the United States in God's grand design for the human race becomes visible."[17] Shriber is writing, here, of European travel writing, but travel south was also invested with historical and national significance. While travel to the continent meant an encounter with a civilizational past, though, most U.S. travelers to Latin America thought they were entering a place with no significant history at all. So if travel within the United States was fashioned as a pilgrimage to places yielded providentially to the United States, as John F. Sears has argued, Latin American travel was more of a mission.[18] Just as the mission is the evangelical counterpart to the pilgrimage—the purposeful journey to where the good news has not yet been proclaimed, as opposed to a worshipful voyage to its place of origin—travel to Latin America was a form of national self-definition characterized by an emphasis on newness and wilderness.

These two categories are more different than they might initially appear, however, since travel to Latin America was most often understood as an encounter with nature, either in its pristine state as a garden, or in its dangerous power as a wilderness. So even though Church's inclusion of a pair of devout figures seems like a clear allegory of the cultivated "garden" of Eden, critics who read his Andean landscape as primeval or "pre-Adamic" conflated the two categories of ecological primitivity. The conflation of garden and wilderness shows how tropical nature could be simultaneously invoked as both a sublime aesthetic object and a morally suspect and potentially dangerous ecology. This contradiction is an example of what Smith calls the "ideology of nature." Drawing a dialectical

link between "universal nature," nature as sublime object of contempla-
tion, and "external nature," or nature as an object of labor, Smith writes
that they functioned together in a logic of exploitation: "The hostility
of external nature justified its domination and the spiritual morality of
universal nature provided a model for social behavior." We can see this
dialectical contest at work in Segur's treatment of Venezuelan nature as
simultaneously ravaged and majestic, spiritually soothing for the very
people whose ravenous appetites are destroying it. As Smith argues, the
abstraction of the natural world's human producers are the distorted
products of this ideology of nature: "Nature, not human history, is made
responsible" for inequality, death, violence, cruelty, hunger, and so on,
while "capitalism is treated not as historically contingent but as an inevitable and universal product of nature."[19] As the continued popularity of
arguments like Landes's shows, this is not an artifact of a more benighted
age, but one that endures in contemporary attempts to account for, and
apologize for, the uneven development of the globe.

In Latin America travel writing of the late nineteenth and early twentieth centuries, the poverty of the global South appears as *homogeneous*
and *natural,* rather than *heterogeneous* and *social.* This essentialist understanding of space can be seen in much of the U.S. regionalist fiction of the
same era, as Hsuan Hsu writes, which treated the underdeveloped spaces
of the United States as repositories of a cultural past being subsumed
by the technology and alienated social relations of capitalist modernity.
Hsu shows how the consolidation of global commodity markets conditioned literary regionalism in the latter half of the century, a moment
of dynamic spatial transformation that nevertheless yielded essentialist
thinking about space. Even local scenes like the "pristine" Maine woods
of Sarah Orne Jewett's fiction were perforated by the globalizing labor
and commodity flows that conditioned them, like the growing timber
industry that captured more and more of Maine's fir trees.[20] In the Latin
American tropics, this contemplative idealization tended to confirm,
rather than question, the virtues of U.S. modernity. In 1907, for example,
another visitor to Venezuela considered the interlocking histories of the
two countries. Joseph Hampton Moore accompanied House of Representatives Speaker Joseph Cannon on a public tour of the Caribbean,
and his account is an excellent example of the two interlocking "souths,"
the environmental and temporal, at work in the period's inter-American
travel literature. In Caracas, Moore summarizes his view of the city's past
and future prospects with a textbook example of what Mary Louise Pratt
calls the "monarch-of-all-I-survey" perspective of the Victorian travel

writer. Moore stands upon Ávila, the mountain that overlooks the Venezuelan capital, and reflects grandiosely on what the city means. He begins with what seems at first like surprising humility:[21] "I wondered if we, as a nation, whose growth and prosperity has been so marvelous, had not perhaps 'looked down' upon these people, whose very demeanor, seemingly morose and sullen, bespoke the spirit of resentment," he writes. What seems like an ironic self-critique of an Anglo-American figuratively "looking down" on Latin America evaporates in the next sentences, though. Chicago "was not on the map when Caracas was 250 years old," but it dwarfs it today. Universal nature, unconquered by man in South America, explains the difference. Citing a meteorologist, Moore concludes that "in the North the human tendency is to delve and hustle; in the tropics it seems to be to wait and dream." From atop Ávila, Moore sees "the line between contentment and fear, between progress and idleness, between the doing and the leaving undone." The climate makes the difference.[22]

Travel Writing, Fictive Travel, and the Moral Geography of Climate

Travel writing was one of the rare literary genres of the time (other than dime novels) that devoted sustained attention to Spanish America, especially when professional academic study of the region was almost nonexistent.[23] Before the consolidation of an "expert class" of Latin Americanist intellectuals, travel writers offered historical, political, and cultural information unavailable elsewhere. Travel writing was also one of the nineteenth century's most popular literary genres, shaping everyday readers' attitudes about other latitudes. Most international travel in mid- and late nineteenth-century North America was to Europe, particularly England.[24] Cuba and Mexico, while less popular than England and Italy, were far and away the most written-about foreign destinations in the Americas.[25] Between 1850 and 1900, 75 books of travel to Cuba were published in the United States—of these, 26 directly treated the 1895–98 Cuban War of Independence and the U.S. intervention in the form of correspondents' accounts and soldiers' memoirs. During the same period, 122 books were published about Anglo-Americans' Mexican travels (of these, nine recounted visits to both Mexico and Cuba).[26] No other country in the hemisphere matched their popularity, although Puerto Rico and the cities of Caracas, Rio de Janeiro, Buenos Aires, and Montevideo were relatively popular destinations.

Travel writing also exists within a broader late nineteenth and early twentieth-century travel culture that Kristen Hoganson calls "fictive travel": the virtual consumption of foreign locales in social contexts like formal and informal travel clubs, literary societies, women's clubs, and in visual and written media like visual art, travel books, stereographs, and newspaper spectacles. Nellie Bly's "stunt journalism," for example, took her to Mexico for six months and around the world in seventy-two days. Documenting hundreds of travel clubs nationwide, Hoganson writes that the significance of this era of fictive travel is its elaboration of a global scale of consciousness, a "planetary scale of being." Along with "foreign" food and entertainment that made inroads in U.S. domestic life, fictive travel helped shape a global consciousness among middle-class white women, the primary members of the travel clubs of the era.[27] This planetary consciousness was consumerist in essence, matching up well with the largely nonterritorial empire that U.S. commerce was building in Latin America, through the isthmian canal project, the invasion of Cuba, and the penetration of Central American fruit trade. The fictive travel movement thus set up the foreign as an object of consumption, but just as important, it was bound up with images of domesticity that hierarchically organized foreign cultures in terms of their approximation of bourgeois Anglo-American life.[28]

The weather and the landscape were important factors in this hierarchical organization of American cultures. For the modern reader, a surprising characteristic of the era's travel writers is their outright hostility or relative indifference to what most attracts modern-day northern visitors to the Caribbean—the warm weather. "The climate," for the U.S. traveler of the late nineteenth and early twentieth centuries, meant a combination of things: the unchanging tedium of tropical warmth, the lack of seasonal variation in temperature, and the diseases, like yellow fever and malaria, that thrived in the Caribbean basin. "The man who comes to Cuba for the first time," wrote James Steele, a former diplomat who wrote tartly of his time as consul, "does not find the Cuba of his pictures and dreams. He has not encountered the deep stillness of a tropical forest." Instead, he lamented, "It is summer without the hay-making; May, lacking the freshness and flowers."[29] In Port of Spain, Trinidad en route to Caracas, William Eleroy Curtis described tropical nature as an allegory of the Fall. He recounts a stroll through the city streets, where men "are too lazy to work, but always seem to be eating something, generally fruit, which is as cheap and plenty as dirt."[30] Curtis repeats a common cliché of the era's travel writing—this is a genre awash in clichés, of course—in claiming that tropical weather encouraged idleness, not simply because of the enervating effects of heat but because of the moral effects of nature's overabundant fertility. "Where food is everywhere abundant, extensive clothing unnecessary, and the soil excessively fertile," Maturin Murray Ballou wrote of Cuba, "there is no incentive for hard work."[31] What for the modern tourist is an appealing break from the speed and stress of modern urban life, in other words, was for the Victorian traveler evidence of the insalubrious nature of the region. The climate was invoked as an explanation for *caudillismo* and political instability in the Caribbean and South and Central America, as well. It explained political intrigue in *Three Gringos in Venezuela and Central America,* a rollicking narrative from the popular turn-of-the-century novelist, journalist, and travel writer Richard Harding Davis—from whom we will hear more in chapter 3. "The value of stability in government is something they cannot be made to understand," Davis wrote of Hondurans. "It is not in their power to see it, and the desire for change and revolution is born in the blood. They speak of a man as a 'good revolutionist' just as we would speak of some one being a good pianist, or a good shot, or a good executive officer. It is a recognized calling, and the children grow up into fighters; and even those who have lived abroad, and who should have learned better, begin to plot and scheme as soon as they return to their old environment."[32] Davis identifies revolution as a racial inheritance "in the blood," but also something endemic in the environment, like a contagion that one can catch when he comes back from colder climes. This tendency to upheaval was a consequence, paradoxically, of the lethargy promoted by the climate and, relatedly, of the mixed racial inheritance of Spanish America. If the weather encouraged revolutions, as Davis suggests, it was not because hot weather promoted hot heads, but because the absence of winter discouraged the long-term planning of a more mature, temperate society less given to impulsive acts.

In ascribing such a variety of moral and historical traits to the weather, late nineteenth-century writers were working in a longer tradition in which climate was imbued with racial and moral meaning.[33] The moral geography of climate manifested itself in the associations of moisture and miasma with disease in an era before the wide acceptance of germ theory, and in the long-standing racist claim that whites were ill-suited to manual labor in warm latitudes. The association of the tropical climate with these related scourges of filth, evil, indolence, and vegetal decline exemplifies the popular "climatic determinism" of the age.[34] Here, the etymological slippage between temperate and temperance becomes a moral conviction. The changing of the seasons and the arrival of spring appeal to a Christian faith in renewal and repentance, Catherine Cocks writes, while the thrift and industry made necessary by winter contrast with the "indolence" that a constantly warm climate encourages.[35] In Mexico's Yucatán, the languorous climate was, ironically, only too busy doing its decadent work on the built structures of Mayan civilization, according to the naturalist Frank Baker. "Ruin and decay have been steadily at work," he writes at Uxmal, "and before many years have passed, this famous relic of the ancient Mayas will be a thing of the past. Over all the buildings a rank vegetation is struggling for the mastery, and the end is inevitable."[36] Before the celebration of the tropics as an elixir of regeneration and youth—a transformation Cocks attributes to the growth of tourism as a national industry in the twentieth century—travel writers foregrounded Latin America as a place of poverty and deprivation; of cultural otherness (Catholicism and indigeneity being the most popular markers of difference); and of a spectacular and beautiful, but dangerous and morally suspect natural landscape.

Food, and U.S. tourists' struggle with it, was one place where these three features converge. Mexican and Central American travel accounts are rife with complaints about curiosities like the tortilla and the arepa (the Spanish food served in Cuban and Puerto Rican hotels was often better suited to Anglo-American travelers' tastes). In his 1857 book, the Frenchman Arthur Morelet expressed a sentiment his U.S. colleagues in Mexico would probably have recognized when his book was reprinted in 1871: "The necessity of being surrounded by so many offensive animals and noxious insects, which, not content with sharing your bed and mingling in your food, invade your person and prey on your flesh, it must be admitted, detracts somewhat from the poetry of tropical adventures."[37] The experience of hardship is part of the drama of the travel narrative, of course, and it also exemplifies the "ideology of nature" writ small: the "poetry" of universal nature was locked here in a miniature struggle with external nature, the mosquitoes that must be subdued. In 1886, Helen Sanborn published an account of the trip she took through Belize and Guatemala as interpreter for her father, a U.S. coffee importer. She dismissed the arepa as an anachronistic survivor of biblical times: "They are made from corn which is ground between two stones, just as it was in Egypt in the time of the Israelites. . . . [I]t was exceedingly fortunate that we were not Epicureans."[38] Howard Conkling, meanwhile, complained of the "everlasting grease and spice that characterize ordinary Mexican cookery."[39] Yet even these culinary deficiencies could be explained by climatic factors that promote acquiescence instead of industry, as when William English Carson complained that Mexican cuisine was itself poorly suited to the country's climate. Unaccustomed to struggling against the coming of winter, they are ruled by habit: hence, he says, the lack of a Mexican wine industry, a fact explainable only by "indolence."[40] Albert Zabriski Gray, a Protestant minister on a tour of Mexico, read history in the fruit market: after indulging in the "luxuriant insipidity" of pineapples and mangoes, he longed for an apple. "For character and strength," after all, "you must go to the sterner, severer North—and thus we have much of the moral of history!"[41] Bly's introduction to a chapter of Mexican recipes in her book *Six Months in Mexico* was at least modestly complimentary, reversing the "insipid" charge: "Probably some one would like to make a few of the dishes most common to the Mexican table," she wrote. "Of course you will think them horrible at first, but once you acquire the taste, American food is insipid in comparison."[42] In the decades before the boom in tourism in the 1920s, travel to places like Panama, Cuba, Mexico, and beyond was practically difficult, a fact reflected in these exaggerated hardships and in the tourist itineraries that literary travelers followed: ruined Mayan temples hidden in the Yucatecan rainforest, Cuban prisons and sugar plantations, Honduran *cafetales* accessible only by mule.[43] If travel was meant to provide education and self-improvement, these virtues came from the confrontation with extremities of material poverty and natural wildness in Latin America, rather than with examples of cultural wealth and natural grandeur, as in Britain or Italy. Some of these hardships, clearly, were gastronomic.

Beyond the moral degeneration that many associated with the tropics, the land itself was also held to be rife with disease. During the U.S. occupations of Cuba, Puerto Rico, and Panama in the first decades of the twentieth century, popular notions of tropical disease were informed by an uneven mixture of the moralism of miasma and the relatively new science of germ theory, which was slowly replacing popular understandings of illness that traced it to the "bad air" or vapor called "miasma" that emanated from diseased places. "Disease," Mariola Espinosa writes, "was therefore an attribute of place; the location itself was sick." Marie Gorgas, whose husband was the Panama Canal Zone's sanitation director, held "Nature herself" responsible for making the isthmus "the headquarters of the worst manifestations of the human spirit. The whole forty-mile stretch was one sweltering miasma of disease and death," connecting landscape, sickness, and morality as mutually reinforcing obstacles to the canal project.[44] When U.S. Army physicians working on yellow fever were able to prove Cuban physician Carlos Finlay's theory of mosquito transmission, they developed aggressive mosquito-eradication measures in the knowledge that it was the infection the mosquitoes carried, and not the moisture itself, that was dangerous.[45] Some saw this breakthrough as evidence of an impending "tropical renaissance"—if climate was "blameless" in the spread of malaria and yellow fever, then arguments about the tropics' inhospitality to "civilization" might be baseless as well.[46] At the same time, this advance in scientific knowledge could paradoxically play upon the same moral preoccupation with "filth" as a carrier of disease, since mosquitoes thrived in the same moisture that also produced miasma. Here, as with "temperance" in climate science, the moral and scientific meanings of "filth" were not easily disentangled.[47]

The work of John Snow on the 1854 London cholera epidemic and Louis Pasteur's work in the following decade on fermentation and the growth of microorganisms contradicted the miasmatic theory of disease, but popular accounts of Latin America by travel writers and journalists trailed the vanguard of scientific research, relying instead on conventional racial, class, and national homologies between moral and physical health. Randolph DeBenneville Keim's 1870 book of travel to the Dominican Republic attributed the nation's health to its high elevation, which ensured that "no miasmatic vapors spread over the land to generate epidemics."[48] In the run-up to the invasion of Cuba in 1898, the *Chicago Tribune* hopefully asserted that "yellow fever in the South and yellow fever in Cuba are said to be two totally different things," presuming that the disease had a character that respected national boundaries. Later that fall, the *Tribune* described yellow fever outbreaks in the south as Cuban invasions that would finally be stopped by American ingenuity and generosity: "Spaniards and Cubans know nothing and care nothing about microbes, but the American government both knows and cares."[49] In Charles Melville Pepper's postoccupation *To-morrow in Cuba* (1898) one still reads of "calenture," the fever said to afflict northern soldiers in tropical climes. And a Canal Zone school primer over a decade later urged teachers and students to remember that "bad air" did not cause disease.[50] What these examples show is the persistent entanglement of scientific and miasmatic—that is, empirical and moral—understandings of tropical disease. The lessons many U.S. Americans drew from this were likewise both technical and moral: if diseases like malaria and yellow fever that thrived in the moist, warm air were the greatest obstacles to the United States' administration of the isthmus, then the conquest of these obstacles proved not only the technical achievement, but also the justice and wisdom of the occupation.

Besides "fever," the tropical climate also had more mundane, deleterious effects on the bodies and especially spirits of white people from the temperate zone. One 1899 visitor to Puerto Rico alleged that the Caribbean heat was different than that of the southern states, not so much in intensity but in a uniquely ineffable character. To borrow a key word from the discussion of tropical fruit above, the Caribbean air is "insipid": rather than leaving the tourist invigorated or hot-headed, as more contemporary stereotypes have it, the tropical climate made him physically weak and mentally dull. "It is not the intense heat, for, measured by the thermometer, the heat is not so very intense, and in most palaces it is tempered by a breeze which elsewhere would doubtless be refreshing," writes the author of *The Porto-Rico of To-Day.* "But it is hardly so here. The air is dull and heavy, and one grows listless. Physical exertion of any kind becomes a bore, and mental exertion becomes almost an impossibility."[51] The Brownsville, Texas, *Daily Ranchero and Republican,* an Anglo paper from a border city, complained to its readers in 1872 that its "glorious summer weather" produced a condition of "general debility": the "liver is more or less affected, the bowels are either constipated or too much relaxed, the stomach but half performs the work of digestion, the appetite is poor, and the spirits depressed."[52] While this "glorious summer weather" was debilitating for the healthy, it made the tropics a popular site for convalescence, especially for consumptive patients. Guidebooks were published for this burgeoning market, and few healthy travelers to Cuba, probably the most popular Latin American destination for consumptives, failed to note the pathetic sight of tubercular patients gasping on the ship decks and in Havana's hotels as they sought the warm, moist air of Cuba.[53] This seeming contradiction—the Caribbean region was a vector of plagues and also a place to recover from them, a place of both insipid depression and fortifying recovery—seems to prove the general rule of identifying the tropics generally with disease, either its transmission or its exorcism. It is as if the Caribbean air worked its health effects in reverse there: only if you were fatally unhealthy *already* could the humidity be invigorating.

Instead of offering the spiritual regeneration that modern-day tourists attribute to it, the Caribbean climate most often delivered moral dissipation to Victorian travelers. It was this dissipation that the U.S.-led modernization of Cuba, Puerto Rico, and Panama was said to repair. As the swamps were cleared, the harbors cleaned, and the streets disinfected, the dreaded tropical fevers would subside, many writers and officials confidently proclaimed.[54] But what about the "dull and heavy" air, the "listless" atmosphere, which no public works project would ever fix? In the Caribbean, sanitation became a practical concern that became identified with modernity and the United States itself, a story I will revisit in chapter 3, on the invasion of Cuba and the postwar occupation. The reconstruction of the Panamanian landscape during the building of the canal proved that the United States was itself an evenly developed country, and it was evidence, as well, that its prosperity, technique, and science could be exported around the globe.[55] And while yellow fever may be different in the north and south, according to the *Chicago Tribune,* sewers are the same everywhere. That is, even though the underlying conditions of backwardness are inflexible, resting in the hotter, wetter regions of the earth, the great hope of the U.S. modernizing mission in the Caribbean lay in the presumption that its modernity was exportable and reproducible. Given the prevailing theories about the moral geography of race and climate, however, it becomes clear that beneath the hemispheric Pax Americana and its ethos of technical progress was an inflexibly hierarchical ethno-racial order. Just as Panama's backwardness could be traced to its heat and humidity, U.S. know-how and modernity was, in turn, identified with its temperate climate. And no amount of street-sweepers could turn Panama into Connecticut. Climate, in other words, was destiny.

Place, Race, and Cultural Difference in the Moral Geography of Climate

The geographer David Livingstone has described a "moral discourse of climate" that explained racial and ethnic judgment in the scientific discourse of empirical geography.[56] This discourse expresses a faith that "backwardness" was responsive to technical transformation as well as a racialist conviction that it inhered in the landscape, if not exactly in the people themselves. In *Civilization and Climate,* Huntington argued for the specifically climatic roots of moral degradation, idleness, and other afflictions found in the tropics. This meant that the roots of the economic gap between north and south were predominantly environmental and therefore not exclusively racial. Even whites, once transported to the tropics, begin to show its deleterious effects, he claimed. An anecdote (despite his fondness for maps, graphs, and tables, Huntington relies heavily on anecdote) proves the point. A northern U.S. expatriate in Nassau says, "'Until I came to the Bahamas I never appreciated posts. Now I want to lean against every one that I see.'" This determining influence of the environment also explained the poverty of the U.S. South, disproving slights against the intellectual and moral level of the southern populace.[57] Here again, though, the U.S. South is used as a point of comparison from which the poverty of the greater "tropical" south may be measured and ultimately distinguished from that of the United States. Huntington's scientific framework meant that the United States' wealth was also circumstantial, rather than providential. "We must determine," Huntington charged his readers, "how much of our European and American energy, initiative, persistence, and other qualities upon which we so much pride ourselves is due to racial inheritance, and how much to long residence under highly stimulating conditions of climate."

Huntington's criteria for these "stimulating conditions" were precise: the optimal conditions for physical and mental exertion, he determined, are daytime temperatures between 60 and 65 degrees Fahrenheit with mild frosts overnight. Whether the final determinant of such conditions is God, as the creator of the nature that shapes human destinies, or impassive nature itself is unclear here. As the contemporary geographer Livingstone observes, it hardly matters, since "nature," as the universal nature preceding man, and God, as creator that precedes human intervention, amount to the same ahistorical force rooted in an abstraction called "the tropics."[58] "The races of the earth are like trees," Huntington wrote. "Each according to its kind brings forth the fruit known as civilization."[59] Given the epochal, metaphorically arboreal pace of historical change in this model, there is little to be done to transform or accelerate it—it can only be managed. One of Huntington's contemporaries, Ellen Churchill Semple, drew the pessimistic conclusion: "The conquering white race of the Temperate Zone is to be excluded by adverse climatic conditions from the productive but undeveloped Tropics, unless it consents to hybridization."[60] For all of Huntington's claims of "place" as prior to "race," as Gary Okihiro notes, the "development" of the tropics was a risky economic and civilizational imperative, whose ultimate danger lay in "miscegenation."[61] The solution lay in the careful management, not only of disease and sanitation infrastructure, but of the integrity of whiteness in the tropics, just as it did for the Cuban annexationists decades earlier—for all of Huntington's supposedly scientific innovations, this had scarcely changed.

Development discourse later replaced this colonialist view of "undeveloped" nations hostile to the "conquering white race" with the proposition of an immanent sameness between nations, waiting to be realized in the course of modernization. Victorian-era travel writers also noticed a convergence between the United States and Latin America, but instead of deferring it to the future, they projected it into the past the United States had left behind. The signs of what we would now term uneven development were understood as persistent remnants of the past of the civilized world and, therefore, of the United States. Describing the difference between north and south in such terms inevitably required finding analogies between them, a figurative technique of comparison that at times could confuse the cultural distinctions otherwise being drawn. While outlining the difference between home and the foreign is the bread and butter of travel writers, analogy is a narrative technique by which this difference is made legible. When Columbus, for example, uses the "orchards of Valencia in April" to describe the landscape of the New World in the diary of his third voyage, he does so, as Mary Campbell puts it, "to convert features of an alien territory into more or less grotesque collages of the familiar."[62] As she argues, this use of analogy is a practice of domestication, an imaginative reconquest. Yet analogy can work the other way, as well, to defamiliarize, or at least to critique, the familiar. For North Americans, unlike Columbus, Latin America was not entirely *foreign,* not a distant "new world," but a close neighbor. U.S. travel writers often emphasized the magnitude of the scale of the hemisphere to assert the breadth of cultural differences within it. At the same time, implicit in these transgressions are more intimate, psychological "crossings," in which "the otherness within," as Bruce Harvey has written, "becomes projected onto a foreign topography and its inhabitants."[63] Imaginative foreign topographies like the "third world" produce the difference they describe through their management of what Pratt calls interaction or "copresences," the "interlocking understandings and practices, often within radically asymmetrical relations of power" that shape the contact between travelers and "travelees."[64] The "backwardness" we see in these turn-of-the-century accounts of Latin America is therefore more complex that it may initially appear. In the foreignness of Latin America, U.S. authors see a reflection of themselves: their recent past, their possible future, the continental America that a porous and only recently fabricated border cannot completely contain. A traveler to the western borderlands, for example, might take the geographic and therefore temporal ambiguity of the area as his subject. In his 1893 book *The Land of Poco Tiempo,* the journalist Charles Fletcher Lummins calls New Mexico territory the "anomaly" of the republic, the "National Rip van Winkle—the United States which is not the United States."[65] New Mexico had been settled by Europeans a century earlier than the eastern states, yet it was, along with the rest of Latin America, the land of *"mañana,"* where the industry and timeliness of the newer east did not apply. It appears, to Lummins, to have been asleep all that time, arrested in a state of development preceding the modern United States. Rather than disavowing the Mexican presence in the southwestern United States, as contemporary nativists might do, Lummins read New Mexico as an anachronistic copresence that could not be swept away but would need, at some point, to be synchronized with the rest of the national space.

Susan Schulten has shown how Latin America was represented on U.S. maps well into the twentieth century as a region, rather than as a set of autonomous nations, making the physical continent—not the historical nation-states—the primary unit of cartographic identification.[66] Likewise, a popular theme of nineteenth-century North American writing about Latin America, from settlers' accounts of *californios* to travel writing from Peru and Mexico, was the Latin Americans' apparent stagnation in a state of nature. According to this view, the Spanish American masses lacked prerequisites for civilization, while the elites were enervated from indolence and overcivilization. Yet Frederick Pike's argument that U.S. Americans understood Latin American in terms of a binary opposition between civilization and nature is only partly correct; it is an oversimplification that reflects the triumph of American exceptionalism in the Cold War more acutely than it does the anxious performances of cultural superiority in this period when U.S. dominance of the hemisphere was not yet a given.[67] Latin America was often treated as a mixture of the antique and modern, as a "backward" object of U.S. intervention, but also as an occasionally modern collaborator in the "progress" of the hemisphere.[68] Cuba was an especially good example, given the island's longstanding reputation for modernity, as discussed in chapter 1. As early as 1867, the merchant sailor George Clark raved in his memoir that the country was already prepared to "come under the rule of Uncle Sam." The bustling metropolis of Havana, he wrote, "has gas works, steam cars, aqueducts, hotels, and billiard halls."[69] As up-to-date as Havana sometimes seemed, though, rural Cuba was also described by many travelers as reminiscent of the U.S. South, especially for those who visited Cuba before the abolition of slavery in 1888. Sugar plantations were a popular stop on the itineraries of many U.S. travel writers, and those who made the short trip by rail or steamship from Havana to the plantations around Matanzas often found themselves moving through an uncanny southern landscape. In *My Winter in Cuba* (1871), Julia Louisa Matilda describes the landscapes and characters that speed past the window of her train. She takes from these briefest of glimpses a deep impression of the character of the Cuban small farmers, who she calls "monteros." Matilda observes how he "in character and so-cial status, much resembles the 'poor whites' of our South."[70] In Matanzas, Richard Henry Dana was stunned to see in a slave-operated sugar mill "a man with an unmistakable New England face in charge of the engine, with that look of intelligence and independence so different from the intelligence and independence of all other persons." He is a mechanic from the manu-facturing center of Lowell, Massachusetts, one of the U.S. technicians who came to Cuba during the harvest season to operate and maintain the com-plex machinery that powered the sugarcane mills. His presence in Matanzas seems to unnerve Dana; perhaps the rural Spanish dictatorship of the lash and New England republican modernity may cohabitate more easily than imagined. In Matilda's southern analogies and Dana's encounter with the Lowell engineer, the copresence of north and south begins to trouble the clear oppositions between foreign and domestic, abroad and home. For Dana, Cuba can be thought of as uncanny in Freud's sense: it elicits the anxiety that, for Freud, is produced by the ambivalent distinction between the familiar and the strange. It is an ambivalence Dana represses, however: after meeting the Lowell man who makes the sugar mills run, he decides that "you can't reason from Massachusetts to Cuba."[71] The two places are an epistemological, if not economic, world apart.

The built environments of Cuba and Mexico challenged travel writ-ers to engage with the country's human and social worlds. In the case of Cuba, the capital city seemed modern while the persistence of slav-ery two decades after emancipation in the United States allowed visitors from the United States to identify it as a vision of the southern past still alive in the present. In the case of Mexico, the country's large indigenous population and its architectural antiquity reanimated a "vanished" in-digenous United States while providing the hemisphere with an ancient built environment unconnected to Europe. The wealth of tropical nature, and the ruination it brings; the antiquity of Mexico and the modernity of its capital; the backwardness of Cuban slavery and, for some Southern-ers, the beautiful future it still promised, even after the U.S. Civil War: these contradictions all show how the emerging distinction between a modernizing United States and "backward" Latin America had to be disentangled from a much more knotty set of cultural and historical ties.

Making a Surrogate South: The Case of Eliza McHatton Ripley, a Confederate Exile in Cuba

Relatively accessible by steamship from New York, Charleston, and New Orleans, Cuba's plantation society offered a pleasing combination of both the exotic and the familiar. Matthew Pratt Guterl has shown how some Southern travelers' accounts of Latin America looked hopefully to a pan-Caribbean plantation culture centered around Havana and New Orleans that transcended U.S. borders and sectional politics.[72] Nostalgia for slavery is a major theme of South Carolinian George Williams's *Sketches of Travel in the Old and New World* (1871), which included a detailed account of an 1854 trip to Havana; *Petals Plucked from Sunny Climes* (1880) by Sylvia Sunshine, the pseudonym of the Floridian Abbie Brooks; and Eliza McHatton Ripley's *From Flag to Flag: A Woman's Adventures and Experiences in the South during the War, in Mexico, and in Cuba* (1889), the bulk of which is devoted to her Louisiana family's exile on a sugar plantation near Matanzas during the Civil War.

As they traveled though Cuba, many Northerners (and some Southerners, as we shall see shortly), felt they had been there before; the island recalled an economy and a set of cultural habits that, in the United States, were ascribed to the slave-owning plantocracy of the Southern states. Visitors to Havana and its outskirts combined their wonder at Cuba's architecture and ecology with this sense of recognition. Often, the moral geography upon which these authors drew was the same in each place: as Jennifer Rae Greeson has argued, Reconstruction-era travel accounts of the U.S. South by Northern authors defined the Southern states with the same natural and moral vocabulary that travel writers used for the Latin American tropics, as both naturally fertile and morally indolent. Edward King's 1870 *The Great South,* a travelogue of the postbellum Southern states, does so by means of analogy, by reading the South "in the context of underdeveloped regions around the globe," writes Greeson. The analogy between the South and Spanish America legitimated U.S. expansion in the American hemisphere by invoking a shared history of foreign domination and subjugation, one that in looking backwards at the "belated" U.S. South looks forward to a U.S.-ruled hemisphere defined by a shared experience of defeat, hardship, and eventual triumph. This comparison framed the link between the U.S. South and Spanish America as a historically intimate tie distinct from that of Europe to its African colonies. This imagined intimacy positioned the United States as the virtuous, empathetic administrator—rather than colonial exploiter—of the underdeveloped regions both within and outside its borders.[73]

The Louisiana-born Ripley's narrative of her failed exile in Cuba is an example. She and her husband, a sugar planter, fled their plantation outside Baton Rouge in December 1862 as Union troops approached the city. Sending their family's slaves to a relative's plantation—save Eliza's personal slave Martha—the Ripleys went first to Texas, and then Mexico, before finally settling in Cuba on a plantation worked both by Black slaves and Chinese indentured workers. Published in 1889, *From Flag to Flag* is a narrative of compounded defeats: first of the Confederacy, then of its attempted revival in Cuba. Cuba was both a refuge and an opportunity to reinvent the plantation society Ripley's family had lost in Louisiana, but the failure of this enterprise returns her to the country she had originally left behind. Ripley reflected on her refuge, exile, and return: "Thus faded the Confederacy. We prayed for victory—no people ever uttered more earnest prayers—and the God of hosts gave us victory in defeat. We prayed for only that little strip, that Dixie-land, and the Lord gave us the whole country from the lakes to the Gulf, from ocean to ocean—all dissensions settled, all dividing lines wiped out—a united country forever and ever."[74] Indeed, Ripley's memoir seeks to join her Dixie patriotism and her planter-class nostalgia to a renewed, unified Americanism, one that relishes the traditions that she had preserved in Cuba while banishing that island's backwardness from its collective memory. Given this narrative arc of exile and deliverance, it is appropriate that the Ripleys named their Matanzas plantation "Desengaño"—literally "undeception" or "disillusion"—since it is their exile in the Cuban master class that ultimately restores their nation to them. As Guterl argues, Ripley's memoir is, on the one hand, illustrative of the contradictions of the postemancipation era, when "debates about labor, land, race, and citizenship were then as much transnational as national." Despite the text's grounding in the politics of emancipation and its aftermath, Guterl suggests that there is also something more familiar about Ripley's desire for land and cheap labor abroad. "One generation's slaves and coolies have evolved into another's H-2 workers and third world dispossessed," he writes, "and Eliza's brutal chauvinisms are a crude precedent for the breezy and callous corporate style of the modern-day executive, relentlessly folding up factories and moving them to ever cheaper sites with little regard for the human cost."[75]

After their arrival, the Ripleys are quickly flummoxed by the management of their enslaved laborers and their inability to reproduce the paternalistic slavery ideal that Martha embodies for them. Writes Ripley, "Never can I forget the horrors of the early days at Desengaño. When the black woman, in a dirty, low-necked, sleeveless, trailing dress, a cigar in her mouth, and a naked, sick, and whining child on one arm, went about spreading the table, scrupulously wiping Royo's plates with an exceedingly suspicious-looking ghost of a towel, the prospect for dinner was not inviting."[76] If Martha represents an ideal of slaveholding domesticity, Cuban slave femininity threatens to undo it with what Ripley and other Anglo-Americans regarded as the indiscipline of Cuban racial mores, in which the phallic cigar in a slave woman's mouth is a recurring nightmare image.[77] (Compare Ripley's disdain here with J. Milton Mackie's in his 1864 *From Cape Cod to Dixie and the Tropics,* in which Black women on the Havana streets smoked cigars "cocked up as jauntily as any hidalgo, and were also expert in the art of holding it between their teeth through all their chattering, grinning, and even ha-ha-ing.")[78] As it was for Judge Ballard in *Blake,* the Cuban cigar is a potent metonym of tropical danger, representing insolence and an "intemperate" lack of restraint nurtured by Cuba's aristocracy, its climate, and its too-loose racial codes.

The division of labor at the Ripley plantation aimed to address both of these cultural and climatic deficits. Eliza's husband takes charge of the farm, setting imported U.S. plows and "energy" to land neglected by local elites like her neighbor, a "marquis" who ignores his suggestions of agricultural innovations. As her husband manages the cane fields, she conquers the plantation house, both of them working, Ripley writes, "with an energy, born of a more vigorous clime, that amazed our apathetic neighbors." "We had never dug nor plowed, but Lamo knew how it ought to be done," writes Ripley, referring to her husband by an Anglicized contraction for *el amo,* "master," in what she means as a charming transliteration of her slaves' locution. Ripley's mockery of her Cuban neighbors' embalmed feudalism helps, ultimately, to justify her disavowal of Cuba. In one revealing episode, Ripley invokes Walter Scott, the novelist who Mark Twain comically accused of causing the Civil War, to mock her Cuban neighbors at a plantation dinner party she attends uncomfortably.[79] Scott's ponderous glorification of chivalry earned him devoted imitators, Twain said, among the South's self-styled aristocracy, and Ripley references him in the same way to mock her neighbors' obsolete preening: "It reminded one of the feudal feasts Scott so loved to describe, where the honored guests sat above, and the followers of the chief below, the salt."[80] Like tropical vegetation that never dies back in a winter that never comes, the plantation aristocracy and the Afro-Cuban classes of these travel narratives seem to produce almost nothing, to prepare for less, and yet are everywhere present. The plantation house's name is auspicious: her time in Cuba is a story of disappointment, but also of "disillusion" with a resurrected Dixie in the Caribbean.

Ripley's time in Cuba concludes with the dispersal of her household, beginning with her son's departure for boarding school in the United

States. Martha leaves the family after their return to the States and settles near their new home. Ripley's emotional ending combines her nostalgia for slavery with an abrupt return of the South's entanglement with Latin America, which Ripley came to identify with the violent dismemberment of the United States. "Martha returned to the United States with us," Ripley writes, "and, when she married, her savings were found sufficient to purchase a lot and pay for the building of a comfortable house in Virginia, near enough for us to see her almost every year, when she could take our daughter, already taller and larger than herself, in her loving arms, and call her "'my Mexican baby.'" Ripley cannot purge the lingering memories of a Confederate Latin America from her family or her text. It was Mexico and Cuba, after all, that ultimately gave her the "whole country from the lakes to the Gulf, from ocean to ocean . . . a united country forever and ever."[81]

Conclusions: Tropicalization in the Age of Development

If Cuba was the Latin American nation that best reflected the past of the U.S. southeast, Mexico represented the past of the U.S. Southwest and, for some antiquarians, the American hemisphere as a whole. Since at least the 1840s, when John Lloyd Stephens authored some of the first written eyewitness descriptions of Mayan antiquity—and then attempted to remove much of its relics to the United States—Mesoamerica's pre-Columbian past was cited as a broadly American cultural heritage independent of the Old World.[82] Travelers to Mexico emphasized the country's large indigenous population and its grand antiquity, neither of which could easily be assimilated into a U.S. typology of social and racial development, as Cuba's plantation society often was.

Yet like Havana, Mexico City was also described as a brilliant example of modern urbanism. The Mexican capital, wrote Isaac Ford in 1893, is "well built, paved, and flagged, has a fine water supply, is lighted with electricity and gas, and has an excellent police." Yet the problem, as in Cuba, was the dramatic poverty of the provinces, where "tropical" idleness reasserted itself. Guadalupe, miles away from the Distrito Federal, is "incongruous," Ford writes, "with its pulque-drinking lazy population sunning itself in the plaza."[83] Indeed, as Jason Ruiz has argued, the characteristic "ambivalence" with which U.S. travelers viewed Mexico—as "*almost* but *not quite* modern"—allows them to plot themselves as uplifting protagonists in the country's unfolding economic future during the Porfiriato.[84] Travelers to Mexico exploited Mexico's apparent contrast between antiquity and modernity when they described Mexico's pre-Columbian architecture. Ford, however, shuns nostalgia, dismissing the relics of Aztec civilization near Mexico City as "grossly overrated." He looks sunnily forward, to a progressive, modern Mexico exploiting its historic ties to the United States and following the "work of civilization" already begun. Ford ridicules the know-nothing tourists who come only to look backwards at ancient, crumbling buildings, mindless of the progressive movement of history. Their attention should instead be on the work that modernization, which is to say the United States, is doing. "Civilization is doing great work in that benighted land," he writes, "and Americans have a large and increasing share in it. Commercial union between the two great silver-producing countries of the world is the order of modern progress." The order of modern progress begins to resemble the immanent sameness promised later by modernist development—all that progress requires, for Ford, is the time to reveal itself, in a future yet to come.[85]

The discourse of Latin American decadence thus worked on two related registers. Climatic determinism spatialized the temporal categories of progress and belatedness, producing a moral geography in which the hard-working north lives in what Hazard called an "era" of progress, while the tropical south languishes, awaiting a "*mañana*" that never arrives. Believing as they did that particular racial types could only be fully acclimatized to particular latitudes, climatic determinists, Livingstone writes, were anticosmopolitans that charted a global geography of ethnic and moral difference.[86] And Cocks argues that the claims of geographers like Huntington actually paved the way for notions of cultural pluralism we regard as modern, since his antiracist theory of tropical cultures identified developmental difference as circumstantial, rather than innate.[87] Climatic determinism's argument—that racial or ethnic differences are in fact the result of external stimuli and environmental factors, rather than essential racial traits—resonates with a theory, more acceptable today, that says cultures all share an essential equivalence, but move at a different pace.

The association of the tropics with belatedness and languor survived the turn of the twentieth century. It remains an irresistible metaphor for writers interested in the political intrigues of both domestic and global Souths: see, for example, Joan Didion's 1987 book on the Florida exile community, *Miami:* "I never passed through security for a flight to Miami without experiencing a certain weightlessness, the heightened wariness of having left the developed world for a more fluid atmosphere, one in which the native distrust of extreme possibilities that tended to ground the temperate United States in an obeisance to democratic institutions seemed rooted, if at all, only shallowly."[88] The democratic institutions "grounded" in the developed world of the mid-Atlantic find less solid footing in the humid Caribbean. Didion suggests in the developmentalist terms of the late twentieth century that "the place came first," that the Caribbean's "fecund," fluid geography was political and cultural fate. Earlier, and with less irony, John Dos Passos's 1963 travel book *Brazil on the Move,* shows climatic determinism's suitability for an explicitly developmentalist Cold War perspective. The 1930s radical turned 1950s Cold Warrior imbues the tropics with a combination of beauty and benightedness, as the Brazilian joke with which he begins his book shows:

> When the Lord Jehovah has finished making Brazil he can't help bragging a little to one of the archangels. He's planted the greatest forests and laid out the world's biggest river system and built a magnificent range of mountains with lovely bays and ocean beaches. He's filled the hills with topaz and aquamarine and sowed the rivers with gold dust and diamonds. He's arranged a climate free from hurricanes and earthquakes which will grow every conceivable kind of fruit.
>
> "Is it fair, Lord," asks the archangel, "to give so many benefits to just one country?"
>
> "You wait," says the Lord Jehovah, "till you see the people I'm going to put there."

The new Brazil, though, is "on the move"—its geography and consequently its people are being remade by the postwar nation's modernization project, symbolized by the monumental modernist capital, Brasília, then under construction. Brasília is to be built, Dos Passos reminds us, on a high plateau blessed with a cool climate where "animals of the temperate zone, including European man, would flourish." As he sits in a little hotel bar near the future site of the capital, in a provincial town that will soon see large-scale investments, he shoos away flies and pores over blueprints and brochures for new construction projects (this is a book whose hero is a highway builder, Bernardo Saya). Dos Passos imagines the Brazilian hinterlands going under asphalt as a twentieth-century version of the United States' wagon trails. "This must have been, I kept thinking, how our early enthusiasts for the North American West talked and glowed, sitting in some rickety tavern on the site of Washington City, when the subject turned to the Ohio or the great dimly discerned prairies west of the Mississippi."[89] Brazil's present is the U.S. past, and its future is the U.S. present. The "lethargy" to which the tropics were condemned by nature can be overcome by the leveling force of capital and technology. Yet Dos Passos retains some of the climatic determinists' faith that culture and development spring forth like roots from a hospitable environment—Brasília, after all, is a symbol of modernization in part because, he says, its climate is unlike the rest of the country.

These days, of course, travel writers, historians, and others devoted intellectually to explaining the differences between north and south, rich countries and poor, no longer speak in terms of hierarchies, at least not explicitly. "It would be a mistake," Landes reminds us, "to see geography as destiny. Its significance can be reduced or evaded, though invariably at a price. Science and technology are the key: the more we know, the more can be done to prevent disease and provide better living and working conditions." Landes retains the modernist faith in development as the technical improvement of the premodern. Yet the seeming empiricism of this sentence is undone by Landes's subsequent claim that "in general the discomfort of heat exceeds that of cold," an obviously subjective position. The product of a more enlightened age, Landes is sensitive to the importance of cultural pluralism—for this reason, he ventriloquizes his moral geography through an unnamed "Bangladeshi diplomat." "I have always felt reinforced and stimulated by the temperate climate," the native informant confides to his friend.[90] I have spent so much time with travel authors because in their work we can see more clearly the culturalist biases that also pervade the self-consciously scientific claims of Landes, Huntington, and others. The fantasy of "the tropics" as a place of moral degradation and an object of technical transformation persists in the U.S. imagination as a place of ruin and abundance, a region reflecting the still-unmet desire for mastery of the unruly torrid zone.

3   Latin America at War

The Yellow Press from Mulberry Street to Cuba

ON JULY 3, 1898, as General William Shafter's Fifth Army Corps massed outside Santiago de Cuba, the *New York World* gave its readers a detailed look at the eastern port city whose imminent capture by the United States would, all agreed, deal the final blow of the two-month-old war with Spain. The unattributed article, entitled "Santiago, Shafter's Goal, Brought Home to New York," attempted to educate American readers about the Cuban city by superimposing a map of Santiago de Cuba upon a plan of downtown Manhattan. The image dominates the page; inset type highlights the locations of Santiago's notable attractions in relation to New York's geography and underscores the Cuban city's inferiority both in size and in the quality of its failing infrastructure: "St. Thomas Street corresponds to our 6th Avenue Shopping District," notes one of these captions, yet "is only 17 ft. wide—sidewalks on our avenues are wider." "Mosquitoes and flies swarm" just south of an area corresponding to West 4th Street near the Hudson River. Just off the Plaza del Catedral—corresponding roughly to lower Chinatown and the edges of the financial district, still a site of working-class tenements and homeless encampments in 1898—we learn that "the drinking water is bad." It is so bad, in fact, that as the article goes on to say, "it looks, smells and tastes a good deal worse than that occasionally served to Brooklynites."

The map includes statistics on Santiago's diminished wealth and its shrinking wartime population—forty-two thousand at the time of the American invasion—alongside the paltry collection of its four-hundred-volume library (the grand New York Public Library on 42nd street, which the *World* had championed in a populist fundraising campaign, was still under construction). On either side of the double map are two contrasting images from New York. One article, "Mamie, Water Rat," juxtaposes the wharves of the two islands by depicting a typical girl of the New York tenements, perched in a diving posture at Manhattan's Battery pier: "Mamie is a little girl from the east side. Her 'sure nuff name,' as she herself expresses it, is Mary Rafferty. But she is known to all the habitués of the New York swimming baths as 'Mamie, the Water Rat.'"[1] Mamie, as the short accompanying article informs us, has discovered in the free baths of the Battery a talent for swimming and a moral discipline lacking in the downtown urchins she otherwise resembles in body and speech. Opposite Mamie—and immediately adjacent to the road on which Shafter's men approached Santiago—is an illustration of one Pauline Marr, a bourgeois young woman from uptown Manhattan who cycles and dances ballet. Marr and Rafferty are from opposite ends of New York and its class system, but Santiago de Cuba and the politics of reform symbolically unite them. As the army marches to Santiago, this article suggests, it brings relief and modernity in its wake to the suffering city. The uplift of the tenement girl and the freedom (here limited to leisure and high art) of the middle-class woman serve as stark contrasts to a Spanish regime whose cruelty was routinely sentimentalized in the U.S. press in terms of moral outrages against Cuban womanhood.[2]

Eight years later, a cartoon in the *Cleveland Plain Dealer* also relied on a metaphorical comparison between Cuba and the tenement. The cartoon appeared as the United States was preparing an invasion of independent Cuba, one of the many justified under the terms of the Platt Amendment that limited Cuba's sovereignty after its formal independence in 1898, guaranteeing the United States the right to unilaterally intervene to preserve "life, property, and individual liberty" on the island.[3] In the *Plain Dealer* cartoon, a group of young boys depicted in blackface are gathered behind a wall reading "Cuba Libre," as they divide up the spoils of a recent theft. As a policeman resembling Uncle Sam peeks around the corner, the boys scatter, shouting "Cheese it! Here comes the cop!" in the Bowery *argot* well known (even in Cleveland, apparently) to readers of reform literature, comic strips, and dime novels. The slum analogy positions Cuba as needy, childlike, and undisciplined, overseen by the firm hand of Uncle Sam. Yet while the *World*'s comparison between Santiago and New York betrayed a competitive anxiety about the advancement of Manhattan and Brooklyn, in the *Plain Dealer* cartoon there is no doubt about who is in charge. And while propaganda for the 1898 invasion of Cuba consistently personified the island as white and adult (and thus deserving of sympathy), here in the *Plain Dealer* cartoon the island is represented by a crude stereotype of blackness and youth.[4] What

Map of Santiago. Shafter's army entered Santiago on a road marked to the upper-left of the article "Bike, or Ballet?" *New York World*, July 3, 1898. (Courtesy of David M. Rubenstein Rare Book & Manuscript Library, Duke University)

cultural logic explains the flexible, sometimes contradictory combination of racial, geographic, and national analogies deployed here?

For one thing, both images read Cuba's underdevelopment in the terms set by North American tropes of urban class and race difference. Like Mamie the Water Rat, sympathetic Cuba was impoverished, virtuous, and female, with an ethnically marked whiteness. An unsympathetic, underdeveloped Cuba was criminal, male, and visible in terms of an ethnic difference that fell on the wrong side of the color line. In its Santiago map, the *New York World* made a visual analogy between Cuba and the slums—one in the heart of the great cities and the other just ninety miles from American shores, yet both of them foreign and unfamiliar like Irish Mamie and her working-class vernacular. In the comparison, we can see how the backwardness of the tenement—with its routine social problems of disease, overcrowding, sanitation, lack of recreation and culture, and for many journalists its intense heat—is graphically displaced onto urban Cuba.[5] The 1898 War[6] in Spain's three remaining colonies—Cuba, Puerto Rico, and the Philippines—marked the United States' political ascendancy in the Americas, establishing the United States as a global power from the Caribbean to Asia. On an ideological level, the displacement onto Cuba of North America's own uneven urban development was part of this assumption of hemispheric dominance. Through its invasion and occupation of Cuba and Puerto Rico, the United States seized the authority to cast the Caribbean islands' uneven development as a peculiarly *Latin* characteristic. The 1898 war was the beginning of what Henry Luce, the magazine publisher, would later call "the American Century"—the era in which the "triumphal purpose of freedom" would complete its march across the globe under the leadership of the United States. If the twentieth century is that "American Century," however, then its origins lay on the battlefields of Cuba, Puerto Rico, and the Philippine Islands, and in the newsrooms and boardrooms of New York.[7]

As war loomed in 1897 and early 1898, a popular theme in American culture was the possibility of a nationally unifying campaign. The war brought "dudes" and "chappies" out of the Ivy League and into a collective national effort. Theodore Roosevelt led his Rough Riders in camp renditions of "Fair Harvard" as the *World* trumpeted the patriotism of Uncle Sam's "Gilded Youth" who served alongside army regulars and plebeian volunteers.[8] Roosevelt's unit, according to the popular legend, was a collection of wealthy heirs and workers united in common cause; they were as famous for this cross-class symbolism as they were for their apocryphal charge up Santiago's San Juan Hill. The myth of the unit's republican equality was well established in advance of the invasion of Cuba, as a story from the Tampa embarkation base makes clear: a captain told a *World* correspondent that the Rough Riders were made up of "millionaires, owners of ranches, cowboys, 'cow thieves' . . . miners, doctors, merchants, dentists, lawyers, and about everything you can think of, including watch thieves, as I found out at San Antonio, where my watch was nabbed from my blouse.'"[9] William F. Cody, the impresario known as "Buffalo Bill" then at the height of his fame, claimed that thirty thousand Indian soldiers were ready to fight in Cuba to avenge ancient Spanish cruelties in North America, an example, as well, of popular entertainers' widespread readiness to exploit the conflict.[10] Coney Island incorporated the war into its entertainment options and its bathing fashions (stars and stripes were a popular look that summer), and its war-themed attractions are another example of how the war fever redirected domestic racism toward Spanish targets. The *World* reported on revisions made to a popular carnival game in which contestants threw baseballs at the head of a Black man peeking through a hole cut in cloth. The new game, "Kill the Spaniard," added patriotic purpose to this gruesome entertainment.[11] The *World* reports one striking example of the ways that domestic racism and imperial adventurism could triumph over old regional divisions, as well: a patriotic "darky show" put on by the Professional Women's League featured stage actresses in blackface who altered the lyrics of the Union war anthem, "Marching Through Georgia," to suit the unified white republic's imperial mood. The new lyrics read: "And our battle-cry shall be, / 'Don't forget the Maine!' / While we are fighting for Cuba."[12]

Northern and Southern papers welcomed the restorative powers of a new war that would leave the Civil War and its resentments behind. "The Bourbon who cherishes civil-war bitterness on either side of the old line is now as ridiculously out of date as a last year's bird's nest," the *New York World* editorialized.[13] Popular songs and doggerel verse composed for the conflict trumpeted the new union of North and South with titles like "'Dixie' Up to Date," "Massachusetts Greets Maryland," and "Gettysburg, 1898."[14] Many Black newspapers initially supported the war as an opportunity to improve race relations in the armed forces and the nation at large, an argument white newspapers often made as well. The *World* touted "Black soldiers and white in the trenches together" as a sign of what they called a democratic "people's war."[15] At the same time, Cuba seemed to provide an opportunity for white racial revitalization after Reconstruction's end. The most infamous Southern nationalist novel of the era, *The Leopard's Spots,* posed a question that generations of American expansionists had also asked, "'Shall the future American be an Anglo-Saxon or a mulatto?'"[16] Amy Kaplan observes how that novel portrays the war with Spain as a revivifying racial adventure, serving as a "*deus ex machina* to unify white men in chivalrous rescue of white women from Black men and of the white nation from Black Reconstruction." In this way, writes Kaplan, 1898 war culture exploited a foreign conflict in order to ideologically repair domestic class tensions. Though a reading of Roosevelt's memoir of the war, *The Rough Riders*, Kaplan argues that popular accounts of the 1898 War threatened to collapse the boundaries between the foreign and domestic even as they worked to solidify them. The spectacle of Black soldiers on San Juan Hill, instead of symbolically purging the Civil War from the American psyche, revived old fears of Black uprising and national collapse. Accounts of the war that foregrounded the heroic white male body—the soldier and the war correspondent—thus deliberately sidelined those actors, like Cubans and Black U.S. soldiers, who might threaten the coherent boundaries of a white imperial republic. As she writes, "Just as Roosevelt and others supported the black troops as long as they were led and represented by white officers, the white male pictured alone in the wilderness of empire on San Juan Hill comes to displace, appropriate, and incorporate the agency of nonwhites in the empire and at home." Kaplan emphasizes how, in popular accounts of the 1898 War, domestic conflicts condition popular representations of the war with Spain; Black soldiers, in her reading, would "destabilize this hierarchy" of white men and nonwhites in the Caribbean empire.[17]

Yet journalistic representations of the war were far more dysfunctional than Kaplan's compelling treatment allows. In her illuminating account of the circulation of Rudyard Kipling's "White Man's Burden" in turn-of-the-century America, Gretchen Murphy warns against assuming that "the movement for empire abroad was inspired by, consistent with, and modeled after the domestic racial social order of the Southern United States," rather than a "counterweight or complication" of it.[18] In the case of Cuba, the island's classification as "nonwhite" was less straightforward than Kaplan's analysis suggests. In fact, as we can see from the *World*'s map of Santiago, part of what made Cuba both attractive and unsettling to white American observers was its similarities, racial and otherwise, to the United States. We have already seen the origins of this ambiguous racial position in the Cuban annexationist movement. The island was, in many accounts, wealthy, white, and modern. At the same time, however, Spanish Cuba was a racialized foreign body:

its Catholicism and its "off-whiteness," to use María DeGuzmán's term for Spain's racialization in the United States, repelled American visitors as much as this cultural difference also attracted their interest.[19] In other words, in the nineteenth century Cuba was never entirely consigned to the "outside" of the United States, but occupied a liminal position of racial identification and familiarity. To Americans, Cuba was not an unambiguously foreign space, and beneath the claims of humanitarian sympathy for Cubans and Puerto Ricans was a tenuous racial identification that did not extend, for example, to the people of Spain's colony in the Philippines.[20] Therefore, while we will find ample examples of Cuba's racial and national "othering" by U.S. writers during the war, the graphic identification of Santiago de Cuba and downtown Manhattan with which I began shows that representations of Cuba were also involved in a fraught dialectical contest with representations of working-class European immigrants *within* the United States. It is this contest that helps explain why the *World*'s comparison of Santiago to New York even needed to be made in the first place. Weren't the width of "our streets" and the only relative cleanliness of Brooklyn's fetid water supply in fact evidence of a *rivalry* with the Cuban city?

Beyond these historical questions of Cuba's historical intimacy with the United States is a methodological one of literature's specific value as evidence in more broadly historical arguments. As a cultural formation, literature plays a dynamic and often contradictory role in "scripting and in interrogating fictions of racial identity," as Murphy argues.[21] Representing a historicist tendency to read literature as too much of the former and too little of the latter—that is, as a script, rather than an interrogation—the historian Louis Pérez treats metaphor as a representational machine that shapes cultural trends and dominant assumptions. He describes metaphors of Cuban youth and immaturity as the central means by which American imperial designs were reframed as idealistic, indispensable, and altruistic. This instrumental reading of metaphor, however, overlooks the complications it inevitably raises. Like the travel writer's analogy, metaphor is a figure of comparison, which relies on the transfer of meaning from one thing to another, muddling its terms even as it distinguishes them. The metaphor of the Cuban as slum-dweller positions Cuba as child (in which Uncle Sam is a tutor or parent), but also, implicitly, as a kind of "American" type. Elsewhere, the slum metaphor designates Cuba as heroic mother (in which Uncle Sam is savior or suitor) or as incorrigible delinquent (in which Uncle Sam is policeman or father). "Metaphor," therefore, does not make up a coherent ideological system, but a contradictory and flexible representational practice. The Cuban warfront was understood and interpreted not only in terms of Cuba's cultural difference, but its resemblance to the United States—this is why the metaphorical comparisons even made sense in the first place.

Such resemblances, between Cuba and the United States, between the domestic war on the slums and the foreign campaign against the Spanish, and between the internal volatility of the republic and the expansive boundaries of an overseas empire shadowed even the most jingoistic accounts of the Cuban war. Attorney General Richard Olney's famous 1894 remark that the nation stood on the "ragged edge of anarchy" reflected a broad sentiment that the United States was in stark disequilibrium during the 1890s.[22] The decade remembered as the "Gilded Age" or the "Gay 90s" was also a time of violent confrontations between labor and capital in the north and west and the march of white supremacy in the South, as Henry James lamented the "abyss of inequality" in what he claimed were formerly peaceable relations of men and women.[23] It was a decade, as well, in which the "tenement problem" in Manhattan's vast, overcrowded slums became a crucial issue in New York politics. At the turn of the century, reform and militarism were mutually reinforcing discourses often difficult to distinguish from one another; the title of Jacob Riis's 1902 best-seller *The Battle with the Slum* reflected the tenor of the era. As urban reform was militarized in rhetoric and in form—as a "war" on dirt, disease, and crime, pursued by paramilitary squads of police and sanitation workers—the military invasion of Cuba was characterized as an urban reform operation.

For this reason, the postwar American occupation drew upon the expertise of urban reform administrators Roosevelt, chief of the NYPD before the war, and sanitation engineer George Waring, who had organized the "White Wings" cleaning brigades in downtown Manhattan. Writers like the novelist Stephen Crane, the journalist Henry Mawsom, and James W. Buel, an author of frontier tales, Arthurian legends, and city mysteries, moved from chronicling slums to recording and reporting the war.[24] Crane filed a dispatch that used one as an analogy for the other from the eastern Cuban town of Siboney, where U.S. forces landed on June 25, 1898, to mount the assault on Santiago de Cuba. Sounding a common note for U.S. journalists in its portrayal of Cuban insurgents as famished, dull, and indifferent, Crane makes an additional, revelatory analogy:

> The Cuban soldier, indeed, has turned into an absolutely emotionless character save when he is maddened by battle. We feed him and he expresses no

joy. When you come to think of it, one follows the other naturally. If he had retained the emotional ability to make a fuss over nearly starving to death he would also have retained the emotional ability to faint with joy at sight of the festive canned beef, hard-tack and coffee. But he exists with the impenetrable indifference or ignorance of *the greater part of the people in an ordinary slum.*[25]

Here, Crane foregrounds class conflict in the United States in order to make Cubans legible to his readers. The popular claims about the United States' "redemption" of Cuba, understood as both a moral duty and a military mission, must be understood in the context of a growing debate around class conflict and the politics of reform in the United States, which derived much of its own rhetoric and its persuasive force from a similarly moral appeal and a rhetoric and practice of "war" on behalf of an abject population. So Cubans were made legible by tropes familiar to readers of reformist representations of the immigrant poor, particularly the tenement woman. However, unlike young Mary Rafferty—and most of the tenement characters in Crane's work—the Cuban in Crane's example cannot be addressed in a common language and cannot be incorporated into a national family.

Genres of Uneven Development: Crane's City Sketch and Martí's *Crónica*

In 1882, the struggling *New York World* newspaper was purchased by Joseph Pulitzer, a Hungarian-born newspaper publisher from St. Louis. Taking the model of sensationalist advocacy journalism he had introduced at his *St. Louis Post-Dispatch,* Pulitzer's New York paper successfully combined a staff of business managers, editors, and reporters, a colloquial tone, and a pioneering use of illustration, color ink, advertising, and entertaining weekend supplements. The *World* published a weekend women's section, a Sunday magazine, business and financial reporting, metropolitan and international news, and a pioneering comics page; it was also the first newspaper to organize a separate sports section. With this reorganization of the paper into sections came a new class of specialist writers ("reporters") to fill them. The *World's* specialization of content is such a familiar feature of modern print journalism that the medium is now practically defined by it, but at the time it was a departure from the editor-driven newspapers that preceded it. His critics and rivals called it the "yellow press," but Pulitzer called it "modern journalism," "western-style journalism," and "journalism for the masses."[26] As the last of these terms suggests, populism and advocacy distinguished the new tabloid medium: the *World* and its crosstown "yellow" rival, William Randolph Hearst's *New York Journal,* contained "serious" editorials and financial news alongside private scandals and popular crusades.[27] Pulitzer launched campaigns against tenement landlords and Standard Oil, and Hearst called for the paving of Fifth Avenue. Both papers also took up the crusade to "save" Cuba from Spanish dominion, investing significant resources and infrastructure to bring dispatches from the battlefield. The 1898 War is often described as the "newspaper war" or the "correspondents' war" for the ways in which this jingoistic, activist press spoiled for war with Spain. They were also debuting, on a global stage, a model of journalism they regarded as modern and transformational, both in the medium and in the world at large. Despite the term's survival in the present day as a pejorative for jingoistic or frankly partisan media, the "yellow press" was in fact a progressive form. Unabashedly imperialist, sensationalistic, partisan, and self-promoting was the yellow press; nevertheless, its self-consciously "modern" war journalism was not the retrograde form that the sobriquet implies, but rather the anxious performance of a media, and a nation, whose modernity was still unproven.

For the novelist and critic William Dean Howells in 1902, the jury on the modernity of New York and its press was still decidedly out. "A study of New York civilization in 1849 has lately come into my hands, with a mortifying effect," he writes, "which I should like to share with the reader, to my pride of modernity." He is referring to *New York in Slices,* George Foster's sensational guidebook to New York. Not only had New York's material depravity not changed much since 1849, Howells concluded, but its intellectual professions, and their interest in these bawdy, violent subjects, had evolved only slightly. With the rise of the telegraph and the Associated Press at midcentury came the new figure of the reporter, a class of writer who was subordinate to the "editor" and whose job was to interpret and organize information that came over the wire. As Howells reflects, "Fifty-odd years ago journalism had already become 'the absorbing, remorseless, clamorous thing' we now know, and very different from the thing it was when 'expresses were unheard of, and telegraphs were uncrystallized from the lightning's blue and fiery film.' Reporterism was beginning to assume its present importance, but it had not yet become the paramount intellectual interest, and did not yet 'stand shoulder to shoulder' with the counting-room in authority."[28] The rise of "reporterism" and of business-minded newspapers where the "counting room" ruled alongside the writers were only escalations of the "remorselessness" of newspapers a half-century before. Howells tempered his suspicions, however, by seeing the newspaper as a potentially democratizing medium; the "labor" of the writer might potentially enrich and embolden his "art."

For many others, this growing division of intellectual labor made journalism a sign of the vulgarization of authorship and intellectual life. "The multitude, I am more and more convinced," wrote Henry James, "has absolutely no taste—none at least that a thinking man is bound to."[29] James's Cuban contemporary Julian del Casal likewise disdained what he called "scribbling" for the masses and for pay. In one essay he called journalism a "repugnant mass of local excrement which, like rotting food on golden dishes, is served up daily by the press to its readers." He went on: "Journalism can be, in spite of its intrinsic hatred of literature, the benefactor that puts money in our pockets, bread on our table and wine in our cup, but, alas, it will never be the tutelary deity that encircles our brow with a crown of laurel leaves."[30] Casal's metaphorical play on the body of the literary writer, sublimely quarantined by a "tutelary" spirit, captures his sense of journalism's invasion of the author's personal integrity. As Aníbal González writes, it was journalism's "emphasis on novelty, speed, and objectivity over familiarity, reflection, and analysis" that so unsettled Casal. Journalism's emphasis on empirical truth over imaginative personality meant it could never do more than put money in a scribbler's pocket.[31]

The Latin American genre that is most representative of this process of specialization in the intellectual professions at the end of the nineteenth century is the *crónica,* or chronicle, a genre that Casal worked in and which José Martí mastered during his New York exile from Cuba. Susana Rotker defines the chronicle as "literature under pressure": a hybrid journalistic form that, while tied to the eventfulness and temporality of "news," aimed to preserve the stylization, subjective authorial voice, and "timelessness" of the literary essay.[32] Julio Ramos sees the *crónica* as a heterogeneous literary form that indexed the crisis to which Casal responded so bitterly. In the chronicle, he writes, "literature would represent (at times anxiously) its encounter and conflict with the technologized and massified discourses of modernity."[33] The changing division of labor in intellectual life in the 1880s and 1890s in the Americas is visible in Crane's city sketches and war reporting as well as Martí's journalism from New York. Martí's chronicles, assembled in his complete works as the *Esenas norteamericanas* (North American scenes), treated famous figures like Walt Whitman and Buffalo Bill, technologies like

New York's subways and the new Brooklyn Bridge, and events like President Garfield's assassination and the Haymarket riots. They appeared in Spanish-language newspapers in Argentina, Mexico, New York City, Venezuela, and elsewhere, always in the dense, poetic prose for which Martí is famous.

In 1888, the Newark-born Crane got his first writing job contributing to his uncle's summer news service at the seaside resort of Asbury Park, New Jersey. After he moved to New York City, he began reporting on city life and police news for publications like the *New York Journal, McClure's,* and *Arena.* Crane wrote for the "yellow press" in Cuba and for some of its professed rivals, like *The New York Press,* at home; my point here is not that Crane's journalistic was purely a product of the "new journalism," but rather of the crisis in journalism those "yellow" papers demonstrated. While in New York, Crane wrote his first novel, the slum romance *Maggie, a Girl of the Streets,* while the book that made him a celebrity, the Civil War novel *The Red Badge of Courage,* was first serialized in abridged form in the *New York Press* and *Philadelphia Press* in December 1894. By the time he went to Cuba, Crane came to represent a hybrid literary-journalistic ideal that combined factual reporting from the site of extreme experience—the battlefield and slum—with a literary narrative style. Fascinated by timely events like New York municipal elections, he also sought to make these the stuff of timeless aesthetic endeavor. Crane's journalistic work, as well, was "literature under pressure." Both Crane's 1890s sketch and Martí's *crónica,* I argue, can be fruitfully compared as genres of uneven modernity, given their overlapping subject matter—New York's mixture of modern and underdeveloped spaces—and the hybrid form with which they approached them.

Urban poverty and class conflict were popular subjects for New York reporters. And while Crane and Martí have very little in common stylistically, they were attracted to some of the same urban phenomena. Consider, for example, both men's representation of mass transportation in the metropolis. The common trope of monstrosity that Crane and Martí used to describe city life shows some of the generic similarities, as well as differences, between the Martían *crónica* and the Crane city sketch. In "Coney Island," published in Bogotá's *La Pluma* in December 1881, Martí introduced his readers to the Brooklyn amusement park and the U.S. culture of mass entertainment that for him it represented. Martí describes the subway train that brings the hordes of pleasure-seekers to the beach as "a monster emptying out its entrails into the ravenous jaws of another monster." As he writes, "This immense crush of humanity squeezes onto trains that seem to groan under its weight in their packed trajectory across the barren stretches to cede their turbulent cargo to gigantic ferries, enlivened by the sound of harps and violins, which carry the weary day-trippers back to the piers and pour them out into the thousand trams and thousand tracks that crisscross the slumbering city of New York like iron veins." For Martí, monstrosity—the ravenous beast of the subway, whose iron veins wind through the body of the city—represents the grotesque commercialization of leisure at Coney Island. With this comes the corruption of "culture" by mass amusement and spectacle, which metaphorically mechanizes the very lifeblood of the city.[34] Here, fifteen years later, is Crane on Broadway's streetcars: "The cars, by force of column and numbers, almost dominate the great street, and the eye of even an old New Yorker is held by these long yellow monsters which prowl intently up and down, up and down, in a mystic search."[35] The monstrous here is the metaphorical means by which the city's mundane traffic becomes the stuff of literary—here, "mystic"—transcendence. Clearly, Martí and Crane have distinct political and aesthetic responses to the New York traffic—for Martí it is a sign of aesthetic corruption, and for Crane an unlikely source of metaphysical depth. Moreover, the economy and irony of Crane's prose scarcely resembles the dense verbosity and moral seriousness of Martí's. Yet Crane's "sketches," like the Cuban's *"esenas,"* struggle to maintain a "literary" posture that can situate a given newsworthy place of event in a universal "aesthetic" realm that it is the task of the author—no mere scribbler—to uncover. Crane's sketches, both as a police reporter in New York and later on the warfront in Cuba, exhibit this tendency to impressionistic specificity that often promises informational "coverage," before finally withholding it from the reader. One such article consisted entirely of quotes "overheard" in front of the *Press'* "Stereopticon," a magic lantern that projected election results onto the paper's headquarters. With little analysis or editorial commentary, the article was pure "information," but without any authorial intervention to clarify what the information "meant," the article reads almost like a taunt to Crane's editors—it's just the facts, so much so that it reads like poetry.[36] In these uneven formal characteristics, necessitated by their professional obligation to report and their vocational desire to imagine, both men's urban journalism approached the everyday life of the city and the new media of capitalist urban life as both the subject and the vehicle for aesthetic representation.

Yet despite Howells's framing of the specialization of the New York news media as an example of modernity's slow, uncertain advance, the "yellow press" has not been read in the sort of formal terms that Latin Americanist critics have used to treat the newspaper work of *cronistas* like Casal, the Nicaraguan Rubén Darío, and Martí, where issues of "uneven modernity" are routinely at stake in most critics' appraisals. Instead, U.S. historians of journalism tend to view the heterogeneity of U.S. journalistic discourse at the turn of the century in teleological terms specific to the United States, as a sort of interregnum between the patrician journalism of the nineteenth century and the commercial journalism that prevailed in the twentieth.[37] Of course, the national question asserts itself much more obviously in the work of exiles like Martí or Darío, who wrote about it constantly from the perspective of colonial or peripheral economies in which they did not live. Yet what if we read the "modern" journalism of the U.S. 1890s, which was itself so anxiously preoccupied with the United States' international profile and its urban uneven development, as similarly motivated by concerns about the integrity and modernity of the nation? And what if we consider the generic heterogeneity of 1890s newspaper writing less as an interregnum, anticipating and preparing what came after, and more as a reflection of a decade of crisis in both the country and its intellectual professions? In other words, what if we read these "sketches" of slum life and wartime as Latin Americanist critics of the *crónica* have done, as a genre of uneven development—both of the press and the society it chronicles?

A leading critic of Crane's journalistic work, Michael Robertson, offers one approach, reading the uneven distribution of journalistic "information" and literary stylization in turn-of-the-century papers as productive of what he calls a "fact-fiction" discourse.[38] This is legible on the pages of the *World* during the war in Cuba: a reported dispatch from the Cuban battlefield could share space, for example, with a fantastic illustrated piece on how "To Change Earth's Climate and Freeze Out Spain."[39] Phyllis Frus interrogates the aesthetic categories of "fact" and "fiction" in Crane's newspaper article and his later short story, "The Open Boat," on the sinking of the *Commodore* off the Florida coast, on its way to deliver arms to the Cuban rebels. The short story concentrates on the existential crisis of the sinking ship and its sailors; the news story is a narrative account of the ship's voyage that largely overlooks the sinking. Frus reads this discrepancy as an example of realism's ahistorical aestheticism: "Realist and naturalist narratives, though originating in anti-literary impulses, are easily described in aesthetic terms because these narratives downplay historical and political contexts," she writes. "They empty reality of its history and substitute 'nature' or universal human nature."⁴⁰ Yet even if Crane does not or cannot explain it explicitly, his uncertain professional status as a newspaper writer, and the brittleness in 1890s journalism of what strike us now as commonplace distinctions—between "history" and "nature," politics and aesthetics, fact and opinion or fiction—are themselves a part of the "historical and political contexts" of his writing. Indeed, war correspondents like Crane and Davis recognized this, when they invoked "universal human nature" to contest what they saw as their editors' reduction of historical experience to the banality of journalistic "events." In 1899, Davis reflected on his Cuban experience in *Harper's,* lamenting the press bureau's demand for "information": "They wanted the news, all the news, but nothing but the news. The last words of a dying man were not important to them. His name, spelled correctly, and the letter of his troop, were to their employers of the highest value." The lowly war reporters in Key West, Jamaica, or Santiago de Cuba, writes Davis, "were anonymous, and their work, which was at times both brilliant and of historic value, was sunk and lost under the leveling head-line of a press bureau, a machine which would make all men equal, and for which writers sell their birthright of originality and humor and personal point of view."⁴¹ Davis bristles, here, with Casal's contempt at the mess of pottage for which his authorial birthright has been sold to the newspaper. Of course, Davis and Casal emerge from different intellectual professions and traditions; Rotker discusses the heterogeneity of the chronicle as a consequence, in part, of the slow detachment of the press from the state in much of Spanish America, a state of affairs without a clear equivalent in the United States.⁴² By contrast, Ramos reads the *crónica* "mediating between modernity and the areas modernity has excluded or run over,"⁴³ and Gerard Aching describes the *modernista*'s cultivation of an "exquisite" prose style not as a rejection of politics, but as an "aesthetic practice embedded in local and transnational cultural politics and institutions," showing how the *cronistas*' self-conscious stylization was inextricable from their professional status.⁴⁴ Crane, Davis, Casal, and Martí perform this professional anxiety in quite different ways, and they may locate modernity in different places, but they shared a common investment in stylization as a mark of literariness and intellectual autonomy in a modernizing profession that endangered both.

Crane and Martí's journalism, therefore, belong to hybrid literary-informational genres that treat the space of the city as a site of conflict between modernity and its others—the ones it is running over. For Martí, New York' poor neighborhoods exemplify the historical process of modernization in its unruly violence, while Crane tends to see the problem of urban modernization in national exceptionalist terms, as the great irony of confinement and over-urbanization in a nation with so much "open space." The slum was a local opportunity to view the modern United States' metaphorical "outside"—hence his repeated comparisons between the Tenderloin, the North American west, and Cuba. We can see these differences and similarities at work in their common fascination with the tenement roof, where residents escaped their stifling apartments on summer evenings. In an article on New York's rooftops written for the *Washington Post,* Crane describes a late-night drinking session with a local "Johnnie" in a sketch on the rooftop gardens of the metropolis. He begins with an elegant rooftop soiree uptown before turning downtown, where the tenement roofs provide fleeting relief from heat and overcrowding. "An evening upon a tenement roof," Crane writes, "with the great golden march of the stars across the sky and Johnnie gone for a pail of beer, is not so bad if you have never seen the mountains nor heard, to your heart, the slow, sad song of the pines." The underdeveloped spaces in the heart of the United States' biggest city are intelligible for Crane only by analogy to some temporal or geographic limit case, like the wild hinterlands of the western mountains. Martí describes a similar scene from the much more detached point of view of a witness on street level, an outsiders' perspective that contrasts with Crane's more intimate, patriotic lament for "Johnnie" and the western wilderness: "The New York summer is not odious because of how hot it burns, but rather for that which torments the unfortunate people that have no more park than the roofs of the houses, heated by the daylight, or the cool of the floor tiles, which by the light of the moon seem less broken and miserable," writes Martí. "From the roofs of the neighborhood houses, which are many in the poor slums, hang bunches of legs." Shifting his gaze from the disembodied legs above to the broken bodies lined up on the apartment stoops below, Martí describes the local inhabitants in gothically monstrous terms: "From below, far below, one sees up there in the heights of a seventh floor, a colored shirt that raises a white glass full of beer, like a drop of blood into which has fallen another of milk. The moon gives a tint of sulphur to the yellowed ladies, and streaks their pallid faces with bile. From one chimney to another, searching for less-burning bricks to recline upon, pass half-naked men, like goblins, these exhausted workers, their hair tangled, mouths open, swearing and staggering, wiping off with their hands beads of perspiration, as if they were unsewing their own entrails."[45] In Martí's telling, the poor are brutalized even at home and at leisure. These workers have no interiority; they stagger like zombies, repeating the violence done to them as they unstitch their "entrails" (*entrañas*), one of Martí's favorite metaphors for an intact self threatened by exploitation and mechanization. He imagines exploited workers disemboweling themselves either as a sign of their degradation by city and industry, as here, or as a passionate refusal of dehumanization, as in his elegy for the Haymarket martyrs, in which he imagines the anarchist Albert Spies' charismatic appeal to industrial workers: he thrust his hand "into those rebellious, hirsute chests," wrote Martí, "and he brandished before their eyes, squeezed out, and made them smell their own entrails." For Martí, the downtown tenements, the piths of the Brooklyn Bridge (which he imagined as tombs for the "unknown workers," the "entrails of greatness" who died building the bridge), and the monstrous subway cars were the true "insides" of the United States. There is no sentimentality for "Johnnie" or his far-off pines here; these examples do not show the United States' exceptional "outsides," but rather its disgorged bowels—uneven development in all its grotesque putrescence.[46]

The War on the Slum and the Battle for Cuba

In 1896, Crane had written a series of sketches on the downtown Manhattan neighborhood known as the Tenderloin for Hearst's *New York Journal*. The sketches treat everyday life in the vice district, whose boundaries extended from 14th Street north to 42nd Street and from genteel Murray Hill west to Seventh Avenue. Where Crane used the expansive mountains of the west as a counterpoint to the stifling tenements, Buel draws a different comparison, describing the heart of the Tenderloin in 1883 by analogy to the wild frontier decades before. "California in the worst days of '49 to '56," worried Buel, "was a sovereign millennium compared with the civilization of such places as Baxter, Water, and Bleecker Streets of Gotham, or in the district bounded by Fourteenth and Twenty-Second streets and Fourth and Seventh Avenues, known as the Twenty-Ninth precinct."[47] Waves of police reform in 1890s New York, however, were transforming the area, bringing it into historical equilibrium with the rest of the metropolis. After the election of a Republican mayor briefly displaced Tammany Hall Democrats in 1894, Roosevelt was appointed chief of the New York Police Department on a reform mandate. Under his leadership, the department was reorganized along paramilitary lines to combat corruption and political clientelism, its two most notorious problems under the Tammany machine. The NYPD adopted the British military box-coat and U.S. Army leggings, instituted military discipline, rankings, surprise inspections, and standardized pistols and ammunition, and reorganized the detective bureau as an intelligence service.[48] (This enforcement of hierarchy and technical specialization paralleled, in a sense, what Pulitzer was doing at *The World,* with his division of reporting, editorial, and business staff, and the creation of discrete sections of expertise for reporters. Like the reformed police, war correspondents in Cuba also styled themselves as soldiers.) If a pacified Tenderloin was brought up to date with the rest of the city, Crane suggests, it will also lose its unique character, as he observes in terms that are easily recognizable to twenty-first-century readers for their tone of bohemian lament. "To the man who tries to know the true things there is something hollow and mocking about this Tenderloin of to-day, as far as its outward garb is concerned," Crane sighed in an 1896 article. "The newer generation brought new clothes with them. The old Tenderloin is decked out. And wherever there are gorgeous lights, massive buildings, dress clothes and theatrical managers, there is very little nature, and it may be no wonder that the old spirit of the locality chooses to lurk in the darker places."[49] In his slum journalism, Crane was especially interested in these "darker" places, and in the two years before he left for Cuba many of his sketches treat with regret the pacification of downtown areas like the Tenderloin or Minetta Lane, the enclave of African American saloons in Greenwich Village.[50]

One Tenderloin sketch from December 1894, "The Duel That Was Not Fought," comically dramatizes the still-incendiary atmosphere of the partly pacified Tenderloin. It is also Crane's first writerly encounter with Cuba. The story depicts a barroom dispute in a lower Sixth Avenue bar between an effete, mannered Cuban and gruff Irishman from Cherry Street on the Lower East Side. Patsy's use of a "careless and rather loud comment"—presumably an ethnic slur—angers "the Cuban," who challenges Patsy to a sword duel that the Irishman eagerly accepts in spite of his total ignorance of swordsmanship. The Cuban, here, is treated as a genteel European, his pretension setting off the Irishman's plebeian bluster. Patsy directs a confused mixture of racial insults at the Cuban, calling his "olive-skinned" antagonist "Yeh bloomin' little black Dago." Crane ironically presents Patsy's ready eagerness to fight as an example of a vigorous and aggrieved—if often misdirected—national temperament that rises to every aggressor's challenge, no matter how absurd. "'Git yer swords," Patsy says in the downtown patois Crane loved to record. "Get 'em quick! I'll fight wi' che! I'll fight wid anything, too! See? I'll fight yeh wid a knife an' fork if yeh say so!'"[51] Despite a pages-long exchange of escalating threats, the duel never takes place, and Patsy's foolhardy bravado is never tested. A policeman with a "distinctly business air" breaks up the dispute and carries off the hotheaded Cuban, who has insulted him as well. A potentially interesting international incident, therefore, is anticlimactically interrupted by efficient police work.

For Crane, the climax of this story would be delivered in Cuba three years later. While his 1894 Tenderloin sketches betray an ambivalent attitude toward the police and their domestication of downtown, the Cuban revolution that began in 1895 created a new source for the literary inspiration that the police were chasing out of the Tenderloin, just as the Cuban occupation offered a new international stage for the police reforms themselves. Comparing Roosevelt's police reform in New York and the imperial "police mission" of the 1898 War, Christopher Wilson calls the former "a blueprint not just for the NYPD, but for future Latin-American policy."[52] On the eve of the invasion, a *New York World* reporter made the same connection. In an article entitled "'Army Fit for Cuba, Say People Who Watch Police Parade," the journalist wrote, "Our policemen looked more martial than soldiers yesterday in their annual parade. There was a new note in the display, the note of militarism. Not once, but scores of times, spectators exclaimed: 'There's an army that could drive all the Spaniards out of Cuba.'"[53] The remainder of this essay will investigate what Wilson and this anonymous scribbler both suggest, that in the martial culture of the American 1890s, Latin America—and especially Cuba, for decades the United States' familiar Latin synecdoche—began to replace the northern slum as the site not only of literary vitality, but of the "war" the nation and its intellectuals were waging against disorder, dirt, and violence.

In an 1887 article in the Buenos Aires daily *La Nación,* Martí gives a comical account of a newsman's Brooklyn funeral, where the deceased is buried and eulogized by his competitors. Describing the scene at the cemetery, Martí writes, "Here they don't fear death much. The journalist, above all, seems to look upon it without any dread: The journalist has so much of the soldier within him!" When their passenger ferry returns to Battery Park, however, Martí notes an abrupt change in the tenor of the afternoon: "valor, like a sword returned to its sheath, docked at its broad pier." The guild parts ignominiously, Martí tells us, when the ferry docked—once on dry land, every mourner dried their tears, broke into a run, and raced to be the first to file a story on the funeral.[54] Martí's mocking use of the metaphor of the reporter as soldier plays on popular caricatures of the huckstering, hustling newspaper reporter, but it is particularly appropriate for the culture of North American police and war journalism at the end of the century, when the reporter-soldier analogy was so widespread. The yellow press's perceived indecency was the subject of much suspicious mockery, as Martí's account would suggest. *Truth,* a satirical New York weekly, joked on the popular association of both Havana and Hearst with filth by maligning the latter by comparison with the former: "They spread a yellow journal over a yellow fever case in Cuba, and the fever pales into whiteness by the contrast and flees away."[55] These newspapers were the targets of so much criticism for tawdry sensationalism that James Creelman, a *New York Journal* correspondent in Havana and Manila, began his autobiographical history of the yellow press on an immediately defensive note. He defined it as "that form of American journalistic energy which is not content merely to print a daily record of history, but seeks to take part in events as an active and sometimes decisive agent."[56] If the yellow press struck for alluring sensation, it was not afraid, as Creelman writes and as Martí and *Truth* mockingly suggest, to be down in the muck as well.

Journalists from the United States had been reporting from the figurative "muck" of the Cuban insurgency since it began in 1895, and the New York press dominated the scene. Crane, already famous as a war novelist, began reporting for the *World* in 1898 and later, after he was fired, for the *New York Journal*. Besides Creelman and Crane, reporters like the *New York Herald's* George Rea, the *World's* Sylvester Scovel, and the *Journal's* Richard Harding Davis and Grover Flint were the first of the war's celebrity correspondents. Scovel, for example, was briefly imprisoned for espionage by Spanish officials, an experience that did no harm to his professional reputation. On May 17, 1898, the *World* boasted on its front page that two of its correspondents, Charles Thrall and Hayden Jones, had been captured as spies and released in a prisoner exchange.[57] In 1897, Davis extolled the bravery and fighting spirit of the Cuban insurgents in his *Journal* dispatches and a book-length collection, *Cuba in War Time,* which called for U.S. military intervention. However, in the illustrated histories and memoirs by correspondents that appeared after the war, reporters generally described Cubans as disorganized, sullen, and ungrateful. In one example of the ways in which the "battle with the slum" and the "war in Cuba" could figuratively intersect, Crane characterized Cuban ingratitude by ironically mocking both the sanctimonious charity worker and the thoughtless indigent of the New York slums: "Everybody knows that the kind of sympathetic charity which loves to be thanked is often grievously disappointed and wounded in tenement districts, where people often accept gifts as though their own property had turned up after a short absence. The Cubans accept our stores in something of this way."[58] To other correspondents, Cubans were hardly more than shadows. The correspondent H. Irving Hancock recorded his initial impressions of Cuban dress in revealing terms. Cubans were outfitted, he wrote, "in a kind of ecru-colored linen, the raggedest uniforms conceivable. Of the straw hats that they wore, though it may sound like a bull, there is only one phrase that will do them justice, and that phrase is uniform nondescriptness."[59] John C. Hamment, a *Journal* photographer, suggested in his memoir that Cubans were so nondescript as to be almost invisible: they "so closely resemble the bark of a royal palm or the stump of an old tree in colour that it is impossible to recognize a native unless you are very close to him."[60] Crane repeated the common charge that Cubans were indifferent to their own cause and paraphrases what he said were the common feelings of U.S. troops: "They came down here expecting to fight side by side with an ally," Crane recounts, "but this ally has done little but stay in the rear and eat army rations, manifesting an indifference to the cause of Cuban liberty which could not be exceeded by some one who has never heard of it." He went on: "The American soldier, however, thinks of himself often as a disinterested benefactor, and he would like the Cubans to play up to the ideal now and then. His attitude is mighty human. He does not really want to be thanked, and yet the total absence of anything like gratitude makes him furious."[61] Crane's characteristic irony here suggests that the propaganda underlying the U.S. campaign—as humanitarian relief campaign—is itself a humbug that Cubans are failing to adequately play along with.

Yet male intellectuals like Crane and Davis also viewed Cuba as a place where they could realize heroic exploits of newsgathering that were themselves newsworthy, dangerous, and even adventurous. Davis made explicit the connection between the policemen working to pacify New York's streets and the correspondents toiling in the battlefield abroad: "When you sit comfortably at your breakfast in New York with a policeman at the corner," Davis wrote in *Cuba in War Time,* "and read the despatches which these gentlemen write of Cuban victories and their interviews with self-important Cuban chiefs, you should remember what it cost them to supply you with that addition to your morning's budget of news."[62] Cuba was a place where heroism was possible, virtue could be put into action, and war was redemptive, even for patriots who only fought with pen and paper. Indeed, slum reporting in the late 1880s and 1890s routinely featured the explicit or implicit theme of battle. Progressive commentators on the slums viewed reform itself as a war against an especially determined enemy. In Riis's 1902 *The Battle with the Slum,* the author reserved particular praise for police chief Roosevelt, writing of the slum as a battlefield for civilization in which "we win or we perish."[63] In his autobiography, he called his first forays to the slums "raiding parties," where he made pioneering use of German flash powder, a highly combustible compound that made it possible to take photographs indoors and in low light. Riis's first experiences with the powder resemble a military invasion: "The flashlight of those days was contained in cartridges fired from a revolver. The spectacle of half a dozen strange men invading a house in the midnight hour armed with big pistols which they shot off recklessly was hardly reassuring, however sugary our speech, and it was not to be wondered at if the tenants bolted through the windows and down fire-escapes wherever we went."[64]

Besides celebrating Roosevelt's accomplishments in the NYPD, Riis's *The Battle with the Slum* heaps particular praise on Colonel George Waring, the sanitation engineer whose portrait graced the book's frontispiece when it was reprinted as *The Ten Years' War* after his death in Cuba. Disease and sanitation were routinely cited as primary obstacles to the U.S. war effort and as projects of the humanitarian occupation, and Waring's task as sanitation engineer became singularly important.[65] The popular association of tropical climate with diseases in late nineteenth- and early twentieth-century U.S. culture was a major feature of preinvasion reporting, and fears of illness were inevitably bound up with cultural assumptions about Caribbean indiscipline and hygiene, as we saw in chapter 2. Like Roosevelt, Waring came to his post in Cuba from New York City's post-Tammany administration. He was an agronomist and Civil War veteran from Rhode Island who was appointed chief of the city's Department of Sanitation. He famously organized the city street-cleaning brigade, which became known as the "White Wings" for their striking, all-white uniforms. The street cleaners cut a prominent profile in the downtown streets, where they stood out for their appearance and their military discipline, as an Edison film of a 1903 parade of White Wings shows. The men march down Fifth Avenue in formation, five across, with each group accompanied by a uniformed policeman; the cleaners themselves are dressed in their white uniforms with matching constabular helmets. In the Edison film, the organized procession is followed by a "cavalry" of drivers leading the horse-drawn carts the Wings employed to haul away garbage and ashes.[66] In June 1898, the *World* reported that a parade of the Ninth Army Regiment down Broadway was escorted not by the police, but by the White Wings, whose machine sweepers were mounted "like a heavy artillery. Everybody saw the point, and the transfer of street sweepers to the proud position usually occupied by the police was acknowledged here and there by a cheer."[67] What was "the point"? As Waring himself put it, his street sweepers were "soldiers of cleanliness and health," whose "trophies" were the clean pavements of the metropolis.[68] He took this military approach to sanitation from New York to Santiago and Havana when President McKinley appointed him to direct the sanitation efforts in occupied Cuba.[69] A brigade of "White Wings" was organized in Santiago, with straw *guajiro* hats replacing the New Yorkers' helmets, and plans were developed to repair the city's sewage system and dredge Havana's sheltered harbor. Unless something is done, Waring wrote in his report to the president, "commerce will carry the terror and the terrible scourge of yellow fever to our shores, until we rise again in a war of humanity, and at all costs wipe out an enemy with which no military valour can cope."[70]

Ironically, Waring died of yellow fever in Havana and was eulogized as a "martyr" in a great cause. Cleaning up Havana and Santiago were widely celebrated as the postwar occupation's most celebrated accomplishment and a major justification for the invasion.[71] The colonel's posthumous report painted a rather bleak picture of overcrowding in Havana, where the bulk of U.S. attention shifted after the capture and occupation of Santiago de Cuba: "The surroundings and customs of domestic life are disgusting almost beyond belief," he wrote. "Sixteen thousand houses, out of a total of less than 20,000, are but one story high and at least 90 per cent of the population live in these—averaging say 11 to each house. . . . According to the general—almost the universal—plan, the front rooms are used as parlours or reception rooms. Beyond them is a court, on which open the dining-rooms and sleeping-rooms. Beyond these, on another court, are—I might say is—the 'kitchen, stable, and privy, practically all in one.'"[72] This multipurposed, improvised domestic spatial organization was typical of working-class housing in New York, as well, and Riis had written in similar terms about domestic life in tenement apartments, where work and home mingled indiscriminately in dangerously overcrowded spaces.[73] In Havana, however, it is "almost universal"; the Cuban capital is like one big tenement.

Waring's point of comparison, though, was not New York, where he had made his reputation, but the England of generations past. "Havana is no dirtier than many another city has been," Waring wrote. "In England, in the olden time, the earthen floors were strewn with rushes. When these became sodden with filth, fresh rushes were thrown over the old

A squad of Cuban "White Wings" photographed in Santiago de Cuba. The New Yorkers' constabulary helmets have been replaced by broad-brimmed Cuban peasants' hats. From Buel and Mawsom, *Leslie's Official History of the Spanish-American War*, 1899. (Courtesy of General Research Division, The New York Public Library, Astor, Lenox and Tilden Foundations)

ones, and these in turn were buried, until the foul accumulation was several feet deep. . . . These conditions remained until repeated visits of the great sanitary teachers—the plague, the black death, the cholera, and other pestilences, which devastated cities and swept whole villages out of existence—had taught their hard lessons."[74] Waring thus extracts Havana from a history that the United States shares, and he places it in the past of Euro-American civilization and, even more abstractly, in a literary "olden time." (Meanwhile, in August 1898, the new commissioner of the New York Street Cleaning Department denounced the city's practice of dumping garbage at sea as "a survival of barbarism," while in September a *World* headline screamed, "Typhoid Germs in Montauk Water!"[75]) Where U.S. intervention in Cuba's war had been justified by political sympathies with the revolution, the occupation was conducted through the protodevelopmentalist discourse of colonial trusteeship, in which Cuba's present was comparable to the United States' past, and its advancement a matter of *technical* improvement in areas like sanitation. Before, many Americans had viewed Cuba in terms of shared interests, such as slavery (or abolition), sugar, and republicanism, or an imagined geopolitical threat, like slave revolt, the Confederacy, or Britain. In 1898, however, the U.S. government disavowed any material interests in Cuba, and U.S. popular discourse dismissed American similarities with the island. With the ongoing reform of North American cities, the social problems once associated with the northern slum were addressed in Santiago and Havana in the moral terms of their "redemption" by the United States. "Before the American era," proclaimed a postwar illustrated almanac below one of the "before" and "after" street-scene photographs common in such books, "there was no such thing as underground drainage in Santiago, and all such work was a revelation to the inhabitants."[76]

After these "revelations" in Santiago, Waring looked forward to redeeming the capital: "Havana can be freed from her curse," he wrote. "The price of her freedom is about $10,000,000. Can the United States afford to redeem her? For once humanity, patriotism, and self-interest should be unanimous and their answer should be, Yes!"[77] When "reform" became militarized, with the police and public works promoted as warriors for the public good against an implacable enemy, it became easily exportable as a tool of imperial expansion. The soldierly posture of the newspaper correspondent in suffering Cuba gave a narrative form to this ethic of reform, where reporters could not only transcribe events but help to shape them for the good. And when the war with the slum went to Cuba, Stephen Crane followed it.

From Mulberry Street to Daiquirí

The third and final war for Cuban independence began in February 1895, and a small force including Martí, president of the Cuban Revolutionary Party, and Máximo Gómez, commander-in-chief of the rebel army, landed in rural eastern Cuba two months later. Under the leadership of Gómez, the general Calixto García, and another veteran of Cuba's first independence war, Antonio Maceo, the outnumbered *independentistas* spread the conflict from the remote eastern districts throughout the island. By February 1896, the "ever-faithful isle" was in a state of total war, as the new Spanish captain general, Valeriano Weyler—who would become well-known to U.S. newspaper readers as "the Butcher Weyler"—instituted a radical policy of *reconcentración* (concentration) of the rural population, a measure intended to disrupt the proindependence forces and demoralize their supporters. The evacuation of villages into concentration camps and the destruction of crops and cattle caused massive suffering, which made it into U.S. newspapers and even stereographs; despite this repression and the deaths of both Martí and Maceo, the colonial forces were on the defensive by the first of 1898. Weyler had been recalled in late 1897 when a major offensive failed to weaken the insurgency, and a subsequent Spanish proposal of Cuban "autonomy" within the empire was rejected by the revolutionaries and denounced as a betrayal by Cuba's remaining loyalists. Most historians now agree that the revolutionary forces were on their way to likely victory; while the U.S. intervention in April 1898 considerably hastened Spain's capitulation, the decisive damage to Spain's military and political position in Cuba had already been done.[78] On April 20, 1898, two months after the explosion of the U.S. warship *Maine* in Havana harbor, President William McKinley signed a Joint Resolution of Congress that committed the United States to war with Spain without recognizing the Cuban republic-in-arms. To placate Cuban opposition and congressional critics, the resolution included a compromise measure, known as the Teller amendment, which disclaimed any territorial designs on the island by the U.S. government. From the beginning, then, U.S. intervention in the war was framed as a humanitarian gesture to a sister nation.

The U.S. war with Spain began in earnest in the first week in May, when the Pacific fleet of Commodore George Dewey began its assault on Manila Bay in the Philippine Islands. On June 22, the American Expeditionary Force landed on the beach at Daiquirí, near the eastern city of Santiago de Cuba, where they met no resistance from Spanish forces, aided by Cuban harassment of nearby Spanish units and the revolutionaries' occupation of the village and the nearby beach. Yet the Cuban role in supporting the landing was barely acknowledged by correspondents and military officials at the time, each of whom repeated a story of passive, even entirely absent, locals. Admiral Sampson, commander of the U.S. Navy squadron that landed that day, later described the lack of Spanish resistance at Daiquirí as "a mystery."[79] Hancock in his memoir wrote that after the American soldiers waded ashore, "as if by magic, Cubans now appeared on the beach," where they passively watched U.S. soldiers fight the surf.[80]

This treatment of Cubans as either apparitions or absent altogether was a persistent trope of U.S. accounts of the campaign, but these derisive portrayals were not consistent for the entire conflict. *Truth,* for example, ran numerous admiring photographs of the Cuban rebel military staff in issues published earlier in the spring; by August, it joked that the Cuban nation was itself a phantom. "When the war is over," one article quipped, "a searching party will have to be organized to go over Cuba and find enough patriots to organize a government with."[81] The same dichotomy exists in the *World*'s depiction of Cuban combatants before and after the U.S. invasion. In a spectacular electrogravure illustration from the *World*'s May 15 Sunday edition, Cuban insurgents embrace the Americans like old friends on the beach. After the U.S. invasion of Cuba, the Sunday section headline read, "Landing U.S. Marines in Cuba, greeted on the shore by insurgent troops gathered to protect them from Spanish attack." The absent Cubans of later American myth-making are decidedly present here, armed and in seeming control of the beach where the U.S. troops are landing. Even so, the U.S. flag in the craft bobbing in the waves suggests that this image is a celebration of U.S. military might. Yet notice, here, how the image frames the arrival of U.S. troops from the Cuban perspective, inviting a New York reader to imagine herself on Daiquirí Beach watching the landing. The Cuban men, furthermore, are white, but of a slightly darker complexion than their U.S. counterparts; they are mustachioed, while the Americans are clean-shaven. Rather than marking a clear racial distinction with their American allies, though, the men in the foreground form a symmetrical pair, the Cuban's bandolier setting off the sailor's neckerchief, their crisp white uniforms difficult to distinguish from one another, each man's gestures of greeting mirroring the other. Far from the ragged, "nondescript" soldiers of Crane, Hamment, and Hancock's accounts months and years later, Cubans here are upright, disciplined, informed soldiers, framed for the *World*'s readers not only as allies but as doubles of the Americans. Meanwhile, bright, tropical foliage frames the picture, climbing up the right side and eventually garlanding the paper's masthead, bringing the tropics "home to New York" and figuratively entangling them both in a single *New York World*.

Just over a month later, on June 24, the *World* depicted the Daiquirí landing quite differently, with a drawing of grateful, ragged women and children emerging from "caves" near the beach. Still ambiguously racialized in their "off-whiteness," the Cuban figures in the image are no longer upright allies, but forsaken victims. This image is stylized and allegorical—a woman, representing Liberty and suffering Cuban nationhood, leads her wide-eyed companions in a melodramatic gesture of welcome and gratitude. The highly speculative nature of these images meant that they reflected the prevailing editorial sentiment about the war and its purposes, and in their visual style they resembled popular

The cover of the *New York World*'s Sunday supplement, May 15, 1898, a full month before the Daiquirí landing. The caption reads, "Landing U.S. Marines in Cuba. Greeted on shore by the insurgent troops gathered to protect them from Spanish attack." (Courtesy of David M. Rubenstein Rare Book & Manuscript Library, Duke University)

representations of the urban poor and the fallen woman. The fallen woman and the prostitute were themselves fixtures of urban chronicles all the way up until the 1890s, in dime novels and melodramas like Alice Wellington Rollins's *Uncle Tom's Tenement,* which relocated Harriet Beecher Stowe's novel to the Bowery of 1888, and Edward Townsend's 1895 *Daughter of the Tenements,* in which Italian immigrants scrupulously shield their daughter from the temptations of the Bowery. She also emerged in self-conscious critiques of the slum romance, like Crane's *Maggie,* which aimed to avoid what its author called "preaching."[82] She appeared in the "charity writing" of Protestant reformers like Thomas de Witt Talmage, who in *The Night Sides of City Life* and *The Masque Torn Off* preached against the vanity of the "woman of pleasure" and praised the humble poverty of "the voices of the street."[83] Buel, in *Mysteries and Miseries of America's Great Cities,* viewed the slum as a place distinguished by the disgrace of womanly virtue. Riis was also attuned to the slum environment's degradation of domestic peace. As he wrote, "Back of the shop with its wary, grinding toil—the home in the tenement, of which it was said in a report of the State Labor Bureau: 'Decency and womanly reserve cannot be maintained there—what wonder so many fall away from virtue?'"[84] While Riis's and Crane's general rejection of the moral accounting of earlier writers on the slum and their studied attention to ethnographic detail marked a departure in U.S. writing about the urban poor, both writers also worked within a long tradition of chronicling urban degradation with the body of the slum woman, especially the mother and the prostitute.[85] The melodramatic language of slum fiction served as a natural accompaniment to war stories not only through the sentimental language of heroic rescue they often shared, but also because of the popularity of "realistic" tales of extreme spaces, like the slum and the battlefield.

An illustrated page in the September 25, 1898, Sunday *World* featured a full-page illustration of a wounded soldier's return in "Home Coming of a Regular Army Hero." The story, subtitled "A Picture from Life," tells of a wounded soldier who nearly perished on the squalid transport ship home (medical care for wounded soldiers was one of the paper's *causes célèbres*). The ending is a good example of Robertson's "fact-fiction discourse," in that it is a plainly sentimental melodrama drawn "from life": "The joy on the faces of the mother and sister and of the old war veteran, his father, over the fact that Uncle Sam has sent back even a part of the fine, strapping youth . . . is full of piteous truth," the anonymous author writes. A young man tips his cap to his small, bespectacled mother, who embraces him; his sister stands aside, her hands clasped in prayer, while his father stands proudly in the door of his humble yet respectable home. On either side of the illustration are two columns with the kind of "true romances" that fascinated yellow-press readers: "True Romance of Chinatown: A Story of Real Life" and "Hall Caine Hunts for Queer People for Novel on New York Slums," a story about the British novelist employing "character detectives" downtown.

The *New York Journal*'s story of one Cuban woman's escape from a Spanish prison in 1897 fit squarely into this "fact-fiction" tradition and in fact constituted a kind of international escalation of the contemporary domestic war on prostitution. For U.S. readers of the popular press the riveting story of the imprisonment and escape of Evangelina Cosío y

One month after the image in the previous illustration was published, on June 24, 1898, the *New York World* reimagined the Cuban welcome at the coastal town of Daiquirí. The caption reads, "Starving Cubans Welcome American Army of Invasion." (Courtesy of David M. Rubenstein Rare Book & Manuscript Library, Duke University)

Cisneros was the single most important event of the Cuban insurgency other than the *Maine* explosion. Cosío (newspapers at the time always used her maternal surname Cisneros) was charged with seducing a Spanish colonel to lure him into an insurgent trap. In her New York–published, English-language autobiography, *The Story of Evangelina Cisneros, as Told by Herself,* she claimed that she had been sexually assaulted by Berriz, who was beaten by fellow Cubans who came to her aid.[86] The *Journal* described her plight this way: "This girl, delicate, refined, sensitive, unused to hardship, absolutely ignorant of vice, unconscious of the existence of such beings as crowd the cells of the Casa de Recojidas, is seized, thrust into the prison maintained for the vilest class of abandoned women of Havana, compelled to scrub floors and to sleep on bare boards with outcast negresses, and shattered in health until she is threatened with an early death."[87] Although Cosío herself came from a prominent Puerto Príncipe family (she was related to Gaspar Betancourt Cisneros, the annexationist coeditor of *La Verdad*), her imprisonment told a familiar story for American readers: like Crane's Maggie and so many white heroines of the slum romances, she was portrayed as a good, honest, sexually chaste woman, corrupted by men and circumstance and nearly condemned to "harlotry" and racial disgrace. Julia Ward Howe, the New England educator, composer, and women's suffrage activist with a long interest in Cuba, asked "All Good Men and True Women" in an article in the *Journal,* "How can we think of this pure flower of maidenhood condemned to live with felons and outcasts . . . ?"[88] Cosío was broken out of prison by agents of the *Journal,* perhaps by simple bribery; the paper publicized its own account of its reporter's daring rescue raid, in which he sawed the iron bars off of her prison window and laid a plank into her cell from an adjacent house.[89] Cosío toured the United States at the *Journal's* expense, sold out a reception at Madison Square Garden, and met President McKinley. Missouri's governor suggested that the *Journal* might as well just send five hundred reporters to free the whole island.[90]

A preface to her autobiography written by Karl Drecker, the reporter who reputedly rescued her, neatly captures the gendered fiction of humanitarian empire that permeated 1898 war culture: "It was a national demand that this young girl be saved from the infamies of Spanish prison life," wrote Decker. "The *Journal* has done its part. Miss Cisneros is now the ward of the American people." In another introductory chapter, Julian Hawthorne (son of Nathaniel) wrote, "In the person of Evangelina Cisneros, Cuba appeals to us."[91] The *World's* image of the grateful Cuban welcome at Daiquirí and the *Journal's* exploitation of Cosío played on these popular representational logics of the fallen woman and the chaste heroine. In the *World's* illustration of the aftermath of the Daiquirí landing, the Cuban woman—who is racially ambiguous in the drawing, and dressed in tattered rags—reaches out to her American deliverers in a gesture of welcome and supplication, while prostrate children look on in astonishment. One of the characters of Buel's *Mysteries and Miseries of America's Great Cities* reaches out for salvation at a heavy wooden door emblazoned with a sign, "Knock and it shall be opened unto you," her eyes directed in a similar gaze of faithful expectation of her Christian deliverance. (Buel would later recount the 1898 War in his *Leslie's Official History of the Spanish-American War.* Buel's coauthor, Henry Mawsom, was another journalist who covered both the tenement and the battlefield.) De Witt includes a similar image of dignified poverty "appealing" to a sympathetic reader in an illustration entitled "The Voice of the Street," in which a neatly dressed street sweeper raises her right arm in a salute that suggests her dignity amidst the squalor that her ragged clothing otherwise indicates. Most representations of Cuban womanhood drew on this available generic vocabulary of sympathy, feminine virtue, and sexual transgression amidst the dangers of the city, and a visual vocabulary of poverty, passivity, and supplication. This was combined, of course, with the erotic "appeal" that Hawthorne implies in his tribute to Evangelina Cosío y Cisneros. Yet the American representation of Las Recojidas and Daiquirí also set up female oppression as a particular mark of Spanish, and Cuban, barbarism. To return to our initial example, how would the Pauline Marrs and Mary Raffertys of the world thrive in such a place, without American intervention?

One episode from Crane's career in Cuba and Puerto Rico demonstrates how the inequality of American urban life was symbolically displaced onto Cuba in the coverage of the 1898 War. Much of Crane's war reporting consisted of anecdotal episodes of combat and camp life. He resorted to the symbolic and racial vocabulary of the slum to interpret the Cuban other—a literary strategy that both fixed Cubans as inscrutable and foreign, yet paradoxically did so in a form that rendered them easily recognizable. This unsteady contradiction nearly spirals out of control in one of Crane's dispatches from the front. As Crane and Sylvester Scovel climbed the mountains outside of Siboney with a Cuban guide, they arrived at an insurgent camp. After a "typical" scene of Cuban indiscipline—at dusk, scouts file in to report to their captain, "lazily aswing" in his hammock—Crane reports the following encounter:

A "fallen woman" seeks solace in a city mystery authored by J. W. Buel. Above the door a sign reads, "Knock and it shall be opened unto you." *Mysteries and Miseries of America's Great Cities, embracing New York, Washington City, San Francisco, Salt Lake City, and New Orleans* (San Francisco: A. L. Bancroft & Co., 1883.) (Courtesy of The University of Chicago Library)

A street sweeper: "The Voice of the Street." From Thomas de Witt Talmage's
The Masque Torn Off, 1882. (Courtesy of General Research Division, The New
York Public Library, Astor, Lenox and Tilden Foundations)

One barefooted negro private paused in his report from time to time to pluck various thistle and cactus spurs from his soles. Scovel asked him in Spanish: "Where are your shoes?"

The tattered soldier coolly replied in English: "I lose dem in the de woods." We cheered.

"Why, hello there! Where did you come from?" To our questions he answered: "In New York. I leve dere Mulberry street. One—t'ree year. My name Joe Riley."

This passage works as an uncanny return of the slum itself, in particular Mulberry Street, New York's most infamous tenement address. In this scene, the implicit and often explicit racialization of the slum—"darkest New York," as at least one writer called it—emerges ironically in the person of Joe Riley, a Black West Indian who can blend with ease into either downtown Manhattan or insurgent Cuba.[92] The two reporters initially delight at the pleasure of encountering an English speaker from "home" in such remote surroundings. Journalists like Crane frequently expressed a kind of confusion and disorientation, not always unpleasurable, at the foreignness of the New York tenements, the tongues and the novel cultural forms of European or southern American migrants. Riley would have been just such a curiosity on Mulberry Street, but in Cuba he now seems refreshingly familiar to Crane and Scovel. However, the moment of happy recognition that Joe Riley originally promised quickly passes, as Crane becomes perplexed by his Irish surname and then abandons the man's story entirely. He abruptly ends this episode of his dispatch with an exasperated hyphen that interrupts the sentence and never delivers the expected factual explanation: "I have heard of a tall Guatemalan savage who somehow accumulated the illustrious name of Duffy, but Riley—"[93]

The encounter disturbs Crane's otherwise conventional war chronicle of two brave correspondents traveling with disorganized Cuban insurgents, while U.S. volunteers do the hard fighting elsewhere. Crane reports Riley's appearance with little commentary; he seems to find the man simply uninterpretable. In other texts of the 1898 War, like Cosío's autobiography, Col. Waring's report, and much of Crane's own reporting, tropes and characters of the slum narrative and the sentimental novel displace impoverishment and urban underdevelopment onto the Cuban body politic, where it becomes a symptom of Latin backwardness in general, rather than part of a shared history or an exceptional feature of each country's patterns of development. In the story of Joe Riley, by contrast, we can see this sleight-of-hand breaking down under the weight of its own contradictions. Crane's account undercuts the blustering self-confidence of his and most other reporters' account of the 1898 War, in which the thesis of American futurity and generosity and Latin belatedness and ingratitude dominated headlines and postwar accounts. Here,

"Society for the Prevention of Cruelty to Children, Two Ragamuffins 'didn't live nowhere,'" Jacob Riis, ca. 1890. (Collection of the Museum of the City of New York)

"Four Little Cubans of Havana." From a stereograph
published by Underwood and Underwood, New York,
1899. (Courtesy of the American Antiquarian Society)

however, Jacob Riis's "Other Half" and the Latin "Other America" bleed
confusingly into one another on the page.

The American Century and the Third World Imaginary

The war culture of 1898 forms a crucial episode in the creation of a
third-world imaginary in the United States. By "third-world imaginary,"
I mean the constructed image of a geographically distinct world that requires the cultural and economic training of the modern United States. In
Cuba, backed up by an army of occupation and unable to communicate
with his Cuban hosts, Crane's analogy of poverty and abjection became
affixed to the constructed identity of Cubans as passive recipients of U.S.
benevolence, even when his ironic voice at times undermined that comparison. His dispatches from the Cuban front resemble his anecdotal,
impressionistic method of chronicling the Tenderloin and the Bowery,
a self-consciously "literary" mode of reporting that he and Davis stub-
bornly defended against the "journalistic" impartiality demanded by their
editors—a relatively new perspective in news-gathering that would not

have made space for the Joe Rileys of the 1898 War. If the material of such irreducibly, mysteriously "literary" insight came from places of extremity and heroic action—such as the slum, the west, or the warfront—Crane's conflation of the two "frontier" spaces in this article places them on a similar level of abstraction. Thus abstracted, the Cuban war and the battle with the slum are removed from their immediate historical context, and they enter a realm of myth—the human hardship, collective struggle, and unblinking masculine heroism that was increasingly located abroad. The U.S. invasion of Cuba, which borrowed the rhetoric and repertoire of 1890s urban reform, justified the invasion as a moral responsibility to a "suffering" people. The disappointment that Crane and his colleagues felt in the Cuban insurgents they found comes from the expectations of foreignness and deprivation that militant reformers encouraged in those who sought to know how the other half lived and died—and yet who felt secure in the knowledge that the other half indeed made a whole. Mary Rafferty, "the water rat," could, in time, be reconciled with the progress of Pauline Karr. By contrast, the popular press confronted the Cuban other and found her familiar, yet inscrutable in her poverty, cultural habits, race, and language.

Correspondents like Crane could not communicate common ground with such a Cuban population whose "impenetrable indifference" was analogous to the residents of "an ordinary slum." This impenetrability, however, came to appear unbreachable in the context of the war and occupation—Crane's ignorance of Spanish, of course, did not help matters (not that he cites this as a reason). Before the invasion, Cuba was celebrated as a would-be republic, worthy of U.S. solidarity and sympathy. Americans brought energy and modern methods to Cubans who were, many authors observed with disappointment, ill-equipped for the blessing. Yet urban poverty and rural "backwardness" were North American problems, too: indeed, Crane, J. W. Buel, and the artist Fredric Remington (who traveled on Hearst's payroll to Cuba) had made their careers representing these "wild places" of the urban north and frontier west. Cuba's poverty was framed in print in terms familiar to U.S. readers who knew these places, or thought they did. Note, for example, how John Kendrick Bangs's *Uncle Sam, Trustee,* a celebratory chronicle of the postwar occupation, praises General William Ludlow for crushing a strike by Havana workers following "the example of the Chicago anarchists." Ludlow's response demonstrated "a thorough understanding of the best method of dealing with a race which had been long subjected to tyranny, and which, though aspiring to liberty, did not comprehend its limitations and responsibilities." What is notable here is the way in which Cubans' ancient racial limitations can only be explained in terms of an event that took place ten years before in Chicago.[94]

The gap between modernity and underdevelopment would in the twentieth century no longer lie within the borders of the United States—instead, it is what divided the United States from Latin America. The persistent dialectic of intimacy and foreignness structured U.S. representations of revolutionary Cuba; the intimacy of the United States and its new colonies in the Caribbean was framed as a paternalistic relationship between a powerful nation and its weaker neighbor. Cuba, once so close to the United States as to be nearly a state in the union, now belonged to another time, indeed, almost another world. After Shafter's armies brought brooms and the blessings of independence to Cuba, they left an "underdeveloped" country in their wake.

4　Latin America and Bohemia

Latinophilia and the Revitalization of U.S. Culture

Do Oaxaca and Tepoztlán really have more fun than Middletown?
—Stuart Chase, *Mexico: A Study of Two Americas* (1931)

The civilization shown is curiously different from our own, yet quite understandable.
—Anita Brenner, from a review of Waldo Frank's
Tales from the Argentine (1931)

Bohemian Tautologies

IN HIS 1931 best-seller *Mexico: A Study of Two Americas*, Stuart Chase asked the rhetorical question above about the subject of Robert Staughton Lynd and Hellen Merrell Lynd's classic 1929 ethnography of Muncie, Indiana, *Middletown: A Study in American Culture*. Chase interpreted the Lynds' discussion of class division, social mobility, and incipient consumerism in a Midwestern town as an indictment of a culture in decline. If Middletown was a synonym for America's cultural ills—its conformity, propriety, its Protestant dullness—Mexico, wrote Chase, offered a ready alternative. Mexicans had preserved folk cultures, local economies, and traditional skills that in the United States, he thought, had withered under the pressures of possessive individualism and industrial capitalism. In the representative Mexican village of Tepoztlán, Chase never saw a belligerent Mexican drunk, an impolite Mexican child, or a Mexican housewife who preferred store-bought to hand-ground cornmeal. In addition, he never saw a Mexican without his hat on. Unlike American men who had begun to go hatless to preserve their hair, Mexicans never sacrificed propriety for vanity—and they were doubly right to do so, he adds, because he never saw "a bald Indian." This last point raises an obvious question: If they always wore hats, how did he know if they were bald or not?[1]

The point is, of course, tautological. This style of circular reasoning about the cultural attributes of the foreign is common, especially when the attributes of that culture are cited so selectively in the service of a foregone conclusion about the "home" culture. "Development" often exhibits the same structure: development is the process by which the poorer nations reach development, which is itself an ideal version of what developed countries like the United States imagine themselves to be. Steven Clark mentions a much earlier example: the tautology that undergirds the etymology of "cannibal," a word derived from the language of the indigenous inhabitants of San Salvador. The word was used by Columbus as a name for the island's people, who he called "Caribs," and, of course, for their presumed "cannibal" savagery. The native meaning of the word recorded by the Spaniards as "canibales," however, has been lost.[2] The two words, Carib and cannibal, are now synonymous, with no way to break out of the tautological bind in which the meaning of each circles back to the other. Willa Cather, a contemporary of Chase, wrote in a similarly circular way in her 1927 novel *Death Comes for the Archbishop,* whose protagonist reflects on the early years of New Mexico Territory: "The Mexicans were always Mexicans, and the Indians were always Indians." Like Chase's sombreros and Columbus's cannibals, Cather's tautology seems to affirm an ontological truth for which no proof is possible or required. Or, consider the Beat poet Lawrence Ferlinghetti in his 1970 volume *Mexican Night:*

> And I am what I am
> And will be what I will be
> Sobre las playas perdidas
> del Sur[3]

Ferlinghetti affirms that it is only in Mexico (and in the language of Mexico) that he can comprehend his own essential being—that he is, in fact, what he is. Latin America's dense landscape, full of poetic meaning, provides both clarity (the ability to see things as they really are) and opacity (the realization that those things, once seen, are impossible to see clearly). The tautological structure of this conclusion—the clarity that makes apparent the opacity, and the opacity that demands the clarity once again—justifies the voyage. Only in Mexico could he come to the realization that he needed to be in Mexico, a point made repeatedly by Sal and Dean, the heroes of Jack Kerouac's 1957 novel *On the Road,* whose final chapters capture a postwar bohemian ideal of Mexico as a place of mystery and license. When the two men cross the border at Laredo, Texas, Sal shares this insight: "Just across the street Mexico began . . . [t]o our amazement, it looked exactly like Mexico."[4]

Since a tautology only brings you back to where you began, quotes like these suggest an old complaint about tourism and about much travel writing, which is that it serves to confirm what the author already knew before she left. This circularity also has the effect of undermining the dynamism that postwar development was meant to convey, as critics of development discourse have pointed out: That is, if development is the process and the end point of the process, can the process ever actually end?[5] In the quotes from Cather and Ferlinghetti, the tautology of foreign encounter underscores an ontological cultural difference, in which the self or some collectivity like "the Mexicans" contains an essential quality that separates them from others. At the same time, however, the tautological structure of these conclusions emphasizes that the self-knowledge one discovers elsewhere cannot be easily articulated, only fleetingly grasped. The revitalization that Latin America offers to the enervated, alienated, or nostalgic northerner is appealing precisely to the degree that it is tautological and therefore logically baffling: its elusiveness justifies the search because it is the elusiveness of Latin American culture that marks it as resistant to commodification and to the descriptive techniques of modern intellectuals. To prove the moral claim that Latin American indigenous peoples possessed a richer culture was not only impossible, but beside the point: if you could not grasp its importance instinctively, then you were too arrogant or too blinded by the "machine culture" to understand it properly. The circular, self-proving logic of this argument meant that it was frequently presented as an article of faith, as in Carlton Beals's opaque assertion that the "Indian world of Perú is, all told, a world of weird beauty and potential greatness. Let not the makers and masters of machines sneer or feel too superior."[6] Or William Spratling in the travel book *Little Mexico:* "For those who have a feeling for this country, Mexico is Mexico," he wrote, "and, in itself, sufficiently special, sufficiently intense not to need further justification of remote connections."[7] In other words, if what you knew before you left was that you do not know, the voyage south confirms your ignorance (or rather your knowledge of your ignorance). This conclusion, at least, cannot be dismissed simply as the provincial xenophobia of the tourist, who is typically unaware of his ignorance—indeed, it is this indifference to knowledge that typically marks the casual "tourist" and distinguishes him from the searching "traveler." What, then, distinguishes the latinophile from the mere traveler?

Latinophilia: An Introduction

By "latinophilia" I am referring to the twentieth-century American enthusiasm for Latin America as a revitalizing force for Anglo-American culture. Latinophilia, as I mean it, articulates a twofold desire: to break with a putatively imperialist past in cultural relations with Latin America and, in doing so, to revitalize an American culture perceived to be in decline. Latinophilia is both *comparative* and *compensatory,* in that it draws on the differences between north and south to remedy a perceived lack in the United States. Latinophilia is exoticist in its fetishization of racial, national, and ethnic difference, anecdotal and observational in its use of evidence, and generally popular rather than scholarly in tone. Scornful of the tourist, it cultivates and celebrates an "insider" form of knowledge of Latin American society, gained only after direct experience, rather than book learning. Finally, the intention of the latinophile is to critique the perceived failings of the home culture. Since one of these is the spiritual decline said to come with a mechanized and overdeveloped society, latinophilia thus prefers experience to expertise, or rather prefers the expertise of experience, for reasons specified above: the genius of the folk one seeks to emulate, after all, is instinctual rather than intellectual, learned but not taught. This reliance on experience rather than expertise does not mean that experts (however credentialed) cannot be latinophiles, but that their observations enter the realm of latinophilia only when they are rendered in the experiential terms particular to a passion. For this reason, the literature of latinophilia is largely a lay one, crafted for popular audiences. It also conforms to the logic of a tautology: the latinophilic journey in Latin America confirms, rather than repairs, the American cultural decline that it also diagnoses.

In the period between the end of the Mexican revolutionary war in 1920 and the decade following World War II, folklorists, modernists, bohemians, tourists, and political radicals "discovered" Latin America as a revivifying supplement to a modern American civilization crumbling (to varying degrees, depending on whom one asked) under the weight of bourgeois culture, mass culture, and class conflict. Mexico, in particular, with its large indigenous population, its simmering revolutionary energies, and its radical modern art movement, became the site of the most intense latinophilic interest in cultural revitalization. This is the era, Helen Delpar writes, of "the enormous vogue of things Mexican": the fascination by American intellectuals with Mexican folklore and revolutionary culture.[8] The Mexico City–based magazine *Mexican*

Folkways, edited from 1925–37 by the U.S. ethnographer Frances Toor, was a bilingual journal of Mexican craft and popular (often indigenous) art and one of the leading interlocutors between the Mexican and U.S. art worlds (*Mexican Folkways* published essays in Spanish, but to judge from its advertising, which directed readers to Mexico City's only soda fountain, English-speaking art dealers, and summer courses in Spanish, it addressed a mostly U.S. audience). The magazine published or reviewed the work of many of the leading lights of Mexico City's expatriate intellectual community, like Beals, Anita Brenner, and Redfield, along with the photographers Tina Modotti and Edward Weston and the painters José Clemente Orozco, Carlos Mérida, the Guatemalan muralist who often illustrated the magazine, and Diego Rivera, who served as art editor and was so regularly featured that he was often identified simply as "Diego."[9] At the same time, Toor excoriated "sentimental" romantics who, she thought, exploited Indian artistry while at the same time articulating her own fears that the old traditions were disappearing. In an editorial written in 1935, at the height of the Depression, she provided a taxonomy of American consumers of Indian art. Reflecting on the gradual disappearance of Indian customs and crafts, she wrote, "There are two classes of North Americans to whom this realization is appalling. First, the sentimental unthinking ones, who at all costs to the Indian, would like to see him remain picturesque and producing lovely handmade things for their delight, without wishing to pay for their value. Second, those who think and feel but have before them the terrible example of a highly industrialized and mechanized civilization in their own country."[10] This second, thinking class, argues Toor, looked to Mexico and saw its uneven development as a sign not of backwardness (or not only that) but, more positively, as a sign of a cultural resistance to the leveling force of capitalist modernity. Toor went on: "Think of those glorious and complacently rich United States of America before the crisis, when there were 'full dinner pails', bathtubs and automobiles for the average worker; for the middle classes, several automobiles and for the rich automobiles without limit! But those people with so many material comforts had to keep radios going when they were not going themselves; people with no calm, no inner peace. And now, one of the many problems facing the country, is what to do with the leisure forced upon it by the crisis. Thus the sight of the Indian sitting for hours without doing anything and then producing something beautiful, seems to them a miracle."[11] Toor's analysis reproduces a familiar bourgeois response to alienation—resistance understood as escape, and a desire for individual, psychic solutions ("inner peace") rather than collective ones. This approach is jarring in juxtaposition with criticism by Rivera, who wrote in an earlier issue of Mexican handicraft as the creative expressions of a rural proletariat coming into self-consciousness.[12] Whatever one thinks of Rivera's proscriptive class analysis, it allows one to see how much Toor's connoisseurship is concerned with Mexico as a lens through which to read the United States: the interests and improvement of the U.S. consumer, on the one hand, and the broader social problem of protracted, even irreversible American decline, on the other. If U.S. capitalism could no longer be counted on to provide either bread *or* roses, suggests Toor, then perhaps Latin America, so often dismissed as primitive, backwards, and unstable, could offer an alternative path.

The era between the Mexican and Cuban Revolutions is a broad period about which it is difficult to generalize in either U.S. or Latin American historical terms, including as it does official patronage of Latin American culture in the United States during the Good Neighbor Policy of the 1930s and 1940s, other revolutionary moments in Mexico, Cuba, and Guatemala, and the rebellious culture of U.S. bohemia. The romanticism of traveling intellectuals often positioned themselves against the vulgarity of mass tourism—"My foreboding," Chase writes in his book, "is concerned with the American tourist." This anxiety about cultural decline from outside was, in turn, itself a product of the model of national culture that tourism engenders.[13] Toor and the art historian Brenner, after all, both penned travel guides marketed to Americans traveling to Mexico. Latin America was marketed to prospective travelers as belated, on a different temporality from the progressive United States. Yet where once this was evidence of Latin backwardness, after the 1920s this belatedness becomes valorized as pleasurable, even instructive.

The Good Neighbor Policy, a major foreign and cultural policy initiative in effect from 1928 to 1947, was an attempt to replace the aggressive nationalism represented by Theodore Roosevelt's "Big Stick" with a more cosmopolitan, regional ethic of cooperation that became a strategic necessity as the conflict with Fascism escalated in the 1930s. As Amy Spellacy has argued, the Good Neighbor Policy proposed a new, flexible construction of scale for the Americas—that is, a new way of ordering and imagining the uneven development of capitalism in the Western Hemisphere. This new scale relied on the central trope of the "neighbor," a metaphor that figuratively shrinks the hemisphere, rendering its international community more intimate both in size and in affiliation, like the "neighborhood" of an ideal town. Chase, of course, drew on this close form of affiliation in comparing Middletown and Tepoztlán. The "good neighbor" trope abounds, as well, in the popular culture of the era, from Hollywood studio films and Disney productions to travel writing, fine art, and even school primers educating young U.S. schoolchildren on their hemispheric "neighbors." One such book, *Pan-American Day: An Anthology of the Best Prose and Verse on Pan Americanism and the Good Neighbor Policy,* was intended for use by teachers in planning curricula around this now-forgotten holiday. Organized thematically into plays, poems, and brief essays, the book implored students to "be hemisphere conscious" and to "be willing to share the title *American* with our Good Neighbors in the Pan-American sphere."[14] By constructing inter-American relations in the neighborly terms of "civility" and curiosity—and, in this case, in the child's terms of "sharing"—the "good neighbor" metaphor, Amy Spellacy argues, authorized U.S. authority in that imaginary neighborhood without acknowledging the exercise of power such authority would require.[15] Thus, schoolchildren were instructed, "American needs soul to-day. Money and vast organization of capital are the possessions of the northern sphere," a textbook Latinophilic self-critique of an acquisitive North America. Meanwhile, "to the south, the great hemisphere is rich in feeling, conscious of cultured and polite inheritance, placing a great emphasis upon pleasures, fine arts and gentlemanhood, not without attention to friendship and easy human relations unknown to a like degree in the brisker, more abrupt north. These, too, are needed."[16]

To return to the opening question of whether Tepoztlán has more *fun* than Middletown—whether its cultural life is richer and more satisfying, and whether its community feeling is more natural and nurturing—Chase answers in the affirmative: "I think they do. They take their fun as they take their food, part and parcel of their organic life. They are not driven to play by boredom; they are not organized into recreation by strenuous young men and women with badges on their arms and community chests behind them; they are not lectured on the virtues of work and the proper allocation of leisure hours."[17] This is the cultural power of economic underdevelopment. Oaxaca and Tepoztlán do not lack regimentation and hierarchy, but they organize social life "organically," through a local tradition freely accepted, rather than by a coercive central authority or through the subtler forms of commercial, educational, or political bureaucracy. In comparing Middletown to its Mexican counterparts, however, Chase was careful not simply to highlight points of difference. The idea of the book, in fact, was to encourage Americans to rediscover those parts of this organic communal existence they too possessed, but had forgotten. In the not-so-recent past, Middletown *had* at least as much fun as Tepoztlán does now. Thus, the contrast between the peoples is not so stark, much less absolute, than it may appear, and as it routinely was for past travel authors. See, for example, Spratling's account of a riverboat journey in *Little Mexico:* as the boat wanders through the wilderness, "the day passes, slowly, but without monotony. The Indians talk almost not at all. This is their country and their life. Monotony does not exist for them."[18] Spratling cites many of the telltale marks of economic backwardness—isolation, backcountry travel, idleness—but the local people are indifferent to the judgment that outsiders might pass on them, and "monotony," for others a sign of a lethargic society off the pace of modern life, does not exist. For Spratling, the moral deficiencies of "indolence" became the moral advantages of community, leisure, and tradition.[19] Mexicans' talents of handicraft, their ability to socialize freely without neurotic complexes, their independence from the tyranny of the working day, and their intimate connection with history and the land: these were all repressed in an U.S. personality that had once embraced them.

Instead of describing village economies in terms of the *difference* between Latin indolence and Yankee industry, Chase offers a travel writer's analogy. Mexico can be understood in historical and temporal terms as the past of the United States. Yet where many travel writers made this comparison in order to triumphantly distinguish the latter from the former, Chase draws a less salutary conclusion. This distinction, between "backwardness" and "tradition," is crucial to the aesthetic of latinophilia.[20] Chase repeatedly cites his New England childhood in Mexico to make uncanny comparisons and draw unhappy contrasts: the village maize harvest resembles the old-time barn raisings of times gone by, Oaxacan folk dancers look "remotely like the figures in New England country dances," and corn lies deep in Massachusetts' collective memory too (even if Mexican food overall, tasty yet "innocent of pie," remains a challenge for him). After making the valuable point that most foreign travelers base their conclusions of peasant laziness on the testimony of their bosses, with whom the writers tend to have the most personal contact, Chase argues that Mexicans in fact work quite hard but have developed an aptitude for rest that has become unfortunately underdeveloped in the United States, where it is misconstrued as a lack of effort. "There is much to be said for consigning unpleasant business to an endless mañana," wrote Chase. It was no less an authority than Mark Twain, he continues, "who held all his incoming letters for six months, and was amazed and delighted at the small percentage which then required answer. The clock is perhaps the most tyrannical engine ever invented. To live beyond its lash is an experience in liberty which comes to few citizens of the machine age."[21] The idea that Latin Americans were indifferent to the clock was (and still is) a cliché, and it was nothing new for U.S. writers to draw the primary contrast between themselves and Latin America in temporal terms. Yet in the 1920s and into the Depression era, for latinophiles like Chase this temporal and material advancement is less secure than ever.

The grammar of "latinophilia" is essential to its logic of racial and national differentiation. The circular reasoning of tautology tends to emphasize cultural difference and the racialized mystery of Latin America (its "weird beauty," as Beals puts it), but it always literally circles back to the self that one sees reflected in the strangeness of the foreigner. For writers and critics preoccupied with the United States' supposed economic, political, and moral decline, looking at Latin American underdevelopment felt increasingly like looking at the United States' future—and for critics of the "machine age" and middle-class propriety like Chase, that future did not look so bad. This is why latinophilia means something different from what Elisabeth Mermann-Jozwiak calls "Mexicanism," a Latin Americanist version of Said's orientalism.[22] While Mexico certainly occupies a prominent place in the American imagination as a place of the exotic and premodern, unlike the Orient in Said's account of European thought, Mexico and Latin America more broadly also figured as part of a hemispheric consciousness, shot through with imperial ambitions and colonial legacies, but also with the intimacy, here, of the "neighbor." This hemispheric consciousness—the legacy of inchoate borders, Pan-Americanist policy initiatives, and cultural solidarity movements—helps shape the critique of capitalist modernity that emerged from some latinophilic work.

The topic of U.S. representations of Latin American tradition and modernity between the wars is a broad subject; I thus limit myself, in this chapter, to a representative sampling of latinophilic engagement with Latin America, particularly in Mexico. These examples differ in their genre, medium, and in politics, but they are informed, directly and otherwise, by the cultural politics of the Mexican Revolution. There were folklorists like Toor, whose *Mexican Folkways* received funding from post-revolutionary Mexico's Ministry of Education. Another influential interlocutor between Mexico and the American intelligentsia was Anita Brenner, a Mexican-born art historian and folklorist raised in the

United States by parents exiled by the revolution. She not only wrote one of the most influential works of Latin American art criticism of the 1920s, the book-length essay *Idols behind Altars,* but also authored an impressionistic photographic history of the Mexican Revolution and a guidebook for U.S. travelers. Earlier, the circle of "Young America" cultural nationalists of the teens and 1920s looked to Latin America as an example of a vibrant vernacular culture that had thus far avoided the "jungle" of modern "machine culture." This group includes Lewis Mumford, who saw Orozco's mural work as a cosmopolitan example of regional cultural vitality, and Waldo Frank, one of the most popular U.S. intellectuals in Latin America at this time.

Most of the errors these latinophiles commit—romantic primitivism, superficial attention to structural economic issues, the idealization of poverty, a tendency to universalize U.S. experience, and an unsophisticated understanding of racial politics within Latin American societies—will be apparent to the contemporary reader. Some of these errors were apparent at the time, to readers like the novelist Katherine Anne Porter, an expatriate in Mexico City whose acerbic review of *Mexico: A Study of Two Americas* was rejected by the *New Republic* as too negative to print. "Mexico is not really a place to visit any more, or to live in," Porter lamented. "The land has fallen prey to its friends, organized and unorganized; its art and customs are in the dreadful convulsions of being saved, preserved, advertised and exploited by a horde of appreciators, amateur or professional. They swarm over the place and eat the heart out of it like a plague of locusts."[23] Porter's sarcastic dismissal of Chase shows how much skepticism there was even in the Depression decade about idealized celebrations of the "authentic" folk, something Sonnet Retman has observed in her study of the invention of U.S. folk culture, and its often satirical approach to "real folks."[24] Yet Porter's bitter irritation that Mexico, now discovered by the newcomers, is what we might call "over," is also the classic complaint of the bohemian discoverer to those arriving in her wake. More compelling than pointing out the obvious ethnocentric blind spots of authors like Chase, therefore, is considering the desire that their work activated and helped satiate in Anglo-American cultural consumers. In the decades before the elaboration of modernization theory and developmentalism in U.S. universities, middle-class Americans were skeptical about the extent and the worth of their own country's modernity. In the midst of a worldwide depression, latinophiles wondered whether industrial civilization was anything more than a passing mirage, and whether the nation's cultural underdevelopment might actually prove to be the most permanent legacy of the United States' industrial achievements.

A Culture in Need of Revitalization

Many of the Victorian travel writers discussed in chapter 2 conflated morality and climate, and the occupation planners in chapter 3 linked economic and cultural underdevelopment, viewing the former as a function of the latter. American latinophiles rejected the terms of the travelers' moral geography—or, at least, their coordinates—and began to draw a distinction between cultural and economic progress. In viewing Mexican "backwardness" as cultural wealth, they were asserting a widely held belief among U.S. intellectuals on the left: that the United States was a society in atrophy. In the 1920s and into the years of the Great Depression, the cultural critique of capitalism by intellectuals of the left often took the form of a denunciation of materialism as having replaced more spiritual and cooperative values. In a typical vein, Van Wyck Brooks wrote bitterly of Americans' "atrophied personality." "How," he asked, "can one speak of progress in a people whose main object is to climb peg by peg, up a ladder which leads to the impersonal ideal of private wealth?"[25] Many on the Marxist left like Michael Gold understood Mexico's "premodern" culture as a function of its place in the world capitalist market. Gold, the *New Masses* editor and Communist Party intellectual, chided those who emphasized only the Mexican Revolution's cultural policy and misunderstood its economic assault on land ownership. But neither, he said, was an aesthetic critique of bourgeois civilization incompatible with revolutionary opposition to capitalism. A wholesale social revolution would leave nothing unchanged, not least the "gray commercialism" and the "shallow, eager competitiveness" of capitalism's "so-called culture."[26] Chase, of course, did not understand Tepoztlán in these terms, but instead in the idealist terms of civilizational progress and decline: Mexico today, he writes, is the result of the "toboggan slide" of Mexican civilization, a four-hundred-year process beginning with the Conquest. The misplaced winter sledding metaphor, used as a device to describe Mexican history, actually emphasizes the point Chase is making: the U.S. may be starting its own slip down the same slope. "We Westerners may even now be on the brink of a gorgeous toboggan slide. A people like the village Mexicans—done with 'civilization' for four hundred years, sturdy enough to keep going without economic lifts and nose dives; with sense enough to make beautiful things with their hands, to see a fair world about them, to produce the best behaved children on earth—may leave something to be desired, but only an ignoramus may sneer at them. These people possess several qualities the average American would give his eyeteeth to get; and they possess other things completely beyond his purview—human values he has not even glimpsed, so relentlessly has his age blinded and limited him."[27] Yet in spite of this admiration, latinophilic literature in the interwar period was not quite a break with the racist chauvinism of generations past. Instead, it drew on earlier antecedents that had begun to disarticulate the particularly cultural *pleasures* that "primitive" societies offered from the cultural *backwardness* that made them "primitive" in the first place. When Francis Hopkinson Smith's 1889 travel guide *A White Umbrella in Mexico* describes the nation as "a semi-barbarous Spain," she uses the adjective approvingly, as a rough equivalent of what modern travel guides, using an ecological rather than cultural lexicon, would likely call "unspoilt."[28] Yet the irony of the position that writers like Chase, Spratling, Brenner, and Toor would assume, that Mexico is both underdeveloped and in the ascendancy, requires further elaboration.

In his 1916 essay "Young America," Brooks made a point that others in his circle of young dissident American intellectuals would repeat: the United States was corrupted by a materialistic culture that valued little more than the accumulation of wealth. He compared U.S. culture to "a badly motivated novel, full of genius but written with an eye to quick returns. . . . *So undeveloped we are,* save in the little private role we set ourselves, so unhabituated in the more comprehensive relationships of life, that it is as if we lived in relief, as it were, only half cut out."[29] Brooks attributes the United States' cultural "undevelopment" to the absence of a unifying tradition and the materialism of a society that overvalues commerce. In his well-known essay "On Creating a Usable Past," Brooks assessed "our existing travesty of a civilization" and saw a need to invent a "usable" collective past that could nourish an American literature beyond the shallow roots of commercial popular culture and the bloodless elitism of cultural gatekeepers he calls "the professors." In a nation that lacks the unifying national traditions of Europe, national art varies between sentiment and scholasticism: "We want vitality, and we have intellectualism," Brooks writes. "We want emblems of desire, and we have Niagaras of emotionality."[30] Spratling, the author of the memoir and travel book *Little Mexico,* moved to the town of Taxco, where he invested in its long-dormant silversmithing industry and marketed its products to the growing tourist and handicraft market of the United States. Where for Chase, "Middletown" was the mediocre, alienated foil of Mexican village life, Spratling drew on Sherwood Anderson's short-story cycle *Winesburg, OH,* which portrayed life in a solipsistic, Mid-western town. *Little Mexico,* which contained several sketches of distinc-tive Mexican types, included this one, of a teacher: "His hands are very brown and quite small, with slender, sensitive fingers, hairless and as smooth as those of his own baby. They are beautiful hands, not unusual for Mexico, and indicate a very different sort of man from the gentle-man from Winesburg, OH who has a story written about him. Because this one is not only quiet, but has decision."[31] These uses of small-town middle America as an analog for alienation suggest that it is in these pros-perous, Anglo-Saxon places, not the immigrant cities or the Black Belts of the south and north, nor in the slums, reservations, or tenant farms, that U.S. culture decays. Sidestepping racial and class conflict in its critique of the contemporary United States, the analogies of Taxco/Winesburg and Middletown/Tepoztlán underscores Spellacy's point about ideolog-ical stakes of the "neighborhood" as a model for the hemisphere. Its flexibility—subjective by definition, a "neighborhood" can be as large or as small as one likes—could allow for the Tepoztláns and Taxcos of the Americas to serve simultaneously as exotic foils and familiar, accessible relations. For Spellacy, this served a larger geopolitical purpose, shrink-ing the hemisphere by "creating a manageable, contained space out of what would otherwise be an unwieldy collection of geographically dis-tant and culturally distinct nations."[32] It also maintains its critique of U.S. capitalism on relatively safe, culturalist grounds—the United States' problem is that it is too middle class.

"Desiccated culture at one end, and stark utility at the other," Brooks wrote in his jeremiad *America's Coming of Age.* The most advanced the-ory of America's cultural decline came from the so-called Young Ameri-can cultural nationalists of the 1920s, especially writers like Brooks, Waldo Frank, Lewis Mumford, and Randolph Bourne. Bourne and Brooks, writes Casey Blake, "hoped to reestablish the organic unity of preindustrial cultures on a modern, democratic basis."[33] In his 1931 book *The Brown Decades,* Mumford reflected the pessimism of his own age in looking back at the postbellum era as one marked by a growing indus-trial economy and shrinking culture of the time: "In the new coal towns, the national banner itself, after a few days' exposure to the air, changed its red, white and blue to brown, grey and black," he wrote. "But even more the Brown Decades were created by the brown spectacles that every sensitive mind wore, the sign of renounced ambitions, defeated hopes."[34] Three years later, Mumford offered a more hopeful vision, encouraged by the debut of the Mexican muralist José Clemente Orozco's contro-versial frescoes at Dartmouth College, *The Epic of American Civiliza-tion.* "So the chestnuts are coming back," began Mumford's review in the *New Republic:* "So too, perhaps, our regional cultures, which were blasted by a ruthless and over-rapid industrialization and undermined by attacks of metropolitan 'prosperity,' may be putting forth fresh stems from their buried but still vital roots."[35] The unlikely connection be-tween the vanishing native New England tree and the audacious Mexican painter is Mumford's subject here: he argues that Orozco's work signals a revival of New England's buried spiritual roots. Taking Orozco's sub-versive title seriously—as a hemispheric epic that also provincializes the United States as a mere part of the "America" of the title—Mumford reads the frescoes as an indictment and yet also a revival of a declin-ing New England tradition of "spiritual vitality." Mumford's celebra-tion of a Mexican revolutionary artist as the best embodiment of a New England spirit is a striking example of the importance that the Mexican art revival had for U.S.-based intellectuals. As Anna Indych-López has argued, the muralists' popular sensibilities and scorn for Europhilia pro-vided a model for U.S. painters and critics in search of their own national artistic vocabulary.[36]

Frank and Bourne sought out the redemptive possibilities of the United States' vernacular culture. Writing during the midst of World War I, Bourne's essay "Transnational America" criticizes the resurgent nativ-ism directed at German and Scandinavian migrants. He admires these immigrant communities for retaining the "vernacular literature" and a "central cultural nucleus" that Anglo-Americans have sacrificed to com-mercial culture and nationalism. Surveying Anglo-American life, Bourne finds mostly the "tasteless, colorless fluid of uniformity" and "the down-ward undertow of our civilization with its leering cheapness and falseness of taste and spiritual outlook, the absence of mind and sincere feeling which we see in our slovenly towns, our vapid moving pictures, our pop-ular novels, and in the vacuous faces of the crowds on the city street."[37] Bourne sees the solution to this "downward undertow" in the United States' "transnationality," by which he meant the unexploited veins of folk cultures from Europe. Bourne saw U.S. culture as both too com-mercial and too provincial, constrained on the one side by the uniformity of mass culture and on the other side by a provincial nationalism. How-ever, Bourne, like Frank and Brooks, has little to say about the African American south or the Latino southwest, for example, apparently seeing these as unsuitable sources of a "national" vernacular. For two of these left cultural critics, to mine the "transnational" veins of a revived U.S. culture, you had to stake your claim on foreign soil.

Frank and Beals took these critiques of America's commercial "machine culture" and used them to interpret Latin America's lessons for northern readers. Frank was a cultural critic who developed a following in Cuban and Argentinean intellectual circles for his theory of a vigorous, inspired Latin America that might also provide what Frederick Pike calls the "cultural superstructure" for a materialistic United States.[38] Beals was a prolific travel author and muckraking journalist who made his name as an author of travel books on Mexico, Peru, and Bolivia, and authored a journalistic exposé of Cuba's Gerardo Machado dictatorship. In his 1933 book *The Crime of Cuba,* Beals viewed the island as a culturally rich victim of the colossus to the north. With what he called "its brooding saturated with mystery, its lifeways so alien in source and actuality," Cuba's promise of regeneration was under threat.[39] In *Our America,* Frank had said of Americans: "We are clever. We are literate. We are materially advanced. But, facing the mandate of our hour, the recreation of a world, we are more backward than the Magyar or the Slav, because we lack that spiritual substance which creates Faith and which moves mountains." Frank's comparison of Americans to "Magyars" and "Slavs" performs an ironic rhetorical move he would make repeatedly. Even as it implicitly accepts the essential differences between "backwards" and modern peoples, it proclaims the particular cultural advantages of the former—their "spiritual substance"—as a distinct advantage.

This distinction between cultural and economic development, between Anglo-American materialism and Latin American aestheticism is an old critique in Latin American letters.[40] In 1839, one of the first Cubans to write firsthand about the United States, Guillermo Lobe wrote, "The American of the North has no other object, no other stimulant, no other sensations, breathes no atmosphere other than that of commerce, speculation, and sordid interest: he fixes his glory, his happiness, his exclusive object on acquiring, possessing, and increasing his riches."[41] A version of this complaint was realized in its most canonical form by José Enrique Rodó, the turn-of-the-century Uruguayan *letrado* whose essay "Ariel" was written in the wake of the U.S. invasion of Cuba and Puerto Rico in 1898. Rodó allegorized Latin America as the Shakespearean sprite of *The Tempest* held captive by the North American sorcerer, Prospero. Rodó criticized the United States as a society dominated by the "utilitarian spirit."[42] Frank's *arielista* disdain for his country's "cult of material acquisition" opposed a spiritually deficient materialism to the liberatory possibilities of art, a critique of U.S. culture that found support in Latin America, especially Cuba and Argentina, which he visited frequently throughout the 1920s and 1930s.[43]

The Cuban essayist Jorge Mañach lamented with Frank the "cultura aritmética" (arithmetic culture) of the United States, whose influence on the island threatened to turn Cuba's rich national culture into a uniform monoculture.[44] The Cuban ethnographer Fernando Ortíz diagnosed this sentiment as "pesimismo criollo," or national pessimism. According to Ortíz, the *pesimiso criollo* was closely linked the feeling of disillusionment among many in the intellectual class frustrated with the persistence of political corruption and economic dependency after the long fight for independence.[45] Citing Cuban literacy statistics, Ortíz wrote, "Today as perhaps never before, the most cultured peoples are the strongest, and only in true culture can one find the necessary strength to live without servitude." In *Our America* (the reference to Martí's canonical essay of the same name was apparently unintentional), Frank identified the United States in similar terms: as a spiritually decrepit people, in danger of cultural bankruptcy and in need of revitalization. Instead of illiteracy and corruption, though, the United States' malaise came from its *cultura aritmética,* which threatened to replace vernacular traditions with ephemeral material goods. Mañach's introduction of Frank before the Instituto de Cultura Cubana-Hispana treated this malaise as a multilingual transnationalism of pessimistic intellectuals. Referring to Frank as a "minorista," the name adopted by the group of Havana avant-garde intellectuals to which Mañach belonged, he wrote, "We have taken from North America not its best side of democratic intent, but those excrescences which Frank has called the 'cults of Power' and which threaten to destroy its own creative and organic virtue. We need to learn, from this minority American, that all that glitters is not gold or rather, that what glitters is indeed too often gold."[46] Frank's critique of the United States' spiritual crisis was well received in Cuba because he echoed *vanguardistas'* own complaints about Cuban national culture under the American neocolony.[47]

Mexican Modernity: Indigeneity, Art, and Living History

Despite the popularity of Cuba as a travel destination and intellectual center in Latin America, for the generation of latinophiles of the interwar era it was Mexico that had the greatest appeal. The appeal of Mexico to this generation of American cultural nationalists, bohemians, artists, and folklorists lay in the country's large and, since the Mexican Revolution, newly visible indigenous population. While the intellectual life of avant-garde Havana provided the most receptive audience for Frank's critiques of American alienation and modernization, Mexico served as the richest example, to Frank and others, of (1) an authentic, autonomous *American* culture and (2) a living folk culture, embodied in the indigenous population (Cuba's "folk," being Black, did not offer the same broad appeal). In other words, Mexico's indigenous antiquity was requisitioned by Americans keen to discover a New World heritage independent of Europe. The work of Winold Reiss, the German-born photographer of the Montana Blackfeet and revolution-era campesinos in Mexico, serves as a useful example of the appeal of the Mexican Indian to American audiences. As Oles observes in *South of the Border,* Reiss's portraits of indigenous people in Montana and Mexico are roughly contemporary, but stylistically very different. The Blackfeet, by the 1920s confined to reservations and subjected to the assimilationist pressures faced by all native peoples in the United States, are photographed in their traditional costume as relics of a past time. This nostalgic portrayal of the "vanishing Indian" contrasts with his Mexican portraits, which are more informal and make little effort to present their subjects as "traditional." While the Blackfeet are "history" in the colloquial sense of "finished," the enduring appeal of indigenous Mexicans lies in the fact that they are "historical" in a different sense: they offer living contact with the past in the present.[48]

The appropriation of Mexican indigeneity offers one example of the point that "transnational" cultural work is not inherently, or even usually, politically antinationalist, much less radical. As Steven Park notes in his account of "Mesoamerican modernism," the citation of the Maya as a model for Anglo-Americans appealed broadly, to self-described "militant modernists" like the little magazine *Broom,* which cited the Maya as a weapon against realist convention, as well as ostensible antimodernists like Robert Stacy-Judd, the principal ideologue of the Mayan revival in architecture. In the latter case, the effort to claim Mexican indigeneity as a broadly "American" antiquity shared by the United States was a kind of antiquarian jingoism. The Mayan revival, which peaked in the mid-1930s, aimed to incorporate motifs of Mayan design into a truly "American" architecture. Stacy-Judd, a British-born architect and amateur archaeologist, was the movement's chief exponent and propagandist. He began a manifesto of the movement by lamenting the "American tragedy" of unoriginality in architecture: "We are a tragic figure in this, the World School of Architectural Classics," claimed Stacy-Judd. "A host of geniuses lie buried beneath a pile of gross materialism, iron-bound custom and its attendant inhibitions." In order to arrest this inexorable decline and release the creative energies of U.S. architects, Stacy-Judd proposes an "All-American Architecture" based on the Mayan. For Stacy-Judd, as Park writes, not only can the United States lay claim to Mesoamerican antiquity, the United States was actually its "rightful heir."[49] In an excellent example of the power of the "neighborhood" trope to license cultural appropriation, Stacy-Judd outlined, under the heading "Americans and Mayans Analogous," the two great similarities between the Mayan empire and the United States: both are heirs of a foreign conquest, and the Maya were also "a commercial, businesslike people with an ideal government." Left alone, this utilitarian sensibility atrophies into a cult of business. Yet the Mayan execution of "stupendous undertakings" and their tendency to build for "mass groupings" of people would serve the United States, as it supposedly had for the pre-Columbian Maya, as a burst of restorative, unifying energy. Appropriately, therefore, Stacy-Judd illustrates his call to action with Mayan-derived designs for places of religious ritual like the First Baptist Church, built in Ventura, California, in 1931, as well as secular temples like the never-completed plan for a combined department store, office building, hotel, theater, and arena complex in Hollywood.[50]

Frank claimed that Americans should look to Mesoamerica not *only* because it was appealingly different, but also because we are similar in ways that our technical civilization prevents us from seeing: "The practical tradition has its technic: we have studied it, in studying our Jungle and its Cults of Power. Its passionate commentators fill our daily sheets, crowd the air and the movies; subtly bend the young to their way by dating the American from Washington and Franklin, rather than from Columbus and Roger Williams, or—more properly still—from the native cultures of Maya and Pueblo."[51] The reference to the Pueblo of the American southwest, whose architecture and craftwork was enjoying a vogue in American artistic circles in the 1920s and 1930s, only underscores the heightened significance of Mexican antiquity: only those native peoples who built permanent structures bequeathed a cultural legacy to the modern nation. Mexico's ancient structures became more accessible than ever during this period. After Mexico's revolution, new roads and government restoration projects allowed more and more tourists to visit the temple ruins of the Yucatán Peninsula, which had been left, as one travel guide enticingly put it, "unvisited in the silence and obscurity of the wilderness."[52] According to Brenner, the prominent place of the macabre in Mexican life would be instructive for visitors from a utilitarian, austere civilization. She begins her travel guide, *Your Mexican Holiday,* on a Pan-Americanist note, emphasizing the cultural links suggested by American agriculture. Without Mexico's ancient mastery of quintessential products—she cites corn, tobacco, rubber, and cocaine—"modern America and modern civilization are inconceivable," she writes. This shared agrarian legacy, Brenner continues, has "helped to make us far more different than we think, from our European parent-stock, and which create a stronger bond than we are conscious of between the three Americas." She balances this appeal to an ideal hemispheric unity, though, by underscoring the cultural and epistemological divisions that subsequent history has produced. In her travel notes on Mitla, the Zapotec temple city and burial site, Brenner writes to her Anglo-American readers that "the attitude implicit is too diverse from our own habits and feelings to be clearly grasped. Briefly, it is a mixture of awe, fear and fascination, and an attempt to solve the mystery by giving it a recognized and accepted place, instead of—as we do—running away from it and trying to forget it."[53]

Frank attempts to bridge this cultural gap by yoking together the Maya and the religious dissenter Roger Williams as counterpoints to the utilitarian Franklin and the nationalist Washington. Yet he cites the Maya as examples to Americans in two seemingly contradictory ways in *The Rediscovery of America.* Firstly, the Maya as a living people were not yet shackled by the uniform culture of modernity. At the same time, they were a metaphor for the ruin that awaits a United States in decline. Part of this paradox comes from the Maya people's popular image as a civilization represented not by their contemporary culture but by their ancient architecture. Part of it also comes from Frank's own complicated cultural politics: he was an erudite cosmopolitan who disliked the provincialism of popular culture but also an antielitist who scorned Europhilia. The folk, for him, could be both the wellspring of a collective national tradition as well as an army of philistines. The Maya in their literal "jungle" are drawn into an extended metaphor by which Frank denounces the figurative "American jungle" of machine culture and consumer capitalism. "In lieu of tarantulas and banyan trees," he writes in *The Rediscovery of America,* "we have machines; in lieu of the action on us of storms and unguessed myriads of bacteria and insects, we have the intricate pull and stress of economic forces."[54] The indigenous people of the Yucatán thus occupied for Frank the strange position of a patient in an advanced state of disease and the best remedy for the sickness. The defeated Pueblo and the surviving Maya, with all their metaphysical deficits, still serve as an antidote to the practical traditions that have created a metaphorical economic "jungle" even more tangled and oppressive than its literal counterpart in the tropics. But then, the Maya are once again heralded as metaphors for the slow rot of United States civilization: "Far more than we suspect," concludes Frank, "we are like the Mayans who house their asses in priestly tombs."[55] This contradiction is typical of the latinophilic gaze: based as it is on a celebration of poverty and under-development, it is unable to transcend the cultural hierarchies that are its foundational premise. The title of Frank's book—*The Rediscovery of America*—perfectly encapsulates this contradiction. In summoning the romance of discovery, it suggests the violence of Columbus's conquest while pretending at the same time to decry it.

Brenner, somewhat more sensitive than Frank to the dangers of cul-tural appropriation, often made her own relationship to Mexico and its indigenous cultures a theme of her writing, drawing on her own origins in Mexico while emphasizing her distance from the nation and especially its indigenous society. In a *Mexican Folkways* article on the *petate,* the traditional reed bedroll of the Mexican and Central American peasantry, Brenner regrets her distance from the tradition the *petate* represents in a way that also underscores the superficiality of a modern art clientele that can never assimilate it. "In a New York apartment," she writes, "it may be an ornament, but it is also a reproach. It is too real for a fantastic [and] overwhelming Brobdignagia; it is too cheap to be of value where all things are measured by one standard; it is too sober for a bewilder-ing, admirable, matchless, efficient chaos of white lights and luxurious garments. . . . And I am forced to accept that, in spite of the fact that I brought a *petate* with me I left the *petate* far beyond me."[56] Brenner's comparison of U.S. culture to Swift's Brobdignag—the land in *Gulliver's Travels* occupied by giants—provides a wonderfully literalized figure of overdevelopment that is alienating and overpowering. Such a fantasti-cally overbuilt place, populated by creatures of grotesquely large scale, cannot comprehend something as simple as a *petate,* the product of a regional genius.

Brenner's work, from *Idols behind Altars* to *Your Mexican Holiday: A Modern Guide* advances the argument that because of its residual re-gional cultures, Mexico is the place of "modern, important, new-world doings in art." *Your Mexican Holiday* summed up the difference between Mexico and the United States with a curious visual metaphor: "So mod-ern Mexico is a cinema of human history seen backwards or forwards, though it is often hard to tell which is the savage," she wrote. "As New York displays every race, Mexico cradles every age."[57] In a reversal of what Marx described in the *Grundrisse* as capitalism's "annihilation of space by time"—where New York would represent the contraction of the globe into a single space and a uniform temporality—Mexico offered the appeal of space triumphant once again. For Brenner, Mexico's interest derived from its retention of indigenous and "premodern" cultural forms in close proximity to modern ones. Her comparison of Mexico and New York neatly captures the linear direction of progress that the concept of underdevelopment encodes in its syntax. Yet it is significant that she compares two very unlike things—the nation of Mexico, on the one hand, and the United States' largest and most wealthy city, on the other. This indicates once again the problem of the national scale of underdevelopment: it is nations, and not regions or cities, that are underdeveloped. Thus, New York can stand in for the "modern" United States, while Mexico is irreducibly Mexico. Moreover, modernity lies in art and the local, rather than in technology and the scale of the global. It is Mexico's wealth of *local* practices—the *petate,* the *huipiles* of Veracruz, the silversmithing of Taxco, even the muralism of Orozco, Rivera, and Siquieros—that lent it this privileged cultural modernity. This aesthetic reversal of the terms of modernization and backwardness—in which Mexico's advancement comes out of its regional fragmentation—reframes Mexico's poverty as the maintenance of tradition, its unevenness as the preservation of cultural possibility. In *Idols behind Altars* Brenner described indigenous cultures as organically integrated—a relic of premodern division of labor. "Land, labor, gods, skill, and personal honour are indivisibly linked, and further fixed to place," she writes. Labor is also not alienated—except, as she hastily adds about the Porfiriato, when it is simply taken.[58]

However, even as she defended Mexico's importance to Americans in terms of its compensatory function—that is, Mexico's difference, and its ability to offer an example of a revitalized culture for enervated U.S. Americans—Brenner herself emphasized Mexico's uniqueness. Describing what she awkwardly calls Mexico's "dominantly artist" character, Brenner describes the Mexican artist's intimacy with form, history, and landscape as an essential aspect of the national character. "The need to live, creating with materials; the need to set in spiritual order, the physical world; the sense of fitness—these are components of an artists' passion, and these are the Mexican integrity. That is why Mexico cannot be measured by standards other than its own, which are like those of a picture; and why only as artists can Mexicans be intelligible."[59] Brenner's formalism asserts, by way of a tautology, that just as a picture can only be interpreted in its own terms, Mexico itself has the irreducible "integrity" of an art object. Her claim that Mexico "cannot be measured by standards other than its own" exemplifies Neil Larsen's point that to the metropolitan reader, Latin American culture is too often meaningless outside proscribed coordinates. Latin America and the global South "figure not only on a spatial map," writes Larsen, but on a "'hermeneutic map' as well, a 'map' that already plots the South as intrinsically meaningful but beyond whose coordinates all possibility of meaning is canceled. In directing its attention elsewhere, the North necessarily concedes something about its own sense of identity and authority, its own position on the hermeneutic map."[60] The tautological logic of latinophilic critique redirects the northern subject back to itself. Mexico is different, irreducibly so, but in Brenner's argument here, it is understandable according to the criteria we already have for misfits, bohemians, and artists in the United States. The gap between a Mexican people on the move and a U.S. "machine culture" in stagnation can be breached, Brenner suggests, by finding this artistic Mexico, a Mexico that returns us to ourselves, the Mexico inside of "us."

The Ethics of the "Earthborn": Latin American Folk in U.S. Fiction

The apparent chasm between the "machine culture" of the United States and the culture of revolutionary Mexico, several examples of which we have seen above, was a popular theme of latinophilic writing on the U.S. Southwest in the first decades of the twentieth century, as well. An important early example was the work of Mary Austin, whose 1903 book of sketches of southwestern life, *The Land of Little Rain,* explored the lives of what she called the "earthborn" in a Chicano California town called Las Uvas. "We breed in an environment of asphalt pavements a body of people whose creeds are chiefly restrictions against other people's way of life," writes Austin of Anglo-Americans, "and have kitchens and latrines under the same roof that houses their God." By contrast, "At Las Uvas they keep up all the good customs brought out of Old Mexico or bred in a lotus-eating land; drink, and are merry and look out for something to eat afterward; have children, nine or ten to a family, have cock-fights, keep the siesta, smoke cigarettes and wait for the sun to go down."[61] Here and in other work like *American Rhythm,* her book on Native American music, Austin described these "good customs" as a racial and regional inheritance, and like other latinophiles Austin saw the richer spiritual life of the "earthborn" as a sublimated national trait as well—the chasm might be breached between Las Uvas and the Anglo "we."

In this final section of this chapter, I consider three U.S. modernist novels that accounted, in different ways, for the difference between U.S. metropolitan modernity—the "we" who come from the "asphalt" of the coasts—and the "earthborn" of Latin America. Willa Cather's 1927 *Death Comes for the Archbishop,* Ernest Hemingway's 1952 *The Old Man and the Sea,* and Jack Kerouac's 1957 *On the Road* take as their subject a vanished, or vanishing, social world distinguished by a close spatial proximity to the modern-day United States (or, in the case of the Mexican migrant farmworkers with whom Kerouac's Sal lives for a brief period, a tenuous place within it). Cather's novel depicts a remote Catholic parish in New Mexico territory after the Mexican-American War, as the region is slowly absorbed economically and politically by the United States. Hemingway and Kerouac's novels, on the other hand, address a postwar middle-class imaginary of Latin America, as a place where premodern forms of labor persist just a short distance away from the bourgeois United States. *The Old Man and the Sea* chronicles a peasant fisherman outside Havana, marooned in a subsistence economy in the shadow of a tourist paradise. Kerouac's novel shows the enduring appeal of Austin's racial taxonomy with his selective exploitation of Mexicans, Chicanos, and African Americans as talismans of a lost cultural authenticity. In varying ways, these novels question the distance—cultural, geographic, and otherwise—between the "underdeveloped" and "us."

Cather was Austin's contemporary and with her, one of the most well-known chroniclers of the American borderlands within U.S. literary modernism. For many of the artists and writers who flocked to New Mexico in the teens and 1920s, adobe architecture was a potent symbol of its resistance to the leveling force of modernity. As Mabel Dodge Luhan, the wealthy patron of the Taos, New Mexico, artist colony, wrote of an adobe fireplace in one of her newly built houses: "It looked, when it was ready, as though it had been made with hands, as did all the houses in that country. Uneven surfaces, irregular lines, true as hand and eye could make them, but not mechanically squared, not *contracted!*"[62] Cather wrote in much the same way about the preindustrial craftsmanship of 1850s New Mexico in *Death Comes for the Archbishop.* "The thick clay walls had been finished on the inside by the deft palms of Indian women," Cather writes, "and had that irregular and intimate quality of things made entirely by the human hand. There was a reassuring solidity and depth about those walls, rounded at door-sills and window-sills, rounded in wide wings about the corner fire-place."[63] As a regional specialty literally constructed from the soil, adobe is an ideal example of what Austin saw as the territorialized, regionally rooted culture of the "earthborn." As Philip Joseph has written, however, despite her conventional affection for adobe fireplaces, Cather's vision of the Southwest's regional culture was significantly at odds with Austin's, as the latter complained (it was also, I will argue, more sophisticated). After allowing Cather the use of her Santa Fe house to draft *Death Comes for the Archbishop,* Austin was displeased with the results, which she found insufficiently committed to imagining the region's autochthonous cultures as intact and self-contained. "I was very much distressed that she had given her allegiance to the French blood of the archbishop," she wrote in her autobiography; "she had sympathized with his desire to build a French cathedral in a Spanish town."[64]

Cather's novel chronicles a French cleric, Father Latour, who comes to New Mexico territory to build a pastorate (and, later, a cathedral) shortly after the U.S. victory over Mexico in the 1848 war. The protagonist's death comes sometime in the late 1880s, but while the novel spans the U.S. conquest of what was coming to be called the American Southwest, the politics of the outside world barely impose upon the archbishop's remote flocks. Cather describes in detail the vast, sparse environment of the Southwest, lending it the character of a hermit's wilderness: a place without pretense or affectation, full of moral meaning, if little else. The idealism of this historical vision lends itself easily to a racial essentialism rooted in the soil.[65] At the heart of my interest in this novel is a sentence I quoted above: "The Mexicans were always Mexicans, and the Indians were always Indians." It is an example of latinophilic tautology: a circular reasoning about the cultural attributes of "the foreign" whose idealism—a commitment to transhistorical forces beyond the material and political world—reveals it as a strategy, ultimately, of self-legitimation. In their commitment to clear national difference, such cultural tautologies are structurally similar to what I described in the introduction as the historical tautology built into the "grammar" of development. Development is the process that poor nations undergo in order to attain "development," which, like the ideal version of the U.S. past that latinophiles sought in the Mexican village, is itself an ideal version of what U.S. Americans imagine themselves to be in the present. The preservationist impulse in latinophilia is at odds, of course, with development's forward thrust: the vanishing point of unity between the traditional "foreign" and the modernized "domestic" space is, in the bohemian vision, projected into an idealized past, where in the developmentalist mode, it lies just out of reach in the future. What these formulations of history and geography share is the elusiveness that justifies the search, for either the distinct virtues of the earthborn or those of a global liberal capitalist modernity. In each, meaning simply circles back to the self that is the true object of the inquiry: the latinophilic treatment of Latin America, like the classic developmentalist account, usually tells us as much about the U.S. author as it does anything else. Cather's treatment of the cultural history of the Southwest demonstrates another possible reading of tautology, with different historical and political connotations—its confounding of clarity, its resistance to meaning. Indeed, as Joseph argues about this novel, it is Cather's "ambivalence" about the territorial and historical rootedness of New Mexico's regional culture that bothered Austin so much.[66] This makes Cather's novel a sophisticated challenge to the more simplistic geographic essentialism of most latinophilic readings of Latin America.

Cather's novel, melancholically chronicling the decades after the Gadsden Purchase, fits nicely into the tradition of what John A. McClure has termed the "late imperial romance." Such texts, he writes, "sharply interrogate the popular romance of the civilizing mission of 'development' and relate in its stead a counter-romance of descent into realms of stubborn strangeness and enchantment."[67] *Death Comes for the Archbishop* depicts the modernization of a peripheral region of the country treated in this novel as more Latin American than "European" or Anglo-American. It contains only one Anglo character—the dime-novel hero (and real-life federal Indian agent) Kit Carson, who appears as a simple, brutal conqueror, one who cannot read a printed page but is "quick to read a landscape or a human face." As Audrey Goodman writes, the history of perception—the means of "reading" the landscape and its people—is inseparable from conquest in *Death Comes for the Archbishop*. Yet this landscape is opaque and resistant to interpretation, a fact that reflects both the land's "stubborn strangeness and enchantment" as well as the multitude of geographical and cultural registers from which the novel's French, Anglo, and Mexican characters approach it. "The novel's Southwest defies landscape convention," writes Goodman. "It cannot be comprehended in a glance."[68] Perspective as well as history change it: as the Archbishop lies near death, he reflects on "this peculiar quality in the air of new countries," which "vanished after they were tamed by man and made to bear harvests. Parts of Texas and Kansas that he had first known as open range had since been made into rich farming districts, and the air had quite lost that lightness, that dry aromatic odour. The moisture of plowed land, the heaviness of labour and growth and grain-bearing, utterly destroyed it; one could breathe that only on the bright edges of the world, on the great grass plains of the sage-brush deserts."[69] As Goodman argues, Cather's framing of the southwestern air as a weighty, material substance reflects not just a yearning for a landscape prior to or beyond commodification. It also reflects the fact that as a treatment for tubercular patients the New Mexican air, like the Cuban, was itself already a commodity in 1927. Her awareness that the development it laments proceeds at multiple scales—both of geography and perception—makes Cather's work a more nuanced treatment of the relationship between development and the landscape than that of latinophiles like Austin, who aimed to preserve a territorialized ethnic authenticity, or Chase, who imagined a dormant past of village domesticity.

Cather writes, "Father Latour often said that his diocese changed little except in boundaries. The Mexicans were always Mexicans, the Indians were always Indians." Walter Benn Michaels has made much of the tautological second sentence, reading the novel's Catholicism as a nativist response to the failure of assimilation. Cather, he writes, dramatizes the 1920s problem of the "Americanization" of immigrant aliens by replacing national assimilation with Catholic conversion. "In the context of a novel explicitly concerned with the possibility of transforming people—that is, after all, what the missionary Father Latour has come to New Mexico *for*—the persistence of race marks the point beyond which no transformation is possible," writes Michaels. "Replacing Americanization with conversion, Cather will imagine the Catholic Church as an institution committed to preserving rather than obliterating" ontological cultural difference.[70] Besides misconstruing "Mexican" as a race, Michaels's selective misreading of Cather's "nativist" cultural politics ignores both the verb tense and context of his central evidentiary sentence. Goodman observes that Cather's novel treats the landscape as exactly that, a landscape—a representation of space subject in the novel to being "read." What we must notice here is that Latour is contrasting, perhaps too wistfully, the peripheral underdevelopment of his parish—"a quiet backwater, with no natural wealth, no importance commercially," he thinks—with the "great industrial expansion" that his colleague Father Vaillant encounters in his Denver parish, which "developed by leaps and bounds and then experienced ruinous reverses." The Mexicans *were* always Mexicans, that is, until New Mexico changed. They will not always *be* what Latour calls "Mexicans," a nationality and ethnicity distinct at the moment from "Americans." In this way, Cather's novel is a modernist attempt to imaginatively reconstruct the enchantment thought to reside in United States' domestic underdeveloped landscapes. Yet her ambivalence about the authenticity of regional culture—a source of her conflict with Austin—leads Cather to recognize the futility of Latour's reconstructive desire. As she puts it, "the country was still waiting to be made into a landscape"—that is, it was not yet an environment that could be aestheticized and vulgarized in a book like Stuart Chase's.[71] Thus Father Latour's tautological sentence, "the Mexicans were always Mexicans," is less an affirmative statement of an attainable horizon of cultural authenticity than a circular evasion of meaning—it is a tautology, after all. In dodging solid ground and clear-eyed perception, Cather's sentence reveals the uselessness of attempting to realize impermeable, territorialized racial and ethnic cultures, which would reinvigorate the center with the cultural wealth of the periphery.[72] In the next section, I turn to the work of Ernest Hemingway and Jack Kerouac, who learned a much different lesson from their travels to Latin America.

Looking South in the Age of the Organization Man: *The Old Man and the Sea* and *On the Road*

In the postwar era, as the Good Neighbor Policy gave way to a Cold War politics that consigned Latin America to a "backyard" of insurgencies, client states, and holiday destinations, the United States' literary chroniclers of Latin America looked less for points of analogy and shared histories, and redrew lines of difference in bright lines. Two popular authors wrote accounts of Latin America that have exerted broad popular influence in this era: Hemingway's *The Old Man and the Sea* and Kerouac's *On the Road* revived fantasies of a Latin American primitive far removed from the United States' industrial civilization. "Machine culture" was the buzzword of latinophiles of the interwar generation, but postwar alienation in these texts came from leaving the factory and fields behind. The symbols of cultural stagnation in the 1950s were less working class than middle class, less industrial and more highly technical: nuclear fusion replaced the assembly line as the technological symbol of fear and isolation, and while mass consumption remained a target of scorn for rebellious intellectuals, the urban and suburban "organization man" in a "grey flannel suit" became the icon of alienated masculinity. The notion that Americans were anxious and frightened was a commonplace of 1950s and 1960s cultural critique. The critic Leo Gurko made this point about Hemingway in particular, in an essay published the same year as *The Old Man and the Sea*: "The era dominated by the atom and hydrogen bombs, by the cold war with Russia that gives every sign of becoming chronic, by the struggle for individual survival within the matrix of hugely mechanized societies, appears to be exactly the universe repeatedly described by Hemingway," he wrote.[73] Calvert Casey, the Baltimore-born Cuban novelist, lamented the growing "Americanization" of the island in a 1956 article for the Havana literary journal *Ciclón*. This transformation was distilled, for him, into the growing popularity in Havana bars of whiskey and soda, the drink of the U.S. executive. Casey says that in Mexico, where one finds grinding poverty and "methods of work and living whose evolution stopped in the 17th century," one still does not find the "anxiety [*intranquilidad*] and tedium" of U.S. life.[74] He defends its opposite: a Cuban "gregariousness" and communal spirit that would have found a ready ear in the pages of *Holiday* or *Esquire* magazine, which printed Hemingway's and A. J. Liebling's tales of fishing or eating their exuberant way across the Caribbean.[75]

When in 1952 Ernest Hemingway published *The Old Man and the Sea,* his portrait of a Cuban fisherman's battle with a giant marlin, most reviewers ignored what would seem to be an important detail: the nationality of its main character. Contemporary reviewers rarely noted that it took place in Cuba, and the few who did mentioned it in passing.[76] Instead, critics read it as a universal parable: *The Nation*'s reviewer, Harvey Breit, called the novel "tragic and happy," a tale of frustration and sorrow that "reads a little like a fable." He elaborated: "In 'The Old Man' the mystique of fishing, with its limited triumphs and tragedies, is transposed into a universal condition of life, with its success and shame, its morality and pride and potential loss of pride."[77] First published in *Life* magazine, *The Old Man and the Sea* concerns a poor, elderly fisherman in Cojímar, a fishing town east of Havana. While out at sea during a long luckless streak, he finally lands an enormous marlin, the greatest catch of his career. But the grueling battle with the fish carries him far out to sea, and before he can tow his prize ashore it is devoured by sharks. Santiago's glimpse of a Miami-bound jet flying over the Florida straits, and the appearance at the novella's end of U.S. tourists gawking over the marlin's ravaged carcass, only underscore its portrayal of Cuba as a place at the interstices of the developed and underdeveloped world, a Latin American nation "so close and yet so foreign," as a famous tourism poster of the era proclaimed.

Despite reviewers' lack of interest in the title character's Cubanness, the appeal of *The Old Man and the Sea,* I argue, rests on its careful characterization, particularly Santiago's delicate, sometimes confusing balance of foreignness and familiarity. Santiago's simplicity and his proximity to the natural world are what make him not-American. Yet one is allowed to forget that Santiago is Cuban, as well, and so he became for many critics "universal," since in the U.S. market, the price of the ticket to universality is to be recognizably American. Santiago is never identified racially in the text (in the successful 1958 film adaptation, however, he was played by Spencer Tracy, a white actor speaking unaccented English). Hemingway deals awkwardly with the issue of Santiago's spoken language. He makes the elderly Cuban a surrogate American by a peculiar linguistic slight-of-hand that depicts Santiago as just foreign enough to interact with nature in the sort of life-or-death way that fewer North Americans presumably can, while familiar enough to allow English-speaking U.S. readers to identify with him. This task is accomplished primarily by baseball. Baseball is the cultural currency shared by the Cuban character and the U.S. reader, a pivot between the two nations. In the text itself, it is also a secular religious motif, an object of Santiago's faith and the bedrock of his sense of justice. "The Yankees cannot lose," he declares in the stilted, grandiose tone in which he always speaks (a tone of voice that surely enhances the allegorical, religious significance many readers find in it). His young apprentice, known only as "the boy," replies with the same high seriousness:

> "But I fear the Indians of Cleveland."
> "Have faith in the Yankees my son. Think of the great DiMaggio."
> "I fear both the Tigers of Detroit and the Indians of Cleveland."
> "Be careful or you will fear even the Reds of Cincinnati and the White Sox of Chicago."[78]

This dialogue is far from the unadorned realism for which Hemingway was famous. It is quite formal, as Robert Gorham Davis, the *New York Times* literary critic, noted favorably: "Santiago speaks in those formalized idioms from the Romance languages which in so many of Hemingway's stories have served to express ideas of dignity, propriety, and love."[79] This effect comes from Hemingway's habit in much of his Cuba writing of directly transliterating Spanish syntax when Cubans are talking.[80] The conversation between Santiago and the boy preserves the use of the indefinite article, correct in Spanish but out of place in English, as when Santiago discusses "the baseball" with his young friend. The Spanish possessive form—the Detroit baseball club would be called "los Tigres de Detroit," for example—sounds stiffly, even biblically formal if rendered literally in English, giving this banal conversation the kind of ponderous tone that Davis observed.

An innocuous discussion of the American League standings could not easily ascend to such spiritual heights were these two English-speaking New Yorkers talking, of course. It is the two Cubans' distance from Yankee Stadium that lends the conversation its gravity, and this in turn gives the "great DiMaggio"—the Yankee outfielder, famously the son of a fisherman—his apostolic status in the old man's imagination. Baseball is also the occasion for the only two instances of quoted Spanish in the novella. A little later, the boy asks Santiago, "'Tell me about the great John J. McGraw,'" the famous big-league manager of a generation earlier. Hemingway then adds, awkwardly, "He said *Jota* for J."[81] Here, it is momentarily unclear whether the boy is meant to be speaking entirely in Spanish, in which case it is oddly redundant for Hemingway to specify only that he said "*Jota*," or if he has only spoken the letter "J" in Spanish, and the rest in English. The sentence seems intended simply to remind the reader that these two characters are speaking Spanish to each other. Santiago's dialogue here, which indexes both his foreignness and Hemingway's decoding of it, is an example of the widespread form of what anthropologist Jane Hill has termed "Mock Spanish," a form of public speech, with origins in the nineteenth century, that incorporates colloquial Spanish speech in a way that indirectly racializes the native Spanish speaker while displaying the egalitarian sympathies of the person doing the quoting. Hill describes Mock Spanish as a "covert racial discourse" that identifies its targets not through direct assault, as in a slur, but rather though "indirect indexicality, messages that must be available for comprehension but are never acknowledged by speakers."[82] The regular citation of "*mañana*," a Spanish word that a monolingual English reader will recognize as a reference to Latin American procrastination, is one example that appeared frequently in chapter 2; a more modern instance is the Hollywood convention of Hispanic characters who pepper their otherwise fluent English conversation with *gracias, sí,* and other widely known Spanish words, seemingly to accentuate their ethnicity. Similarly, the Cubans' speech in *The Old Man and the Sea* is transliterated in a way that preserves an imbalance of epistemic power between the foreign character and the English-speaking reader, whose comprehension of Spanish is flattered by the *jotas*. The novella's mock-Spanish syntax and vocabulary, the plot's simplicity, its ethical focus on labor and love, and the fact that Santiago and the boy are never embedded in any political, family, geographic, or other social specificity, all help explain why early reviewers of the book interpreted the novella to be about "universal," even messianic, themes, rather than national or cultural ones.[83]

In making Santiago a "universal" subject of an existentialist parable, Hemingway has projected onto him the premodern vitality, piety, and intimacy with nature that American subjects of a "machine culture" or "atomic age" no longer possess. Yet the protagonist's devotion to baseball and his ambiguously English speech grounds this universality in the United States, making Santiago a surrogate American—onto whom these nostalgic masculine fantasies can be projected.

Unlike the folklorists and cultural nationalists of an earlier generation—indeed, unlike the Hemingway of his 1936 novel set in Cuba and Key West, *To Have and Have Not*—the Anglo identification with the Latin American here does not require a critique or even an understanding of U.S. habits, politics, or economics, of the kind that showed up regularly in *Mexican Folkways* or Waldo Frank's writing. Also unlike Frank or Toor, Hemingway does not engage Cuban society beyond the level of myth. In spite of his official celebration by the Cuban revolutionary state, his aloofness from and seeming disinterest in the Havana intellectual world was often noted by his Cuban contemporaries. José Rodriguez Feo, the critic and editor of *Ciclón* and *Orígenes,* the most important Cuban literary journal of the 1950s, summarily dismissed Hemingway's macho pretensions in a letter to Wallace Stevens that questioned his belonging in Cuba: "Of course, you know that Hemingway has lived among us for a long time; but I have always maintained that the milieu has not affected him at all. . . . Of course, I have never quite come to admire Hemingway: I mean that if you are a real blood and bone latino, you find absurd and a bit of an affectation those 'virile problems' which seem to bother him so much."[84] In a vitriolic 1967 essay, novelist Edmundo Desnoes described Hemingway's interest in Cuba as essentially colonial: "In Cuba he lived like an Englishman who has retired to one of his colonies," Desnoes wrote, "with sympathy for the Cuban people but watching them from above, from his *Vigía,*" the estate where he lived outside the capital city.[85]

Hemingway became something of a Cold War prototype of the individualistic American abroad, especially in Spain and Latin America, as the 1950s and 1960s progressed. His life in Cuba played no small part, as Robert Manning showed in a 1965 *Atlantic* profile of the writer at home at Cojímar. "Who in my generation," asked Manning, "was not moved by Hemingway the writer and fascinated by Hemingway the maker of his own legend?"[86] In 1968, after the writer's death, Lawrence Ferlinghetti acknowledged this legend as a cliché as he traveled through Mexico: "Up before dawn, writing, I'm some faroff hungup Hemingway character waking in some small Spanish hotel alone, counting my marbles."[87] In between Hemingway's Havana and Ferlinghetti's Cold War wanderings comes Kerouac's *On the Road,* a book that despite its place near the end of this chapter's timeline resembles the Victorian racism of Richard Harding Davis's *Three Gringoes in Venezuela and Central America* as closely as any of the texts that we have considered since.

Despite its unusual narrative structure and its reputation as a subversive text, *On the Road*'s treatment of race and ethnicity is reactionary. The latinophiles of even two decades earlier would have recoiled at Kerouac's unexamined exoticism, his treatment of Mexico as an example of the "basic primitive and wailing humanity that stretches in a belt around the equatorial belly of the world from Malaya . . . to India the great subcontinent to Arabia to Morocco."[88] James Baldwin famously ridiculed the passage in which Sal strolls through a Black ghetto in Denver, peering at the "dark porches of Mexican and Negro homes," fantasizing about the "sensuous gals" therein, and wishing that he were Black, Mexican, or "even a poor overworked Jap." Baldwin responded, "It is still true, alas, that to be an American Negro male is also to be a kind of walking phallic symbol: which means that one pays, in one's own personality, for the sexual insecurity of others."[89] Sal's part-time job as a cotton-picker among migrant Mexican farmworkers in California is punctuated by his affair with a Mexican woman, and indeed a great part of the appeal of Mexico is that it permits both the primitive ideal of licentiousness ascribed to Blacks, as above, without the threat that Black sexuality appears to represent for Sal (in a Mexican brothel Sal and Dean visit late in the novel, a Black prostitute remains an object of fascination that Sal is afraid to approach). Mexico thus serves a double purpose: firstly, the trip to Mexico allows Sal and Dean to realize what Catherine Cocks calls the "pleasures of degeneration" of the global South without a direct confrontation with Black sexuality.[90] Secondly, it allows them to realize their central fantasy of escape from middle-class propriety. Their escape is signified here, as in Chase's book years before, primarily by their rejection of time: the first thing Dean and Sal do upon crossing the border is to discard their watches. Kerouac's novel is extraordinary, though, in the degree to which it relinquishes even the most minimal level of engagement with Mexico as anything other than a screen on which a fantasy of a revitalized consciousness may be projected. To return to the theme of tautology, Mexico is nothing more or less than what Sal thought it was when he arrived, and aside from isolated moments of recognition—as when industrial Monterrey is compared to Detroit—the country remains spectacularly, dramatically other. As Rachel Adams puts it, the real landscape of the travelers' Latin American journey is their own "grandiose subjectivity."[91] They travel through Mexico without ever leaving their own heads.

Adams punctures the rebellious posture of Sal and Dean's flight to Mexico in another way, as well, by showing how the popularity of the southern border crossing for Beats and hippies came at a time when the United States and Mexican governments were aggressively promoting cross-border traffic and foreign direct investment in tourism and manufacturing. These journeys therefore positioned Latin America as a space of fugitive rebellion at a moment when such cross-border journeys were becoming more convenient for those with means. Daniel Balderston and José Quiroga have studied the cultural politics of Gay Sunshine Press' anthologies of gay Latin American literature, which came a generation after Kerouac, in a context of gay liberation. Latin America is not a place of performing one's repressed heterosexuality, but of liberating one's suppressed queerness—"the beautiful and sinister fairyland where jungle fever beckons the marketing machine," Balderston and Quiroga write.[92] The sexual liberation that requires such a displacement abroad is always at some level racist, since a crucial part of the liberation—the satisfaction of one's repressed desire—requires the availability of a racialized foreign body. The Mexican section of *On the Road* proceeds along these predictable lines: it is a whirlwind of sexual escapades and drug-induced visions, exotic reveries and mystical insights. Mexico also revives the two friends' zeal for travel once even the North American west has become exhausted. "Behind us lay the whole of America and everything Dean and I had previously known about life, and life on the road," says Sal as they cross the border. "We had finally found the magic land at the end of the road and we never dreamed the extent of the magic."[93] The homoeroticism of *On the Road* and the fantasy of a queer Latin America in Gay Sunshine Press reproduce similar visions of an available, sexualized Latin America. In each, the silence of the Latin American participant in this pageant is the requirement for the personal forms of rebellion and license that the U.S. authors imagine.

The Cuban Revolution, underway when Kerouac was finishing his novel, showed definitively the political character of the uneven development that he fetishizes as a timeless cultural attribute in *On the Road*. Yet *On the Road* also exemplifies a sort of denouement for both the critique and the desire I have been tracing throughout this chapter: that the United States was *not* the sophisticated, healthy society its leaders claimed it was, and that it was in fact in the midst of a protracted cultural and spiritual decline. This decline came, for most of the authors surveyed here, from the fate of culture under capitalism and from the nativism that blinded Anglo-Americans to the riches of their hemisphere. The desire to reverse this decline into monotony and exhaustion was a journey, whether physical or entirely imaginary, into regions of the hemisphere, and of the psyche, not yet conquered by mass culture. Despite its naiveté and idealism, interwar latinophilia held the United States' modernity up in a hemispheric gesture that compared it, often unflatteringly, to Mexico's. By the time Hemingway wrote *The Old Man and the Sea,* the only thing Americans and Cubans have in common, besides an interest in Major League Baseball, is the novel's pretentious notion of "a common humanity." Kerouac's *On the Road* is latinophilia's nadir: abandoning even Hemingway's liberal-humanist gesture, the Latin American landscape is little more than a projection screen for Anglo-American desires, its people the personification of antiquated fantasies.

5 Latin America, in Solidarity

Havana Reads the Harlem Renaissance

THE NEXT two chapters consider U.S. responses to Latin American radicalism in the cultural field—that is, in literature, film, and other forms of mass culture. These chapters examine the combination of yearning, curiosity, and fear that Latin American political movements held for those in the United States with few personal ties to Spanish America—that is, those whose political attachments to Latin America were affiliative, as Edward Said used the term (in which one links oneself to others by social, political, or professional practices) as opposed to filiative (an attachment to the country of one's birth or one's ancestors).[1] Some of these intellectuals made their work in the spirit of solidarity. Others, as we shall see in chapter 6, were fascinated by the spectacle of the Latin American body in revolt, treating revolutionary politics as dictated by cultural sensibilities, gender conventions, and political pathologies imagined as "Latin."[2]

My focus in these chapters is on those writers and intellectuals for whom these international encounters with radical change challenged or confirmed exceptionalist narratives of American freedom and development. This chapter considers a particular case study: Langston Hughes's trips to Cuba during its Afro-Cuban revival and his reception by *afrocubanista* authors and critics. Hughes and the writers he met in Cuba—poets like Nicolás Guillén and Regino Pedroso, and critics and translators like Gustavo Urrutia and José Antonio Fernández de Castro—identified each other as anti-imperialists and as members of a diasporic avant-garde (although Fernández was himself white). At the same time, they were Cubans and North Americans, citizens of two nations with a long, recent history of conflict, occupying unequal positions in the global cultural economy. In 1927 and 1930–31, Hughes went to Cuba in search of a hemispheric American history of Black struggle and culture, at a moment of anticolonial militancy in the diaspora and beyond. What Hughes found was no instinctual filiation, but the laborious practice of making this affiliative history manifest, through the personal connections he tried to build and the literary translations he made—a labor, in other words, of solidarity.

Solidarity is struggle across lines of filial identity like language, nationality, or race, through which one seeks mutual (and not just common) advantage against shared enemies. It requires one to give up some loyalty in the service of some other, ultimately greater one, as in socialist internationalism's disavowal of nationalism (for example, prioritizing one's status as a worker over one's position as a German); or to expand those identifications (to see oneself as a member of a multilingual, multinational Black diaspora, for example, and not just of a nation or even a national Black community). It requires these attachments, arguing to do otherwise is to condemn yourself to solitary defeat. Hence Marx and Engels's famous call to solidarity in the last sentence of *The Communist Manifesto:* "Working Men of All Countries, Unite!" This line is framed by the ironic pair of sentences that precede it. "The proletarians have nothing to lose but their chains," the *Manifesto* reads. "They have a world to win." (Not how this conclusion is often popularized in an undialectical and more pessimistic form, as if solidarity is a last resort: "Workers of the world unite! You have nothing to lose but your chains."[3]) Because solidarity is not a fixed identity, but a dynamic tool of the oppressed, it is a *practice* of political affiliation that must be constantly remade, lest it become ossified into the orthodoxies it is meant to unsettle, become trivialized as a rote form of cosmopolitanism, or shrink, demoralized, in the face of the defeats inevitably risked by those who have nothing to lose.

The literary grounds of Hughes's and Guillén's collaboration was their common interest in vernacular culture, and particularly music, as the basis of a modern poetic aesthetic. The practice of this aesthetic—which drew upon the African-descended musical forms of the blues and *son* produced by urban migrants from rural plantation zones—involved an implicit negotiation of each country's cultural geography and racial politics. If modernization, in the economic sense, is an aesthetic of progress that envisions a future of evenness and development, then uneven development exposes the seams and inequalities in the production of space under capitalism. At the scale of the nation or the city, the modernist use of the vernacular might involve foregrounding the persistence, as Hughes does in innumerable poems, of the sounds and accents of the U.S. south circulating through the segregated northern metropolis. In "The Weary Blues," one of his most well-known "blues poems," Hughes emphasizes how both the bluesman and Lenox Avenue where he stands are figuratively out of sync with the rhythms of the metropolis:

> Droning a drowsy syncopated tune,
> Rocking back and forth to a mellow croon,
>   I heard a Negro play.
> Down on Lenox Avenue the other night
> By the pale dull pallor of an old gas light
>   He did a lazy sway . . .
>   He did a lazy sway . . .[4]

The setting of the encounter between the singer and the speaker, under the "pallor" of the "old gas light" of Lenox Avenue, is the degraded infrastructure of Harlem. The dangling modifiers in the first two lines—is the "Negro" droning and rocking, or is it "I," the poem's spectator and listener, or is it both?—gestures ironically toward the elusive moment of unity the music makes possible, when singer and audience are one swaying body. This is the reversal implied by the musical term "syncopation": the displacement of the accents in a rhythm from the unaccented part onto the "normally accented," or, as the *Oxford Dictionary* puts it, with an unintentionally biblical ring, so that "the strong beats become weak and vice versa."[5]

The poem's grammatical misalignment suits its setting and its subject matter. That is, if we read "syncopation" as a musical metaphor for both the unevenly developed city and the desire for solidarity it creates in those who live in it, then the syncopated blues, "drowsy" though it may seem, exposes this misalignment and hopes for its reversal. Hughes's "The Weary Blues," read as a poem about both the blues and the uneven development of the city and nation, has much in common with the work of Nicolás Guillén, for whom Cuban music was a product of Cuba's colonial histories and hence its underdevelopment. For example, his poem about the famous Cuban boxer nicknamed "Kid Chocolate" invokes the specter of "our canefields' blood" that haunts the boxer's glamorous career in New York City.[6] In a 1930 newspaper article, Guillén profiles Rosendo Ruiz, a musician unfairly neglected due to what Guillén ironically calls "the extraordinary defect of having never left Cuba." Guillén's larger project in this article is to proclaim the centrality of "vernacular" forms, especially musical ones, in Cuban culture, since they demonstrate the significance of the small and local against the "prurito de lo grande," or an itching, an obsession, a "thing" for what's grand, including praise and acclaim in the world's imperial capitals: "Nothing that has come to us from Paris, or at least from New York, from which, unfortunately, everything comes to us, from shoes to cold weather, has interest for us."[7]

For Hughes and for Guillén, music registers the misalignments between the local and the foreign, the small and the large, the emergent and the dominant, uptown and downtown, the region and the nation, the island and the mainland. Yet at the same time, as Guillén's rejection of "New York" shows, the poetry of uneven development rings differently in Havana than it does in New York, for two broad reasons: the different positions these places hold in a global cultural economy, and the different workings of the politics of race and national identity in each. The homology that many subsequent critics have made since between Black Havana and Black Harlem—and the assumptions of Hughes's "influence" on the former—overshadows what was in fact a vibrant debate about the hemispheric meaning of Harlem, as both a urban space and a global symbol. This chapter treats Cuban responses to Harlem in order to emphasize what is often overlooked in transnational American studies: the place not only of solidarity, but of misunderstanding, mistranslation, and misapprehension.

Motivos de son and Mistranslation from Harlem to Havana

On April 20, 1930, the Cuban journalist Gustavo Urrutia wrote to Langston Hughes in New York to announce the publication of a new set of poems, *Motivos de son* (Son Motifs), by a young Cuban poet named Nicolás Guillén. Urrutia was by that time a major force in Havana intellectual life, particularly in the *afrocubanista* movement, in which Guillén's poems would soon become canonical. *Motivos* was published in *Ideales de una raza* (Ideals of a race), the weekly Black-interest section of the conservative Havana daily, *Diario de la Marina*. Urrutia edited the Sunday supplement from 1928 until 1931, when political pressure from the authoritarian nationalist regime of Gerardo Machado forced the paper to cancel Urrutia's pages. In his 1930 letter to Hughes, Urrutia predicted happily that Guillén's *Motivos de son* would scandalize the local Black bourgeoisie with its frank use of the vulgar slang and popular music of urban Cubans of color. Hughes, who had recently returned from a March visit to Cuba covered by Urrutia's reporters, was well known among the Havana literati for *The Weary Blues* (1926) and *Fine Clothes to the Jew* (1927), parts of which had already been translated in

Ideales and publications like *Social,* Cuba's premier cultural review of the 1920s.[8] Urrutia wrote in his letter to Hughes, "I feel exce[e]dingly happy in this moment on account of *eight formidable negro* poems written by our Guillén in our negro page of to-day. They are something grand. The name of the series is *Motivos de Son.* You know very well what this means. They are real, Cuban negro poetry written in the very popular slang. They are the exact equivalent of your 'blues.' The language and feelings of our dear negroes made most noble by the love and talent of our own artists. I am only sorry that you will be unable to translate, and even understand what these poems mean, but you must know that the spirit of them is [the] same as the blues. Some ones are sad, some are ironical, others are sociological, viz. *Oyé me dijeron negro.*"[9] Urrutia is careful in this letter to translate the meaning of Guillén's work into a U.S. racial vocabulary, insisting conspiratorially that Hughes knows "very well what this means"—"this" could refer either to the importance of Guillén's poems, or to the collection's title.[10] Finally, Urrutia equates the *son*—the Afro-Cuban ballad form of the Havana working class and rural peasantry that inspired Guillén's collection—with "your blues." As scholars of the Hughes-Guillén encounter have done ever since, Urrutia is careful to draw racial analogies between Cuba and the United States, which he then uses to compare the work of the two young writers, inspired as they both were by music, radical politics, and modernist poetics.

This letter has been routinely misinterpreted in North American scholarship, beginning with Hughes's biographer, Arnold Rampersad. He argues that just as Hughes had combined the rhythms and structure of blues forms and popular speech in his *Weary Blues,* Guillén had done the same with the *son.* "For the first time, as Hughes had urged him to do," writes Rampersad, "Guillén had used the *son* dance rhythms to capture the moods and features of the black Havana poor."[11] Many U.S. critics have similarly attributed Guillén's decision to incorporate *son* rhythms and popular slang into "high" poetry to Hughes's influence.[12] The scholarly misinterpretations of Urrutia's letter overlook two important aspects of his communication to Hughes: firstly, his apparent, surely strategic flattery of a famous and potentially powerful advocate for Guillén's work abroad ("You know how much we appreciate you," he gushes, "this explains why I communicate with you on this ex[c]iting matter before I do with any other of my friends"). Secondly, Urrutia is carefully translating, for Hughes's benefit, Cuban racial meanings into a national vernacular—that of "your blues" and "negro poems"—that many U.S. critics misapprehend as a global one. Even Ian Smart, an

American Marxist scholar who admires Guillén, calls the meeting with Hughes a "catalyst" for Guillén's mature poetry and appears to take for granted that the racial "ferment" of the U.S. New Negro movement was an export commodity.[13]

These misinterpretations of Hughes's influence and of the easy commensurability of blues and *son* are critical not only for the relatively rarified fields of Hughes and Guillén scholarship, but for the broader field of diaspora and transnational American literary studies. Most English-language scholarship of Hughes's Cuban ventures rarely considers the unequal relations of cultural prestige and political power between Harlem, New York, and Havana, Cuba. Yet Cuban contemporaries of Guillén, and the poet himself, were keenly attentive to these circumstances. Indeed, Guillén's journalistic writings on Hughes's well-publicized visits to the island, and the prose and poetry he wrote about the African American revival, contain a great deal of sometimes subtle, but often explicit, criticism of his colleagues in the United States. Moreover, as a translator and correspondent of Guillén's, Hughes struggled with the difficulty of translating a specifically Cuban vernacular, as well as the country's racial codes, into an American English idiom. In their eagerness to celebrate this case of cross-cultural solidarity, some literary historians have neglected the cultural *conflict* that makes such partnerships both necessary and difficult to achieve in the first place. Moving beyond speculative fantasies of diasporic unity and unprovable claims of poetic influence, this chapter considers the Hughes/Guillén contact by concentrating on the inevitable miscommunications that accompanied the internationalist desires of the Afro-Cuban New Negro movements (and later, the third-worldism of Guillén's post-1959 career).

These miscommunications—of which the misidentification of *son* and blues is an example—are part of the dynamics of cultural translation. As Emily Apter has argued, in an act of literary translation it is the linguistic inassimilability of the original, and the ever-present prospect of translation failure, that forms a crucial part of the labor of what she calls "transnational humanism."[14] And as Vera Kutzinski points out in her recent book on Hughes's international career, translation is a means of "registering cultural differences and searching for common ground—*not* necessarily similarities."[15] In considering the affective dimension of the Hughes-Guillén partnership, we should read their friendship as a microcosmic example of the slow, unsteady work of cultural translation and cultural struggle, in which failure is ever-present and misrecognition not only inevitable but necessary, as Kenneth Warren has written.[16]

Brent Edwards argues that it is such short-circuits that have helped define the "practice" of making diaspora, where cross-cultural encounters are "characterized by unavoidable misapprehensions and misreadings, persistent blindnesses and solipsisms, self-defeating and abortive collaborations, a failure to translate even a basic grammar of blackness."[17] In the encounter between Hughes and Guillén, and in the "failures" of at least two English translations of Guillén, we will come to see the "transnational" not as a unified *field,* but a set of contradictory and difficult *processes* and *practices,* shaped by empire and exile as well as solidarity and border-crossing, and always by a combination of these. To return to this book's examination of the intimacy of the United States and Latin America, the practice and labor of making diaspora in Cuba and the United States is an explicitly radical and counterhegemonic way of making this intimacy plain. This framework is in stark contrast to William McKinley's invocation of "ties of singular intimacy" between Cuba and the United States—which framed intimacy as the United States' paternalistic obligation to employ "idle men and re-establish the pursuits of peace" on the island—or the latinophiles' celebration in Mexico of the lost vitality of an "American" (in both the hemispheric and, crucially, national senses) past.[18] Both in translation and, in Hughes's and Guillén's cases, in poetic forms derived from music, this intimacy is an elusive object, always in flight. The importance of music to Hughes's experience of Cuba and his collaboration with Guillén is important here.[19] Just as translation is a practice of realizing a linguistic unity that is always just out of reach, music, Shana Redmond writes, "is a method" that "allows us to do and imagine things that may otherwise be unimaginable or seem impossible." Redmond's particular subject, the political anthem, is a musical form less subject perhaps to the obstacles of translation than literary mediations of blues and *son,* as anthems aim to communicate a shared political affiliation that can be felt even apart from lyrical content. Nevertheless, her focus on the "sensory engagement" that music offers beyond literacy, and its particular power this gives music to articulate "shared ambitions," reminds us again of the "spatial feelings" that Hsuan Hsu says moor us to shifting national or, in this case, internationalist geographies. For Hughes and Guillén, the practice of solidarity is an elusive, renewable desire, never a settled achievement, something formally elusive and essentially social.[20]

Urrutia's letter to Hughes, even as it proclaims solidarity between the two men and their movements, eloquently communicates some of the conflicts of the Harlem-Havana circuit: the language and knowledge barriers, uneven power relations, and the simple fact of distance. Another distinction that emerges is that between racial politics in the United States and Cuba. Cuba's comparatively recent experience of abolition and revolution (slavery was abolished only in 1888, and national independence was nominally achieved in 1898), along with its nationalist ideology of racial harmony, indelibly shaped the country's official racial discourse in ways that Hughes, indeed, noted in his own observations of Cuba. Many of Urrutia's editorials for *Ideales,* which appeared in the nation's conservative daily, underlined the multiracial nationalism typical of Cuban political rhetoric, which, as Urrutia often noted, differed from the purportedly more advanced United States where Jim Crow still ruled the south. Given these historical differences, translation imperfectly mediates relationships like the ones between Hughes and his Cuban hosts, underlining the fact that diasporic interconnections are, as Kutzinski again notes, always formed by and though language—they are discursive and highly contingent.[21] In Guillén's letters to Hughes—the two corresponded regularly during the early 1930s, and then intermittently until 1961, the first year of the United States embargo on socialist Cuba—the labor and the pleasure of translation is a major theme. His letters find Guillén groping for English words and then teasing Hughes about his grammatical errors in Spanish. Elsewhere he takes pleasure in teaching his friend *habanero* vulgarities that he insists Hughes study for his return visits ("learn to speak *criollo,*" he demanded in Spanish in one letter).[22] As anyone who has struggled with a friendship in a foreign language knows, the act of interpretation, the work to make oneself understood and to understand, is also a medium of internationalism.

Hughes took this up more deliberately when he and the literary critic Ben Carruthers translated *Motivos de son.* Perhaps the most controversial act of translation in the Harlem-Havana circuit was the rendering of *son,* a rural, Afro-Cuban ballad form that migrated to Havana during the World War I period, as "blues." Like the blues, *son* is a rural, Black popular song genre that migrated with its performers to urban areas around World War I, and it refers to a "mood" as well as a formal structure. Nevertheless, the two styles have markedly different rhythmic structures, instrumentation, and lyrical content. *Son* vocalists are almost uniformly male, and their lyrics are usually ribald, comical, and, given the patriotic content of much Afro-Cuban cultural production in this period, occasionally nationalist—*soneros,* for example, could make claims for the charms of "Cuban women" (of any race) that blues musicians could not make for "Americans."[23] Later Cuban readers of Hughes resisted the equivalence that American readers made between the blues and the *son,* arguing that such translations were simply acts of assimilation that ignored the particularity of the *son,* and hence Guillén's poetic use of it. Yet when Hughes and Carruthers made the first English translation of Guillén's work in their 1948 collection *Cuba Libre: Poems by Nicolás Guillén,* they rendered *Motivos de son* as "Cuban Blues," making an explicit analogy between the blues and the *son* in an effort to situate the Cuban poems in a U.S. context, just as Urrutia had tried to do in his letter to Hughes. In Hughes's drafts, however, he softens the analogy without abandoning it completely. His own tentative title for the collection was "Blue Notes," a title that retains *Motivos de son*'s own notion of poetry improvising on musical motifs (*motivos*) without explicitly identifying the poems as a Cuban version of American blues poetry.

Motivos de son is a very difficult, if not impossible, work to translate because the poems play on a musical form unfamiliar to most English-language readers in the United States, and because the poems mimic a local slang and colloquial pronunciation that can only be reproduced in the terms of some other city's rough equivalents. For example, Hughes's and Carruthers's separate drafts of Guillén's "Ayé me dijeron negro" (literally, "Yesterday Somebody Called Me Black," with the final "r" of "Ayer" left unspoken) struggle with this dilemma, and their published, joint translation rewrites the poem in an American English vocabulary, with a rhyming, musical meter—they title it "Last Night Somebody Called Me Darky." Hughes's draft, held in his personal papers at Yale University (it is signed "LH"), attempts a more literal translation that keeps some of Guillén's spelling without removing the poem and its narrator to a U.S. setting; in doing so, however, the translation concedes the impossibility of translating Guillén's use of popular slang and colloquial Spanish pronunciation, the most controversial parts of the poem. Guillén's poem reads: "Ayé me dijeron negro / Pa' que me fajara yo; pero e' que me lo desía / era un negro como yo," in which the final apostrophes—on "pa'" (*para*), for example—signal the elision of the final syllable of various words, in an attempt to reproduce the sound of spoken Caribbean Spanish by an implied Afro-Cuban speaker. Compare the opening stanzas of the two signed drafts: Hughes's above, and Carruthers's very different one (signed "BC"), which appeared in the published book, below:

Hughes:
Yesterday somebody called
me black

just to make me mad—
but the one who said it
was just as black as me.

Carruthers:
Last night somebody
called me darky
jes' to make me fight,
but de one who said it to me
Is a darky, too, all right.[24]

Hughes's translation struggles to be literally faithful to Guillén's original, but in doing so it sacrifices its musicality and colloquial cadences, and hence its locality as well. Their published translation makes a different bargain—in totally rewriting the poem with a North American dialect vernacular, they attempt to translate a formal character of vernacular blackness, while leaving its specific content in Havana. Both translations remind us of the original poems' inassimilability to English; in this productive way, they are both "failures," as they chafe against what Apter calls "the nub of intractable semantic difference" that should be present in the practice of translation.[25]

Most readers of *Cuban Blues* probably could not turn to the Spanish original and could not recognize a Cuban working-class accent. The *Motivos* therefore had to be rewritten to be translated, and even while *Cuban Blues* proposes a vernacular diasporic community capable of transgressing linguistic and aesthetic boundaries, inevitably much was lost or elided in this translation. Some Cuban readers as well as some critics of Hughes's work would come to view this mediation as cultural imperialism. Meanwhile, other English translators of Guillén's poetry would mistranslate his work more explicitly, in assimilating his poems to later political priorities. Indeed, Afro-Cuban critiques of Hughes and Harlem underscore the dialectical antithesis of transnational American literature's desire for cross-cultural community: for example, the imperial images, nationalist resentments, and mistranslations that also constitute transnational cultures. Concentrating on these short circuits and misunderstandings is not a conservative or pessimistic appraisal of such efforts at transnational communication, however. Hughes's searching diaries, his struggles to translate Guillén's work, and even the bawdy Spanish lessons Guillén gave his American friend stress how that misunderstanding and the struggle to overcome it were part of building community. In short, in reading Hughes and Guillén we come to see "transnationality" and cultural translation as an aspiration of cultural struggle, never as an achieved or natural reality.[26]

Hughes, indeed, seemed aware of this at the time, but he took an optimistic attitude toward his unfulfilled internationalist aspirations. Even so, his finest Cuba poem takes a melancholic tone. In "To the Little Fort of San Lazaro on the Ocean Front, Havana," Hughes writes of the yawning gap between the romance of city's picturesque oceanfront fortress and the present-day international threats that it is powerless to turn back. The fort is affectionately addressed by the poet as the city's former protection against pirates, the swashbuckling sort of popular legend. He names a diverse group of three: the Briton Francis Drake, the Frenchman de Plan, and a little-known Havana privateer, Diego El Grillo, known as "El Mulato." In their day, Hughes writes, "when time and ships were slow," the fort conquered.

> But now,
> Against a pirate called
> THE NATIONAL CITY BANK
> What can you do alone?
> Would it not be
> Just as well you tumbled down,
> Stone by helpless stone?[27]

The modern, decidedly unromantic "piracy" of the National City Bank contrasts sharply with the long-gone, well-trod romance of these heroic outlaws. The pirates of Caribbean folklore are gone forever, and this form of itinerant Atlantic citizenship will never come again, if it ever existed. San Lázaro, Hughes suggests, is stubborn but ultimately defeated by the new world of global finance capital—transnational community efficiently displaced by transnational empire.

Hughes visited Havana for the first time in 1927, on a lark before the semester at Lincoln College in Pennsylvania. He would return by steamship in February 1930 as an established, internationally known poet. *Ideales de una raza* devoted most of two issues to Hughes's visit, and *Revista de la Habana*, a major cultural journal, published a critical study to coincide with the trip. He recalled the voyage in his autobiography, *I Wonder as I Wander*, where like every American author who visited

Havana before him, he began his account by describing el Morro, the fortress that guards the Bay of Havana. Ironically, he misspells the fortress as "el Moro" (which in Spanish means "moor," an error motivated by the comparison he makes): "It was suppertime when we got to El Moro with Havana rising white and Moorish-like out of the sea in the twilight," Hughes recalls. "The evening was warm and the avenues were alive with people, among them many jet-black Negroes in white attire. Traffic filled the narrow streets, auto horns blew, cars' bells clanged, and from the wineshops and fruit-juice stands radios throbbed with drumbeats and the wavelike sounds of maracas rustling endless rumbas. Life seemed fluid, intense, and warm in the busy streets of Havana."[28] Here and in his private journals, Hughes noted Havana's brightness, its noise, its musicality, and its blackness. In addition to recording the quotidian details of his trip—like a "fat American from Chicago" in his steamer cabin who "wants to see dirty movies in Havana"—he grappled with Cuba's racial vernacular and the possibilities of fellowship in Black Havana. On his final voyage, in April 1931, Hughes assembled a glossary of Cuban racial terms and slurs and recorded instances of segregation that he witnessed. His diaries also express some of his utopian and everyday hopes for the trip, which included stops in Haiti and Brazil. "To see one[']s own people in banks, shops, fine clubs, high positions," he writes and then notes: "Negro artists—Exchange of ideas musicians and painters, new rhythms, new colors, and faces. Poets and writers—new backgrounds & basis for comparisons. A paradise for Kodak camera fans."[29]

Ideales de una raza used Hughes's visit as an opportunity to show its cosmopolitanism and to make a nationalist defense of racial politics in Cuba against the example of Jim Crow. Urrutia devoted many editions of "Armonías," his column, to the United States' "race problem," which was often compared to Cuba's own, usually unfavorably. The article on Hughes details the poet's run-in with the Ward Steamship Lines in New York, which denied him first-class passage to Havana by first claiming that all seats were sold out, and then by asserting that the Cuban consulate had denied his visa due to exclusion laws for Chinese, Russians, and Blacks of any nationality. Under the headline "The Langston Hughes Incident," the paper reprinted letters of protest from Urrutia and the Afro-Cuban legislator Lino D'Ou to the Cuban secretary of state as well as the subsecretary's letter to Hughes and the NAACP stating that no such exclusion laws existed.[30] *Ideales* discussed the affair as an example of the United States' hypocrisy and of Hughes's admirable determination to resist it. Urrutia's article on the issue asserts as much in terms that simultaneously indicate the Afro-Cuban movement's vexed relationship to Hughes and to the Harlem movement in general: "Another bard less modernist—less virile—than Langston Hughes would now be in Harlem composing some lamentable BLUES, with curses and tearful finales. But this poet who, from Nicolás Guillén's description, swims, boxes, and loves aviation, has stirred up a great excitement around the incident and come to Havana, enjoyed an enchanting vacation, as he told us, and upset the ministries of both countries."[31] Urrutia's praise for Hughes identifies him with a masculine, "modernist" vitality that he contrasts sharply with the effeminate, tearful capitulation of the "lamentable blues," a musical genre closely associated with Hughes's work but criticized as weak and defeatist by some Afro-Cuban critics.

Where Urrutia reflects at a distance on Hughes's modern virility, Guillén's article on the poet's arrival at the Havana docks in the same issue devotes considerable attention to his physical appearance and youth, which seem to defy both his national origins and his artistic sophistication. Guillén introduces the interview with a long anecdote about a false description of Hughes he was given before he met him at the Havana port. The description bears no resemblance to the fist-fighting aviator of Urrutia's account: as he waits for Hughes to disembark, Guillén says he expects to meet a forty-five-year-old man, "extremely fat," almost white in color, with an "English moustache decorating his fine and embittered lips." Guillén confesses how, after reading "The Weary Blues" and "Fine Clothes to the Jew," he also expected a man of imposing physical stature and middle age. Those who know only his poetry, Guillén says, "would attribute to him a physical maturity at which he has not yet arrived and for which he still has long to wait." As he finds out, far from being a corpulent, mustachioed Europhilic modernist, Hughes is a thin, affable, almost comically eager "jovencito" of twenty-six, recognizable to Guillén as a plebeian Cuban type. He describes him sardonically, using a term for a light-skinned mulatto: "He looks just like a '*mulatico*' *cubano*. One of those trivial *mulaticos* that studies for a degree at the National University and spends their lives organizing little parties at two pesos a ticket." Guillén's initial description of Hughes borders on condescending insult.[32]

Rampersad, with some condescension of his own, calls Guillén's tone in this article "cheeky," given what he sees as the Cuban's debt to Hughes. Ellis, by contrast, argues that the article's tone reflects Guillén's "self-assurance" about his own poetic vocation, presumably because he felt threatened by Hughes.[33] However, Guillén's subtle critiques of Hughes are more than simple demonstrations of self-assurance, especially since at this early point, it is unclear what Guillén would have to feel defensive about—*Motivos de son* would not appear in *Ideales* for another month and thus no claims about Hughes's influence on him had yet been made. Guillén's articles on Hughes's visit are notable for their notes of praise and fellow feeling combined with mockery and subtle condescension, but biographical readings of "cheek" and self-assertion do not explain Guillén's critical tone. Hughes is "modernist," Guillén writes, yet unlike T. S. Eliot or Ezra Pound he is down-to-earth and translatable as a Cuban social type; by contrast, this type is young and earnest about racial issues, nearly to the point of banality. Guillén even adds a backhanded compliment regarding Hughes's efforts to learn Spanish: "Mr. Hughes's Spanish," writes Guillén, "is not pretty [*no es muy rico*]. But he tries marvelously."[34]

The rest of the article recounts an interview in which Hughes discusses Black political and artistic movements around the world and his own experience as a traveler, especially his recent trips to Europe, the southern United States, and Africa. "I have no more ambition," Guillén quotes Hughes saying, "than to be the poet of the negroes. The negro poet, do you understand?" Guillén responds gravely in the affirmative: "And I feel rising from the bottom of my soul that poem with which this man opens his first volume of poems," he writes, quoting approvingly from a Spanish translation of Hughes's "Negro": "'Yo, soy negro: negro, como la noche: negro como las profundidades de mi Africa.'" ("I am a Negro: / Black as the night is black, / Black like the depths of my Africa."[35]) Again, however, Guillén moves from this serious note of identification with Hughes to a gentle mockery of his friend's interest in race in Cuba. As the two watch a *danzón* performance in one of Havana's famed *academias de baile* (the euphemistically named "dance academies" known as centers of both *son* music and prostitution), Hughes becomes fascinated to the point of what Guillén suggests is embarrassing exuberance. He describes the North American's reaction, again quoting the poem he earlier celebrated. Here, however, it is not Hughes who is "negro como la noche," but the Black Cuban drummer he watches desirously. "Afterwards," Guillén describes Hughes, "while contemplating the bongo player, 'black as night [*negro como la noche*],' he exclaims, with a breath of unsatisfied anxiety: 'I want to be black. Very black. Black for real!'" ("Yo quisiera ser negro. Bien negro. ¡Negro de verdad!"[36]) Thus ends Guillén's "Conversation with Langston Hughes": in his ironic portrayal, the most famous Black poet in the world, and the honored guest of *Ideales,* eagerly seeks out Black culture like a hungry tourist seeking some local dish.

As Ellis observes, with his article's final exclamation—"¡Negro de verdad!"—Guillén is quoting the last line of his 1929 poem, "Pequeña oda a un negro boxeador cubano" (Small ode to a black Cuban boxer). The poem is an equivocal tribute to Eligio Sardiñas Montalvo, better known as "Kid Chocolate," the Cuban boxing champion of the 1920s. The poem is delivered from the point of view of a skeptical observer who admires the boxer's courage and skill but cautions him not to mistake his fame for freedom. "Pequeña oda" addresses cultural internationalism from the point of view of a nation on the periphery of the global cultural industries. Yet ironically, its acerbic critique of U.S. consumption of Cuban Black culture has, in its English translation, been as severely misunderstood as the titular boxer. The athlete is trapped, the poet says, in a brutal sport in an unforgiving city whose language

> sólo te ha de servir para entender sobre la lona
> cuanto en su verde slang
> mascan las mandíbulas de los que tú derrumbas
> jab a jab
>
> [has only been good enough on the canvas
> to understand the filthy slang
> spit from the jaws of those you waste
> jab by jab]

As in another imported spectator sport, baseball, Cubans appropriated American English boxing terms as their own. In New York, though, "jabs" and "rings" are unforgiving parts of the cold northern cityscape:

> El Norte es fiero y rudo, boxeador.
> Ese mismo Broadway
> Que en actitud de vena se desangra
> Para chillar junto a los rings
> En que tú saltas como un moderno mono elastico.
>
> [The North is fierce and crude, boxer,
> That same Broadway
> Whose vein bleeds out
> To screech beside the rings
> Where you leap like a modern elastic monkey.]

Broadway bleeds into the ring; it is only another place where he must perform for the diversion of a screeching audience. The Broadway that bankrolls the boxer's "fashionable patent-leather shoes" (Kid Chocolate was famous for high living) also

> stretches its snout with a moist enormous tongue
> to gluttonously lick
> all our canefields' blood.

The blood of the cane field rises and bleeds out in the Broadway boxing ring where Kid Chocolate takes beatings and gives them out, but this is a relationship that the boxer cannot see from where he stands.[37]

The poem critiques U.S. economic exploitation in Cuba and laments the lonely fate of a Cuban migrant in the United States, but it also expresses a deep skepticism about the cultural enterprise of Black internationalism itself (in which sports, for Urrutia, Hughes, and many others, played a more important part than is perhaps recognized by many scholars). Guillén and Urrutia both feared a creative and athletic revival without structural change, a criticism Guillén launches here squarely against New York. However, the history of this poem's publication and of its subsequent English translation has tended to obscure Guillén's skepticism about the relationship between Harlem and Havana. Some of the criticism, especially in English, has even reframed his critical position as one of unrestrained exuberance. The original version of this poem contained a stanza that took a jab at Waldo Frank, the left-wing editor and essayist who lectured often in Cuba, and Langston Hughes:

> De seguro a ti
> no te preocupa Waldo Frank
> ni Langston Hughes
> (el de 'I, too sing America')

> [No doubt you
> Are not worrying about Waldo Frank
> Nor about Langston Hughes
> (he of 'I, too sing America')[38]]

This stanza extends Guillén's critique of North American society's exploitation of Kid Chocolate to two of its most famous radical intellectuals. These lines are, on the one hand, a reflection on the boxer's own ignorance and, on the other, an ambivalent critique of the two writers—perhaps the two most famous living U.S. writers in Cuba—who apparently have nothing to say to the likes of Montalvo. Not even Hughes, whose signature poem, the oft-translated "I, Too, Sing America," proclaimed the speakers' "beauty" to a racist nation that disdained it, can address the especially difficult situation faced by a Black Cuban in the United States, and by extension Afro-Cubans in an U.S.-dominated hemisphere.[39] Guillén removed this critical stanza, however, from a revised version published in his book *Sóngoro Consongo* in 1931, perhaps as a concession to a poet with whom he had since become friends (and who was also working to find a U.S. publisher for the translation of *Motivos de son*).

Even without these critical lines, the revised and now authoritative version of "Pequeña oda" still raises the issue of white exoticism in the "vogue" for Black arts and athletics in Harlem and Havana, but like the earlier critique of Hughes and Frank, this point has eluded readers of the poem's English translation. The poem's original ending derides a European fashion for consuming and even assuming the image of blackness. Guillén would repeat its final exclamation in his report on Hughes's arrival in Havana two years later. It reads:

Y ahora que Europa se desnuda
para tostar su carne al sol
y busca en Harlem y en la Habana
jazz y *son,*
lucirse negro mientras aplaude el bulevar,
y, frente a la envidia de los blancos,
hablar en negro de verdad![40]

[And now that Europe disrobes
to toast its flesh in the sun
and seeks in Harlem and Havana
jazz and *son,*
to play black while the boulevard applauds
and, before the envy of the whites,
to talk black for real!]

This stanza has been misunderstood by English-speaking critics who misplace the subject of Guillén's infinitive "lucirse." The Spanish verb means "to show off" or "to impress," and it has been badly mistranslated by Guillén's principal English editors and translators.[41] Robert Márquez and David Arthur McMurray rewrite this stanza as a triumphant declaration of Black internationalism, eliminating Guillén's criticism of white ventriloquism of Black identities. Their translation reads:

So now that Europe strips itself
To brown its hide beneath the sun

And seeks in Harlem and Havana
jazz and son
the Negro reigns while boulevards applaud!
Let the envy of the whites
Know proud, authentic black![42]

Although Guillén creates some ambiguity by separating the infinitive "lucirse" from its modal verb, "busca"—whose subject is "Europe"—Márquez and McMurray mistakenly assign the agency of the verb to "negro," where it definitely does not belong. This new ending completely changes the poem's meaning, replacing Guillén's comic, ironic critique of Euro-American consumption of Black performance with a rather humorless declaration—with exclamation points—of Black nationalist triumph across borders. Notably, this translation appeared in 1972, at the height of left-wing interest in Cuba as a leader of the third world, when Guillén was the "National Poet" of revolutionary Cuba.[43] Guillén, notably, keeps English words like "jazz" and "jab" in roman type but puts the Cuban music term *son* in italics, as if it is a foreign term (a minor but important detail elided in the McMurray and Márquez's transcription of the Spanish original, which does the opposite—it puts the English words in italics and sets "*son*" in roman type). The "toasted" spectators call jazz their own, but the *son* will always be someone else's foreign term, even in a Cuban poem about one of the country's proudest cultural exports.

The poem's final exclamation assembles this criticism of white exoticism into a sarcastic mockery of "authenticity" that Guillén quotes in the final line of his interview with Hughes—both the denizens of the boulevard and Hughes himself want to be, or at least to speak, *"negro de verdad!"* Whether Guillén was intentionally alluding to the poem in his 1930 Hughes profile is impossible to determine. But the echo raises the question once again of the Cuban's distrust of his North American guest. Is Hughes, in consuming the *son* of Havana to reaffirm his own connection to Black Cuba, simply behaving like the European tourists of the "boulevard" who search for jazz and authenticity on upper Broadway? While Guillén removed the sharpest edge of his critique of U.S. intellectuals in 1931, this poem's ending still cuts at the foreign exploitation of Cuban culture—whether in the form of the career of Eligio Sardiñas Montalvo, as the poem emphatically claims, or the patronage of the *son* in Havana.

Nicolás Guillén, *Afrocubanismo,* and the Politics of the Cuban Avant-garde

Rosalie Schwarz argues that activists and writers in Harlem and Havana formed two axes of a new Black internationalism between the wars: "Of all the facets of life in the United States that fascinated Afro-Cubans in the 1920s," she writes, "Harlem cast the most captivating spell. Geographic proximity, long-standing ties between the United States and Cuba, and commitment to social betterment made kindred spirits of activists and writers in the two black communities."[44] Such assessments of seamless allegiance overstate *afrocubanista* writers' enchantment with the United States, however. In fact, for Guillén, "Harlem" was more of a metonym for segregation than it was for cultural and political militancy.

In order to understand the intellectual and political environment in which Hughes traveled in 1930 and 1931, we must first investigate the anti-imperialist avant-garde of which Guillén, and *afrocubanismo* in general, formed a crucial, if frequently marginalized, part. *Ideales de una raza* was part of a politically active, cultural nationalist intellectual movement in 1920s and 1930s Cuba that has been loosely referred to as *vanguardismo,* or avant-gardism. *Vanguardismo,* associated with journals like the *Revista de Avance, Social,* and *Revista de la Habana,* took up the reevaluation of *cubanía,* or "Cubannness," during a period of intense political and economic crisis on the island. In Cuba between 1923 and 1933, economic crisis and the rule of an authoritarian nationalist leader, General Gerardo Machado, provoked a serious crisis in the political order that had governed Cuba since the end of the postindependence U.S. military occupation in 1902. The increasing power of U.S. capital and its culture industries compounded this crisis for the intellectuals of the Cuban avant-garde. They aimed, in short, to "revindicate" the compromised republic and uplift its masses. In its manifesto, the avant-garde Grupo Minorista (the Minoritarian Group) denounced "yankee imperialism" and Cuba's "pseudodemocracy" while demanding the promotion of "the latest scientific and artistic theories" as well as a new "vernacular" art in Cuba.[45] The document synthesizes the main planks of the avant-garde in Cuba: the "renovation" of national values as part of a political-cultural project of liberal nationalism; the improvement and modernization of the cultural level of the masses via a didactic mission on the part of native intellectuals; and finally, the turn to popular culture as the vehicle for anti-imperialist cultural politics.

Afrocubanismo emerged as part of this renewed interest in the vernacular roots of Cuban national culture, from music and anthropology to poetry. Like the *vanguardia* itself, *afrocubanismo* was a loosely organized movement that represented an uneasy truce of divergent political positions, from Marxism and liberalism to a Latin Americanist mysticism, but in the mainstream of the movement, blackness was inseparable from *cubanidad*. Some criticized *afrocubanismo* as antinational—why divide the nation with "Afro-Cuban" poetry, asked the white scholar Alberto Arredondo, when all Cuban poetry is already Afro-Cuban? "The negro's cause," he wrote, "is the cause of nationality."[46] Other white avant-gardists approached Afro-Cuban culture with the same exoticism that Guillén critiques in "Pequeña oda"—the famed cultural anthropologist Fernando Ortíz, for example, began his career as a criminologist researching Black *"brujería,"* or *"witchcraft."* However, other white students of Afro-Cuban culture, like Ortíz's colleague Lydia Cabrera, were motivated by the controversial thesis that Cuban culture was inextricably African.[47] Afro-Cuban nationalism surged in the 1920s and 1930s as part of a movement united around the goal of renewal, independence, and national culture. "To reconstruct Cubanness," writes Alejandro De La Fuente, "thus implied a revalorization of black contributions to the formation of the Cuban nation, for by the late 1920s it was clear that Cuba could not claim to be a white country."[48] In the debates over the content of Cuban national culture of the 1920s and 1930s, *afrocubanismo* was an insurgent intellectual movement that was also subject to co-optation and cultural exploitation. As Robin Moore argues in *Nationalizing Blackness,* the Afro-Cuban movement's challenge to conventional notions of *Cubanness* thus informed high-cultural and intellectual life while also precipitating a white cultural industry exploitation of Afro-Cuban musical performers. Therefore, while Guillén's interest in vernacular song intersects with Hughes's own, his explorations of the *son* were bound up with the Cuban avant-garde's fascination with popular culture, and *afrocubanismo*'s challenge to an orthodox ideology of *mestizaje*.[49]

Guillén would eventually come to be the most famous literary figure associated with *afrocubanismo,* largely on the strength of *Motivos de son* and later works like *Sóngoro cosongo,* which also elaborated on African-derived musical and religious motifs. In his 1931 preface to *Sóngoro cosongo,* Guillén made the definitive statement of the movement's mainstream goals. "For the time being," he wrote, "Cuba's spirit is mestizo. And it is from the spirit—not the skin—that we will derive our true color. Some day we will call it: 'Cuban color.'"[50] Guillén's sense of aspiration—it is not yet called *"color cubano"*—complements his fear that it may never be, that a spirit that is mestizo "for now" may dissipate into prejudice and dissension. Here, the specter of Jim Crow and northern ghettoization loomed large in Guillén's mind, as they did for Urrutia and other Cubans of color who observed the United States. In his *Ideales* article "El camino a Harlem" (The road to Harlem), Guillén argued that Cuba was descending into an American-style racial divide, and he appealed to the heroes of the 1898 Cuban Revolution, with its ideal of racial union, to prevent it. "Harlem" here is not the capital of a renaissance but a metonym of U.S. segregation and inequality. "Senselessly, we are moving apart in many areas where we ought to be united; and as time passes, this division will become so deep that there will be no space for a final embrace. That will be the day when every Cuban community—the day reaches them all—has its 'black barrio,' like in our neighbors to the North. And that is the road that everyone, those who are the color of Martí as much as those of us who have the same skin as Maceo, should avoid. That is the road to Harlem."[51] Guillén's invocation of Martí, the white revolutionary thinker, and Maceo, the mulatto general of the independence wars, as the paired icons of the Cuban nation expresses an ideal of racial democracy that *afrocubanista* intellectuals of color like Guillén and Urrutia defended. The road to Harlem, then, is not a path forward to modernity and militancy but in fact the way backward, the denial of Cuba's unique progressive potential. Here, in other words, Guillén is reversing the conventional terms of cultural development and placing the United States in the belated station typically assigned to Latin America. Guillén's critique of "Harlem" recalls Pascale Casanova's observation in *The World Republic of Letters* that the "irremediable and violent discontinuity between the metropolitan literary world and its suburban outskirts is perceptible only to writers on the periphery, who, having to struggle in very tangible ways in order simply to find 'the gateway to the present' (as Octavio Paz put it), and then to gain admission to its central precincts, are more clearsighted than others about the nature and the form of the literary balance of power."[52] Guillén's skeptical perspective was shared by writers elsewhere in the Caribbean, as well, as Jeff Karem writes in his reading of the Trinidadian novelist Eric Walrond, a migrant to New York who identified with the Harlem Renaissance but whose perspective on it was critically internationalist. In Walrond's short fiction, the United States is a nation of ghettoes from which his African American characters escape to the Caribbean, attracted by the relative freedom of movement there. Yet for a Cuban character in his story "The

Yellow One," an African American Floridian represents, Karem writes, "'the other,' the jealous aggressor against the islands."[53]

While Guillén considers the politics of *afrocubanismo* in a necessarily international context, Hughes early on saw African American identity and "American" nationality as conflicting poles, and saw the former as constantly having to fight its exclusion from the latter. In his essay "The Negro Artist and the Racial Mountain," Hughes framed the situation of the Black artist in the United States as a battle against a particularly racialized form of cultural standardization. He wrote of "the mountain standing in the way of any true Negro art in America—this urge within the race toward whiteness, the desire to pour racial individuality into the mold of American standardization, and to be as little Negro and as much American as possible."[54] Hughes's travels in Cuba appear to have offered him further support for this thesis, as he enthusiastically assessed the opportunities available to Cuban artists and writers of color compared to those of Black artists in the United States. In an article for *Crisis* on the Black Cuban sculptor Teodoro Ramos Blanco, Hughes praises his public monument to "heroic black motherhood," a statue of the Afro-Cuban revolutionary heroine Mariana Grajales set to be unveiled in a prominent park in Havana. The fact that the Cuban government would publicly honor a Black woman as a national figure, with a sculpture by a Black artist, leads Hughes to reflect on how few monuments there are in the United States recognizing the likes of Frederick Douglass or Sojourner Truth. Hughes concludes with a bitter challenge to his peers: "Is it that we have no artists—or no pride?"[55] The Martían ideal of a raceless nation provided the rhetorical space, at the very least, for Afro-Cuban writers such as Urrutia and Guillén to speak for both a racial and national community simultaneously. For Hughes, the apparent vibrancy of the Afro-Cuban avant-garde and the official support given an artist like Ramos Blanco excites his own sense of the United States' comparative injustice. If the Harlem Renaissance aspired to truly Americanize culture in the United States, as Alain Locke argued in his introduction to *The New Negro,* Hughes, back from Cuba, suggests that the nation was not up to the task.

Cuban Responses to Langston Hughes

The year 1931, when Hughes made his final visit to the island, was also the last year of *Ideales de una raza*'s existence. The pioneering publication fell victim to the dictatorship of General Machado, who consolidated his power and eliminated potential enemies, as Cuba's economy worsened and militant opposition increased. Cubans of color—both supporters and opponents of the regime—were swept up in this conflict in particular ways. As *Ideales de una raza* was censored, Afro-Cuban santería religion and even the congo drum were banned from public places on the grounds that they were "antinational" subversive practices.[56] The overthrow of Machado in 1933 by a combined student-military revolt gave rise both to a new militancy on race issues by Afro-Cuban groups and the Communist Party and a racist reaction that took the form of bombings, race riots in Cuban cities, and the mobilization of new organizations like the Ku Klux Klan Kubano. Without entirely abandoning *afrocubanismo*'s appeal to Cuban mestizo nationalism, a new group called the Asociación Adelante (the Forward Association) drew on the wave of revolutionary nationalism of 1933 and the disillusion that accompanied the successful rightist reaction against it. In a climate of intense politicization, its monthly magazine *Adelante* succeeded *Ideales* as Cuba's new leading publication on racial issues.

Adelante published a wide variety of cultural, political, and historical essays. It strove to maintain a broad ideological heterogeneity; at the same time, it voiced a deep skepticism about Cuba's foundational promises of racial equality. The magazine also studiously covered international Black arts and news on a wide variety of subjects, and it added a regular section devoted to feminism. The paper included translations of poetry from the English-speaking world, including Hughes's work, as well as commentaries on culture and sports in the United States. In one issue, a Puerto Rican author, Angel Augier, translated blues lyrics and accompanied them with a Marxist critical essay reading them as southern proletarian poetry.[57] The publication also featured a monthly profile of African American leaders and history: Arturo González Dorticós's biographical sketches chronicled "Federico Douglass," W. E. B. Du Bois, Booker T. Washington, and others. In the pages of *Adelante,* as in *Ideales de una raza,* the Afro-Cuban revival was always understood as part of an international movement that circulated in the United States and elsewhere. Yet this desire to consider Afro-Cuban culture as part of an international movement regularly came into conflict with *Adelante*'s radical nationalism and many critics' resentment of the relative ease and prestige with which African American culture seemed to circulate abroad. While *Adelante* paid keen attention to African American culture and history, several authors in *Adelante* sought to distinguish *afrocubanismo* from what Regino E. Boti, using Frank Lloyd Wright's term for U.S. culture, called its *"usona"* cousin. For his part, Guillén appeared vexed by an early Cuban review that compared *Motivos de son* with Hughes's *The Weary Blues,* which as we have seen has since become a commonplace in Hughes and Guillén criticism. Shortly after *Motivos'* publication and three months after Hughes's second visit to Cuba, Guillén defended his poems' originality and vanguardist credentials. He asserted that his use of vernacular musical form, working-class slang, and impolitic racial language constituted a significant literary and political intervention, and not just in Cuba. In a testy response to a provincial reviewer who objected to *the poems'* vulgarity, Guillén wrote, "From the literary point of view, and in terms of the meaning that popular culture has in the world today, they constitute a mode of being in the 'advance guard,' just like the great Cuban journalist wants."[58] Guillén asserted that *Motivos de son* was not inspired simply by Hughes's blues poetry; rather, they were part of a worldwide turn toward *lo popular.* His response to the journalist links the poetics of the *son* to a global enterprise. Vernacular language, not imitative cosmopolitanism or vulgar nationalism, says Guillén, is the revolutionary stuff of the true "modern" poetry. As he had said in disparaging the *"prurito de lo grande"* of the Cuban cultural elite, however, Guillén sarcastically rejects what he takes to be the conventional terms of being "advanced" on the world stage.

Some of Guillén's defenders also attacked the presumed lineage with Hughes that had already begun circulating, speaking up for their poet's originality with nationalist ardor. An article by Baltasar Dromundo in the May 1936 issue of *Adelante,* "La poesía afrocubana de Nicolás Guillén," celebrates Guillén's "modernity" and his "orgiastic" exploration of the "spiritual jungle of the negro theme" in describing the poet as both a "primitive" and a modernist. The article exoticizes Guillén's poetry in order to distinguish him from a comparatively dour, defeatist Americanism and thereby place him in the vanguard of hemispheric Black literature. Referring to the poet by his first name, the article angrily distinguishes Guillén's modernity from his supposed "precursors"—which is to say, all African American poetry from its origins to the New Negro present. "Distant are the grandfatherly times [*tiempo abuelo*] of Paul Lawrence Dunbar; and further still is the era of Phyllis Wheatley, that of Richard Bruce, Waring Cuney, Edwards Silvers, Countee Cullen, all precursors. . . . Nicolas's poetry is of indelible modernity, transparently honest and of absolute mullato integrity, in the sexual, rhythmic, and human sense. Nothing could be further from this serious poetry of 'jazz' and its sense of historical violation."[59] Despite its blustery overstatement, Oromundo's article recalls Urrutia's more reasoned profile of Hughes upon his arrival in Havana five years earlier. Urrutia had made a similar connection between "modernity" and virility when he praised Hughes's confrontation of a racist steamship company in New York. That article also drew a contrast between poetic modernity and African American popular music. Dromundo sees jazz as dour, old fashioned, and defeatist in its embrace of "historical violation"; the more politic Urrutia had alleged in his profile of Hughes that a less "modern" poet would have retreated after the racist insult at the Ward Steamship Lines offices to compose "some lamentable BLUES," drawing a similar connection between the "blues" and resignation, between American folk expression and an imagined spirit of capitulation in African American politics. This article indicates that a consensus around Hughes's influence had already started to form, even at this early stage after *Motivos'* publication. In response, Dromundo takes particular pains to distinguish the Cuban poet from any "precursors" in the United States, tying Guillén's virile modernity to his nationality and his particularly Cuban originality.

In another attempt to distinguish *afrocubanismo* from African American modernism, literary critic Regino Boti also defended Guillén's originality in an *Adelante* article that echoed other critics' suspicion of jazz and blues. He reads Guillén as a "national" poet in his use of a local popular musical form that transcends its racial, class, and formal particularity to achieve a truly national "resonance." Drawing on José Vasconcelos's concept of the "cosmic race"—a theory of Latin America's ascendant mestizo civilization and the declining fortunes of Euro-America—Boti describes Cuban culture as a transculturation of African and Spanish elements, of which Guillén's poetry is a triumphant example.[60] He delivers a parting shot at critics who, in a misguided attempt to legitimize Guillén's bold experiments, partake in the "zeal to find a genealogy for us": "Since the tone of Nicolás Guillén's poetry seems foreign in Cuba, it became necessary for these detectives to look abroad to find him an ancestry [los pesquisidores de acudir al extranjero para propinarle un ancestro]. And they found it in Langston Hughes. . . . Hughes resembles Guillén as much as one lyric poet could resemble another; and he differs from him as much as one lyric poet must differ from another. . . . The two poets differ, and so do their songs. Hughes's muse waits. Guillén's demands [La musa de Hughes espera. La de Guillén reclama]."[61] Hughes, once praised in *Ideales* for his exemplary "virility," has now been surpassed by his alleged protégé, whose rebellion contrasts with the North American's complacency. Boti's disavowal of Hughes and his influence is, to be sure, chauvinistic in its claims for Guillén's superior, militant "muse"—it should be noted that Guillén himself never wrote of Hughes in such personal terms—even though it yields a convincing account of the forced analogies between the two poets. Yet Boti's resentment complements James Weldon Johnson's theory of African American poetry's frustrated "universality" in his preface to *The Book of American Negro Poetry.* Johnson observed that African American music—especially ragtime, his prime example—had won audiences across national and linguistic borders as "American music." Johnson argued that African American literary artists had not been permitted to transcend the particularity of U.S. racial segregation to write and speak as "American" authors.[62] Boti, by contrast, points to a situation in which poets of color from Latin American countries like Cuba may achieve national prestige but are denied any global cultural "universality"; in order to be read and understood in the centers of world culture, they must take their subordinate place in a Euro-American genealogy. Boti argues that Guillén has become a truly "national" poet in Cuba, unlike Hughes in his country; however, in order to achieve a poetic "universality" that transcends this national particularity, Guillén requires the prestige and sponsorship of a North American ancestor.

In the 1920s and 1930s, both Hughes and Guillén sought to internationalize the "revival" in Black arts in Harlem and Havana. At the same time, both *afrocubanismo* and the Harlem Renaissance fought to nationalize movements often stigmatized by critics in both countries as narrowly "racial" (or, for others, not "racial" enough). Yet as Hughes observed, Cuba's national ideology of *mestizaje* and the relatively recent memory of nationalist revolutionary struggle gave *afrocubanistas* a degree of rhetorical space in which to advocate for the rights and achievements of Cubans of color and conferred institutional legitimacy on such advocacy. Certainly no leading North American white newspaper, much less the national paper of record, sponsored a Black-interest, Black-edited section. As the Harlem Renaissance looked south to Havana, Cuba appeared in both new and old forms. Like many travelers before him, for example, Hughes was enchanted by the sights of Spanish forts on the Havana waterfront. However, what for earlier generations of U.S. travelers to Havana simply summoned the Orientalist romance of a belated, "Moorish" Cuba instead reminds Hughes of the modern buccaneers of finance capital, whose unequal development of the urban north mirrors its underdevelopment of the Caribbean south. Some of his other Cuban poems, like "Soledad: A Cuban Portrait" ("The shadows / Of too many nights of love / Have fallen beneath your eyes") also recall the hackneyed observations of countless breathless tourists.[63] Yet for Hughes, Cuba also offers the possibility of solidarity in resistance to racial and economic injustice. For Cuban intellectuals like Urrutia and Guillén, however, this deeply felt internationalism at times conflicted with a nationalist position that confronted the economic, political, and cultural power of the United States. This nationalist and anti-imperialist strain in the *afrocubanista* avant-garde sometimes took chauvinistic forms, as in the criticism of blues and jazz as music of capitulation. Yet the fact that the literal and cultural translations of Harlem to Havana and back were translation failures, in Apter's sense, does not necessarily make them political failures. Instead, it underscores that diasporic internationalism was never a unified system but always a contradictory practice and desire, marked by utopian hopes and frustration, fellowship and mistranslation, admiration and resentment: there was no transnationalism without empire, and no possibility of community without the struggle of building it anew.

6 Latin America in Revolution
The Politics and Erotics of Latin
American Insurgency

Warmest climes but nurse the cruelest fangs: the tiger of Bengal crouches in spiced groves of ceaseless verdure. Skies the most effulgent but basket the deadliest thunders: gorgeous Cuba knows tornadoes that never swept tame northern lands.

—Herman Melville, *Moby Dick*

Here was a man's man.

—Raoul Walsh on Pancho Villa, *Each Man in His Time*

AFTER HIS famous 1957 encounter with Fidel Castro in a guerilla base in the Sierra Maestra mountains, the *New York Times'* Latin America correspondent, Herbert Mathews, wrote a vivid description of the charismatic leader: "This was quite a man—a powerful six-footer, olive-skinned, full-faced, with a straggly beard." When the film director Raoul Walsh met with Pancho Villa to research his title role in the 1914 film *The Life of General Villa,* he remembered his impressions of the general in his autobiography, *Each Man in His Time:* "He was a big man physically: big black mustache, big head, wide shoulders, thick body, and eyes that reminded me of something wild in a cage," Walsh recalled. "He had the scowl and dark coloring of an Indian and to me was the classic example of a Mexican bandit. . . . I could understand why his men were said to follow him blindly wherever he lead. Here was a man's man."[1] Both men's power over their followers, and their northern interlocutors, derives from their imposing physical presence—their embodiment of charismatic, defiant manhood. In fact, this charisma is all Villa possesses in Walsh's account. His appeal is not political, but simply an extension of his physical being.

Walsh describes Villa with the familiar signifiers of the Mexican "bandit" figure in Anglo-American popular culture: the large moustache, "Indian" complexion, and "wild" eyes denoting a barely contained rage.

The underdeveloped politics of the South here are sexualized and pre-political—that is, they emanate from an intuitive, embodied "passion" that drives these rebellions and inspires their partisans. Six decades later, during his 1968 tour of the third world's revolutionary states, Stokely Carmichael met with Castro in Havana and was as impressed as Mathews with the Cuban revolutionary's stature. "My first impressions of him *personally?*" writes Carmichael—later Kwame Turé—in his memoir, *Ready for Revolution.* "Well, the first thing you going to notice, he's a big dude. I mean, physically imposing. But, y'know, there was nothing overbearing in his presence . . . you could somehow sense his determination, his will, and you could *feel* his energy. I recall a sister whispering, 'Why, he has such kind eyes.' Then I noticed. Yeah, it was true, he did have compassionate eyes."[2] Castro's kind eyes and his strong body index the things that Carmichael wants to celebrate about revolutionary leadership—determination, natural authority, vision, compassion, strength that is not "overbearing"—though his observation of the thing that distinguishes Castro as a humane revolutionary, his gentle eyes, is nervously displaced onto one of Carmichael's female colleagues. The gazes of these various observers of revolution in Latin America are all directed toward the male revolutionary, who embodies revolutionary commitment in his combination of strength, poise, and compassion. For Walsh, of course, Villa's "manliness" was racialized, indicative of not only his impressive stature but also his "wild," underdeveloped psyche and his comrades' unthinking, "blind" devotion. The combination of political passion and unregulated male sexuality that Villa represented for Walsh extends beyond the obviously xenophobic accounts of the Mexican Revolution in U.S. culture, with its common racial stereotypes of "banditry." Indeed, think of "revolution" in the United States, and one tends to think of such fragmentary gestures and sartorial signifiers taken from Mexico, Cuba, and Nicaragua: a broad chest crossed by a bandolier; a phallic cigar clenched between teeth; a uniformed man compulsively arranging a bank of erect microphones, one of Fidel's trademark gestures; Augusto Sandino's hat; and perhaps most of all, a beard.

The homoerotic representation of revolutionary virtue—the word derives from the Latin *virtus,* which referred to a combination of "manliness," "valor," and moral strength—is not unique to the third-world revolutionary wave that Carmichael joined. These all become national images as much as political ones as they circulate within postrevolutionary societies like Mexico, Cuba, and Nicaragua, as well as in the networks of the international left and anticommunist right. John Reed, the

American socialist who chronicled his time with Villa's troops in *Insurgent Mexico,* describes the intensely affectionate solidarity of campesino soldiers: "'We shall sleep in the same blankets,'" a soldier named Longinos Güereca tells Reed one night at camp, "'and always be together. And when we get to the Cadena I shall take you to my home, and my father shall make you my brother.'"[3] In this martial, male world, revolutionary bravery is coeval with a class-inflected campesino virility; this produces accounts of the revolution that are, as Robert McKee Irwin writes about the genre of the Mexican revolutionary novel, "startlingly homoerotic."[4] Héctor Domínguez-Ruvalcaba has described how, in canonical Mexican narratives of the 1910 Revolution, the comradeship of male revolutionaries is made manifest through "a gaze . . . so focused on male bodies that its descriptive principles may well belong to the category of erotic aesthetics." As he points out, the "national romance" theorized by Doris Sommer is a heterosexual project: to found a new nation is to "conceive" a new society, the "seminal" act of making the nation. In the Mexican novel of the revolution, however, the eroticized male body is the most visible form of nationality, and the homophilia of canonical narratives of the revolutionary war coexists with a homophobia that contests the "effeminacy" that this desire might reveal. As Domínguez-Ruvalcaba writes, "the circle of seduction and repression reveals a contradiction that provides the meaning of the national hero: in this phallocentric society, the male body claims its centrality as the hero figure; this centrality makes his body an object of desire."[5] How does this convention—the representation of revolutionary passion as masculine and embodied—change when U.S. writers use it to mark the limits of their nation?

The Latin American revolutions of the twentieth century appeared to a number of Anglo-American critics, filmmakers, and writers as examples of that once vigorous, but now restrained, national virility. North Americans identified various causes for Latin American revolutionary upheavals: for many like Walsh, revolution was the product of a culturally and geographically determined temperament. For Carmichael, by contrast, it was the product of a global anticolonial politics that transcended imperial borders. For many others, though, revolution was also a path to North American modernity, a logic that saw the United States as the endpoint of Latin America's historical trajectory. On Fidel Castro's first visit to the United States after the 1959 revolution, when his political intentions and affiliations were still either opaque or incomplete, he was welcomed by enthusiastic crowds in Washington, DC, and a charmed *New York Times* reporter. "Fidel Castro swept into Washington last

Wednesday night," the journalist wrote, "not only out of another world, the world of fierce Latin passion, but also out of another century—the century of Sam Adams and Patrick Henry and Tom Paine and Thomas Jefferson." Revolution, here, may summon a "fierce" temperament out of "another century," but it is an "American" century nonetheless. Cuba under Castro is seen here repeating the United States' own past example, reliving its own fierce passions. Perhaps, the reporter continued, Castro "stirred memories, long dimmed, of a revolutionary past, and recalled a revolutionary ardor once deeply felt."[6] Elsewhere, as in Walsh's depiction of the "wild" Villa, this ardor was not a point of comparison but rather a mark of cultural difference. Revolution was the irrational eruption of an underdeveloped culture lodged in the past and governed by passions that failed to assert themselves in more modern and moderated climes. It is clear enough that eroticizing revolutionary action is to trivialize it, at least insofar as the erotic is understood to be more or less synonymous with irrationality and impropriety. But why should revolution abroad be represented so consistently through the eroticized male body in the first place? And how is the desire—for the male subject of revolution, or for the radical change he so often comes to signify in mass culture—managed by cultural texts in the United States, given its own revolutionary history?

From the Halls of Santono to the Shores of Nicarania: Revolutions in the "Mythical Kingdom"

We can begin to answer these questions with an illustrative example from one of the many films in the first half of the century that referenced revolutionary insurgencies in Nicaragua and Mexico. The caricature of the venal, impulsive revolutionary is an old one within the United States; we have already seen a nineteenth-century example in Davis's account of the professional Honduran revolutionist in *Three Gringos in Venezuela and Central America,* for whom "the desire for change and revolution is born in the blood."[7] The archetype derives its still-recognizable visual form from the Mexican and Nicaraguan revolutions, which were either filmed themselves (especially in the Mexican case) or referenced in a displaced way by adventure films that used the insurgencies as a backdrop.

In the 1932 comedy *First in War,* made with Hal Roach Studios, the slapstick comedian Charley Chase finds himself unwittingly thrust into battle in the fictional country of "Nicarania." Based transparently but loosely on Nicaragua, where U.S. Marines were then fighting a bloody counterinsurgency against the guerillas of Augusto César Sandino, "Nicarania" was the conventional "banana republic" of popular Anglo legend, signified by dirty streets lined by palm trees and strolled by idle men and "señoritas" in billowing skirts. A year before the final withdrawal of U.S. forces from Nicaragua, and two years before Sandino's assassination, the revolution became a fictionalized slapstick in this film from the popular series featuring the bumbling, "befuddled Everyman," Charley Chase.[8] Sandino's revolt began when he and a number of other Liberal Party supporters began an uprising against a Conservative president, Adolfo Díaz. Díaz had taken power after a coup supported by the U.S. government, which had effectively run the Nicaraguan state between the arrival of the Marines in 1912 and their initial departure in 1925. Sandino, the only Liberal general to reject the U.S.-brokered peace treaty that ended a 1926–27 civil war, was inspired by the Mexican Revolution's campaign for land reform as well as an indigenist nationalism that exalted what he called the "Indo-Hispanic race" and "Indian-American" culture of Nicaragua.[9] In describing his own motives, Sandino used a bodily metaphor himself, that of his blood, in order to lay claim to a mestizo racial inheritance that was the bedrock of the nation. In his San Albino manifesto of July 1, 1927, he wrote, "I am Nicaraguan and I feel proud that Indian blood, more than any other, runs in my veins, which by some atavism contains the mystery of being a loyal and sincere patriot."[10] U.S. newspapers covered Sandino as an elusive, self-promoting "bandit"—itself a term derived from the long-standing Mexican stereotype—and attributed the insurgency to his "blood" in another way, as the product of an innate Latin vanity and apathy. "Publicity has made Augusto Sandino," reported the *New York Times* in 1932. "The bandits are not all 'Nicaraguan patriots' and most of the bands are composed of men who prefer that kind of life to working."[11]

First in War begins in New York, where Charley, an army soldier and musician prone to pratfalls, has gone AWOL on Tin Pan Alley to seek fame as a songwriter. Tossed unceremoniously out of a music publisher's office, he collides with a general from "Nicarania" who has come to hire someone to write his country's national anthem. Charley, thinking quickly, sells the man a slightly altered version of the University of Pennsylvania fight song, updated to urge patriots to "fight, fight, fight for Nicarania!" When the scene shifts to Nicarania, where Charley is stationed in the combat zone, he once again runs into the general, who has been captured by the U.S. Marines. Charley has his mind on more immediate things, however: his barbershop quartet, one member of which has come down with a cold before a scheduled performance. Charley springs his old friend out of prison as a substitute, enticing him with the promise of the "swell muchachas" that will be in attendance. The general oblig-ingly returns to prison once the party is over, but at that very moment, his Nicaranian comrades arrive on their *own* prison break mission. In the film's comic conclusion, *el general* refuses their help: "I am a gentleman of honor," he sniffs haughtily, allowing Charley to escort him back to jail, at which point Charley earns an undeserved promotion for valor.

"Nicarania" was not the only fake country with a fake revolution in U.S. cinemas in the 1910s, 1920s, and 1930s; revolutions in imaginary countries modeled on Mexico, Cuba, or Nicaragua were popular subjects of silent and early sound cinema. *Thunder Below* (1932) starred Talulah Bankhead in a fictional Central American republic called San Mateo, while the Anglo-American protagonist of *The Stoker* (1932) fought a "bandit" named "Santono."[12] For *Captain Macklin* (1915) U.S. script-writers invented "Anduras," and for Douglas Fairbanks's *El Americano* (1916), the tropical republic of "Paragonia"—"a jewel set in the girdle of the Earth," as the intertitles describe it. The tropicalized description of Paragonia—feminized, passive, sexually available—exemplifies the con-flation of political and libidinous passions that animate Latin American politics in these films (not to mention the geographical confusion of a Patagonian inspiration for the film's Caribbean setting). Ruth Vasey's his-tory of the foreign policy of the Motion Picture Producers and Distribu-tors of America suggests that the practice of fictionalizing Latin American countries reflected a studio policy of setting pictures in fictional "mythi-cal kingdoms" to avoid offending foreign censors.[13] However, as the film historian Emilio García Riera shows, many of these earlier revolution films were also based on literary precursors, suggesting that the studio considerations that dictated the "mythical kingdoms" do not entirely ex-plain the trend. *A Man's Man* (1917), for example, was based on a novel by western author Peter B. Kyne about U.S. mine owners fighting revo-lutionaries in "Sobrante."[14] In Davis's 1897 novel (and later film) *Soldier of Fortune,* the American hero thwarts a revolution in the republic of "Olancho."[15] O. Henry, known for his xenophobic writing on Mexico, adapted two of his stories for the screen: *The Changing Woman* (1918) was set in "Macuta," and *The Double-Dyed Deceiver* (1920) took place in "Buenas Tierras."[16] His only novel, *Cabbages and Kings,* in which he coined the term "banana republic," was set in a fictional Central Ameri-can nation named "Anchuria."[17]

Later, more sympathetic treatments of "real" Latin American revolu-tions, like the 1939 *Juarez,* starring Paul Muni as Mexican independence leader Benito Juárez, and the 1949 film *We Were Neighbors,* starring

John Garfield as a sympathetic Anglo-American participant in Havana's anti-Machado underground in 1933, reflect the influence of Hollywood's participation in Good Neighbor politics, when Latin American revolutions were treated sympathetically (if paternalistically) as democratic (and thus "American") rebellions against foreign occupation or dictatorship.[18] The older practice of setting revolutions in "mythical kingdoms" reappeared in the Cold War, when the Cuban *barbudo* replaced Villa and Sandino as the sexualized archetype of insurgency. In *Bananas!* (1971), Woody Allen's familiar comic persona, the sexually frustrated liberal intellectual, unwittingly becomes the clumsy macho dictator of the fictional Caribbean island of "San Marcos." Latin America's "banana republics" are so absurdly unrealistic and clichéd in these films—self-consciously, archly so in *Bananas!*—that one almost doesn't notice the obvious fabrication of place names, so seamlessly do they fit into the farcical exaggeration of the general portrayal. Allen's character, Fielding Mellish, has never heard of "San Marcos" before he becomes its president, just as Fairbanks's character in *El Americano* has never heard of "Paragonia" when he accepts an invitation from a U.S. mining executive to suppress a revolution there. (Indeed, this obliviousness becomes a running joke in *Bananas!*; none of the New York leftists demonstrating at the UN "in solidarity" with San Marcos know where it is.) Given the geographical illiteracy and political naïveté Allen satirizes, it hardly seems necessary to invent phony nations. A significant part of a U.S. film audience would have known, however, there was no such place as "San Marcos" or "Nicarania," and be wise to the irony that it is at once no place, and yet every place "south of the border."

The real subject of such U.S. films is therefore not revolutionary Latin America, much less the foundational fictions of its modern states; rather, what we see in these texts is an Anglo-American fantasy of an undifferentiated, "underdeveloped" Latin America, the belated cross-border relation of the "modern" United States. What does "underdeveloped" mean in this context? In the United States, reframing revolution as "banditry," and politics as romance, positioned Latin American politics as impulsive and individualized, rather than organized and even bureaucratized. Here, underdevelopment means the political immaturity of unstable societies unable to channel their political conflicts via the depersonalized and thus disembodied bureaucratic institutions that ostensibly prevail in the United States, where the political supposedly remains safely impersonal. At the same time, to judge from their publicity materials and reviews (many of the earliest films have been lost), cinematic responses to the

Mexican and Nicaraguan insurgencies also drew on desires for heroism and decisive action that this bureaucratic Anglo-American consensus seemed to foreclose.

This pattern of desire and disavowal has much in common with what Frances R. Aparicio and Susana Chávez-Silverman have called "tropicalization": "a mythic idea of *latinidad* based on Anglo (or dominant) projections of fear."[19] For an example of this dialectic of fear and desire, take the 1915 film *Captain Macklin,* written by Davis and based on his novel of the same name. Like his contemporaries Stephen Crane and Jack London to a degree, Davis treated Latin America as a politically volatile theater of a reinvigorated U.S. masculinity. According to a synopsis of *Captain Macklin,* which is lost, the title character is an undisciplined West Pointer who, once disgraced at the military academy, travels to Honduras in search of adventure. There, he becomes involved in a political intrigue to restore García, the president, who has been deposed by a rebel named Alvarez, whose uprising is sponsored by a U.S. shipping corporation that García had attempted to tax.[20] In spite of the plot's apparent implied critique of U.S. imperial diplomacy, an ad for *Captain Macklin* describes the film as a spectacle that would satisfy viewers' desire for "soldiers and cannons and half-breeds and excitement." An ad for cinema proprietors in *Moving Picture World* offered the following description of the film: "Captain MACKLIN by Richard Harding Davis is a wonderful picture for red-blooded humans. For this four reel majestic Master-Picture is full of soldiers and cannons and half-breeds and excitement. From the time Cadet Macklin in dropped from West Point until two months later when he becomes Vice-President of Honduras, there's nothing but vital, gripping action."[21] But even as it draws an implicit racial contrast between a "red-blooded" Anglo-American audience and "half-breed" Honduras, the advertisement frames the film's appeal in terms of the bloodless politics of the United States and the full-blooded vitality of affairs south of the border. This American "bloodlessness" was the unfortunate price of modernity, as Louis Reeves Harrison argued in his review of the film later that spring in *Moving Picture World.* Harrison argues that Latin America has something the developed north increasingly lacks, especially in politics: romance. He goes on to explain why such political romances cannot take place in the United States:

> South American republics, like the 'Zenda' kingdoms somewhere in the Balkan regions, furnish a background for picturesque romance and military costumes, and they permit the intrusion of love stories into affairs of state. We cannot

locate modern romance within our own boundaries and get away with it, not so much because it would be incongruous as because affairs of state are too disagreeably practical for those of love and adventure, and then revolutions are altogether too infrequent for the purpose of a story. Why bother about it when the republics of Central America furnish an abundant supply of battle scenes and swift change of governmental control?[22]

The critic's point is twofold: first, that the best "modern romances" involve affairs of state and of the heart. Secondly, Latin America (Harrison uses "South American" and "Central America" interchangeably) is the best location for this modern combination because it is there (along with the Balkans) that the political passions barred from the "disagreeably practical" U.S. state still can be found. These passions are the product of a leader's frustrated libido and his adherence to codes of aristocratic "Hispanic" propriety, and so they are registered for the viewer and reader primarily on the body. That is, the revolution is represented as a physical, erotic, experience, a romantic object of desire that is simultaneously disavowed as synonymous with chaos, upheaval, and disorder.

Critical in these depictions of revolutionary masculinity is the absent presence of the Latin American female body. In *Devil with Women* (1930), Humphrey Bogart's character, a U.S. soldier of fortune, "lends his sword and swagger to a banana republic which is sadly troubled by guerillas," wrote a reviewer, and he exploits his enemy's susceptibility to "coy señoritas" in order to defeat them.[23] Like the "swell muchachas" who facilitate Charley Chase's triumph in Nicarania and the fictional sister whose rape motivates Villa to take up arms against the government in *The Life of General Villa* (1914), the corollary to the male revolutionary hero is the absent or passive female character, who is everywhere present yet who disappears into the background of the films. The 1947 John Wayne film *Tycoon!* is another case in point, set in the fictional Andean country of "Tenango." Wayne does not play a revolutionary in this film, but rather a heroic engineer developing the country's wilderness by blasting a railroad through it. Named Johnny Munroe, in an unsubtle reference to the Monroe Doctrine that justified U.S. intervention in Latin America, he falls in love with Maura, the cloistered daughter of a local railroad tycoon. As Lindsey Collins has argued, Munroe's profession and his pursuit of Maura become linked in an unsubtle sexual allegory for benevolent U.S. domination of the hemisphere, a Monroe Doctrine for the early Cold War. While building a railroad tunnel through a "virginal" mountain landscape, Munroe is also attempting to liberate the suppressed Latin American womanhood of popular U.S. myth, repressed by aristocratic codes of etiquette retained in "Spanish" America.[24] In films that use the Latin America of the present as a projection of the underdeveloped U.S. past—either of revolutionary passions or an unconquered landscape—the Latin American woman, Maya Mendible writes, is "figuratively disembodied: present only in familiar metaphorical relation to the imagined national self."[25] The Latin American mythical kingdom is a place of political romance and of virile adventure, in which women figure only metaphorically.

These imaginary countries are places where a man can *really* be a man, where sexual and political possibilities no longer available in the modern United States can still be achieved, without the dissimulations and calculations of professional politicians. Depoliticizing Latin America's political revolts as the expression of inarticulate, irrational urges allows Americans to imagine themselves governed by a democratic consensus where disagreement never descends to "uncivil" expressions, where violence resides only outside the law. Yet the familiar tactic of representing the Latin American revolutionary as a desiring male body serves a double, seemingly paradoxical function of estranging us from the revolution by bringing us closer to the revolutionary. Instead of making the personal political, the political becomes purely personal in these stories, and ever-more distant from the horizon of U.S. life. Here is the paradox of intimacy, which I described in the Introduction as the combination of recognition and disavowal that characterizes the pendulum swings of U.S. images of underdevelopment. When Latin American revolution is made accessible and even seductive to Americans by being sexualized, it is also made irretrievably foreign. In the sections to follow, I trace this combination of desire, for the "modern romance" and the revolutionary past it summons, and disavowal of the revolutionary romance's homophilic eroticism. This pattern plays out in the U.S. culture industry's mediation of the three great Latin American revolutions of the twentieth century: the Mexican Revolution of 1910–20; the Cuban Revolutionary triumph of 1959; and the victory of Nicaragua's Frente Sandinista de Liberación Nacional in 1979.

The Mexican Revolution and the Legends of Pancho Villa

The 1910–20 Mexican Revolution was a complex set of regional revolts and coups d'état set off by the challenge of the liberal Francisco Madero to the regime of the long-standing dictator, Porfirio Díaz. The assassination of Madero and seizure of power by his rival Vitoriano Huerta escalated into a peasant rebellion that challenged Mexico's semifeudal system of peonage and large estates inherited from the colonial era. After Madero's assassination, the defenders of the *maderista* reform, known as the Constitutionalists, took up arms against the *federales* loyal to Huerta. The complexity of the conflict, known to the American public at the time as "The Mexican War," is in a way beside the point for the purposes of this chapter, since for the U.S. reading and film-going public it was not complex at all. Instead, the revolution was distilled into a single alluring, dangerous figure on the border: Francisco "Pancho" Villa, leader of the Division del Norte in Chihuahua state.[26] The revolution thrust Villa into the American popular consciousness, where he has remained ever since.

Villa was a sensation in the United States from 1913, at the height of his power in Chihuahua and his popularity in the United States, until early 1916, when the so-called Punitive Expedition led by U.S. Army General Jack Pershing pursued his army across the border after its raid of a United States armory in Columbus, New Mexico. He was the subject of fourteen medium and long features in 1914 alone, most of them sympathetic portraits of an unlettered, impulsive, promiscuous "peon in politics," to use Reed's admiring description of him from *Insurgent Mexico*.[27] During Villa's revolutionary career, he was celebrated in the United States as a plainspoken hero, decried as a bandit, misrepresented as a chivalrous aristocrat, and slandered as an impulsive rogue. His film analogues were brave and full of indignation, class conscious but politically inarticulate, rebel and thief in equal, often indistinguishable measures. These film depictions of Villa are recognizable by at set of familiar, iconographic signifiers, like bandoliers across the chest and the broad-brimmed hat of a Mexican *charro*. Zuzana Pick argues that these images of a redemptive and threatening Villa are inextricable from his broader historical legacy. "Only spectacle and romance could contain the paradoxes that overdetermined the legend," Pick writes, referring to Villa's legend as bandit and revolutionary in the mass cultures on both sides of the border.[28] In the United States, as Carlós Cortés argues, movie Mexico has alternated between a good, if opaque, neighbor and a menace on the border. Given this flexibility, the country has most consistently served as a metaphor, he writes: "a backdrop for American activity, a foil for displays of American superiority, a stage on which Americans conduct their own personal morality plays, and sometimes a surrogate for political and ideological struggles within the United States."[29] As Juan José Alonzo argues, Anglo-American representations of Villa typically collapse these conventional images of the Mexican bandit and revolutionary into a single recognizable character.[30]

The common denominator between these paradoxical characters is an impulsive, impassioned masculinity. Villa's humble upbringing lent itself to competing myths about both his native "savagery" and his instinctual generosity. Yet even though he possessed almost no formal education, his notoriety in the United States was in large part due to his canny exploitation of the new technology of the moving image.[31] The deal Villa negotiated with Mutual president Harry E. Aitken guaranteed the studio exclusive access to Villa's army and the right to screen its films in the United States, Canada, and all Mexican territory occupied by the División del Norte. Cameramen and directors would receive safe passage, secure transportation, and room and board for employees and horses. In return, the División would receive 20 percent of profits from exhibitions, and footage would be subject to approval by Villa's officers.[32] Spectators would thrill at footage taken directly from the Mexican battlefield, as Mutual advertisement claimed in a 1914 advertisement in the *Moving Picture World*. Mutual trumpeted the lucrative potential of the Mexican Revolution and Villa himself, "the greatest military genius since Napoleon." The ad urged exhibitors to strike quickly: "The Iron is hot! Villa is getting more famous every day! There is three times more about him in the newspapers than about any other man alive!"[33] An anecdote from the same magazine in 1914 shows how popular the Mexican Revolution was among cinephiles that year in the United States. A projectionist from Norwich, Connecticut, writes a letter to the editor of a regular column to request a copy of the magazine's handbook: "The other two I have had, I have presented to my assistants, so that now I am 'Handbookless' unless you heed this S.O.S. and rush one *poco pronto, Quieh Sabe Senor?* (Mexican stuff is all the rage now. Can't grab the poco part, but I'm wise to the rest.—Ed.)"[34] The "rage" for Mexican Revolution pictures had not improved the projectionist's Spanish, but it had clearly infiltrated the trade in ways both extraordinary and mundane. These heroic and villainous Villas, the "Napoleonic" genius and the unlettered "peon," the revolutionary redeemer and the scurrilous bandit, cohabited simultaneously. Even his "savagery" was out of sync with the conventional temporal hierarchy that word would suggest; the *New York Times,* in its unfavorable coverage of Aiken's film deal, referred to the general as a "savage," but of a particularly modern kind—it was his film contract that made him so.[35] Villa was "stern and savage," the *Times* argued, because "even the most morbid seeker for horrors might be shocked, if not by the sight of carnage, at least by the thought that it has been commercialized in this particularly cynical way."[36] Other U.S. observers drew the opposite conclusion, mocking what they assumed was Villa's untutored inexperience in front of a camera. One critic of the Mutual films dismissed the revolution "as a lot of poor peons, more or less badly armed, fighting for they do not know what, and murdering each other like bands of savages," while mocking Villa and his lieutenants as amateurs who "posed as meekly as any novice before a camera and obediently took off their hats when told to do so by the photographer," ignoring the fact it was Villa who had invited the photographers in the first place.[37] The pair of anecdotes tell us little about Villa, but they are a reminder of what Pick, Cortés, and Alonzo argue above about Villa's durability as a projection screen for U.S. fantasies about the modern national self and the immature, disorderly Mexican "other," whose revolution is a tendency to upheaval and impatience bred in the blood.

The Mutual contract led to the 1914 silent picture *The Life of General Villa,* now lost, directed by Christy Cabanne and starring Walsh as the title character. The project helped establish the image of Villa as "righteous bandit"—a thief with sympathy for the downtrodden, but without an organized politics. A contemporary synopsis of the film describes the title character as "a young rancher living alone with his pretty young sister and doing well," a misrepresentation of Villa's impoverished upbringing that places the film in the recognizable, romantic landscape of "Old Mexico": aristocratic, mannered, rural, peninsular in habits and culture. A newspaper summarized the film this way: "One day a young lieutenant of the Mexican Federal army came to that locality with another young officer. The lieutenant became smitten with Villa's sister, and with the aid of his companion abducted her and ruined her. The sister, after telling her brother, died, and Villa journeyed to the garrison town and killed the lieutenant, but the companion escaped. Villa then sold his ranch and with a small body of his men escaped to the mountains, vowing warfare on all mankind in revenge for the death and ruin of his sister."[38] Thus began the Mexican Revolution, according to the Mutual Film Company. *The Life of General Villa* elides Villa's poverty to imagine the revolution as the kind of political romance that Harrison had argued was so appealing to U.S. audiences.

A Species of Mexican Man (dir. Romain Fielding, 1915) treats the revolution as a cross-border romance, showing how the "righteous bandit" character could play on either conventional manifestation of Latin American masculinity: either hypersexualized or excessively proper, either un-controlled by social restrictions on sexuality or unnaturally restrained by them. Of this film, also lost, a weary critic wrote, "The details of the plot have to do with a Mexican 'Man on Horseback,' a mysterious being, high in the ranks of one of the warring factions, who crosses the border in order to procure arms and ammunition for his comrades. Once in the United States, he promptly walks straight into a romantic adventure, the charming American girl whom he rescues from peril, becoming his bride and the future Mrs. President of Mexico." Coming the year before Villa's invasion of New Mexico, the "Man on Horseback" is a visionary hero who unites his country's people with his leadership and unites North America with his rescue of the "charming American girl" who will be-come his wife. This critic was not convinced, however, and dismissed the film as a trite American fantasy:

> If the living prototype of the man that Romain Fielding has made the central figure of the three-reel drama, "A Species of Mexican Man," is to be found anywhere in Mexico, the people of that war-torn and misgoverned country would do well to seek him out and, following the hint given them by the playwright, seat the gentleman firmly in the presidential chair. As conceived by Mr. Fielding, his leading character is one of those unfortunate beings who is equally at home leading an army on the field of battle, playing the polished courtier to some fair dame, or directing the affairs of a nation—a veritable Count of Monte Cristo, 1915 brand. This will undoubtedly insure him a warm welcome. The love of romance is still strong within the better part of us, and we admire and applaud the deeds of these heroes of the pictured story, even when our hard, practical sense keeps telling us that there aren't any such chaps.[39]

Retreating to a "practical" sense of realism about the desire for "such chaps," Weitzer reads the Mexican Revolution, and the U.S. film audi-ence's craze for it, as evidence of misguided romance that prevails among Mexico's ruling elite but which is, happily, limited only to the United States' film-going public. "We" know that there are no longer "any such chaps," the critic suggests, but we want them just the same—and if there are any to be found, they can be most likely found in Mexico.

If this revolutionary romance symbolically unites north (the Anglo-American woman) and south (the virtuous Mexican man), this cross-border romance is a rare possibility foreclosed after 1916. As García Riera and Orellana have written, Villa's prominent place in U.S. popu-lar culture of the 1910s was subject to shifts in U.S. foreign policy. His

1916 invasion of Columbus, New Mexico, certified him as an enemy in Washington and in the film industry. Villa was no longer either a chivalrous hacendado or righteous bandit, but rather a randy, undisciplined thief. Consequently, the U.S. Army's so-called Punitive Expedition against Villa took the symbolic form of a police mission that punishes this indiscipline and "cleans up" the disorder it spread. In one 1916 cartoon short, *The Long Arm of Law and Order,* Uncle Sam reaches over the border to grab Villa, tossing him into the same garbage can with Emilio Aguinaldo, the Filipino guerilla leader who had fought the U.S. military occupation a decade earlier.[40] And in the *Colonel Heeza Liar* animation series, the title character—a composite of Baron Munchausen and Theodore Roosevelt who has outlandish adventures across the globe—joins the punitive campaign in northern Mexico.[41] In *Heeza Liar Captures Villa* (1916) Heeza Liar cross-dresses to seduce and disarm his adversary, thus turning Villa's strength—his exaggerated heterosexual virility—into his tactical weakness. Certainly, the political shift in U.S. sympathy for Villa between 1914 and 1916 shaped Villa's cultural representations. Claire Fox argues that U.S. filmic accounts of Villa produce a particular U.S. "point of view" by means of "the cultural codes conveyed though humor, captions, iconography, and framing that assert the dominance of the United States vis-à-vis Mexico, and that manifest this difference through the depiction of middle-class Anglo citizens as 'model spectators.'" Yet can this "point-of-view" account for the desire by U.S. audiences and studios for Villa as something more than a negative marker of cultural difference? Villa also circulated in U.S. popular culture as a "Napoleonic genius," a righteous outlaw, or even, as Christopher Wilson notes of some U.S. press accounts, a plainspoken, Mexican "Old Hickory."[42] Fox argues that after the Punitive Expedition, Villa's once-heroic masculinity is compromised by Pershing's emasculating pursuit. Representations of Villa on the run, she argues, are a way of symbolically feminizing him and invigorating Pershing in turn. Yet this sort of seamless cultural transaction—in which Mexico is gendered one way, and then abruptly reframed in response to geopolitical calculations—is too neat an account of a messy cultural history in which Villa's masculinity was also always an object of desire as well as disgust.[43] How to disentangle the entwined strands of sympathy and disgust, desire, and contempt here?

As David Eng has argued in another context, psychoanalysis helps articulate sexuality and "underdeveloped," or what Freud called "primitive," psyches. The primitive, Eng writes, is one "whose mental thoughts pass directly into action," and the mark of "civilized" man is therefore the deliberation that comes between idea and action. In his reading of Freud's *Totem and Taboo,* Eng points out how, in Freud's thought and in Eurocentric anthropological discourse more generally, "what marks the primitive psyche as such, beyond all other distinguishing characteristics, is its propensity for sexual impropriety."[44] Caricaturing political rebellion as coeval with ungoverned sexuality is one way of marginalizing it, treating political grievances as individual and impulsive rather than social and deliberative. The eroticization of insurgency derives, as well, from a Eurocentric association of unregulated bodies with ungoverned bodies politic, as film historian Charles Ramírez Berg has argued about the "Latin lover" film archetype, which he traces to the Italian-born actor Rudolf Valentino. Berg enumerates the convention's typical traits: "eroticism, exoticism, tenderness tinged with violence and danger, all adding up to the romantic promise that, sexually, things could very well get out of control."[45]

The enduring association between ungoverned sexuality and Latin American political radicalism endures even after the "Latin Lover" has faded into the realm of embarrassing kitsch. The hypersexualized "bandit revolutionary" reappeared in the Italian-made spaghetti westerns of the 1960s and 1970s, for example, where Villa's reputation as a class-conscious rogue lent itself to film treatments that treated contemporary third-world insurgencies with the visual style of the classical Western. The righteous bandit's reputation for a fearless instinct to take up the gun—whether for socialism or for gold—suited a political moment in which revolutionary agency seemed to have shifted to the global South. Misnamed as "Zapata westerns," these films, set in a landscape resembling the arid northern plains (rather than the tropical Chiapan highlands), feature main characters indebted to the Villa legend and the conventions of the Mexican War film.[46] In *A Bullet for the General* (dir. Damiano Damiani, 1966), *A Fistful of Dollars* (1964), *The Good, the Bad, and the Ugly* (1966), and *Duck, You Sucker* (also known as *A Fistful of Dynamite* (1971), a heavyset, mustachioed bandit leader is often advised by a white American "soldier of fortune" (in a politicized variation on this convention, in *Duck, You Sucker* he is an exiled Irish Republican Army operative). In each film, the Villa analog transforms his mercenary theft from the state into a politicized campaign against it.[47] In some of these films, the hero's inchoate class consciousness manifests itself in sexual violence, as in Telly Savalas's painful turn as a sex-addicted, monstrous despot in 1972's *Vendetta* (originally titled *Pancho Villa*), who poses constantly for film crews and literally tosses the women he beds out of hotel room windows. His revolutionary sentiments are never articulated as ideas, but are rather linked, as ever, to his fleshly impropriety. This film takes this theme to absurd lengths when Savalas intones to a physician who scolds him for his poor hygiene: "I've been busy changing the government, doctor. No time to change the underwear."

Gustavo Pérez Firmat shows how post-1959 Hollywood treatments of Cuba also used the campy excesses of the Latin lover to satirize the macho postures of the revolutionary.[48] In one of his examples, *Up the Sandbox* (1972), Barbra Streisand plays an Upper West Side housewife who accuses Fidel Castro of sexism at a speech in New York. Castro, seemingly impressed by her boldness, invites her to his hotel room, where he opens his shirt to reveal a woman's breasts—the charismatic male rebel is revealed as a woman. Fidel's breasts, to Pérez Firmat, prove the phoniness of his masculine public persona and political project. His revolutionary zeal, which often manifests itself as virile swagger, is a sign of repressed femininity.[49] In *Bananas!*, when the New Yorker Mellish stumbles into the San Marcos guerilla base, he catches a long glimpse of a soldier, bearded and dressed in olive green. The man's upright figure is framed through Allen's trademark glasses, the sign of his intellectuality, his sexual frustration, and thus his distance from the potent man of action refracted through the lenses. Later, once Mellish is incorporated into the unit and sent abroad to raise money for the revolution, the mettle and sexual charisma he never had extend from the long prosthetic beard he wears to disguise himself as a *comandante* in the San Marcos revolution. With plots that spoof the gender conventions of the macho revolutionary, films like *Bananas!* and *Up the Sandbox* self-consciously reconfigure the trope of the revolutionary, masculine Latin lover, mocking its ethnocentric kitsch only to reaffirm, ultimately, the assumptions at its heart: middle-class Americans are disciplined and rational, but also occasionally uptight and alienated; Latin Americans, by contrast, are romantic, implicitly male figures, hot-tempered, driven and dominated by their unruly bodies.

To the category of the "primitive" that marks the separation of north and south, civilization and barbarism, we can also add the sexualized category of the "monster." In a discussion of sexual identities and policing in Brazil, Jorge Leite Júnior discusses the distinction between the figure of the "abject"—the vile, disgusting, repugnant person that has been expelled from the body, discharged as 'Other'"—and the monstrous as a category of social definition. Unlike the "abject," the monster's transgressive properties provoke not only fear but also fascination.[50] Villa's exaggerated eroticism distinguished him, for these filmmakers, as a "primitive" acting upon unregulated instincts. Yet this eroticism makes figures like Villa and the Castro of *Up the Sandbox* objects of mockery as well as desire. Foucault argues that the monster's transgression is a specifically sexual one, making him or her "intelligible," a magnification of everyday deviations rather than a vile, abject Other.[51] Jeffrey Cohen notes the word's etymological link to the Latin *mostrare*, to show—the monster serves as a warning to "keep out" of the forbidden spaces he roams. The monster, in addition to being a category of social exclusion, is also a geographically liminal figure: monsters belong to the margins, both socially and spatially, where they are banished outside the city gates, in a haunted castle, an enchanted forest, or the border. Outside such spaces, the nonmonstrous may move peacefully, but inside they take their chances. "To step outside this official geography" of social belonging, writes Cohen, "is to risk attack by some *monstrous border patrol* or (worse) to become monstrous oneself"—an appropriate metaphor for our purposes. Once "contained by geographic, generic, or epistemic marginalization," he concludes, "the monster can function as an alter ego, as an alluring projection of (an Other) self."[52] Monstrosity thus describes something horrifying and repugnant, but crucially also fascinating and intimately familiar. If Castro and Villa's sexuality is depicted as monstrous, it is in this double sense of being both unknown and yet familiar, both transgressive and restorative, both a sign of ethnic and geographical otherness and of intimacy.

It is appropriate, as Fox argues, that Villa's notoriety derives from his actions along the border: it is precisely where the real boundaries between the United States and Mexico are most ambiguous that the cultural boundaries are policed most aggressively. Because of the territorial and cultural ambiguity of the border, it becomes a synecdoche of the nations it divides. And while monsters, who operate in spaces where "normal" rules don't apply, set limits to normative behavior, limits are just that, limits—they are not "outside" that which they define, but on its edges. The monstrous Villa is an alter ego, a projection of our other selves that, like Frankenstein's monster, we have created for ourselves and then disavowed. In this way, the sexualization of revolution imposes a cultural and geographic hierarchy, of "primitive" monsters who dwell at the southern margins of the nation. To return to Fox's argument, then, the intimacy of Villa's monstrosity helps explain why his hyper-masculinity legitimizes U.S. intervention even as it invites admiring sympathy from U.S. observers and flattering comparisons to U.S. presidents. Monstrosity lacks the clear sense of difference attributed to the "primitive"; monsters, like the revolutions they make, walk somewhere among us.

The desire to find this revolutionary spirit at home motivated Mexican Revolution literature on the U.S. left. Reed's description of Villa as a "peon in politics" was sympathetic, a reference to Villa's humble origins and to his unlettered intelligence, which shaped his opposition to the conventional wisdom of an educated elite he aimed to overthrow. "He couldn't see why rich men should be granted huge tracts of land and poor men should not," Reed writes. "The whole complex structure of civilization was new to him. You had to be a philosopher to explain anything to Villa," suggesting that instead of an ignorance of politics, it was rather a radical inclination to question it, to pull it up from the roots, that motivated him.[53] We have already seen how, in Reed's reportage from Mexico, the martial culture of the revolutionary army produced an erotics of revolutionary solidarity. Other examples exhibited a similar fascination with the revolutionary body without the disgust that shadows the monstrous Villa caricature. Jack London's story "The Mexican" allegorizes the revolution as an international boxing match in Los Angeles, fought before a corrupt Anglo referee, between a youth known only as "the Mexican" and an Irish-American brawler. The Mexican's triumph emerges in his ability to resist both the corruption of the law (embodied by the referee), the hostility of the "innocent" bystanders (the audience howling for blood), and the brutality of his opponent to score a revolutionary victory on U.S. soil. The Mexican's physical strength, here, is resolutely chaste and motivated—his body is an instrument of the revolution. In "Memoir of a Proud Boy," Carl Sandburg imagines the death of an Anglo-American volunteer in Villa's army. The boy represents the links of solidarity between the western U.S. working class and the Mexican campesino, and his death proves the remoteness of both from the eastern elites of an U.S. culture industry that would turn Villa's campaign into a sentimental romance. The dead volunteer is a young poet, miner, and idealist "with no mother but Mother Jones," Sandburg writes. He "went to Chihuahua, forgot his old Scotch name, / Smoked cheroots with Pancho Villa / And wrote letters of Villa as a rock of the people." The boy is shot dead on a dusty road, where his corpse rots as a boy throws stones to keep the pigs away: "There is drama in that point / . . . the boy and the pigs. / Griffith would make a movie of it to fetch sobs. / Victor Herbert would have the drums whirr / In a weave with a high fiddle-string's single clamor."[54] Sandburg depicts the Mexican Revolution as pure "drama" best understood in contrast to a bourgeois

United States where only cheap sentiment remains—like the dramas D. W. Griffith, producer of *The Life of General Villa,* churned out "to fetch sobs." The drama bowdlerized in cinema melodramas and Tin Pan Alley songs remains in places like Chihuahua and the mining camps of Montana: the uneven places of the world, including those of the United States. For Sandburg and London, the revolution is a body, sometimes broken and sometimes indestructible, that inhabits the same temporal frame and even the same territory as the "modern" United States. More commonly, however, the embodiment of revolutionaries like Villa simply fixed him as a monstrous anachronism not fully assimilated into modern life, but not yet fully disowned. These representations of revolution and the "passions" that provoke it are involved in a dialectical contest with U.S. self-understandings: when Americans look south, they are usually looking at themselves.

Cuba: Solidarity and the Revolutionary Body

Sandburg and London use the Mexican revolutionary body as a symbol of conviction and strength, the irreducible sign of a radical desire elsewhere trivialized as sentimental romance. The 1959 Cuban Revolution refined many of the revolutionary signifiers that we have seen above. Images of Fidel Castro and Che Guevara have now come to serve as icons of a revolutionary kitsch from a global "1960s," but they also circulated in the United States as part of a longer mass-cultural tradition of revolutionary Latin American masculinity that arguably began with Villa. In his work on the image of the Cuban Revolution in U.S. culture of the 1960s, Van Gosse has theorized solidarity as a component of what he calls "prepolitical" forms of identification. Foregrounding the often forgotten revolutionary enthusiasm of the postwar liberal left in the first two years of the Cuban Revolution, Gosse writes that "'politics,' so-called, stem as much from crises of identity that are real conditions of everyday life—of masculine solidarity and anxiety, for instance—as from consciously ideological intent and geopolitical and political-economic necessity."[55] To many sympathizers in the United States, the young guerillas who rode into Havana in 1959 were the image of charismatic rebellion, drawing upon nostalgic fantasies of the U.S. past as well as more modern middle-class fantasies of rebellion and adventure. Norman Mailer, for example, embraced Castro and Ernest Hemingway as complementary, paired figures of historical renewal and political promise. In his notorious essay "The White Negro," Mailer had defined this sense of radical possibility as "the Hip," a posture and mood of rebellion based on Mailer's reading of African American jazz style. Describing the United States' metaphorical flesh, Mailer writes, "A stench of fear has come out of every pore of American life, and we suffer from a collective failure of nerve."[56] Note, in the central metaphor of the United States as a squalid, malodorous body, how the bodies of men of color return as the imaginative site of political radicalism and reinvigoration, from the active "nerves" out to the nervous pores.

In the postwar era that Mailer saw as paralyzed by paranoia and isolation, political transformation could only be imagined taking place in and through the body. Gosse suggests this critique is not necessarily either reactionary or apolitical. Rather, it can be a nascent form of political consciousness. "At a time of no politics," Gosse writes, "the 'political' could at first be reclaimed only as the 'personal,' and so, at first, solidarity with the Cuban rebellion could express itself only in the most subjective terms."[57] In his study of Beat culture's encounter with the Cuban Revolution, Todd Tietchen adds that political mobilization in Cuba exposed, in turn, the political limitations of the Beat movement's subjective values of spontaneity and subcultural rebellion.[58] Amiri Baraka (then Leroi Jones) drew this conclusion in "Cuba Libre," his first-person 1960 essay about a U.S. delegation to revolutionary Cuba. Jones's essay is an introspective account of a sometimes cathartic collective experience in which he describes himself surrounded at all times by a crush of other people, few of whom are ever named. It explores the "subjective terms" in which he first grasped Cuba's revolutionary enthusiasm, and self-consciously critiques the bourgeois subjectivism of those very terms. "The idea of 'a revolution' had been foreign to me," writes Jones. Using the Spanish term for North American to emphasize the chastened sense of national self-awareness the trip has given him, Jones goes on: "It was one of those 'romantic' and/or hopeless ideas that we Norteamericanos have been taught since public school to hold up to the cold light of 'reason.'" His trip to a political rally in the Sierra Maestra leads him to compare rebel "beards," who simply affect cultural radicalism without any real political convictions, and revolutionary *barbudos,* who manage both (a comparison that again, however, understands both as implicitly masculine pursuits). "The rebels among us," Jones says, "have become merely people like myself who grow beards and will not participate in politics. Even the vitality of our art is like bright flowers growing up through a rotting carcass," he concludes, invoking yet another bodily metaphor for the counterrevolutionary United States.[59] In a March 1961 dispatch from Cuba for the democratic socialist magazine *Liberation,* Lawrence

Ferlinghetti likewise slammed the solipsism of rebels without causes in the United States. He recounts a conversation about the Beats with the Cuban poet Pablo Armando Fernández, who "read a lot of Kerouac and others and dug their weird dissent," Ferlinghetti says, "but has lately gotten disillusioned with them since they won't come far enough out of their private lives and commit themselves." Ferlinghetti then adds a parenthetical indictment of Kerouac's suburban self-involvement: "(Before I left the States, Kerouac told me on phone from Long Island: 'I got my own Revolution out here—the American Revolution.')"[60] And while the Cuban revolution could represent a homosocial space of revolutionary fantasy to sympathizers like Mailer, the United States' developmentalist alternatives to Cuban socialism—like Kennedy's Alliance for Progress and the Peace Corps—also drew on their own "logics of desire and intimacy," Molly Geidel writes, countering the revolutionary with their own hero figure. As she argues, "American social scientists . . . articulated and assuaged their own anxieties about the affluent, atomizing, repressive society of the 1950s by creating intimate yet hierarchical masculine fantasy spaces of development while also offering to cooperative 'underdeveloped' nations and populations a homosocial vision of belonging." One of these "fantasy spaces," the Peace Corps, was embodied in a heroic, typical male volunteer, devoted not to revolution but to development—less *barbudo* than "beard," to borrow Baraka's taxonomy. Yet as Geidel argues, liberal development programs and "militant solidarity practice" were mutually, if contentiously, constitutive," drawing on similar rhetorics of seduction and revitalization centered on heroic male figures. (Sargent Shriver's taxonomy was, of course, unlike Baraka's: his analog for the Peace Corps volunteer was the nineteenth-century pioneer, Geidel explains. The Corps would resurrect a "pioneering spirit" in an affluent society gone "soft."[61])

Cuba's official veneration of the charismatic male *barbudo* combined a homophilic celebration of the male revolutionary body with an official homophobia. Allen Ginsberg reportedly learned this lesson during his 1965 trip to the island, when he pointed out the latent homoeroticism of the Cuban revolutionary vanguard, personified by young *revolutionaries* like Guevara, Castro, and Camilo Cienfuegos. Accounts of his transgression vary, but Ginsberg told an interviewer in 1972 that "the worst thing I said was that I'd heard, by rumor, that Raul Castro was gay. And the second worst thing I said was that Che Guevara was cute." Ginsberg's impolitic remarks, he said, resulted in expulsion from the country.[62] The tension between official codes of revolutionary sexual morality and the "subjective" terms of solidarity also plagued the Venceremos Brigades, the U.S.-based solidarity organization that in 1969 started bringing U.S. leftists to aid in in the sugar harvest. That year, Fidel Castro had mobilized the country for a record ten-million-ton sugar harvest. Whatever contributions these inexperienced cane-cutters made to the failed national crusade for the "ten million," the trip's primary objective was of course political.[63] In published accounts of *brigadistas*, the work of solidarity is meant to bridge the psychic barriers between the first and third worlds. The means of transgressing this psychic boundary, however, are physical—the manual labor of cutting cane. As an introductory essay to one collection of Venceremos Brigade testimonies, the project was framed in Guevarist terms as part of the moral transformation of alienated North American radicals into socialist revolutionaries no longer motivated by material incentives or competition. "The Venceremos Brigade has given the movement a unique opportunity," the editors wrote, "a chance to come together in an 'ordinary' revolutionary situation and see if it is possible for American radicals, with all of their hangups, to realize Che Guevara's concern that revolutionaries 'must struggle every day so that their love of living humanity is transformed into concrete deeds, into acts that will serve as an example, as a mobilizing factor.'"[64] Principally, these hangups constituted a resistance to hard manual labor; racial or ethnic prejudice, specifically a reluctance by white radicals to follow orders from people of color; and egotism or individualism (on this last, the brigade took the rather extreme step of forbidding *brigadistas* from staging competitive games to make the cane-cutting go faster). This sort of class-based self-critique has much to recommend it; unlike much of what we have already seen thus far, here are Anglo-Americans granting to Latin Americans the respect of political leadership. But it also attributes a uniformity of material comfort (and thus psychic hangups) to North Americans and psychic health (and thus material discomfort) to Cubans, an equation that plays into notions of sexual "deviance" and normativity associated with each. The mislaid critique of "egoism" led at least one participant to unnecessary anguish. "I cannot sustain any sort of energy level and I need the times I am depressed to collect again the energy for another struggle," Frances Holt confessed. "Is Communism simply an act of will?"[65] Her struggle to account politically for her depression indicates a tautological problem in understanding revolution in such moralistic terms. For how can socialism ever come to the United States if the revolution in values it requires can only be experienced under socialism?

The brigade's understanding of the relationship between physical labor and political subjectivity played upon the association between radicalism and charismatic heterosexual masculinity, which the FBI exploited in its efforts to harass the group. The Cuban revolutionary leadership made similar associations, of course, as the notorious UMAP (Military Units to Aid Production) camps showed. The pretense of the UMAP camps was to rehabilitate through labor gay or other gender nonconforming Cuban citizens: "individuals whose attitudes and behavior were perceived as being nonconformist, self-indulgent, and unproductive," as the historian Ian Lumsden writes.[66] Ian Lekus's discussion of queer politics and homophobia in the Venceremos Brigade argues that it operated under homophobic assumptions about Cuba, in which "the nascent gay liberation movement in the United States represented an unacceptable, imperialist challenge."[67] Lekus argues that in this context, homosexuality was framed within the Cuba solidarity movement as a white, bourgeois, first-world problem. He records the story of an African American man, later unmasked as an FBI provocateur, who perpetrated violent attacks on white gay *brigadistas* to sow discord within the group: one member recalls that the FBI was very canny, "because nobody could cause problems more than an FBI plant who was a Third World person in that kind of environment."[68] These dangers derived in part from a gendered, Guevarist political ideal of physical hardship and self-abnegation. If the politics of solidarity also involve the embodiment of revolution as a masculinist passion, then this desire *for* revolutionary passion was always shadowed, as with Villa, by its estrangement as a "third-world" characteristic.

"A Man in the Street with a Gun": Photography and the Repertoire of Revolutionary Gestures

A man in the street with a gun was the most vulnerable act,
and yet a tremendous affirmation, so if I made an image, I frame it,
I saw it as a heroic moment.

—Susan Meiselas, *Pictures from a Revolution*

This opposition between an ethic of austere, typically masculine authenticity and a sentimental, feminized self-indulgent bourgeois culture continued after the height of the New Left and its early embrace of revolutionary Cuba. This interpretive framework was amplified, as it had been since Villa's day, by the visual technologies of representing the revolutionary body. By the time Managua fell to the Nicaraguan revolutionaries of the Frente Sandinista de Liberation Nacional (FSLN) in 1979, these technologies were themselves the subject of metafictional commentary. Not only were Villa, Castro, and Sandino "man's men," but the men photographing them were as well.

Journalist protagonists have had a prominent place in popular films about Latin American revolution and counterrevolution, like *Under Fire* (dir. Roger Spottiswoode, 1983), set in 1979 in Nicaragua, *Salvador* (dir. Oliver Stone, 1986), set during the civil war there, and *Missing* (dir. Costa Gavras, 1982), about Pinochet's Chile, as well as films from elsewhere in the third world, like *The Killing Fields* (dir. Roland Joffé, 1984), set in communist Kampuchea. The journalist, and especially the photographer, serves a convenient ideological role as truth-teller and surrogate for a virtuous audience insulated from the terror on screen. The war between El Salvador's FMLN guerillas and the U.S.-sponsored military regime; the Guatemalan insurgency against that country's military tyranny; the Honduran dictatorship; and the Sandinista Revolution and the long "Contra" war that followed: all of these became diffused, as Neil Larsen writes, into a familiar visual repertoire of terror and destitution. As he argues, the naturalist conventions of the journalistic genre emphasize the sensational violence of modern warfare. At the same time, central to these films about journalists is a suspicion of the sensationalism that occasions the narrative. In *Salvador*, for example, this suspicious posture frames representation as inevitably deceptive, either in the form of mainstream U.S. journalists' disinformation or in the case of one character, a photographer who fanatically aspires to emulate Robert Capra by capturing the iconic snapshot that will sum up the war. The result, argues Larsen, is that despite the truth-telling posture of the journalist in films like *Salvador*, revolutionary change here is reframed as an ahistorical abstraction, as the tragedy and terror that cannot be made legible narratively or in images.[69] Like the make-believe Central American revolutions of the 1910s and 1920s, where Charley Chase and Captain Macklin found redemption, Stone's 1980s Central America serves as the background for the personal revolution of the rejuvenated U.S.-born protagonist. Revolutions become a third-world export to be consumed by a U.S. audience long since accustomed, in the post-Vietnam era, to associating tropical landscapes with this visual repertoire of terror and violence.

The visual archive of Latin American revolution in the twentieth century has been refined even further by two photographs of Guevara. The first is the "Heroic Guerilla" picture taken in Havana in 1960 by the Cuban photographer Alberto Korda, which has crossed the globe and been reproduced on all manner of commercial products. The heroic subject is carefully cropped so that his torso and face fill the frame, with a gray sky behind him serving as a blank background, devoid of any geographic or culturally specific signifiers; his smooth, dark windbreaker, zipped up to the neck, helps grant the image the idealized, almost sanitized austerity that distinguished Guevara's reputation for revolutionary morality and at the same time also invites a viewer to imaginatively inhabit his place. The second such photo is the snapshot of his corpse, taken by an unknown Bolivian soldier after the defeat of Guevara's ill-fated guerilla campaign there in 1967. John Berger discusses the importance of Guevara's body as revolutionary example in his well-known reading of the photographs. The Korda photo, he argues, contains a gesture of revolutionary virtue that can be imitated and admired—hence its wide circulation as the image of internationalism. In contrast to the clean simplicity of Korda's photo, though, the image of Guevara's corpse is cluttered: several soldiers idle around a table, upon which Guevara's emaciated, shirtless body is laid, his eyes staring lifelessly at the ceiling. Depending on who looks, the autopsy photo offers either decisive evidence of the futility of revolution or evidence of a revolutionary life faithfully followed to one of its two possible conclusions, as Guevara himself had written—victory or death.[70] Berger, noting the tableau's resemblance to Rembrandt's painting *The Anatomy Lesson of Professor Tulp,* observes that unlike a painting, which "we can regard . . . as almost complete in itself," a photograph takes its meaning from the multiple and changing ways in which it circulates. The autopsy photograph therefore makes a unique demand on the viewer. "In face of this photograph we must either dismiss it or complete its meaning for ourselves," Berger writes. "It is an image which, as much as any mute image ever can, calls for action." The stark image of a broken body is crucial to this demand, Berger writes, because it makes "actual" the possibility of death that grants a revolutionary life its moral justification.[71] This body demands that we, the sympathetic viewers, be willing to take its place.

As the career of Korda's most famous photograph shows, however, this identification is often not so demanding. Instead, it can position revolutionary movements as the product of singular, charismatic leaders living in heroic times. In a brief essay on the work of Susan Meiselas, the great U.S. photographer of the Nicaraguan Revolution of 1979–90, Diana Taylor writes that her photographs of Sandinista fighters invite the viewer to identify with the "powerful, recognizable, and quotable social gestures that performed the revolutionary hope of the late 1950s,

'60s, and '70s throughout Latin America. Youthful Davids throughout the region fought to unseat a continent of authoritarian Goliaths backed by the U.S. military and economic forces."[72] By "social gestures" Taylor refers to Brecht's notion of quotable, nonvocal instances of socially significant communication. His most famous example is the moment in *Mother Courage and Her Children* when the title character, suffering the loss of her son and unable to speak lest she condemn one of her other children, turns to the audience and emits a silent scream.[73] *Gestus* is Brecht's term for the combination of physical gestures that reveal a character's social relations—the social origins and effects of an individual's suffering and struggle. Instead of treating revolutionary action as solitary, singular heroism, Meiselas's photographs treat the Sandinista insurgency as inherently social, partly just by presenting revolutionary acts—isolated in time and space though they are in the photographic frame—as both collaborative in execution and open-ended in their result. Despite Meiselas's interest in the bare simplicity of "a man in the street with a gun," as she put it in her documentary film *Pictures from a Revolution* (dir. Susan Meiselas, 1991), one always learns from her pictures that that man, or woman, is never alone. One such photograph of a single man with a rifle—captioned "Popular forces begin final offensive in Masaya, June 8, 1979"—presents an FSLN guerilla gesturing to unseen comrades out of the frame. His face is blurred and partially obscured by his signaling arm; we may admire his bravery, even identify with it and hope to emulate it, but the man himself—like his comrades—is opaque to us. Another of Meiselas's pictures emphasize how this revolutionary *gestus* relied as much on what is shown as on what is hidden, on the anonymity as much as the open display of the unadorned body. Her photograph for the cover of the *New York Times Magazine* of July 30, 1978, depicted three young revolutionaries training with practice bombs, looking directly into the camera while wearing masks typically used for an indigenous cultural festival. The masks hide the revolutionaries' identity from the National Guard and curious metropolitan readers alike.[74]

Unlike the Korda photo of Guevara, where the image's sparse visual details and lack of context allow a viewer to project himself onto its vision of a heroic future, Meiselas's images are full of movement and often crowded, with people, blood, and the detritus of both combat and the consumer quotidiana of postmodern Managua. In what is probably her most famous photograph from Nicaragua, a young, bearded man in jeans, an olive-green shirt, and a beret hurls a Molotov cocktail at

"Sandinistas at the walls of the Estelí National Guard headquarters." This is the iconic photo of Pablo Arauz, also known as "Molotov Man." From Meiselas's book *Nicaragua,* 1981. (Susan Meiselas/Magnum Photos)

an unseen enemy as a crucifix swings from his neck, its angle aligned with the burning bottle in his hand. The young soldier's beard and beret evokes Guevara, who had already passed into myth; the Sandinista is also positioned at the center of the frame with a grey, cloudy sky behind him, just like the "Heroic Guerilla." The man is not alone, however, and as the eye moves from his head down to the ground we see not only the two soldiers at his side, but the sandbags and bullet casings that interrupt the clean simplicity of the top half. Even his uniform transforms along the vertical axis—his jeans belong to the same late-1970s international consumer culture as the soda bottle in his hand. The viewer's eye is drawn to the Pepsi logo on the Molotov cocktail burning in his hand, an ironic sign of U.S. hegemony now repurposed as an anti-imperialist weapon. The heroism of the picture's top half contrasts with this quotidian realism on its lower half, and the Guevarist romance degrades as the viewer's eye moves downward. The weaponized Pepsi bottle and the rage on the man's face are full of danger and possibility: he may have hit (or missed) his target, or he may have been dead only moments after her shutter closed. A viewer, therefore, cannot overlook the dangerous circumstances in which these insurgent gestures take place, and the moment in time, full of possibility, hope, danger, courage, and fear in which they took place.

Performance, Taylor writes elsewhere, underscores a problem of archival instability that the Nicaraguan experience makes poignantly clear in other ways: the body of Augusto Sandino, the revolution's namesake, was never found after his capture and execution, a fact that made him paradoxically ever-present as a martyr and symbol. And one of the most popular counterinsurgency tactics of the Anastasio Somoza dictatorship was "disappearing" its enemies, kidnapping them and disposing of their bodies in secret. How does one record and make use of a past that you know is there, but that has been made forcibly to vanish? Such socially significant gestures belong to what Taylor calls the performative category of the "repertoire," which differs from the printed, written, and recorded media of the archive in that it "enacts embodied memory—performances, gestures, orality, movement, dance, singing—in short, all those acts usually thought of as ephemeral, non-reproducible knowledge."[75] The embodied nature of this knowledge, she continues, makes the past "available as a political resource in the present." Meiselas's work in Sandinista Nicaragua is partisan in its desire to be a political resource and "ephemeral" in its refusal of narrative to easily translate the gestures she captures into a stable and reproducible political or aesthetic meaning. Her photographs are remarkable for vivid gestures that showcase a popular irruption by the scorned, invisible masses into a national politics that always excluded and degraded them. They are also remarkable for what they leave out: faces hidden or bodies destroyed, like a mutilated torso in a roadside body dump or the wall graffiti that makes a poignant, enraged, anonymous demand: "Donde está Norman Gonzales? que contesta la dictadura" (Where is Norman Gonzales? let the dictatorship answer.)

Her pictures also lack the narrative content that comes so often in documentary photography from ironic juxtaposition or captioning. As an example: one photograph depicts three guerillas behind a barricade, two of them crouching in active combat against an unseen enemy, and one standing upright, calmly playing a clarinet. What does this image mean? Is this an allegory of "bread and roses," the importance of culture in revolutionary struggle? Is it absurd, the kind of improbable moment that indicates that a profound social upheaval is underway? Or is it simply uninterpretable? Meiselas interviews one of the two crouching combatants in *Pictures from a Revolution,* in which she revisits the subjects of

"Sandinista barricade during last days of fighting in Matagalpa." From Meiselas's book *Nicaragua,* 1981. (Susan Meiselas/Magnum Photos)

her pictures after the FSLN's 1990 electoral defeat. The soldier explains in the film that Meiselas's photograph was taken just after Somoza had fled the country. Yet die-hard *somocistas* fought on, obfuscating the moment of victory: the revolution had triumphed, but the war continued. It was thus an ambiguous moment of celebration and combat, a document of a peculiar moment in time that also anticipates the years of bitter conflict that awaited the revolutionaries, for whom the war with the Contras and their sponsors in the United States government never ceased. In keeping with the elegiac tone of her film, Meiselas recounts the photo as a document of a moment in time whose primary characteristic was uncertainty, and whose primary protagonists were individual bodies that stood for something, in a double sense: as symbols of revolution, but also as hopeful builders of a better nation themselves. The so-called Molotov Man, who became an iconic, endlessly reproduced image of revolutionary courage, had a name: Pablo Arauz. He survived the revolution and told Meiselas after the FSLN defeat in 1990 that despite all the setbacks, "My conscience is Sandinista until death."[76] Through their careful concentration on the vulnerable body, Meiselas's photographs capture this conviction and sense of possibility legible in these embodied gestures, significant in a war in which physical disappearance was one of the Somoza regime's most formidable weapons of terror. Her humble subjects, unlike most of the Latin American figures that we have explored in this chapter, are allowed to appear, not as projections of an Anglo-American self, nor as monstrous fantasies of marginal "others." They are, instead, the courageous and hopeful protagonists of their own unfinished story.

Coda

The Places of the "Third World" in Contemporary U.S. Culture

THE PLACES of this book's writing have been of utmost importance for me. The local senses of a place, shaped as they sometimes imperceptibly are by the global and regional scales of uneven development and capital accumulation, have both shaped and sometimes undermined the national fantasies I have attempted to trace here. The work that became this book began in New York City with its indispensable archives and its indelible (though many have tried to elide it) Latin American history. But the notion of "underdevelopment" as a comparative, ideological, and U.S. concept, rather than just a national, empirical, and foreign one, took shape in the aftermaths of Hurricane Katrina in New Orleans and Fordism in Detroit. Underdevelopment, as I hear it most often today in the United States, is a synonym for "decline": rather than a belated state of social and economic progress elsewhere, it is an arrested state of progress interrupted or reversed here. Its power comes from the analogy thus made between the world of progress in the global North and the misery thought to reside in the South.

In the aftermath of Hurricane Katrina, as I sat in my apartment in Queens watching news of the calamity playing on the TV, the only way, it seemed, for popular journalism to render the scale of destruction was by analogy to underdeveloped nations abroad. The comparisons, in all their crudeness, had a grain of historical truth. New Orleans has been and is still a cultural and economic transit point of the Americas; its history is a Caribbean one. Yet the narrative of the disaster that quickly emerged was that of a "national tragedy" taking place in a "great American city." So the comparisons of New Orleans to the "third world" illuminated little about New Orleans's transnational history but revealed much about a U.S. nationalism that denies that such a history exists. Because there was seemingly no domestic equivalent that would make the tragedy intelligible, many journalists resorted to analogies to a generalizable abstraction called "the third world." The New Orleans I saw on TV and read about in the press that summer was "America's third world"; it was compared variously to Baghdad, to Sierra Leone, to Congo, and to Haiti, its residents, in turn, compared to the "refugees" thought in the United States to be the unique problem of such places.[1]

The first use of the term "third world" was probably the Frenchman Alfred Sauvy's in August 1952, in the magazine *L'Observateur:* "This ignored, exploited, and distrusted Third World, just like the Third Estate, wants to be something," he wrote. In Sauvy's usage, the ordinal number "third" directly referenced the French Revolution, suggesting a political rather than pathological understanding of the anticolonial movements mobilizing this "third world." As Todd Shepard argues, however, the term was also from the beginning deeply racialized, connected to a pseudoscientific, anti-cosmopolitan view of racially distinct populations linked to distinct geographies, a version of which we have seen in the environmental determinists of chapter 2. Thus, even though the "third-world" idea was successfully reclaimed as a *political* identity of cross-racial anticolonial unity, the concept also has a colonial, racist lineage, which it has never entirely lost.[2]

For Vijay Prashad, for whom the third world was (in the past tense) "not a place but a project," its importance lay in its expression of a political and secular desire, by a union of the former colonial peoples for a more equal distribution of the world's material and intellectual wealth.[3] "Third world" had a political valence less present in cartographic terms like "global South," and this geographic unspecificity was the point. The "third world" was everywhere, and it therefore offered the possibility of uniting disparate peoples divided by language, race, and religion under a common secular banner of social progress. This was the vision famously captured by Richard Wright in *The Color Curtain,* his report from the 1955 Bandung conference of postcolonial nations: "The despised, the insulted, the hurt, the dispossessed—in sort, the underdogs of the human race were meeting. Here were class and racial and religious consciousness on a global scale. Who had thought of organizing such a meeting? And what had these nations in common? Nothing, it seemed to me, but what their past relationship to the Western world had made them feel."[4] Wright, in his typically dialectical framing, sees the "third world" as a negation of the idea of "the West," formed in opposition to it and its exploitation by it. This formation, as Prashad says later, is nothing *but* a political project, since the countries meeting at Bandung had no filiative loyalties of race, language, or religion in common.

Wright's moment, the Bandung moment, has passed. What has replaced it is less clear. More recently, some critics, like the Marxist economist Aijaz Ahmad, have argued that the term "third world" is empirically inaccurate, that "we live not in three worlds but one"; dividing the world into three obscures the systematic networking of global capitalism.[5] Others, like Arif Dirlik, concede the term's empirical weakness but want to retain the political project central to the "third world" as a revolutionary banner. Most important for my discussion here—which centers on the way in which "third world" and related terms are invoked to describe U.S. imaginings of "underdevelopment" in a post-Cold War moment of austerity and economic crisis—is what Dirlik describes as the term's "residual" character, which summons the long history I have traced in this book. "The Third World was a residual category," says Dirlik, "a dumping ground for all who did not qualify as capitalist or socialist. But the idea had its lineage. This was the world that Marxist radicals had described in the years after World War I as the world of colonialism and semi-colonialism. It was the world that a hegemonic social science emerging in the 19th century alongside capitalism and colonialism had viewed as the world of primitives and of civilisations 'vegetating in the teeth of time.'"[6] The emergence of a socialist decolonization in the interwar period made the "third world" a challenge to but not a clean break with these earlier imaginative geographies, with their meaning of cultural belatedness. Like "development" and "underdevelopment," the third world's historical specificity as a progressive political project tends to obscure this longer history. Indeed, underdevelopment and other terms of geographic and temporal difference in widespread use—"refugee," "third world," and "banana republic"—inevitably recapitulate older cultural geographies even as they invent new forms for them.

"Refugee" became the source of a significant controversy in the aftermath of Hurricane Katrina. As a term reserved in colloquial American English for displaced people from the global South, the term "refugee" carried an implicit racial meaning when U.S. journalists used it to identify New Orleans's displaced residents. Since most were African Americans in a historically impoverished region of the United States, the comparison to the third-world "refugee" was widely regarded as a slur, a rhetorical reinscription of the second-class national status the hurricane winds first laid bare. As I argued in the Introduction, the controversy over describing displaced New Orleans residents as "refugees" from an "underdeveloped country" showed how the term's racial and national associations outstripped any literal correctness it had. On one level, if "refugee" merely refers to someone displaced from her home by disaster or political circumstances, the term is obviously denotatively correct in an example like post-Katrina New Orleans. The fact that "refugee" is so often used for transnational displacement then seems like an arbitrary distinction—as if only military conflicts between nation-states can produce involuntary exile, as if cross-border exile was the only kind. Of course, the controversy in New Orleans revolved around the cultural and national *connotations* of the term in a U.S. racial and regional context. Here, the word emphasized the exclusion of Black southerners from the privileged, self-reliant "nation of futurity" to which others, safe in suburban cul-de-sacs and coastal cities, belonged without controversy. "Refugees," by contrast, reside in underdeveloped places elsewhere.

The logic of transnational analogy, as I described it in chapter 2, typically has worked the other way around—Latin American otherness is made legible by comparison to the familiar, modern United States. At the same time, the internal uneven development of the United States can be made legible—and, paradoxically, exceptional—by comparing it to underdevelopment abroad (hence the repeated invocation of New Orleans as both a city of "refugees" and a "great American city"). In the early Cold War, the construction of systemic poverty as "underdevelopment"—and therefore foreign—led many liberals, even before Katrina, to make the kinds of analogies between the impoverished urban "ghetto" and the underdeveloped world that have often characterized coverage of post-2006 New Orleans and post-2008 Detroit. See, for example, Jane Jacobs's classic critique of urban renewal, *The Death and Life of Great American Cities,* which employs Cold War foreign aid as a metaphor for misbegotten slum "improvement" projects in East Harlem: "Much as the generosity of a rich nation might well extend massive aid to a deprived and backward country," she wrote, "into this district poured massive 'foreign' aid, according to decisions by absentee experts from the remote continent inhabited by housers and planners."[7] Jacobs, writing in the year of the Alliance for Progress, compares the aloof indifference of the urban planner and the cold war diplomat, but she also draws an analogy between the spaces trammeled by each. The recourse to national otherness to make sense of domestic inequality plays on the longstanding racialization of the urban ghetto, whether we are discussing Harlem, New Orleans, or, as we saw in chapter 3, the Lower East Side of a century ago.

These examples might suggest to a skeptical reader that "we" in the United States are not so different from "them" in Honduras, Haiti, or any other "deprived and backward" country of our collective national fantasies. New Orleans, after all, has been closer to Port-au-Prince and Havana than to Washington, DC, for most of its history. This was the reason, in the 1960s and 1970s, why radical college activists of color claimed the label of "third-world students," and why the Black Power movement located itself within a third-world context. Geoffrey Whitehall and Cedric Johnson argue that many hostile reactions to use of the term "refugee" in 2003 defended African American New Orleanians' industriousness and good citizenship against the implicit "third-world" comparison, an argument that they argue reflects the triumph of integrationist liberalism in civil rights discourse.[8] The framing of poverty and racism as "national" problems responsive to national relief institutions (rather than, say internationalist political movements) also reflects the similar construction of underdevelopment as a national problem responsive to nationally specific technical applications.[9] Lisa Marie Cacho's reading of the "refugee" trope argues that all the negative, "residual" connotations attached to "refugee" became transferred in mainstream media usage to the African American population of the Gulf Coast. The racial connotations of "third world" and "refugee" are bound up with the Caribbean and Latin American pathologies, like tropical "indolence," the zeal of the "revolutionist," and the violence of the bandit. As "refugee" becomes identified with color and rescue with whiteness, its use reinscribes the colonial meanings encoded in its history.[10] Nicole Waligora-Davis argues that even as "refugee" conveyed this racist ideological disposition to identify African Americans with criminality and helplessness, the term also expressed a "material reality" of social disenfranchisement. The "severed social relationships, the stripped political and legal privileges, the alienation from both the public sphere and the nation-state" were the painful meanings, she writes, "[that] these survivors refused, but what their experiences nonetheless evidenced."[11] This is one legacy of American exceptionalism that the "refugee" controversy makes clear: given the perception of refugees as "foreigners," it was difficult to find a national vocabulary for the uneven development that produced the domestic exiles of the Gulf Coast: all of our available terms, at least within the conventional vocabulary of liberal political discourse, were "foreign" ones.

Consider NPR correspondent Joe Mesca's chain of analogies in a report that focused both on the humanitarian crisis in New Orleans and the controversy over "refugee." Mesca defended the use of the term as affectively correct: that is, he did not use it in any politically or historically cogent way, but as a metonym that seemed to *feel* right in that time and place. In New Orleans, he wrote, "you couldn't help but think of Haiti or Kosovo." Note his self-exculpatory balance of a Caribbean and European comparison here, and his suggestion that his reaction was not ideological, but inevitable—you "couldn't help" but notice it. Mesca went on: "If you watched this situation on television, you might not realize how dirty and foul-smelling these people were. There was a reluctance on the part of the rescuers to touch the people. There was a total unwillingness to walk among them. The reaction was understandable. Many of the people they were trying to help had swum through sewage water to get here, and no one was showering anytime soon."[12] Mesca's anxious emphasis on his emotional response—disgust, the reluctance to touch or to approach the people, and so on—summons what Dirlik describes above as the colonial concept of the primitive that lurks amidst postcolonial invocations of the third-world "refugee." Of course, Mesca is sensitive enough to avoid this invocation directly, and so his most pointed observations are displaced onto "rescuers" or buried in unattributed passive constructions, as in "there was a total unwillingness to walk among them." Mesca's struggle to come up with frames of reference for homegrown forms of catastrophe shows how ideological are the concepts of the "underdeveloped," the "third world," and the "refugee," and how fantastic, therefore, is their presumption to always describe national spaces off of the United States' shores or in its past. To be a "refugee" means that wherever you stand physically, you reside in the "third world," that portion of humanity for whom natural disaster, violence, and corruption come, if not naturally, at least normally.

This book was mostly written in Detroit, where I moved in 2007, just before the foreclosure crisis further ravaged the economy of an already chronically depressed city. From the vantage point of Detroit the federal and state neglect of New Orleans never seemed so exceptional as to require international comparison—all I had to do to see something similar was step outside and look in virtually any direction. One of my neighbors in southwest Detroit, a native of central Mexico, told me a joke about his arrival in the city. He and his family had been living for several years in Orange County, California, but when the California exurbs grew too expensive, they followed a cousin and drove to Detroit, a city they had never seen and knew little about. Entering the city from the west on Interstate 94, their family's van would have sped through light traffic across the suburban sprawl that consumes most of southeast Michigan. Approaching the city, they might have glimpsed the smokestacks of Ford's River Rouge plant in Dearborn, still in operation but no longer the largest industrial facility on earth. And once they entered Detroit's west side on the sunken expressways that carve like canyons through the city, my neighbors would have passed some of the vacant houses, empty factories, and shuttered warehouses lining the streets above, their former tenants long since departed to suburbs, *maquilas,* or oblivion. The punch line to my friend's story was an ironic question: "Are we still in America?" he recalls nervously asking himself, laughing now at the memory, with a Detroiter's sense of self-deprecating sarcasm.

This anxious first impression of Detroit summons what Smith, elaborating upon Gunder Frank's phrase, calls the development of underdevelopment: an ongoing process of expansion and contraction that proceeds at the three major scales of capitalist organization: urban, regional, and global. As capital moves from one "developed" space to an "underdeveloped" one at another regional or national scale, seeking lower wages, more "flexible" labor laws, or some other geographical advantage, it underdevelops the spaces left behind. Even though this process takes place at multiple scales—Paul Clemens's recent book, which follows the detritus of a shuttered automobile factory from Detroit to industrial Brazil, Mexico, and India, traces this movement—we typically experience it at a single one, the place where we live or where the visual evidence, like ruined buildings and vacant streets, makes the strongest impression.[13] These ravaged urban and regional spaces can either represent or undermine a cognitive map of the "national" space of which they are a part: in my friend's case, the stark contrast between Detroit city and its suburbs called into question what he had always been told about the country. From a more provincial perspective, Detroit's poverty can easily be misunderstood as a local problem of the city's own making, an exception to rather than a reflection of the nation at large. One famous example of this perspective comes from Ze'ev Chafets, in his 1990 book *Devil's Night and Other True Tales of Detroit.* The book is mostly remembered for its use of a novel analogy: Detroit, wrote Chafets, has "all the trappings of a third-world city—showcase projects, an external enemy and the cult of personality" around its charismatic African American mayor, Coleman A. Young.[14] Black Detroit, just like post-Katrina New Orleans, became a third-world breach in a first-world country. The naïveté of Chafets's analogy is in part the subject of my neighbor's joke, which in addition to poking fun at the city's dereliction also mocked the optimistic expectations of his younger, newly arrived self. Detroit's poverty is of course perfectly "American." Yet this was also not "America"—the national fantasy that, for John O'Sullivan's age as much as for our own, "belongs to the future only."[15] In this way, the "development of underdevelopment" is also an ideological process, fabricating not just national space but our consciousness of how national space is made and unmade.

Scrutinizing U.S. conceptions of Latin American's uneven development requires what Heidi Tinsman and Sandhya Shukla rightly call "an insistence that we formulate questions that scrutinize the winner's terms and not begin the story at its end."[16] My claim that Latin American "underdevelopment" is the projection abroad of the United States' own uneven development excavates the colonial etymology of these terms, in their older forms and in some of their newest iterations. One such term, "banana republic," has recently emerged among liberal and conservative critics of the U.S. political establishment as a shorthand for the perceived insolvency, instability, and decline of the recessionary nation. "It is total confusion—a banana republic," said Rep. Peter King, Republican of New York, in response to a 2015 episode of political gamesmanship and dysfunction in the House of Representatives.[17] In a subtle variation, the 2016 campaign of Donald Trump was turning the "developed" United States into "bananalandia," one *Wall Street Journal* columnist argued, painfully attempting the xenophobic rhetorical feat of labeling the nativist candidate as a "Latin" politician.[18] Expanding Chafets's international analogy from an exceptional city to the country as a whole, Arianna Huffington's best-selling 2011 book *Third World America* denounced what its book jacket calls "our country's steady descent from 20th century superpower to backwater banana republic."[19] The *New York Times* compared the United States to a "banana republic" fourteen times in 2013; the pundit Nicholas Kristof uses the term almost as if it is a technical category of economic science when he writes that "the United States now arguably has a more unequal distribution of wealth than traditional banana republics like Nicaragua, Venezuela and Guyana."[20] The term "banana republic" comes from O. Henry's 1904 novel *Cabbages and Kings,* where he used it to describe a fictionalized version of Honduras. His coinage named what Kirsten Silva Gruesz describes as "a specific regional trope of comic ineptitude and political corruption" in the post-1898 U.S. imperium in Latin America. Unlike Huffington's apparent confidence that the United States really isn't—or shouldn't be—a "banana republic," Gruesz argues that the term is used in *Cabbages and Kings* not simply to mock Anchuria's tropical ineptitude, but rather to "suggest to

U.S. readers how they, too, are linked with it in a new world order."[21] The image of Latin American underdevelopment, in other words, reflects U.S. exceptionalism's short-circuitry, rather than its confident expression. In contemporary uses of the term, shaped as they are by a nostalgic memory of a Cold War U.S. world order, this linkage is often more hidden. Instead, the international analogies foreground racial and temporal meanings inherited from the colonial schemata of "advanced" and "backwards" peoples, the climatic hierarchy of "indolence" and "industry," and the modernist opposition of "tradition" and *techne*. With its slow transformation into a "traditional banana republic," the United States' confidence and privileged status is therefore in decline from its perceived glory days. Implicit in the accusation that the United States is a "banana republic," in other words, is a nostalgia for an imagined age of virtue and prosperity at home, and unquestioned dominance over the "real" banana republics abroad. Taken together, "third world" and "banana republic" summon fleeting impressions, as we have seen: bearded *comandantes*, "filthy" streets, alluring and available women, and in the case of bananas, the tropical plant that signifies both the vegetative beauty of countries known only for the fruit they grow as well as the vestigial cultural habits of the population that grows them. These impressions remind us, once again, of the first meaning of "underdeveloped" as a kind of *image-making*: an overexposed photographic plate that makes an image too brightly lit and with too little contrast to be discernible in any meaningful details.

Comparisons between the United States and "banana republics" also show how narratives and metaphors of historical time naturalize the spatial incongruities of capitalist development. This temporalization of geographical space reframes underdeveloped spaces as latecomers, relics, or ruins.[22] The popularity of these analogies to the global South in the post-2008 United States has increased as popular confidence in the United States' promise of futurity appears to be in danger; hence the outrage in books like Huffington's that the United States is abdicating a claim on the future. By focusing on normative, dominant conventions of U.S. representations of Latin America, I have been arguing that the imaginative geography of "underdevelopment" reveals the intimate entanglement of Latin America and the United States even as it presumes, as in the examples above, to name a clearly demarcated, even natural difference. I end this book, then, with four recent interventions—three literary, one political—that engage this contradictory history of the intimacy of the hemisphere and its manifestations in the present.

Take, for example, Jimmy Santiago Baca's "Invasions," an account of the southwestern landscape that works against the temporal framework of progress and nostalgia. In Baca's poem, the land is subdued by an illusory "peace" that buries its violent history. The Latino speaker describes himself as a descendant of Spanish *conquistadores*, Moors, and the Pecos that once called the area home. He fishes with store-bought bait, engaging in a mass-produced, recreational simulation of the subsistence labor of those ancestors. Baca is no Hemingway, though, seeking refuge from bourgeois propriety in angling rituals of laboring authenticity. Instead, his speaker reflects on the conquests buried in the landscape.

> Trout flails like a saber
> dangling from scabbard stringer
> tied to my belt,
> chop-whacking long haired weeds.
> Peace here now. Bones
> dissolved, weapons rusted.
> I stop, check my sneaker prints
> In moist shady bank.
> Good deep marks.[23]

The chain of metaphorical associations in this sequence is striking. Baca begins with the "good deep marks" his sneakers make in the soil, which he admires with a connoisseur's relish, disturbing in light of what they harken back to—he continues with the fish's "chop-whacking" in the weeds, the dying trout flailing on his belt like a sixteenth-century saber blade. These metaphorical wounds are made in land that contains a distant memory of the human history that has not yet faded into the riverbank and the terrible violence that has not yet been lost in the weeds. The poem considers the silence of the landscape as a natural "peace" as well as a product of the violent pacification of those that once inhabited it. The poem ends with the speaker scouting up an incline and surveying, "as my ancestors did," the development of the southwest by a "new invasion" of vacation homes and RVs.

Lorna Dee Cervantes's poem "Freeway 280" does something similar, imagining the "development" of San José, California, as a chronotope rather than a chronology, as Raúl H. Villa has argued.[24] The chronotope, writes Mikhail Bakhtin In *The Dialogic Imagination*, expresses "the intrinsic connectedness of temporal and spatial relationships that are artistically expressed in literature."[25] Like Baca, Cervantes understands the destruction of the southwestern "natural" environment not as a pastoral romance, but as historical excavation, one that challenges the "winner's terms" presupposed by most teleological chronologies. For Cervantes, the physical dismemberment of the landscape by urbanization summons the displacements of her predecessors by Anglo settlement. She writes:

> Las casitas near the gray cannery,
> nestled amid wild abrazos of climbing roses
> and man-high red geraniums
> are gone now. The freeway conceals it
> all beneath a raised scar.

The "raised scar" of the freeway means that the earth beneath is not a passive landscape that can be framed aesthetically, as with Humboldtian travelers, but an injured body that may repair but cannot erase its wounds. The poem continues by naming, in Spanish, the edible greens that flourish in the soil upturned by the freeway construction, and by crediting the labor of the "viejitas," the women that transform this waste into nourishment. What seems like a urban pastoral ends, however, with the speaker's confession that

> Once, I wanted out, wanted the rigid lanes
> to take me to a place without sun,
> without the smell of tomatoes burning.

This confession, of a desire to leave the "blighted" geography behind for cooler, straighter, more developed places, is then ambivalently rejected:

> Maybe it's here
> en los campos extraños de esta ciudad
> where I'll find it, that part of me
> mown under like a corpse
> or a loose seed.

The speaker does not quite repudiate her earlier contempt for the empty lot and its scavengers, acknowledging that it may still be there, like the corpses of the ancestors she wants to remember, or the serendipitous seeds that sustain her neighbors. Rather, the underdeveloped U.S. landscape is something uncanny. It is a place left "behind" as the future beckons on the freeway, a familiar part of her that she still recognizes as alien, just as these empty lots in ostensibly booming San José are "extraños," both "foreign" and "strange." Indeed, the phrase "los campos extraños de esta ciudad," like the poem's other Spanish words, is integrated without italics into the English grammar of the stanza. Yet it also stands out from the English surrounding it. In rendering this sentiment in Spanish, where "extraño" refers to both nationality and normativity, Cervantes identifies uneven urban development as seemingly "foreign," but in fact as comfortable in the soil of California as anywhere.[26]

Junot Díaz's 2007 novel *The Brief Wondrous Life of Oscar Wao* extends this uncanny sense of the United States as a Latino country and an unevenly developed one with a humor that turns the uncanny into common sense. Spanish and "Spanglish" vernacular are regularly interspersed throughout the text without warning, italicization, or translation, as if the narrator, a Dominican American man named Yunior, assumes that no reader should be foolish enough at this point to find this strange. Yet Yunior is also aware of the dissonance between his own common sense and the broader conventions of "American" (that is, U.S.) identity, which would treat the novel he is narrating as a minority report or as a magical realist fancy. The novel tells the story of Oscar, an ostracized, science-fiction-obsessed teenage son of a Dominican immigrant mother in deindustrializing Patterson, New Jersey. Oscar's family history of violence and pain extends deep from north Jersey to the cane fields of Hispaniola, a history, Yunior explains in an opening chapter that begins with Columbus. The "fukú," says Yunior, is a curse first brought to America with the Conquest that has endured in the perverse dictatorship of Rafael Trujillo, the Dominican Republic's ruthless U.S.-supported tyrant. Later infiltrating the battlefields of Vietnam to strike down U.S. soldiers, fukú is a legacy of imperial violence but also a weapon of its victims and their descendants. Yunior explains:

> But the fukú ain't just ancient history, a ghost story from the past with no power to scare. In my parents' day the fukú was real as shit, something your everyday person could believe in . . . in those elder days, fukú had it good; it even had a hypeman of sorts, a high priest, you could say. Our then dictator-for-life Rafael Leónidas Trujillo Molina. No one knows whether Trujillo was the Curse's servant or its master, its agent or its principal, but it was clear he and it had an understanding, that them two was *tight*.

Díaz also writes against the temporalization of space that consigns the "third world" *elsewhere* to a residual time *before*. The past of deindustrializing New Jersey is inseparable from that of the Dominican Republic, and the mythologies of the Antilles are New York's, too. "Why do you think the greatest power in the world lost its first war to a third-world country like Vietnam?" Yunior asks, invoking the "third-world country" insult ironically, tauntingly, identifying as he does with one.

He concludes, "That's right, folks. Fukú."[27] Indeed, fukú is precisely the kind of belief that would have been dismissed as residual "tradition" by Walter Rostow, an architect of the Vietnam War, that developmentalist catastrophe whose justifications and technologies, Díaz says, could not restrain the curse.

The intimacy of Latin America and the United States in Baca, Cervantes, and Díaz can refer to the impermeability of the national boundaries that separate the United States and Latin America—and the cultural knowledges, historical memories, family stories, sustaining traditions, and marvels (like Díaz's fukú) that bleed across its shifting, policed borders. As William McKinley used the term in the aftermath of the defeat of Spain in 1898, it meant something altogether different, of course. When he invoked the "ties of singular intimacy" that bound the United States to Cuba, he did so in a paternalistic fashion that framed the United States as a tutor and policeman, setting and guaranteeing the terms for Cuban development after its separation from the Spanish empire. Later, the unfolding of an "American Century" that made its debut in Cuba, Puerto Rico, and the Philippines retooled John O'Sullivan's ideal of the United States' "magnificent domain of space and time" for the twentieth century—claiming the future as the United States' own domain, but now extending it to others without O'Sullivan's territorial ambitions. U.S. dissidents in solidarity with the revolutionary Cubas of 1933 and 1959 have thus had to confront the fact that these "ties of singular intimacy" were also an imperial bind, John Gronbeck-Tedesco has written, "cut from a cloth stretching back generations."[28]

As I was completing this book, Cuba was the scene of a combined funeral and exorcism—Barack Obama's historic visit to the island in March 2016, where he declared his aim to "bury the last remnant of the Cold War in the Americas" and dispel its bitter spirit. (One might argue, here, that Cuba is in this way treated not as an archetype for a dominant U.S. image of Latin America, as I have suggested it is, but rather as an anachronism, a relic of a conflict finished everywhere else. Yet Central Americans, for example, might well ask when their Cold War will be buried—rumors of its death have been exaggerated before, and we should be skeptical this time, too.) Obama's conciliatory address in Havana's Gran Teatro, the climax to his state visit, felt like something new. Firstly, Obama conceded to revolutionary Cuba some of its most salient historical points about the United States—of an international history marked by exploitation and deceit rather than fraternity and trust. And he gave voice to the bound histories of Cuba and the United States, in families and friends dispersed across the post-1959 diaspora. Much of the rhetorical force of the speech turned on Obama's reframing of McKinley's paternalistic "intimacy" as fraternal "blood": "The United States and Cuba are like two brothers who've been estranged for many years, even as we share the same blood," Obama told his Havana audience, going on to point out that much of that "blood" ran through the veins of slaves and slave owners in both nations. "We both live in a new world, colonized by Europeans. Cuba, like the United States, was built in part by slaves brought here from Africa," Obama said. As Ada Ferrer writes in her account of the visit, this gesture from the president was a gesture of recognition across a long divide of history and of ignorance: "Obama seemed to be saying to Cubans of African descent, I see you, and I understand your centrality in the past and future of your country." It was an observation as striking—coming from a U.S. president—for what it recognized about Cuba as for the impolitic truths it conceded, via the medium of Cuba, about the United States' slave history.[29]

The move from "singular intimacy" to "the same blood" is not insignificant. But, is the difference more than rhetorical? "Intimacy" in the hemisphere has always been partly an ideological repositioning of inter-American conflict as "dialogue." This is undoubtedly true for Obama, who repeatedly turned to that word and to cognates like "debate" to describe the United States' contemporary relationship with Cuba. (As Ferrer points out, in the preparations for Obama's visit, the Cuban state played along, replacing politically combative propaganda billboards around the city with more innocuous slogans, like "Salud para todos" [Good health for all.]) As I argued in the Introduction, Latin America has also served as a mirror that reflects U.S. conceptions of itself. See, again, the "integrity of purpose" and "exercise of the highest wisdom" McKinley saw reflected in U.S. dealings with independent Cuba, and in Obama's case, the kind of open debate and free-wheeling "innovation" that, he claims, invigorate U.S. democracy and the U.S. economy and could do the same for Cubans. "Intimacy" functions in this way as a distorting mirror, but it can also reflect some discomfiting truths, as Ana Dopico points out. In Obama's case, she argues, what is reflected is a tangled history that U.S. politicians never want to concede. "By refusing paternalism, condescension and browbeating, by recognizing U.S. faults, and by underlining Cuban struggle and beauty too," Dopico argues, "the speech started pulling at the knots of shame and suspicion, and acknowledged instead a mutual mirroring, a necessary dialogue. Obama's speech summoned modesty and friendship, a wish to change the narrative and retell the story."[30] The figure in this reflection is, of course, also a Cuban-American one, and Obama's speech was in large part devoted to advancing vision of U.S. and Cuban nationhood in which both Cubans on the island and in the diaspora can recognize themselves. Therefore, the U.S. opening to Cuba is familiar, on the one hand, in that it extends our current episteme of progress—"innovation"—to a socialist nation that has not unleashed its full "potential," as the United States is presumably doing. On the other hand, we can see Cuba's entanglement with the United States acknowledged in a way it has not been before, at least from a U.S. politician.

Obviously, few would view this sort of conciliatory gesture of shared history and struggle without skepticism, even if many also view it with some hope. Oscar Wao's fukú will not be vanquished so easily, even by an exorcist as skilled as the U.S. president. It is, Díaz explains, an inter-American legacy that runs deep in the blood shed and shared by so many generations in the hemisphere. It is a legacy, moreover, that no people—no matter how self-consciously "advanced"—can outrun. Perhaps they should abandon the pretense. "It's perfectly fine if you don't believe in these 'superstitions,'" Díaz writes. "Because no matter what you believe, fukú believes in you."[31]

Notes

Introduction

1. Quijano and Wallerstein, "Americanity as a Concept," 549.
2. Grandin, "Liberal Traditions," 69.
3. See J. Park, *Latin American Underdevelopment*, 5, 198, which chronicles a pattern of "disdain toward the peoples and cultures of Latin America" as well as modernization theory's model of modernity; Pike, *United States and Latin America*, argues that the United States has positioned Latin America as the "state of nature" to the United States' modernity, an oversimplification of the history I will trace here; Streeby, *American Sensations*, 57–58, reads U.S. imperialist discourse in Latin America as "unstable," but only because the U.S. nation-state was; representations of Mexico, in her reading of popular 1848 war literature, seem to serve as a superstructural cultural fix for these internal contradictions.
4. William McKinley, "Third Annual Message," 5 Dec. 1899. Gerhard Peters and John T. Woolley, *The American Presidency Project*, http://www.presidency .ucsb.edu/ws/?pid=29540 (accessed 9 May 2014). Louis Pérez's work—especially *Cuba and the United States*, which draws on McKinley's quotation for its subtitle—has been foundational for reading the historical proximity and political interconnection of Cuba and the United States, against the Manichean divides mandated by the Cold War.
5. Eric Lott's argument about blackface minstrelsy is relevant here. He writes that in white working-class desire for Black cultural forms, a mix of racial and xenophobic animus emanates not only from "age-old racism" but from an "erotic economy of celebration and exploitation." White enforcement of racial cultural boundaries here are "less a sign of absolute white power and control than of panic, anxiety, terror, and pleasure" (Lott, *Love and Theft*, 6).
6. Karem, *Purloined Islands*, 4, 10.
7. See Lowe, *Intimacies*, 17–18. Lowe uses "intimacy" to mean geographic proximity across seemingly distant imperial and national boundaries and a "heuristic" for reading the production of modern forms of subjectivity. Her work

takes on more expansive geography than mine, but it is nonetheless relevant to my reading of "underdevelopment's" separation from the United States. Intimacy, she writes, affords a means to examine the separation of "modern spheres of social life" from those "that are forgotten, cast as failed or irrelevant because they do not produce 'value' legible within modern classifications."

8. Smith, *Uneven Development*, 199–203.

9. Nisbet, *Social Change*, 200–201.

10. Benson, "The Economic Advancement of Under-developed Areas," in *Economic Basis of Peace*, 10.

11. Myrdal, *Rich Lands and Poor*, 7–8.

12. On the term's revival in the contemporary right, see Landes, *Wealth and Poverty of Nations*, 5–7; Lawrence Harrison's use in *Underdevelopment Is a State of Mind*, 1–17, harkens back to the colonial vocabulary of "backwardness." As a footnote on p. 17 helpfully explains, "'development' and 'progress' are used interchangeably in this book." See also David Brooks, "The Underlying Tragedy," *New York Times*, 14 Jan. 2010; Lawrence Harrison again, "Haiti and the Voodoo Curse," *Wall Street Journal*, 5 Feb. 2010, which cites *voudoun* religion as one of Haiti's "progress-resistant cultural influences." Observe the irony of the second article's title, which invokes the notion of a "curse" in order to criticize another culture's silly superstitions. On the term's popularity on the left in the era of dependency theory, see Arndt, *Economic Development*, 170–71. "Neo-Marxists, in Latin America and elsewhere," Arndt writes, "thought much more about underdevelopment than about development."

13. Rodney, *How Europe Underdeveloped Africa*, 22–28; Frank, *Development of Underdevelopment*; Escobar, *Encountering Development*, 47, echoes Gunder Frank's usage in writing that for all its work, development has mostly succeeding in developing "a type of underdevelopment that has been, for the most part, politically and technically manageable."

14. For two critiques of dependency theory from the left, see Laclau, "Feudalism and Capitalism in Latin America"; and Larrain, *Theories of Development*, who regards it as too abstract and too simplified a model, which "may induce the mistaken belief that capitalism in the centre has finally overcome all its contradictions and that it is only in the peripheral systems that contradictions, and the possibilities of socialism, can be found" (145).

15. Arndt, "Economic Development," 460, 463.

16. Harry Truman, "Inaugural Address," 20 Jan. 1949, https://www.trumanlibrary.org/whistlestop/50yr_archive/inagural20jan1949.htm (accessed 8 Apr. 2014).

17. Larrain, *Theories of Development*, 11, discusses three psychological arguments in development literature of the 1960s, like McLelland's *Achieving Society*, 11–19, which singles out a "need for achievement" as a motive force in social progress.

18. Rostow, *Stages*, 26, 20–21.

19. Geidel, *Peace Corps Fantasies,* 17. Geidel is discussing Rostow's 1960 speech "Some Lessons of History for Africa."

20. Saldaña-Portillo, *Revolutionary Imagination,* 24–25.

21. Rist, *History,* 78.

22. Cowen and Shenton, *Doctrines,* 4.

23. Ferguson, *Anti-Politics Machine,* 55.

24. William Neumann, "Debating Chávez's Legacy," *New York Times,* 7 Mar. 2013; Emily Lau, "Hong Kong's Summer of Discontent," *New York Times,* 1 July 2013; Bernard Aaronson, in "Venezuela's Fake Democrat," *New York Times,* 14 Aug. 2004.

25. CBS *Sunday Morning,* 4 Sept. 2005, "CBS News Transcripts."

26. Tipps, "Modernization Theory," 199.

27. Smith, *Uneven Development,* 181; Hsu, *Geography,* 19.

28. Ferguson, *Anti-Politics Machine,* xiii.

29. Ibid., 64, considers how the nation (specifically the LDC, the "Less Developed Country") is framed as the object of analysis under a regime of governmentality. Parker, "Hidden in Plain Sight," in Lewis et al., *Popular Representations of Development,* 93, argues that the national optic of development studies operates at the level, firstly, of data, which are scaled nationally—United Nations development indices aggregate data on things like adult literacy and life expectancy by nation-state.

30. Zamora, *Usable Past,* 19–20; Hegel, *Philosophy of History,* 80, 87. Zamora has shown how the spatialization of progress in the United States was indebted to German idealism and its secular invocation of history as a universal, progressive process. In the *Philosophy of History,* Hegel argued for a "geographical basis of history" that described America—that is, the United States—as "the land of the future." For a discussion of Hegel's overdetermined "amalgamation" of the South American continent's own "multiple points," see Blanco, *Ghost-watching American Modernity,* 152–53.

31. Klein, *Frontiers,* 67–68.

32. Durand, *Week in Cuba,* 62.

33. Curtis, *Capitals,* 1.

34. Dopico, "Picturing Havana," 486.

35. "Springing the Traps," *The Economist,* 2 Aug. 2007, http://www.economist.com/node/9581576 (accessed 10 Apr. 2014).

36. Michael McDonald, *United States Elections Project,* http://elections.gmu.edu/Turnout_2008G.html (accessed 16 Jan. 2014); Organisation for Economic Cooperation and Development, "Society at a Glance 2011: OECD Social Indicators," http://www.oecd-ilibrary.org/sites/soc_glance-2011-en/08/04/g8_co4-01.html (accessed 16 Jan. 2014). While voter participation is not the only indicator of "democracy," of course, it can serve as a useful shorthand. Mexico's 2006 national elections saw a turnout of 59 percent of eligible voters; the United States' hotly contested 2008 presidential elections saw an unusually high turnout of 62 percent.

37. Acemoglu and Robinson, *Why Nations Fail*, 7–9.

38. Escobar, *Encountering Development*, 9.

39. Saldívar, *Border Matters*, 18.

40. Ross, *Fast Cars*, 11–12.

41. Gilman, *Mandarins*, 3.

42. Delpar, *Looking South*, 154.

43. Goldstein, *Poverty*, 90–92.

44. Samuels, "Peace Corps."

45. Goldstein, *Poverty*, 104.

46. S. Park, *Pan American Imagination*.

47. O'Neill refers to this latter point as a "critical mantra" in O'Neill, "On the Limits of History and Hemispheric Literary Studies," 184. Kutzinski, *The Worlds of Langston Hughes*.

48. On the idealist utopianism of transnationalist work, see my "American Studies and the Transnational Ideal"; O'Neill, "On the Limits," 183; Giles, "Commentary," 654; Bauer, "Early American Literature," 251–52. On the politics of antinationalism in Latin American and hemispheric American studies, see López's treatment of Chicana/o literature's negotiation of nationalism as a "function of narrative relation to the past," in *Chicano Nations*, 12.

49. Lazo, "Invention," 768.

50. O'Neill, "On the Limits," 182–83.

51. The "age of development" is conventionally understood as Myrdal and Rostow described it, as a postwar response to imperialism. For Cowen and Shenton, development lent order to the restless movement of progress that preoccupied nineteenth-century thinkers, and Sylvia Wynter argues that it reframes a much older "framework of rationality" in which the underdeveloped languish, "proscribed like the medieval lepers outside the gates of the attained *civitas materialis* of the developed enclaves" (Cowen and Shenton, *Doctrines*, 30, 60); Wynter, "Is 'Development,'" 306. In more economic terms, M. Berger, "Review of Park," calls modernization theory and development initatives, like the Alliance for Progress, projects for "managing capitalist development in the interests of regionalized and internationalized elites."

52. Dalleo, *Caribbean Literature*, 13.

53. John O'Sullivan, "The Great Nation of Futurity," *United States Magazine and Democratic Review* 6, no. 23 (Nov. 1839), 427.

54. Guterl, "Comment," 132.

55. Castronovo, "'On Imperialism,'" 430.

56. Levander, "Confederate Cuba," 828.

57. T. B. Collier, "Development," 38.

58. Césaire, *Une tempête*, 88.

59. Slobodian, "How to See," 327–28, 332.

60. Kaplan, *Anarchy*, 14, 1; see also "Left Alone with America," in *Cultures of United States Imperialism*, 4.

1. Latin America as Anachronism

1. See, for example, "Cuba siempre Española" (Cuba Always Spanish), *Diario de la Marina*, 30 Aug. 1851, which recounted "the shameful retreat to which our valiant soldiers put the traitor Narciso Lopez with his 50 pirates on May 19, 1850."

2. B. Harrison, *Agent*, 3.

3. Bland, *Awful Doom*, 13–14.

4. May, *Southern Dream*, 30; Chaffin, *Fatal Glory*, 6–10; Rauch, *American Interest*, 208.

5. Crapol, "Coming to Terms," 588–89.

6. Rifkin, *Manifesting America*, 35.

7. Meinig, *Shaping of America*, 216.

8. John Quincy Adams to Hugh Nelson, 28 Apr. 1823, cited in *What Happened in Cuba?* 27.

9. John O'Sullivan, "The Cuban Debate," *United States Democratic Review*, Nov.–Dec. 1852, 433–35.

10. Hardy, *History and Adventures*, 5–6.

11. "The Cuban Debate," *United States Democratic Review*, 439.

12. Chaffin, *Fatal Glory*, 10; May, *Southern Dream*, 36–37.

13. Griffin, "Jane McManus Storm Cazneau," 417; Hudson, *Mistress*, 2.

14. Lazo, *Writing*, 84.

15. McGovern, "*From Varela to Martí*," 169. After 1852, Tolón was listed as "redactor en jefe" underneath Cora Montgomery's byline, but McGovern argues that his role in the paper was more uncertain. As she explains, he is described in one contemporary newspaper account (*The Rio Grande Centinela*) as the editor of *La Verdad*, but McGovern contends that his formal role was that of a contributing author. Because *La Verdad* did not have a masthead, it is difficult to know the structure of the paper's editorial staff; the prominent intellectual sponsors of the paper (McManus, Cisneros, and Tolón) likely all had editorial input.

16. *La Verdad*, 30 Apr. 1852.

17. Schwarz, "Brazilian Culture," 16.

18. James, *Black Jacobins*, 392; Fischer, *Modernity Disavowed*, 22. The critique of hegemonic notions of time—backwardness, prematurity, off-beat-ness, reproductivity, and anachrony—has emerged in queer theory as a way of linking temporalized discourses of queer and racial otherness. See, for example, Rohy, *Anachronism and its Others*, 1–21; Freeman, "Introduction," 159–60.

19. Schwarz, "Misplaced Ideas," 19–20, 30.

20. Guerra y Sanchez, *Manual de historia*, 464. Guerra writes that *La Verdad* "circulated extensively in a secret manner throughout Cuba," as the editors themselves asserted. He does not elaborate or cite sources for the claim, however.

21. Betancourt Cisneros to José Antonio Saco, 3 Apr. 1849, *Cartas del Lugareño*, 318. Briareus is a character from Greek mythology with one hundred arms and fifty heads.

22. *La Verdad,* 1 Mar. 1849.

23. *La Verdad,* 1 July 1848 ("Where there is liberty there is its treasure, there is its heart, with Greece as with Poland, with France as with Ireland, with Canada as with Cuba"). Luis-Brown, "An 1848 for the Americas," 438.

24. Ponce de Llorente, *Que es la anexion?* 12. See Schmidt-Nowara, *Empire and Antislavery,* 30, who argues that annexationists regarded Spanish rule as a lethal danger to creole whiteness, while for others Spanishness remained a crucial pole of identity.

25. Portell Vilá, *Narciso López,* 241.

26. As Gerald Poyo, *"With All and for the Good of All,"* 5, explains, "The real dilemma was Cuba's socioeconomic reality, more specifically, slavery."

27. Lazo, *Writing,* 64–65.

28. The editors of *La Verdad* made this position clear in the pamphlet, "Cuestión negrera de la isla de Cuba por los editores y colaboradores de La Verdad" (The negro question on the island of Cuba by the editors of La Verdad), 15: "Our opinion on such a grave measure of such political and social transcendence is that the continuation of the slave trade in Cuba brings the country and its inhabitants to their irremediable and prompt perdition. Whatever method that is taken for slow and gradual emancipation is positively disastrous."

29. Foucault, "Nietzsche, Genealogy, History," in *Foucault Reader,* 81, cited in Coronado, *World Not to Come,* 11.

30. Coronado, *World Not to Come,* 11.

31. Ibid., 18 (italics in original).

32. Fabian, *Time,* 144.

33. José María Torres Caicedo, "Las dos Américas," in Ardao, *Génesis de la idea,* 175–85.

34. Quijada, "Sobre el origen y difusión del nombre 'América Latina,'" 605–6; McGuinness, *Path,* 154.

35. "Miscellaneous: From Hunt's Merchant's Magazine," *Pittsfield Sun,* 22 Nov. 1849. The reprinted article appeared under the subheadline: "Cuba: The Key of the Mexican Gulf: With Reference to the Coast Trade of the United States."

36. Pollard, *Black Diamonds,* 108.

37. Guterl, *American Mediterranean,* 21–22.

38. Pérez-Torres, *Movements,* 12.

39. *La Verdad,* 9 Jan. 1848.

40. The *prospecto,* which references literature and arts—two subjects *La Verdad* rarely touched, aside from occasional poetry—is an example of what Schwarz, in "Misplaced Ideas," 25–26, calls the "bass and falsetto" voice of mid-century Latin American publications. These periodicals spoke in *profundo* of the "purifying torch of the press," on the one hand, while hastening in falsetto to reassure readers of their propriety and recreational "goodnaturedness," on the other.

41. Lazo makes this claim in *Writing to Cuba,* 84.

42. Cora Montgomery, "La Verdad. Periodico consagrado a la politica, a la literatura y a las Ciencias y Artes. Prospecto," *La Verdad,* 9 Jan. 1848. *La Verdad* used accent marks inconsistently in its articles.

43. *La Verdad,* 27 Apr. 1848 (italics in original).

44. Kimball, *Cuba and the Cubans,* 196.

45. José Antonio Saco, "Ideas sobre la incorporación de Cuba en los Estados Unidos" (1848), in Ortíz, *Contra la anexión,* 103.

46. *La Verdad,* 1 July 1848.

47. Sundquist, *To Wake the Nations,* 198–99; Genovese, *Political Economy,* 257; May, *Southern Dream,* 36–37.

48. Kimball, *Cuba and the Cubans,* iii.

49. James Buchanan to James Clayton, April 17, 1849, *Works of James Buchanan,* 360–61.

50. *Boston Post,* 6 June 1850.

51. May, *Southern Dream,* 6.

52. One such partisan was James A. Thrasher, a southern planter in Cuba and the only foreign-born member of the Club de la Habana. In his introduction to his own translation of Alexander von Humboldt's *Island of Cuba,* Thrasher wrote that racial peace prevailed in Cuba as in the U.S. south. He goes on to say, "The extension of our theories of government to Cuba must contribute to their stability, strengthen the ties of our civil policy, increase its moral power, and augment our weight in the family of nations. The accession of Cuba to the Union is not, therefore, merely a Southern question, but it is a question of national gain and of national power" (Thrasher, "Preliminary Essay," 45, 61).

53. "The Cuban Debate," *United States Democratic Review,* 440.

54. Abbott, *South and North,* 58–59.

55. Dana, *To Cuba and Back,* 132. Dana was already well known for his 1840 maritime memoir, *Two Years Before the Mast.*

56. Saco, *Colleción del Papel,* cited in Guerra, *Manual de la historia cubana,* 391.

57. Delany, "Annexation of Cuba," *The North Star,* 27 Apr. 1849.

58. Foner, *History of Cuba,* 10; Paquette, *Sugar Is Made,* 265; Rauch, *American Interest,* 43.

59. Brown, *Black Man,* 90.

60. Delany, *Blake,* 61. Again, the novel's jumbled temporal structure makes this passage somewhat confusing—although *Blake* takes place during Franklin Pierce's 1852 presidential campaign, for his 1859 reader, Ballard's quotation of Chief Justice Roger Taney's 1857 opinion would likely have been familiar.

61. Johnson, *Soul by Soul,* 29.

62. Delany, *Blake,* 63.

63. Benjamin, "Theses," 256–57.

64. Delany, *Blake,* 306.

2. Latin America as Nature

1. Segur, "On a Venezuelan Coffee Plantation."
2. Huntington, *Civilization,* 11.
3. Kamarck, *Tropics,* 15.
4. Dixon, "South of the South," 16. Dixon means the phrase in more affirmative historical terms, aiming for a history of internationalism and struggle among people of color in the Atlantic world, whereas I am focusing on "south" as it is used a marker of poverty, rurality, and underdevelopment.
5. Humboldt and Bonpland, *Personal Narrative of Travels, Vol. I.,* xlv
6. Stepan, *Picturing Tropical Nature,* 36–38.
7. Ibid., 56.
8. Manthorne, *Tropical Renaissance,* 10–11.
9. "Church's 'Heart of the Andes,'" 133.
10. James Somerville, *F.E. Church's Painting "The Heart of the Andes"* (Philadelphia, c. 1859), 11, cited in Manthorne, *Tropical Renaissance,* 17.
11. Manthorne, *Tropical Renaissance,* 17. Manthorne notes that Church replaced a coconut palm in his early sketches with a tree fern in the final painting.
12. Winthrop, *Companion,* 38.
13. "Church's 'Heart of the Andes,'" 133.
14. Winthrop, *Companion,* 29; Sachs, *Humboldt Current,* 101.
15. Winthrop, *Heart of the Andes,* 42.
16. Denevan, "Pristine Myth," 369.
17. Shriber, *Writing Home,* 20–21.
18. Sears, *Sacred Places,* 6.
19. Smith, *Uneven Development,* 28–29.
20. Hsu, *Geography,* 21–23.
21. Pratt, *Imperial Eyes,* 203.
22. Moore, *With Speaker Cannon,* 172, 177.
23. Delpar, *Looking South,* 34. The first college-level course in Latin American history in the United States was taught by Bernard Moses at the University of California, Berkeley, in 1895.
24. Lockwood, *Passionate Pilgrims,* 531–38. Lockwood estimates that fifty thousand people journeyed from the United States to Europe in 1857.
25. H. Wilson, "Bibliography," 422.
26. This figure is compiled from Smith, *American Travelers Abroad.* I have excluded nineteen books that include Mexico as one stop on a larger world tour. Given the difficulty and expense of sea travel abroad, travelers often visited multiple foreign destinations; a voyage to Mexico was often combined with a visit to the Antilles, California, or the continent of South America, just as northern visitors to Cuba sometimes also passed through the U.S. south, the Bahamas, or (on at least one occasion) Haiti en route to some more distant destination.
27. Hoganson, *Consumers' Imperium,* 10. Bly authored a pair of books based

on her journalistic travel: *Six Months in Mexico* and *Around the World in Seventy-two Days*.

28. Wexler, *Tender Violence*, 23. Stereography, a late nineteenth-century media technology, was an important medium of fictive travel. A pair of photographs of a single image—often of some foreign locale or famous landmark—would be combined with a viewing device that gave the illusion of three-dimensional depth. Many Mexico stereographs regularly featured a sizable number of domestic scenes that mix the familiar with the "exotic" in an ironic mockery of Mexican life. One image held in the American Antiquarian Society's collection features a man filling a pail to water outdoors to water his donkey, with an ironic hand-written notation on the reverse reading, "Mexican waterworks." Another, of a farmer holding a baby donkey with the caption "Family pet, Salamanca," mocks the perceived failure of Mexican peasants to police the boundaries of home and work. The caption on the reverse reads: "A good view of Mexican character." These examples were produced by H. A. Doerr, a commercial photographer in San Antonio, Texas (H. A. Doerr, Stereophotograph collection, Mexico [general] Box 273, American Antiquarian Society, Box 272–74).

29. Ford, *Tropical America*, 17, reaches a more positive conclusion. "While there are no trees in the South American woods which can be compared in form and symmetry with the oaks, elms, pines, chestnuts walnuts, and conifers of a northern forest," he writes, "the foliage has richer and deeper tints in its perennial freshness. . . . Nature sets the example of profusion of color in Brazil, and man instinctively follows it in building and decorating the towns."

30. Curtis, *Venezuela*, 227.

31. Ballou, *Due South*, 62.

32. R. H. Davis, *Three Gringos*, 143.

33. Valenčius, *Health*, 235.

34. On climatic determinism's popularity in the early twentieth century, its intellectual and political versatility, and its present-day revival, see Jennings, *Curing the Colonizers*, 9–15; and Livingstone, "Changing."

35. Cocks, *Tropical Whites*, 20–22. See also her "Welcoming Voice of the Southland," in *Bridging National Borders in North America*, 227.

36. Baker, *Naturalist in Mexico*, 46.

37. Morelet, *Travels*, 150.

38. Sanborn, *Winter*, 42.

39. Conkling, *Mexico and the Mexicans*, 70.

40. Carson, *Mexico*, 140–41.

41. Gray, *Mexico As It Is*, 55, cited in J. Park, *Latin American Underdevelopment*, 48.

42. Bly, *Six Months*, 199.

43. Merril, *Negotiating Paradise*, 2. There are many examples of such hardship itineraries. In Cuba, for example, the anonymous author of *Rambles in Cuba*, 10–12, (its author is usually identified as Adeline Noble) took a day trip

to Guanabacoa across Havana Bay to watch Chinese stevedores toil in a sugar warehouse. Matilda's *My Winter in Cuba,* 226, recounts her stay on a Matanzas sugar plantation, where she watched the *ingenio* at night and marveled at its "lurid glow" reminiscent of the "Inferno of Dante, the Hell of Milton, and the Witches' Cave of Macbeth." Howe's *A Trip to Cuba,* 126, recounts how Cuba's repressive gender mores kept her from these sites of deprivation and hardship.

44. Marie D. Gorgas and Burton J. Hendrick, *William Crawford Gorgas: His Life and Work* (Garden City, NY: Doubleday, Page, 1924), 140–41, cited in Greene, *Canal Builders,* 29.

45. Cirillo, *Bullets and Bacilli,* 114–18.

46. Sylvester Baxter, "The Tropical Renaissance," *Harper's Monthly Magazine* 103 (July 1902), in LaRose and Mejía, *United States Discovers Panama,* 201–4. Baxter is one of the rare authors to point out that "the tropics" as a cartographic concept does not exist, given the different climates with widely varying temperatures and fauna in Latin America.

47. Espinosa, *Epidemic Invasions,* 32–34.

48. Keim, *San Domingo,* 312.

49. "Real Foe Fever," *Chicago Tribune,* 1 May 1898; "Yellow Fever in the South," *Chicago Tribune,* 28 Sept. 1898.

50. Panama Canal Zone Health Department, *Mosquito-Borne Diseases,* 3.

51. Robinson, *Porto Rico,* 162.

52. *The Daily Ranchero and Republican,* 14 Aug. 1872.

53. See, for example, Gibbes, *Cuba for Invalids;* Hutchinson, *Under the Southern Cross.* Cocks's *Tropical Whites,* 27–33, chronicles the literature of travel therapy.

54. Rector's *Beautiful Porto Rico,* 45–46, looked forward to the example offered by vigorous Yankee manhood in outdoor pursuits: "Outdoor exercise, embracing athletics, football, etc. will be among the greatest blessings that we can bring to them."

55. Cocks, *Tropical Whites,* 91–92; Greene, *Canal Builders,* 180–225.

56. Livingstone, "Moral Discourse of Climate."

57. The susceptibility of the southern and southwestern United States was an issue of some concern. See, for example, Charles Dudley Warner in *Our Italy* (New York: Harper, 1891), who wondered, "Will Southern California be an exception to those lands of equable climate and extraordinary fertility where every effort is postponed till 'to-morrow?'" cited in Cocks, *Tropical Whites,* 23.

58. Livingstone, "Climate's Moral Economy, 138–39.

59. Huntington, *Civilization and Climate,* 30, 41, 8, 1.

60. Semple, *Influences,* 626–28, cited in Livingstone, *Geographical Tradition,* 236.

61. Okihiro, *Pineapple Culture,* 18–23. For a discussion of Huntington's work, see Livingstone, "Moral Discourse of Climate," 427–30; and Cocks, *Tropical Whites,* 19.

62. Campbell, *Witness*, 177.

63. Harvey, *American Geographies*, 6.

64. Pratt, *Imperial Eyes*, 7.

65. Lummins, *Land of Poco Tiempo*, 3.

66. Schulten, *Geographical Imagination*, 31.

67. Pike, *United States and Latin America*, 47–52. For a similar critique of Pike's work, see Aparicio and Chávez-Silverman, *Tropicalizations*, 7.

68. Salvatore, "Enterprise of Knowledge," 90–91.

69. Clark, *Seven Years*, 353.

70. Matilda, *My Winter*, 88.

71. Dana, *To Cuba and Back*, 59, 132; Freud, "The Uncanny," in *Complete Psychological Works of Sigmund Freud*, 226.

72. Guterl, *American Mediterranean*, 92–113.

73. Greeson, *Our South*, 246–47.

74. Ripley, *From Flag to Flag*, 124.

75. Guterl, *American Mediterranean*, 90–91.

76. Ripley, *From Flag to Flag*, 151–52. The Royos were the former owners of the plantation house.

77. Paravisini-Gebert, "Oriental Imprisonments," 129, discusses the dehumanization of Black women in Cuba travel narratives.

78. Mackie, *From Cape Cod*, 235.

79. Twain, *Life on the Mississippi*, 375–76.

80. Ripley, *From Flag to Flag*, 228.

81. Ibid., 295.

82. Evans, *Romancing the Maya*, 4.

83. Ford, *Tropical America*, 305–7.

84. Ruiz, *Americans*, 57 (italics in original).

85. Ford, *Tropical America*, 293, 408, 322.

86. Livingstone, "Moral Discourse," 416.

87. Cocks, "Pleasures of Degeneration," 216.

88. Didion, *Miami*, 23.

89. Dos Passos, *Brazil*, 1, 44.

90. Landes, *Wealth and Poverty*, 6, 13.

3. Latin America at War

1. "Santiago, Shafter's Goal, Brought Home to New York," *New York World*, 3 July 1898.

2. Marion Kendrick, "The Cuban Girl Martyr," *New York Journal*, 17 Aug. 1897, is one of many examples. The "Girl Martyr" here is Evangelina Cosío y Cisneros, about whom more below.

3. "Treaty between the United States and the Republic of Cuba Embodying the Provisions Defining Their Future Relations as Contained in the Act of Congress. Signed May 22, 1903," General Records of the US Government, 1778–2006, RG 11,

National Archives. http://www.ourdocuments.gov/doc.php?flash=true&doc=55 (accessed 5 Oct. 2015).

4. Cited in Pérez, *Cuba,* 164.

5. Correspondents and soldiers complained about the effects of Cuban heat and humidity, which they considered tactical disadvantages for the American troops. General Shafter, overweight and widely derided as a poor tactician, was often described as wilting in the Caribbean weather. For more on the link between Shafter's corpulence and incompetence, see Andreu, "Sylvester H. Scovel, Journalist," 351.

6. The American war against Spain in late 1898 has gone by multiple names in the United States. The Spanish-American War has always had the greatest currency, but some have sought to restore the absent Cuban role in the conflict by renaming it "The Spanish-Cuban-American War." However, besides its cumbersome overhyphenization this gesture of inclusion excludes the Puerto Rican and Filipino phases of the conflict. Therefore, in the interest of simplicity and accuracy, I use the War of 1898 or the 1898 War.

7. Luce, "American Century," 171. The article originally appeared in the February 17, 1941, issue of *Life* magazine.

8. "John Jacob Astor, Richest Soldier in the U.S. Army," *New York World,* 12 June 1898; "Beautiful Amy Phipps Leaves Family Wealth and Luxury to Become a Nurse in Cuba," *New York World,* 19 June 1898. Amy Phipps was the daughter of Andrew Carnegie's partner in U.S. Steel. See also "The Dandies in War," *New York World,* 15 May 1898, which rejoiced that "American manhood has not been sapped by wealth and luxury; that our 'chappies' are warm-blooded men; that our 'dudes' have among them strong, resolute, courageous fellows who love their country, and that our dandies are mainly athletic and healthy-minded young men, as cheerfully ready to do rough camp work as they are to play rough polo or football."

9. "'Rough Riders' Eat, then Polish Rifles," *New York World,* 15 June 1898.

10. *New York World,* 3 Apr. 1898, cited in Wisan, *Cuban Crisis,* 435. The same point was made in "Indians' Long-Nursed Grudge / They Want to Fight Spain for Sending Columbus to Discover Them," *New York World,* 17 May 1898.

11. *New York World,* 17 July 1898. The article claims that the "negro" was replaced by a "Spaniard."

12. "Actresses Hide Their Beauty in Burnt Cork to Amuse Friends," *New York World,* 13 May 1898.

13. "One Flag—One Pride," *New York World,* 3 May 1898.

14. Witherbee, *Spanish-American War Songs,* 436, 415. See also Doyle, *Poems and Lyrics.*

15. Greenwood, *Smoked Yankees,* 13–14.

16. Dixon, *Leopard's Spots,* 159.

17. Kaplan, *Anarchy,* 121–22, 125, 144–45.

18. Murphy, *Shadowing,* 44–45.

19. DeGuzmán, *Spain's Long Shadow*, xxiv.

20. "The Boston Anti-Imperialist Meeting," 15 Jun. 1898, in Foner and Winchester, *Anti-Imperialist Reader*, 275–80.

21. Murphy, *Shadowing*, 32.

22. Boyer, *Urban Masses*, 124.

23. Henry James, notebook entry, 16 Nov. 1892, cited in Ziff, *American 1890s*, 275.

24. See Buel, *Mysteries and Miseries;* Mawsom, "A Hot Wave"; Buel and Mawsom, *Leslie's Official History*.

25. Crane, "Hunger," (my italics). The article is datelined June 27, while the landing was still underway.

26. Juergens, *Joseph Pulitzer*, xii.

27. Campbell, *Yellow Journalism*, 34.

28. Howells, "Aesthetic New York," 222–23.

29. Matthiessen, *The James Family*, 320, in Robertson, *Stephen Crane*, 20.

30. Casal, *Prosas*, 272, cited and trans. in González, *Journalism*, 86.

31. González, *Journalism*, 88.

32. Rotker, *American Chronicles*, 33.

33. Ramos, *Divergent Modernities*, xli, 271.

34. Martí, "Coney Island," in *José Martí: Selected Writings*, trans. Allen, 94.

35. Crane, "In the Broadway Cars," in *Last Words*, 173. The article originally appeared in the *New York Sun*, 26 July 1896.

36. "Heard on the Street, Election Night: Passing Remarks Gathered in Front of 'The Press' Stereopticon," *New York Press*, November 1894, in Stallman and Hagemann, *New York City Sketches*, 103–7. Stallman and Hagemann do not specify the day of publication for this article, and according to Robertson, *Stephen Crane, Journalism*, 224, the issue has been lost.

37. Campbell locates the transformation in a single year, 1897, when a "class of paradigms" pitted Hearst and Pulitzer's "new journalism" and Lincoln Steffens' "literary journalism" against the *New York Times'* "counteractivist" model. For an opposing view, see Jane Steele, who warns against histories of journalism that "follow a single path of development"; such a model "favors certain newspapers that anticipated the commercial journalism of our own time," she writes, "and ignores other equally significant ones" (Campbell, *Year that Defined*, 6; Steele, *Sun Shines*, xiii, 158).

38. Robertson, *Stephen Crane, Journalism*, 5–8.

39. N. Harrison, "To Change Earth's Climate." This article described an inventor who claimed to have created a device capable of manipulating the earth's rotation with electric current to plunge the Iberian Peninsula into perpetual winter.

40. Frus, *Politics and Poetics*, 28.

41. R. H. Davis, "Our War Correspondents."

42. Rotker, *American Chronicles*, 32.

43. Ramos, *Divergent Modernities*, 120 (italics in original).

44. Aching, *Politics,* 20.

45. Martí, "La bahía de Nueva York," *La Nación,* 3 Aug. 1888, in *Obras Completas,* vol. 12, 22.

46. Martí, "Un drama terrible," in *Obras Completas,* vol. 11, 340; "El puente de Brooklyn," in *Obras Completas,* vol. 9, 430.

47. Buel, *Mysteries and Miseries,* 41.

48. C. Wilson, "Stephen Crane," 273–79.

49. Crane, "'Tenderloin' as it Really Is."

50. Crane, "Stephen Crane and Minetta Lane."

51. Crane, "The Duel that Was Not Fought," in Stallman and Hagemann, *New York City Sketches,* 115. Stallman and Hagemann reproduce the version published in 1898 *The Open Boat and Other Stories.* A version originally appeared in *New York Press,* 9 Dec. 1894.

52. C. Wilson, "Stephen Crane," 306.

53. "Army Fit for Cuba, Say People Who Watch Police Parade," *New York World,* 2 June 1898.

54. Martí, "El monumento de la prensa: los periodistas de Nueva York," *La Nación,* 28 July 1887, in *Obras Completas,* vol. 11, 195–97.

55. *Truth,* untitled article, 10 Aug. 1898.

56. Creelman, *On the Great Highway,* 174.

57. "Thrall and Jones to Be Exchanged," *New York World,* 17 May 1898.

58. Crane, "Hunger Has Made Cubans Fatalists," *New York World,* 12 July 1898.

59. Hancock, *What One Man Saw,* 31.

60. Hamment, *Cannon and Camera,* 122–23.

61. "Stephen Crane's Vivid Story of the Battle of San Juan," *New York World,* 14 July 1898.

62. R. H. Davis, *Cuba,* 117.

63. Riis, *Battle,* 7.

64. Riis, *Making of an American,* 174–75, 295.

65. In a column, "Major-Gen. Joseph Wheeler for the World Reviews the Santiago Fight," *New York World,* 21 Aug. 1898, Wheeler says of Cuba's potential: "The wonderful fertility of its soil, with American ideas of sanitation put in practice, and with American enterprise and energy to develop it, must make it a wonderfully prosperous country."

66. Thomas A. Edison, Inc., *White Wings on Review,* 1903.

67. "Swept All Before the Ninth / 'White Wings,' Not Police, Escort the Regiment Down Broadway—As Effective as Unique," *New York World,* 9 June 1898.

68. Waring, *Street-Cleaning,* 190. Waring even developed a youth organization, the Juvenile Street Cleaning Leagues, who sang a theme song to the tune of "The Battle Hymn of the Republic."

69. For an informative if hagiographic account of sanitation in occupied Cuba, see Hitchman, "Unfinished Business," For a contemporary dissenting per-

spective from the Cuban nationalist elite, see Salvador Cisneros y Betancourt, *Appeal*. Cisneros was a president of the Cuban Republic under the occupation and the uncle of Evangelina. He argued that the sanitation work was undertaken more for the protection of U.S. troops than for Cubans.

70. Porter, *Industrial Cuba*, 156. Porter was the American "Special Commissioner" to Cuba and Puerto Rico, and the book contains an extracted version of Waring's report, which was completed by his aide after the colonel's death.

71. "Colonel Waring, Martyr," *Philadelphia Inquirer*, 30 Oct. 1898; Riis, *Battle*, 270–71.

72. Porter, *Industrial Cuba*, 154–55. The quote is Waring's; the report was drafted by an assistant from the colonel's notes after his death.

73. Riis, *How the Other Half Lives*, 141–43.

74. Porter, *Industrial Cuba*, 156.

75. *New York World*, 25 Aug. 1898; "Typhoid Germs in Montauk Water," *New York World*, 3 Sept. 1898.

76. Olívares, *Our Islands*, 237.

77. Porter, *Industrial Cuba*, 160.

78. Perhaps the first significant revisionist history of the American intervention was the Cuban historian and social critic Emilio Roig de Leuchsenring, *Cuba no debe su independencia a los Estados Unidos* (Cuba does not owe its independence to the United States). For English-language criticisms of the discourses of charity and gratitude in 1898, see Pérez, "Incurring a Debt of Gratitude."

79. Foner, *Spanish-Cuban-American War*, 355; William T. Sampson, "The Atlantic Fleet in the Spanish War," *The Century Magazine*, April 1899, cited in Smith, *Spanish-American War*, 122. The military historian Smith makes no mention of the Cuban efforts to secure the landing-spot, and quotes Sampson without comment.

80. Hancock, *What One Man Saw*, 29. Crane contributed a similar account of Cuban apathy at the landing. "Crane Tells the Story of the Disembarkment," *New York World*, 20 June 1898.

81. *Truth*, 10 Aug. 1898, 5.

82. Stallman, *Stephen Crane*, 73. "You won't find any preaching in *Maggie*," Crane wrote to a friend.

83. Talmage, *Masque Torn Off*, 160, 225.

84. Riis, *How the Other Half Lives*, 180.

85. Gandal, *Virtues*, 62; Norris, "Stephen Crane's Stories of Life in the Slums: *Maggie* and *George's Mother*," *The Wave*, 4 July 1896, cited in Crane, *Maggie*, 151. As Norris writes, *Maggie's* characters were "old acquaintances in the world of fiction."

86. Cosío y Cisneros, *Story of Evangelina Cisneros*, 165, i.

87. *New York Journal*, 24 Aug. 1897.

88. Julia Ward Howe, "To All Good Men and True Women," in Cosío y Cisneros, *Story of Evangelina Cisneros*, 41.

89. Milton, *Yellow Kid*, 199–200. The author offers the bribery explanation, referring to sources at the *Journal*, but omits any citation for the claim.

90. Wisan, *Cuban Crisis*, 329–31. As Wisan writes, the *World* did not let its rival's scoop pass without comment. The U.S. Consul-General to Spanish Cuba, Fitzhugh Lee, complained to the *World* of the *Journal*'s exploitation of her case, arguing that Cosío was, in fact, an insurgent. Given her family's involvement in revolutionary politics (her father was imprisoned for sedition), Lee's conclusion—that she used the *Journal* publicity to promote U.S. intervention—seems plausible. However, because to my knowledge Cosío left no written record beyond her sensationalized "autobiography," her personal motives will remain a mystery.

91. Cosío y Cisneros, *Story of Evangelina Cisneros*, i, 27.

92. For the "darkest New York" reference, see Mawsom, "A Hot Wave Among the Poor," *Harper's Weekly Magazine*, 20 Aug. 1892.

93. "Hunger has Made Cubans Fatalists," *New York World*, 12 July 1898.

94. Bangs, *Uncle Sam, Trustee*, 158–60.

4. Latin America and Bohemia

1. Chase, *Mexico*, 161.

2. Clark, *Travel Writing*, 88.

3. Ferlinghetti, "March 24, '69," *Mexican Night*, 58.

4. Kerouac, *On the Road*, 274.

5. Cowen and Shenton, *Doctrines*, 4.

6. Beals, *Fire*, 348.

7. Spratling, *Little Mexico*, 197–98.

8. Delpar, *Enormous Vogue*, 15.

9. Parker, "*El Nuevo Rivera.*"

10. Toor, "Notas sobre este Número," 4.

11. Ibid., 4.

12. Rivera, "Painting of Pulquerias," 8. "Such is the potency of the esthetic factor in the Mexican rural masses," he writes in the essay's English version, "that even if they had no other as important, it would be sufficient by itself to inspire confidence in the role that they will necessarily play in the future of Mexican organization."

13. Chase, *Mexico*, 187.

14. Hilah Paulmier, "How Young North Americans May Help Promote Pan-American Ideals," in Paulmier and Schauffler, *Pan-American Day*, 108.

15. Spellacy, "Mapping," 44–45.

16. Clayton Sedgwick Cooper, "We Must Win South American Good Will on the Basis of Equality," in *Pan-American Day*, 101–2.

17. Chase, *Mexico*, 206.

18. Spratling, *Little Mexico*, 28.

19. The thesaurus offers no "good" synonym for indolence—lassitude, torpor, languor, and idleness are all negative traits. The moral dimension of work

that structured so many nineteenth-century American accounts of Latin America is still very much with us.

20. Zolov, "Showcasing the Mexico of Tomorrow," 175, cited in Fox, *Making Art Panamerican*, 193. Zolov offers an example of the alignment of modernization with these latinophilic tropes. His account of the 1968 Mexico City Olympics argues that Mexico's Olympic Committee fetishized "tradition" to inoculate it against criticisms that a third-world country was ill-equipped for the Games: the "reification of the 'traditional' as something utterly distinct from the 'modern'" celebrated "'authenticity' at a moment when the tide of capitalist modernization was transforming the planet," he writes.

21. Chase, *Mexico*, 177, 130.

22. Mermann-Jozwiak, "Writing Mexico," 96.

23. "Parvenu . . . Review of *Mexico: A Study of Two Americas* by Stuart Chase," in Alvarez and Walsh, *Uncollected Early Prose*, 253.

24. Retman, *Real Folks*, 2–9.

25. Brooks, *America's Coming of Age*, 176.

26. Irwin Granich [Mike Gold], "Well, What About Mexico?" *Liberator* 22 (Jan. 1920): 28, cited in Delpar, *Enormous Vogue*, 24.

27. Chase, *Mexico*, 208.

28. Smith, *White Umbrella*, 4.

29. Brooks, "Young America," 147 (my italics).

30. Brooks, "On Creating a Usable Past," 338.

31. Spratling, *Little Mexico*, 191.

32. Spellacy, 42.

33. Blake, *Beloved Community*, 99.

34. Mumford, *Brown Decades*, 8.

35. Mumford, "Orozco," 231.

36. Indych-López, *Muralism*, 98.

37. Bourne, "Trans-National America," 91.

38. Pike, *United States and Latin America*, 253.

39. Beals, *Crime of Cuba*, 18–19.

40. Guevara, "The OAS Conference at Punta del Este," in Deutschmann, *Che Guevara Reader*, 217–18.

41. Lobe, *Cartas a mis hijos*, 57.

42. Rodó, *Ariel*, 41.

43. Frank, *Our America*, 231; M. J. Bernadete, "Waldo Frank to Hispano-America," in Bernadete, *Waldo Frank in America Hispana*, 8.

44. Mañach, *La crisis*, 23.

45. Fernando Ortíz, "La crisis política cubana: sus causas y remedios (Resumen de un libro que ya no se escribirá)" and "La decadencia cubana," in Le Riverend, *Orbita de Fernando Ortíz*, 99–101.

46. Mañach, "Presentation of Waldo Frank Before the Instituto Hispano-Cubano de Cultura of Havana," in *Waldo Frank in America Hispana*, 72–73.

Mañach calls Frank an "Americano minorista," using the name for the Cuban "grupo minorista," a circle of avant-garde intellectuals that included Mañach.

47. For more on "Arielism" in the United States, see Pike, *FDR's Good Neighbor Policy,* 76–79.

48. Oles, *South of the Border,* 75–76.

49. S. Park, *Pan American Imagination,* 37, 35.

50. Stacy-Judd, "Wanted," 2–9.

51. Frank, *Rediscovery,* 221–22.

52. Castellanos, "Cancún and the Campo," in Berger and Wood, *Holiday in Mexico,* 243. By the 1940s, several Yucatecan Maya sites were accessible by car, as the result of road construction by Yucatán's revolutionary government, which was aided by Carnegie Institute funding; see Terry, *Terry's Guide,* 580.

53. Brenner, *Your Mexican Holiday,* 5, 176.

54. Frank, *Rediscovery,* 71.

55. Ibid., 74.

56. Brenner, "Petate," 15.

57. Brenner, *Your Mexican Holiday,* 19, 5.

58. Brenner, *Idols behind Altars,* 109.

59. Ibid., 33, 31 (my italics).

60. Larsen, *Reading North By South,* 2.

61. Austin, *Land of Little Rain,* 279, 267.

62. Luhan, *Lorenzo in Taos,* 9 (italics in original).

63. Cather, *Death Comes for the Archbishop,* 33.

64. Austin, *Earth Horizon,* 359.

65. Zamora, *Usable Past,* 23, sees Cather negotiating this boundary, in her use of "unmistakably American spaces" in the west as a staging of "American history as unconscious memory or racial unconscious."

66. Joseph, *American Literary Regionalism,* 118.

67. McClure, *Late Imperial Romance,* 8. Goodman argues for Cather's novel as a late imperial romance in *Southwestern Landscapes,* 140.

68. Goodman, *Southwestern Landscapes,* 155.

69. Cather, *Death Comes for the Archbishop,* 77, 273.

70. Michaels, *Our America,* 78.

71. Cather, *Death Comes for the Archbishop,* 284, 95

72. For a similar reading of this phrase as ironic, rather than a programmatic statement of Cather's view of the Southwest, see Lindemann, *Willa Cather,* 127.

73. Gurko, "Achievement of Ernest Hemingway," 296.

74. Casey, "Apuntes de Vuelo," 57.

75. For Hemingway citations, see below; A. J. Liebling called Havana a "man's city," "Discovering Havana," *Holiday,* Feb. 1949.

76. One such critic was R. G. Davis, "Hemingway's Tragic Fisherman."

77. Harvey Breit, "Hemingway's *Old Man,*" *The Nation,* 6 Sept. 1952.

78. Hemingway, *Old Man and the Sea,* 17.

79. R. G. Davis, "Hemingway's Tragic Fisherman," *New York Times,* 7 Sept. 1952.

80. In Hemingway's travel journalism, see "There She Breaches! Or, Moby Dick off the Morro," *Esquire* (May 1936): 203. Asking a Cuban fisherman to show him another man's fishing "tricks," Hemingway writes, "'Give me the trick of Enrique,' I said, in Spanish."

81. Hemingway, *Old Man and the Sea,* 22.

82. Hill, "Language, Race," 683.

83. For a Christian reading of *The Old Man and the Sea,* see William Faulkner's review in *Shenandoah* (autumn 1952): 55.

84. Rodríguez Feo to Wallace Stevens, Havana, 13 Dec. 1945, in Coyle and Filreis, *Secretaries of the Moon,* 41.

85. Desnoes, *Punto de vista,* 38.

86. Robert Manning, "Hemingway in Cuba," *The Atlantic* (Aug. 1965). http://www.theatlantic.com/past/docs/issues/65aug/6508manning.htm (accessed 28 Dec. 2011).

87. Ferlinghetti, *Mexican Night,* 5.

88. Kerouac, *On the Road,* 280.

89. Baldwin, "The Black Boy Looks at the White Boy," in *Nobody Knows My Name,* 231, 270.

90. Cocks, "Pleasures of Degeneration."

91. Adams, *Continental Divides,* 162.

92. Balderston and Quiroga, "Beautiful, Sinister Fairyland," 89.

93. Kerouac, *On the Road,* 276.

5. Latin America, in Solidarity

1. Said, *World,* 24.

2. On the historiography of Latin America solidarity in the Cold War, see Zolov, "Latin America in the Global Sixties."

3. "Manifesto of the Communist Party," in Tucker, *Marx-Engels Reader,* 500.

4. Hughes, "The Weary Blues," in Rampersad, ed. *Collected Poems of Langston Hughes,* 50.

5. *Oxford English Dictionary,* "syncopation," www.oed.com (accessed 6 Apr. 2014).

6. Guillén, *Sóngoro sosongo,* 18.

7. Nicolas Guillén, "Rosendo Ruiz," *Diario de la Marina,* 26 Jan. 1930.

8. For an account of Hughes's career in Spanish translation, see Kutzinski, *Worlds of Langston Hughes,* 56–85.

9. Gustavo Urrutia, letter to Langston Hughes, 20 Apr. 1930, Langston Hughes Papers. James Weldon Johnson Collection in the Yale Collection of American Literature, Beinecke Rare Book and Manuscript Library. Underlined text in original.

10. For a succinct comparison of Cuban and American racial politics in the 1930s, see D. Davis, "Nationalism and Civil Rights," 35.

11. In his reading of Urrutia's letter Rampersad presumes that Urrutia is comparing Guillén's poems to Hughes's "Weary Blues," rather than to African Americans' lower-case "blues"—as in, "they are the exact equivalent of your [Weary] blues." This interpretation is odd, and exceedingly generous to Hughes, given the lower-case rendering of the word.

12. Rampersad, *Life of Langston Hughes*, 181. See also Cobb, *Haiti, Harlem*; Jackson, "Shared Vision," 90, in which Jackson writes, "Guillén met Hughes in the early 1930s when the latter visited Cuba. Hughes led the Cuban poet away from the Hispanic Modernism of Ruben Dario to Afro-Hispanic blackness," a sweeping assertion—both of Hughes' leadership and of Guillén's modernismo—for which there is no evidence at all. Kutzinski, *Sugar's Secrets*, 151–52, discusses the problematic analogy between American blues and Cuban *son* as black musical styles.

13. Smart, *Nicolás Guillén*, 33–34.

14. Apter, *Translation Zone*, 64.

15. Kutzinksi, *Worlds of Langston Hughes*, 27.

16. Warren, "Appeals for (Mis)recognition," 404–5.

17. Edwards, *Practice*, 5.

18. McKinley, "Third Annual Message," 5 Dec. 1899. Gerhard Peters and John T. Woolley, *The American Presidency Project*, http://www.presidency.ucsb.edu/ws/?pid=29540 (accessed 9 May 2014).

19. "The Trip to Havana," Langston Hughes Papers, Beinecke Rare Book and Manuscript Library, box 492, folder 12436. Hughes's diary of his 1930 trip is full of descriptions of music and the spaces he hears it: of the *son* he writes, "The songs are double in meaning (very dirty often), they are sung to a tropic, mournful rhythm." He visits Club Occidente, where he describes the orchestra with a poetic reverie plus a political critique: "blazing trumpet. Drums like fury; like anger; like violent death. A black orchestra but no black dancers."

20. Redmond, *Anthem*, 1, 13–15.

21. Kutzinski, "'Yo también soy América'," 567.

22. This joking demand took the form of bawdy locker-room banter from Guillén to Hughes quoting their friend José Antonio Fernández de Castro on a recent love interest, using a variety of variously-untranslatable sexual metaphors: Fernández, reports Guillén, was severely broken up over the departure of a women he described as "su 'pelota,' su 'huesito santo' y el 'empapayamiento de su vida.'" Guillén then tells his friend parenthetically: "'¿No entiendes? Pues sufra! Aprenda hablar en criollo." (You don't understand? Then suffer! Learn to speak *criollo*.) Guillén to Hughes, 21 Apr. 1930, Langston Hughes Papers. James Weldon Johnson Collection in the Yale Collection of American Literature, Beinecke Rare Book and Manuscript Library.

23. See the Septeto Nacional's 1927 classic, "Esas no son cubanas" (Those are not Cuban women). For a detailed examination of the form, see Waxer, "Of Mambo Kings," 142–43.

24. Guillén, "Yesterday Somebody Called Me Black," trans. Langston Hughes, and "Last Night Someone Called Me Darky," trans. Ben Carruthers, Hughes Papers, Beinecke Rare Book and Manuscript Library, box 424, folder 94929; Guillén, "Last Night Somebody Called Me Darky," in *Cuba Libre: Poems by Nicolás Guillén.*

25. Apter, *Translation Zone,* 64.

26. Guridy, *Forging Diaspora,* 149, overlooks the critical reception that Hughes received, taking Urrutia's claim about equivalence at face value. In fact, the "diasporic connections" made by Hughes, Guillén, Urrutia, and others were "forged" in a cauldron of anti-imperialist politics that sometimes implicated Hughes himself.

27. Hughes, "To the Little Fort of San Lazaro on the Ocean Front, Havana," in *The Collected Poems of Langston Hughes,* 136.

28. Hughes, *I Wonder as I Wander,* 6.

29. Hughes, "The Trip to Havana," 1930, Hughes Papers, box 492, fol. 12436; "The official daily log book—Jersey to the West Indies—Lang & Zell—via Nazimova," 1931, Hughes Papers, box 492, folder 12437. The authorship of this itinerary is rather ambiguous; the handwriting here appears to be Hughes's, but in *The Life of Langston Hughes,* 201, Rampersad attributes it to Zell Ingram, his traveling companion. I would presume, however, that the two diarists collaborated.

30. Except, as he noted, in the case of Chinese "who do not meet certain requirements," "El incidente Langston Hughes," *Diario de la Marina,* 23 Mar. 1930.

31. Urrutia, "Armonías," *Diario de la Marina,* 9 Mar. 1930.

32. Guillén, "Conversación con Langston Hughes" *Diario de la Marina,* 2 Mar. 1930.

33. Rampersad, *Life of Langston Hughes,* 181; Ellis, "Nicolás Guillén and Langston Hughes," in Brock and Castañeda Fuertes, *Between Race and Empire,* 138.

34. Guillén, "Conversación con Langston Hughes."

35. For Hughes' "Negro," see *Collected Poems of Langston Hughes,* 24.

36. Guillén, "Conversación con Langston Hughes."

37. Guillén, *Sóngoro sosongo,* 18.

38. For the 1929 version of "Pequeña oda," see Guillén, *Obra Poética,* 101; the 1931 version of the poem, with the relevant stanza removed, appeared in *Sóngoro cosongo.*

39. It is worth noting that Guillén, in quoting the poem's English title, leaves the accent off of the "e" in "America," while many of Hughes' Latin American translators rendered this word as "América." This accented América, which

refers to the hemisphere and particularly to Latin America, implies a more inter-American meaning that the poem does not have in the original. Guillén, however, retained the poem's original focus on the United States.

40. Guillén, *Sóngoro sosongo*, 18.

41. Translators like de Jongh, *Vicious Modernism*, 56; De Kaup, "'Our Amer-ica' That Is Not One," 101; and Ellis, "Nicolás Guillén and Langston Hughes," 139, who also notes Guillén's quotation of this poem's final line in his article "Conversación con Langston Hughes," have all misunderstood the poem's ironic ending.

42. Márquez and McMurray, *Man-making Words*, 54–55.

43. The volume is dedicated to Régis Debray, Frantz Fanon, and Angela Davis. Guillén was proclaimed *poeta nacional* in 1961, the same year he became president of the Union of Cuban Writers and Artists (UNEAC), the most impor-tant literary institution in socialist Cuba.

44. Schwartz, "Cuba's Roaring Twenties," in Brock and Castañeda Fuertes, *Between Race and Empire*, 109. Smart and Cobb make a similar argument.

45. "Declaración del Grupo Minorista," *Carteles* 21 (1927), http://www.cubaliteraria.cu/monografia/grupo_minorista/declaracion.html (accessed 5 Mar. 2008).

46. Alberto Arredondo, "El negro y la nacionalidad," *Adelante* (Mar. 1936): 144.

47. Lydia Cabrera, "La influencia africana en el pueblo de Cuba," in Hernandez and Rojas, *Ensayo cubano del siglo XX*, 193–95.

48. De la Fuente, *Nation for All*, 177.

49. Kutzinski, *Sugar's Secrets*, 145, reads *afrocubanismo* as an example of mestizo nationalism's obfuscation of racial conflict, which "had all the makings of a folkloric spectacle whose political effect was to displace and obfuscate actual social problems and conflicts, especially racial ones." For a convincing rebuttal to this thesis, see de la Fuente, *Nation for All*, 185, which argues for the movement's subversive powers. Moore, *Nationalizing Blackness*, 1–3, sees *afrocubanismo* as part of a fundamental "ideological shift" in conceptions of Cuban national identity in the 1920s and 1930s, a product of economic crisis, anti-imperialist sentiment, and the valorization of the vernacular in global modernism. Morejón, *Nación Y mestizaje en Nicolás Guillén*, 154, 166, defends what she calls the "national vocation" of Guillén's poetry, arguing in a Marxist framework that Guillén was not a "negrista" poet in that he does not push for a "cultura negra" or "africana" as such in his work.

50. Guillén, "Prólogo," *Sóngoro cosongo*, 10.

51. Guillén, "El camino a Harlem," *Diario de la Marina*, 21 Apr. 1929, in *Nicolás Guillén: Prosa de Prisa*, 6.

52. Casanova, *World Republic*, 43.

53. Karem, *Purloined Islands*, 163.

54. Hughes, "Negro Artist," 692.

55. Hughes, "Cuban Sculptor," 334.

56. On Machado's repression of Afro-Cuban music, see Sublette, *Cuba and Its Music,* 370; for patronage of *soneros* by the Machado regime, see Moore, *Nationalizing Blackness,* 104.

57. Augier, "Sobre las canciones," 12–14.

58. Guillén, "Son y soneros."

59. Oromundo, "La poesía afrocubana," 24. Oromundo is apparently referring to the poet Edward Silvera.

60. Vasconcelos, *Cosmic Race,* 49.

61. Boti, "La poesía cubana," 352.

62. Johnson, preface to *The Book of American Negro Poetry,* vii.

63. Hughes, "Soledad: A Cuban Portrait," in *The Collected Poems of Langston Hughes,* 57.

6. Latin America in Revolution

1. Walsh, *Each Man,* 89.

2. Carmichael, *Ready,* 586 (italics in original).

3. Reed, *Insurgent Mexico,* 70.

4. Irwin, *Mexican Masculinities,* 129–31.

5. Domínguez-Ruvalcaba, *Modernity,* 63.

6. Kenworthy, "Castro Leaves Big Question Mark."

7. R. H. Davis, *Three Gringos,* 143.

8. Neibaur, *Charley Chase Talkies,* xi.

9. Hooker, "Beloved Enemies," 20. See also Gobat, *Confronting,* 205–6.

10. Augusto Sandino, "Manifiesto, 1 Julio, 1927," in Ramírez, *El pensamiento vivo de Sandino,* 87.

11. Calhoun, "Fighting." The "hard work" in the title refers to that done by the U.S. Marines pursuing Sandino.

12. García Riera, *México visto,* 179. García Riera cites numerous other examples in which revolutionary's names, rather than countries, are subtly shifted

13. Vasey, *World According to Hollywood,* 118–20. Vasey's focus is on the MPDDA, not founded until 1922.

14. Kyne, *Webster—Man's Man,* 66.

15. Hulme, *Cuba's Wild East,* 133.

16. García Riera, *México visto,* 81, 86.

17. O. Henry, *Cabbages and Kings,* 30.

18. Gosse, *Where the Boys Are,* 41; Feeney, "Hollywood in Havana," 226.

19. Aparicio and Chávez-Silverman, "Introduction," in Aparicio and Chávez-Silverman, *Tropicalizations,* 8.

20. This synopsis comes from "Mutual Masterpieces," *The Moving Picture World,* 24 Apr. 1915, 640.

21. *The Moving Picture World,* 24 Apr. 1915, 612–13.

22. L. R. Harrison, "'Captain Macklin'," 739.

23. Hall, "Devil with Women."

24. Collins, "Landscapes," 97.

25. Maya Mendible, "Introduction: Embodying Latinidad: An Overview," in Mendible, *From Bananas to Buttocks*, 9.

26. Emiliano Zapata, operating far from the U.S. border, was fictionalized much less frequently in the United States, although Garcia Riera notes some exceptions: the hybridzed character of Pancho Zapilla, the villain of *The Patriot* (1916) and the bandit *Zapatti* from *The Arizona Cat Claw* (1919), for example.

27. Reed, *Insurgent Mexico*, 126–27. For examples of Villa's representation in U.S. journalism of the day, see Katz, *Life and Times of Pancho Villa*, 323–24; and C. Wilson, "Plotting the Border," 345.

28. Pick, *Constructing the Image*, 93, 69.

29. Carlós Cortés, "To View a Neighbor," 94–95.

30. Alonzo, *Badmen, Bandits*, 53. Alonzo notes that the attribution of the bandit-revolutionary trope to Villa himself can only be made speculatively, since most early western films have been lost.

31. Katz, *Life and Times of Pancho Villa*, 322.

32. De los Reyes, *Con Villa en México*, 41–42; De Orellana, *Filming Pancho*, 43–45; Pick, *Constructing the Image*, 39–41. Citing the text of the contract, held in Mexican archives, Pick disproves the persistent myth that Villa agreed to stage battles in daytime, and even restage them for Mutual if it needed more footage.

33. *Moving Picture World*, 14 July 1914, 20.

34. *Moving Picture World*, "Projection Department," 17 Jan. 1914, 286 (italics in original).

35. *New York Times*, 7 Jan. 1914.

36. "Warfare Is Waged for the Movies," *New York Times*, 8 Jan. 1914.

37. Bush, "Mexican War Pictures," 65.

38. "Right off the Reel," *Chicago Daily Tribune*, 17 May 1914.

39. Weitzer, "'Species of Mexican Man'," 1666.

40. Shull and Wilt, *Doing Their Bit*, 18.

41. Dobson, *Historical Dictionary*, 47.

42. C. Wilson, "Plotting the Border," 341. Besides Andrew Jackson ("Old Hickory") Villa was also compared to Zachary Taylor. Wilson cites a series of photos of Villa with the caption, "Pictures of General Villa that Suggest the Rough-and-Ready Quality of His Leadership," in Marvin, "Villa."

43. Fox, *Fence and the River*, 85, 79.

44. Eng, *Racial Castration*, 8, 11.

45. Berg, *Latino Images*, 76.

46. Gaberscek, "Zapata Westerns"

47. Slotkin, *Gunfighter Nation*, 413, argues that Mexico is the archetypal third-world revolution because it is recognizably American. That is, its revolution can be interpreted and domesticated through familiar tropes and historical analogies like the western hero.

48. Pérez Firmat, *Havana Habit*, 164–65.

49. Rachel Kushner's *Telex from Cuba*—which refers to the rumor of Raúl Castro's homosexuality, but depicts Fidel in a sexual encounter with a male French arms dealer, ex-Nazi, and mercenary—is a more recent rendering of male sexual transgression as a critical commentary on the homoerotics of Castro's *machismo*.

50. Júnior, "Where To?" 3.

51. Foucault, *Abnormal*, 60–61.

52. Cohen, "Monster Theory: Seven Theses," in Cohen, *Monster Theory*, 12 (my italics).

53. Reed, *Insurgent Mexico*, 127.

54. Sandburg, "Memoir of a Proud Boy," in *Cornhuskers*, 50.

55. Gosse, *Where the Boys Are*, 197.

56. Norman Mailer, "The White Negro," *Dissent* (summer 1957), in *Advertisements for Myself*, 304; "Open Letter to Fidel Castro," in Mailer, *Presidential Papers*, 74–75.

57. Gosse, *Where the Boys Are*, 36.

58. Tietchen, "Cubalogues (and After)," 119.

59. Jones, "Cuba Libre," 15.

60. Ferlinghetti, "Poet's Notes on Cuba," 13.

61. Geidel, *Peace Corps Fantasies*, xv; R. Sargent Shriver, "Transcript of Background Press and Radio News Briefing, Monday March 6, 1961, 3:02 p.m.," cited in Geidel, 12.

62. "Interview with Allen Young," in Carter, *Spontaneous Mind*, 328. In a letter to a New York politician, Ginsberg says he only "criticized the police bureaucracy of Cuba for persecution of homosexuals, repressive laws against marijuana use, and harassment of bearded hiply dressed youths." See "Allen Ginsberg to Donald Maness, 22 Dec. 1970, in Morgan, *Letters of Allen Ginsberg*, 360.

63. Elbaum, *Revolution in the Air*, 85. Elbaum describes the Brigades as an important space of movement-building and political education for young radicals, especially those of color, in the United States of the early 1970s.

64. Levinson and Brightman, "Introduction," in *Venceremos Brigade*, 15–16.

65. Ibid., 126–27.

66. Lumsden, *Machos, Maricones*, 65.

67. Lekus, "Queer Harvests," 57.

68. "Reminiscences of Teresa Meade," interview by Ronald J. Grele, 13 Apr. 1984, Columbia University Oral History Research Office, 76–82, cited in Lekus, "Queer Harvests," 67.

69. Larsen, *Reading North by South*, 40, 45. See also Pratt's reading of Joan Didion's similarly titled book of reportage, *Salvador*, in *The Imperial Eye*, 225–27, particularly Didion's trope of the *noche obscura*, which as Pratt writes naturalizes and abstracts the violence of the civil war as the product, not of a specific imperial relation, but of a geographic "heart of darkness."

70. Guevara, "Carta de despedida del Che a Fidel," granma.cu/che/carta/html (retrieved 14 May 2012). In his famous farewell letter to Fidel Castro, Guevara wrote, "en una revolución se triunfa o se muere (si es verdadera)" (in a revolution one either wins or dies [if it is a real one]).

71. J. Berger, "Che Guevara," in *Look of Things,* 46–47.

72. Taylor, "In Memory," 10.

73. Bertholt Brecht, "On Gestic Music," in Willett, *Brecht on Theatre,* 104–5.

74. Meiselas, *Nicaragua,* 57, 23.

75. Taylor, *Archive and the Repertoire,* 19–20.

76. "Interview outtake from *Pictures from a Revolution,* http://www .susanmeiselas.com/latin-america/nicaragua/#id=molotov-man (accessed 16 Oct. 2015).

Coda

1. For example, see David Carr, "The Pendulum of Reporting on Katrina," *New York Times,* 5 Sept. 2005, where he wrote critically of the way in which on cable news, "a third world country had suddenly appeared on the Gulf Coast"; Jeff Koinange, "Katrina: When New Orleans went from developed world to Third World," *CNN.com,* 30 Aug. 2006, http://www.cnn.com/2006/US/08/30/btsc .koinange/index.html?eref=aol (accessed 7 Apr. 2014), which compared the city to Sierra Leone, Uganda, Kenya, and Congo; Alex Alben, "Katrina opened our eyes to America's 'Third World,'" *The Seattle Times,* 29 Sept. 2005, which invokes Tanzania and China. For two other skeptical accounts of the comparison from the popular press at the time, see Mukoma wa Ngugi, "New Orleans and the Third World," *Znet,* 8 Sept. 2005, http://zcomm.org/znetarticle/new-orleans-and-the-third-world-by-mukoma-wa-ngugi/ (accessed 8 Apr. 2014); and Rosa Brooks, "Our Homegrown Third World," *Los Angeles Times,* 7 Sept. 2005.

2. Alfred Sauvy, "Trois Mondes, une planète," *Observateur* 118, 14 Aug. 1952, 14. Shepard, *Invention,* 59.

3. Prashad, *Darker Nations,* xv–xvii.

4. Wright, *Color Curtain,* 12.

5. Ahmad, *In Theory,* 103.

6. Dirlik, "Spectres," 136.

7. Jacobs, *Death and Life,* 307.

8. Whitehall and Johnson, "Making Citizens in Magnaville," in *Neoliberal Deluge,* 64–66.

9. Ferguson, *Anti-Politics Machine,* 64–67; Saldaña-Portillo, *Revolutionary Imagination,* 24–25.

10. Cacho, *Social Death,* 14–15.

11. Waligora-Davis, *Sanctuary,* 139.

12. Joe Pesca, "Are Katrina's Victims 'Refugees' or 'Evacuees?'" *NPR,* 5 Sept. 2005, http://www.npr.org/templates/story/story.php?storyId=4833613 (retrieved 6 Mar. 2014).

13. Clemens, *Punching Out*, 242–66.

14. Chafets, *Devil's Night*, 177.

15. O'Sullivan, "Great Nation," 426.

16. Tinsman and Shukla, "Introduction: Across the Americas," in *Imagining Our Americas*, 19.

17. Robert Costa, "The Speaker Chase: Who's Next?" *Washington Post*, 8. Oct. 2015, https://www.washingtonpost.com/news/post-politics/wp/2015/10/08/the-speaker-chase-whos-next/ (accessed 14 Oct. 2015).

18. O'Grady, "Donald Trump's Latin Role Models."

19. Huffington, *Third World America*.

20. Kristof, "Our Banana Republic." See also Nocera, "Those Banana Republicans"; Krugman, "Austerity Delusion"; and Timothy Noah, "The United States of Inequality: Introducing the Great Divergence," *Slate.com* (accessed 3 Sept. 2010).

21. Gruesz, "Mercurial Space," 144, 151.

22. Connery, "Pacific Rim Discourse," 34; Harootunian, *Empire's New Clothes*, 4.

23. Baca, "Invasions," in *Black Mesa Poems*, 71–72.

24. Villa, "Between Nationalism," 44, 57.

25. Bakhtin, *Dialogic Imagination*, 84.

26. Cervantes, "Freeway 280," in Harris and Aguero, *Ear to the Ground*, 57.

27. Díaz, *Brief Wondrous Life*, 2–4.

28. Gronbeck-Tedesco, *Cuba, the United States*, 4.

29. The White House, "Remarks by President Obama to the People of Cuba," 22 Mar. 2016, https://www.whitehouse.gov/the-press-office/2016/03/22/remarks-president-obama-people-cuba; Ferrer, "Listening to Obama."

30. Ana Dopico, "I'll Be Your Mirror: Obama and the Cuban After-Glow," *Cuba Cargo/Cult*, https://cubacargocult.wordpress.com/ (accessed on 25 Mar. 2016).

31. Díaz, *Brief Wondrous Life*, 5.

Bibliography

Abbott, John S. C. *South and North; or, Impressions Received during a Trip to Cuba and the South*. New York: Abbey & Abbot, 1860.

Acemoglu, Daron, and James A. Robinson. *Why Nations Fail: The Origins of Power, Prosperity, and Poverty*. New York: Crown Business, 2012.

Aching, Gerard. *The Politics of Spanish American Modernismo: By Exquisite Design*. New York: Cambridge University Press, 1997.

Adams, Rachel. *Continental Divides: Remapping the Cultures of North America*. Chicago: University of Chicago Press, 2009.

Ahmad, Aijaz. *In Theory: Classes, Nations, Literatures*. London: Verso Books, 1992.

Alonzo, Juan José. *Badmen, Bandits, and Folk Heroes: The Ambivalence of Mexican American Identity in Literature and Film*. Tucson: University of Arizona Press, 2009.

Alvarez, Ruth M., and Thomas F. Walsh, eds. *Uncollected Early Prose of Katherine Anne Porter*. Austin: University of Texas Press, 1993.

Andreu, Darien Elizabeth. "Sylvester H. Scovel, Journalist, and the Spanish-American War." PhD diss., Florida State University, 2003.

Aparicio, Frances R., and Susana Chávez-Silverman, eds. *Tropicalizations: Transcultural Representations of Latinidad*. Lebanon: University Press of New Hampshire, 1997.

Apter, Emily. *The Translation Zone: A New Comparative Literature*. Princeton, NJ: Princeton University Press, 2006.

Ardao, Arturo. *Génesis de la idea y el nombre de América Latina*. Caracas: Centro de Estudios Latinoamericanos Romulo Gallegos, 1980.

Arndt, H. W. *Economic Development: The History of an Idea*. Chicago: University of Chicago Press, 1987.

———. "Economic Development: A Semantic History," *Economic Development and Cultural Change* 29, no. 3 (1981): 457–66.

Augier, Angel I. "Sobre las canciones de los negros norteamericanos," *Adelante*, June 1936.

Austin, Mary. *Earth Horizon.* Santa Fe, NM: Sunstone Press, 2007.

————. *The Land of Little Rain.* Boston: Houghton, Mifflin and Company, 1904.

Baca, Jimmy Santiago. *Black Mesa Poems.* New York: New Directions, 1989.

Baker, Frank Collins. *A Naturalist in Mexico: Being a Visit to Cuba, Northern Yucatan, and Mexico.* Chicago: David Oliphant, 1895.

Bakhtin, M. M. *The Dialogic Imagination: Four Essays.* Trans. Caryl Emerson and Michael Holquist. Austin: University of Texas Press, 2004.

Balderston, Daniel, and José Quiroga. "A Beautiful, Sinister Fairyland: Gay Sunshine Press Does Latin America," *Social Text* 21, no. 3 (2003): 85–108.

Baldwin, James. *Nobody Knows My Name.* New York: Vintage, 1993.

Ballou, Maturin Murray. *Due South; or, Cuba Past and Present.* Boston: Houghton Mifflin and Co., 1885.

Bangs, John Kendrick. *Uncle Sam, Trustee.* New York: Riggs Publishing Company, 1902.

Barclay, George Lippard. *Little Cuba: Or, Circumstantial Evidence.* Philadelphia, PA: Barclay & Co., 1873.

Bauer, Ralph. "Early American Literature and American Literary History at the 'Hemispheric Turn,'" *American Literary History* 22, no. 10 (2010) 250–65.

Beals, Carlton. *The Crime of Cuba.* Philadelphia, PA: J.B. Lippincott Company, 1933.

————. *Fire on the Andes.* Philadelphia, PA: J.B. Lippincott Co., 1934.

Beals, Carlton, et al., *What the South Americans Think of Us: A Symposium by Carleton Beals, Bryce Oliver, Herschel Brickell and Samuel Guy Inman.* New York: R.M. McBride & Company, 1945.

Benjamin, Walter. *Illuminations.* Translated by Harry Zohn. London: Schocken Books, 1999.

Benson, Wilfrid. *The Economic Basis of Peace.* London: National Peace Council, 1942.

Berg, Charles Ramírez. *Latino Images in Film: Stereotypes, Subversion, and Resistance.* Austin: University of Texas Press, 2002.

Berger, Dina, and Andrew Grant Wood, eds. *Holiday in Mexico: Critical Reflections on Tourism and Tourist Encounters.* Durham, NC: Duke University Press, 2009.

Berger, John. *The Look of Things: Essays by John Berger.* New York: Viking, 1971.

Berger, Mark T. "Review of Park, James William, *Latin American Underdevelopment: A History of Perspectives in the United States, 1870–1965.*" *H-LatAm, H-Net Reviews* (Dec. 1995).

Bernadete, M. J., ed. *Waldo Frank in America Hispana.* New York: Instituto de las Españas en los Estados Unidos, 1930.

Betancourt Cisneros, Gaspar. *Cartas Del Lugareño (Gaspar Betancourt Cisneros).* Ed. Federico de Córdoba. Havana, Cuba: Publicaciones del Ministerio de Cultura, 1951.

Blake, Casey. *Beloved Community: The Cultural Criticism of Randolph Bourne, Van Wyck Brooks, Waldo Frank, and Lewis Mumford.* Chapel Hill: University of North Carolina Press, 1990.

Blanco, Maria del Pilar. *Ghost-Watching American Modernity: Haunting, Landscape, and the Hemispheric Imagination.* New York: Fordham University Press, 2012.

Bland, William. *The Awful Doom of the Traitor; or the Terrible Fate of the Deluded and Guilty the Awful Doom of the Traitor: Being a Full Disclosure of the Character and Selfish Designs of General Lopez, Who Decoyed a Multitude of Our Best and Bravest Citizens to an Awful and Untimely Grave in the Island of Cuba.* Cincinnati, OH: H.M. Rulison, 1851.

Bly, Nellie. *Around the World in Seventy-Two Days.* New York: The Pictorial Weeklies Company, 1890.

———. *Six Months in Mexico.* New York: American Publishers Corporation, 1888.

Bonpland, Alexander von Humboldt, and Aimé. *Personal Narrative of Travels to the Equinoctial Regions of the New Continent During the Years 1799–1804, Vol. 1.* Trans. Helen Maria Williams. London: Longman, Hurst, Orme, and Brown, 1814.

Boti, Regino. "La poesía cubana de Nicolás Guillén," *Revista bimestre Cubana* 29 (May–June 1932): 352.

Bourne, Randolph. "Trans-National America," *Atlantic Monthly* (July 1916): 91.

Boyer, Paul. *Urban Masses and Moral Order in America, 1820–1920.* Cambridge, MA: Harvard University Press, 1992.

Brecht, Bertholt, *Brecht on Theatre.* Trans. and ed. John Willett. New York: Hill and Wang, 1964.

Brenner, Anita. *Idols behind Altars: Modern Mexican Art and Its Cultural Roots.* New York: Courier Dover Publications, 2002.

———. "The Petate, a National Symbol," *Mexican Folkways* (June–July 1925): 15.

———. *Your Mexican Holiday: A Modern Guide.* New York: G.P. Putnam's Sons, 1941.

Brock, Lisa, and Digna Castañeda Fuertes, eds. *Between Race and Empire: African-Americans and Cubans before the Cuban Revolution.* Philadelphia, PA: Temple University Press, 1998.

Brooks, Van Wyck. *America's Coming of Age.* New York: B. W. Huebsch, 1915.

———. "On Creating a Usable Past," *The Dial: A Semi-Monthly Journal of Literary Criticism, Discussion, and Information* 64 (11 Apr. 1918): 338.

———. "Young America," *Seven Arts* (Dec. 1916): 147.

Brown, William Wells. *The Black Man, His Antecedents, His Genius, and His Achievements.* New York: Thomas Hamilton, 1863.

Buchanan, James. *Works of James Buchanan, Vol. 8.* Ed. John Bassett Moore. New York: Antiquarian Press, 1960.

Buel, J. W. *Mysteries and Miseries of America's Great Cities, Embracing New*

York, Washington City, San Francisco, Salt Lake City, and New Orleans. San Francisco. A.L. Bancroft & Co., 1883.

Buel, J. W., and Henry Mawsom. *Leslie's Official History of the Spanish-American War: a Pictorial and Descriptive Record of the Cuban Rebellion, the Causes That Involved the United States, and a Complete Narrative of Our Conflict with Spain on Land and Sea.* Washington, DC: Marcus J. Wright, 1899.

Bush, W. Stephen. "Mexican War Pictures: About Two Reels. The Mutual," *Moving Picture World,* 7 Feb. 1914, 65.

Cacho, Lisa Marie. *Social Death: Racialized Rightlessness and the Criminalization of the Unprotected.* New York: NYU Press, 2012.

Calhoun, C. H. "Fighting in Jungle Means Hard Work," *New York Times,* 21 Aug. 1932.

Campbell, Mary B. *The Witness and the Other World: Exotic European Travel Writing, 400–1600.* Ithaca, NY: Cornell University Press, 1991.

Campbell, W. Joseph. *The Year that Defined American Journalism: 1897 and the Clash of Paradigms.* New York: Routledge, 2006.

———. *Yellow Journalism: Puncturing the Myths, Defining the Legacies.* Westport, CT: Praeger 2001.

Carmichael, Stokely, with Ekwueme Michael Thelwell. *Ready for Revolution: The Life and Struggles of Stokely Carmichael.* New York: Scribner, 2003.

Carpentier, Alejo. *Music in Cuba.* Trans. Alan West-Durán. Minneapolis: University of Minnesota Press, 2001.

Carson, W. E. *Mexico: The Wonderland of the South.* New York: Macmillan Company.

Carter, David, ed. *Spontaneous Mind: Selected Interviews 1958–1996.* New York: Harper Collins, 2001.

del Casal, Julián. *Prosas.* Havana, Cuba: Consejo Nacional de Cultura, 1963–64.

Casanova, Pascale. *The World Republic of Letters.* Trans. M. B. DeBevoise. Cambridge, MA: Harvard University Press, 2004.

Casey, Calvert. "Apuntes de Vuelo," *Ciclón* (July 1956): 57–59.

Castellanos, M. Bianet. "Cancún and the Campo: Indigenous Migration and Tourism Development in the Yucatán Peninsula." In *Holiday in Mexico,* ed. Berger and Wood, 241–64.

Castronovo, Russ. "'On Imperialism, see . . .': Ghosts of the Present in *Cultures of American Imperialism,*" *American Literary History* 20 (2008): 437–38.

Cather, Willa. *Death Comes for the Archbishop.* New York: Vintage, 1990.

Césaire, Aimé. *Une Tempête: D'après "La Tempête" de Shakespeare.* Paris: Éditions du Seuil, 1969.

———. *A Tempest.* Trans. Philip Crispin. London: Oberon Books, 2000.

Chafets, Ze'ev. *Devil's Night: And Other True Tales of Detroit.* New York: Random House, 1990.

Chaffin, Tom. *Fatal Glory: Narciso López and the First Clandestine U.S. War Against Cuba.* Baton Rouge: Louisiana State University Press, 1996.

Champney, Lizzie W. *Three Vassar Girls in South America: A Holiday Trip of Three College Girls Through the Southern Continent, up the Amazon, Down the Madeira, across the Andes, and up the Pacific Coast to Panama.* Boston: Estes and Lauriat, 1885.

Chase, Stuart. *Mexico: A Study of Two Americas.* New York: The Literary Guild, 1931.

"Church's 'Heart of the Andes,'" *Cosmopolitan Art Journal* 3 (June 1859): 133.

Cirillo, Vincent J. *Bullets and Bacilli: The Spanish-American War and Military Medicine.* New Brunswick, NJ: Rutgers University Press, 2004.

Cisneros y Betancourt, Salvador. *Appeal to the American People on Behalf of Cuba.* New York: Evening Post Job Printing House, 1900.

Clark, George Edward. *Seven Years of a Sailor's Life.* Boston: Adams & Co., 1867.

Clark, Steven. *Travel Writing and Empire: Postcolonial Theory in Transit.* London: Zed Books, 1999.

Clemens, Paul. *Punching Out: One Year in a Closing Auto Plant.* New York: Doubleday, 2011.

Cobb, Martha. *1979. Haiti, Harlem, and Havana: A Comparative Critical Study of Langston Hughes, Jacques Roumain, and Nicolás Guillén.* Washington, DC: Three Continents Press, 1979.

Cocks, Catherine. "The Pleasures of Degeneration: Climate, Race, and the Origins of the Global Tourist South in the Americas," *Discourse* 29, nos. 2–3 (2007) 215–35.

———. *Tropical Whites: The Rise of the Tourist South in the Americas.* Philadelphia: University of Pennsylvania Press, 2013.

———. "The Welcoming Voice of the Southland: American Tourism Across the US-Mexico Border, 1800–1940." In Johnson and Graybill, *Bridging National Borders in North America,* 225–48.

Cohen, Jeffrey Jerome. *Monster Theory: Reading Culture.* Minneapolis: University of Minnesota Press, 1996.

Collier, Paul. *The Bottom Billion: Why the Poorest Countries Are Failing and What Can Be Done About It.* New York: Oxford University Press, 2008.

Collier, T. B. "Development in the Dark Room," *The Journal of the Cincinnati Society of Natural History* 13 (April 1890): 38.

Collins, Lindsey. "Landscapes of Gendered Violence: Male Love and Anxiety on the Railroad." In *Philosophy of the Western,* ed. Jennifer L. McMahon and B. Steve Csaki. Lexington: University of Kentucky Press, 2010.

Conkling, Harold. *Mexico and the Mexicans, or, Notes of Travel in the Winter and Spring of 1883.* New York: Taintor Brothers, Merrill & Co., 1883.

Connery, Christopher L. "Pacific Rim Discourse: The U.S. Global Imaginary in the Late Cold War Years," *boundary 2* 21, no. 1 (1994): 30–56.

Cooppan, Vilashini. *Worlds Within: National Narratives and Global Connections in Postcolonial Writing.* Stanford, CA: Stanford University Press, 2009.

Coronado, Raúl. *A World Not to Come: A History of Latino Writing and Print Culture.* Cambridge, MA: Harvard University Press, 2013.

Cortés, Carlós. "To View a Neighbor: The Hollywood Textbook on Mexico." In *Images of Mexico in the United States,* ed. John H. Coatsworth and Carlos Rico. San Diego: Center for U.S.-Mexican Studies, 1989.

Cosío y Cisneros, Evangelina Betancourt. *The Story of Evangelina Cisneros: Told by Herself.* New York: Continental Publishing Company, 1898.

Cowen, M. P., and R. W. Shenton. *Doctrines of Development.* London: Routledge, 1996.

Coyle, Beverly, and Alan Filreis, eds. *Secretaries of the Moon: The Letters of Wallace Stevens and José Rodriguez Feo.* Durham, NC: Duke University Press, 1986.

Crane, Stephen. "Hunger Has Made Cubans Fatalists," *New York World,* 12 July 1898.

———. *Last Words.* London: Digby, Long & Co., 1902.

———. *Maggie: A Girl of the Streets.* New York: W. W. Norton, 1979.

———. *The Open Boat and Other Stories.* London: W. Heinemann, 1898.

———. "Stephen Crane and Minetta Lane, One of Gotham's Most Notorious Thoroughfares," *Philadelphia Press,* 20 Dec. 1896.

———. "The 'Tenderloin' as it Really Is," *New York Journal,* 25 Oct. 1896.

Crapol, Edward P. "Coming to Terms with Empire: The Historiography of Late-Nineteenth-Century American Foreign Relations," *Diplomatic History* 16, no. 4 (1992): 573–98.

Creelman, James. *On the Great Highway: The Wanderings and Adventures of a Special Correspondent.* Boston: Lothrop, Lee & Shapard Co., 1901.

———. *Venezuela: The Land Where It's Always Summer.* New York: Harper and Brothers, 1896.

Curtis, William Eleroy. *The Capitals of Spanish America.* New York: Harper and Brothers, 1888.

Dalleo, Raphael. *Caribbean Literature and the Public Sphere: From the Plantation to the Postcolonial.* Charlottesville: University of Virginia Press, 2011.

Dana, Richard Henry. *To Cuba and Back: A Vacation Voyage.* Carbondale: University of Southern Illinois Press, 1966.

Davis, Darien J. "Nationalism and Civil Rights in Cuba: A Comparative Perspective, 1930–1960," *The Journal of Negro History* 83, no. 1 (1998): 35–51.

Davis, Richard Harding. *Cuba in War Time.* Lincoln: University of Nebraska Press, 2000.

———. "Our War Correspondents in Cuba and Puerto Rico," *Harpers New Monthly Magazine,* May 1899.

———. *Three Gringos in Venezuela and Central America.* New York: Harper & Bros., 1896.

Davis, Robert Gorham. "Hemingway's Tragic Fisherman: The Story of a Humble Man Who Exceeds his Limits and Accepts his Bitter Defeat," *New York Times,* 7 Sept. 1952.

DeGuzmán, María. *Spain's Long Shadow: The Black Legend, Off-Whiteness, and Anglo-American Empire.* Minneapolis: University of Minnesota Press, 2005.

de Jongh, James. *Vicious Modernism: Black Harlem and the Literary Imagination.* Cambridge: Cambridge University Press, 1990.

De Kaup, Monika. "'Our America' That Is Not One: Transnational Black Atlantic Disclosures in Nicolás Guillén and Langston Hughes," *Discourse* 22, no. 3 (2000): 87–113.

Delany, Martin. *Blake, or the Huts of America.* Boston: Beacon Press, 1971.

Delpar, Helen. *The Enormous Vogue of Things Mexican: Cultural Relations Between the United States and Mexico, 1920–1935.* Tuscaloosa: University of Alabama Press, 1992.

———. *Looking South: The Evolution of Latin Americanist Scholarship in the United States, 1850–1975.* Tuscaloosa: University of Alabama Press, 2008.

Denevan, William M. "The Pristine Myth: The Landscape of the Americas in 1492," *Annals of the Association of American Geographers* 82, no. 3 (1992): 369–85.

Denning, Michael. *Culture in the Age of Three Worlds.* New York: Verso, 2004.

Desnoes, Edmundo. *Punto De Vista.* Havana, Cuba: Instituto del Libro, 1967.

Deutschmann, David, ed. *Che Guevara Reader.* Melbourne, Australia: Ocean Books, 1997.

Diamond, Jared. *Collapse: How Societies Choose to Fail or Succeed.* New York: Penguin, 2011.

Díaz, Junot. *The Brief Wondrous Life of Oscar Wao.* New York: Riverhead Books, 2007.

Didion, Joan. *Miami.* New York: Vintage, 1987.

Dimock, Wai-Chee. *Empire for Liberty: Melville and the Poetics of Individualism.* Princeton, NJ: Princeton University Press, 1989.

Dirlik, Arif. "Spectres of the Third World: Global Modernity and the End of the Three Worlds," *Third World Quarterly* 25, no. 1 (2004) 131–48.

Dixon, Melvin. "South of the South," *Calalloo* 8/10 (1980): 15–16.

Dixon, Thomas, Jr. *The Leopard's Spots: A Romance of the White Man's Burden, 1865–1900.* New York: Doubleday, Page, and Co., 1902.

Dobson, Nichola. *Historical Dictionary of Animation and Cartoons.* Lanham, MD: Scarecrow Press, 2009.

Domínguez-Ruvalcaba, Héctor. *Modernity and the Nation in Mexican Representations of Masculinity: From Sensuality to Bloodshed.* New York: Palgrave-Macmillan, 2007.

Dopico, Ana. "Picturing Havana: History, Vision, and the Scramble for Cuba," *Nepantla: Views from South* 3, no. 3 (2002): 451–93.

Dos Passos, John. *Brazil on the Move.* New York: Doubleday 1953.

Doyle, E. A. *Poems and Lyrics Relating to the Spanish and Cuban War.* Winchester, OH: E. A. Doyle, 1898.

Dromundo, Baltasar. "La poesía afrocubana de Nicolás Guillén," *Adelante,* May 1936.

Dunn, Ballard S. *Brazil, the Home for Southerners: Or, a Practical Account of What the Author, and Others, Who Visited the Country, for the Same Objects, Saw and Did While in That Empire.* New York: Richardson, 1866.

Durand, Elliot. *A Week in Cuba.* Chicago: Belford-Clarke Co., 1891.

Edwards, Brent Hayes. *The Practice of Diaspora: Literature, Translation, and the Rise of Black Internationalism.* Cambridge, MA: Harvard University Press, 2003.

Elbaum, Max. *Revolution in the Air: Sixties Radicals Turn to Lenin, Mao, and Che.* New York: Verso, 2002.

Ellis, Keith. "Nicolás Guillén and Langston Hughes: Convergences and Divergences." In *Between Race and Empire,* ed. Brock and Castañeda Fuertes, 129–67.

Eng, David. *Racial Castration: Managing Masculinity in Asian America.* Durham, NC: Duke University Press, 2001.

Engels, Friedrich, and Karl Marx. *The Marx-Engels Reader.* Ed. Robert C. Tucker. New York: W. W. Norton, 1978.

Escobar, Arturo. *Encountering Development: The Making and Unmaking of the Third World.* Princeton, NJ: Princeton University Press, 1995.

Espinosa, Mariola. *Epidemic Invasions: Yellow Fever and the Limits of Cuban Independence, 1878–1930.* Chicago: University of Chicago Press, 2009.

Evans, R. Tripp. *Romancing the Maya: Mexican Antiquity in the American Imagination, 1820–1915.* Austin: University of Texas Press, 2004.

Fabian, Johannes. *Time and the Other: How Anthropology Makes its Object.* New York: Columbia University Press, 1983.

Feeney, Megan J. "Hollywood in Havana: Film Reception and Revolutionary Nationalism in Cuba Before 1959." PhD diss., University of Minnesota, 2008.

Ferguson, James. *The Anti-Politics Machine: Development, Depoliticization, and Bureaucratic Power in Lesotho.* Minneapolis: University of Minnesota Press, 1994.

Ferlinghetti, Lawrence. *Mexican Night.* San Francisco: New Directions, 1970.

———. "Poet's Notes on Cuba," *Liberation* 6 (Mar. 1961): 13.

Ferrer, Ada. "Listening to Obama in Cuba." Available at *nacla.org,* accessed on 28 Mar. 2016.

Fischer, Sybille. *Modernity Disavowed: Haiti and the Cultures of Slavery in the Age of Revolution.* Durham, NC: Duke University Press, 2004.

Foner, Eric. *A History of Cuba and Its Relations with the United States.* New York: International Publishers, 1962.

Foner, Philip. *The Spanish-Cuban-American War and the Birth of American Imperialism, 1895–1902, Vol. II.* New York: Monthly Review Press, 1972.

Foner, Philip, and Richard C. Winchester, eds. *The Anti-Imperialist Reader: A Documentary History of Anti-Imperialism in the United States, Volume I:*

From the Mexican War to the Election of 1900. New York: Holmes & Meier Publishers, Inc., 1984.

Ford, Isaac Nelson. *Tropical America*. New York: Charles Scribner's Sons, 1893.

Foucault, Michel. *Abnormal: Lectures at the Collége De France, 1974–75*. Trans. Graham Burchell. New York: Verso, 2003.

Fox, Claire. *The Fence and the River: Culture and Politics at the U.S.-Mexico Border*. Minneapolis: University of Minnesota Press, 1999.

———. *Making Art Panamerican: Cultural Policy and the Cold War*. Minneapolis: University of Minnesota Press, 2013.

Franck, Harry Alverson. *Working North from Patagonia: Being the Narrative of a Journey, Earned on the Way, Through Southern and Eastern South America*. New York: The Century Co., 1921.

Frank, Andre Gunder. *The Development of Underdevelopment*. Stockholm, Sweden: Bethany Books, 1991.

Frank, Waldo. *Our America*. New York: Boni and Liveright, 1919.

———. *The Rediscovery of America: An Introduction to a Philosophy of American Life*. New York: Charles Scribner's Sons, 1929.

Freehling, William W. *The Reintegration of American History: Slavery and the Civil War*. New York: Oxford University Press, 1994.

Freeman, Elizabeth. "Introduction," *GLQ: A Journal of Lesbian and Gay Studies* 13, nos. 2–3, 159–76.

Freud, Sigmund. *The Complete Psychological Works of Sigmund Freud*. Trans. and ed. James Strachey. Vol. 17. London: Hogarth Press, 1963.

Frus, Phyllis. *The Politics and Poetics of Journalistic Narrative: The Timely and the Timeless*. New York: Cambridge University Press, 1994.

Fuente, Alejandro de la. *A Nation for All: Race, Inequality, and Politics in Twentieth-Century Cuba*. Chapel Hill: University of North Carolina Press, 2001.

Gaberscek, Carlo. "Zapata Westerns: The Short Life of a Subgenre (1966–1972)," *Bilingual Review/La revista blingue* 29, no. 2/3 (2008): 45–58.

Gandal, Keith. *The Virtues of the Vicious: Jacob Riis, Stephen Crane, and the Spectacle of the Slum*. New York: Oxford University Press, 1997.

Gebhard, David. *Robert Stacy Judd: Maya Architecture and the Creation of a New Style*. Santa Barbara, CA: Capra Press, 1993.

Geidel, Molly. *Peace Corps Fantasies: How Development Shaped the Global Sixties*. Minneapolis: University of Minnesota Press, 2015.

Genovese, Eugene. *The Political Economy of Slavery: Studies in the Economy and Society of the Slave South*. New York: Pantheon Books, 1965.

Gibbes, R. W. *Cuba for Invalids*. New York: W. A. Townsend and Company, 1860.

Giles, Paul. "Commentary: Hemispheric Partiality," *American Literary History* 18, no. 3 (2006): 649–55.

Gilman, Nils. *Mandarins of the Future: Modernization Theory in Cold War America*. Baltimore, MD: Johns Hopkins University Press, 2007.

Gobat, Michel. *Confronting the American Dream: Nicaragua under U.S. Imperial Rule.* Durham, NC: Duke University Press, 2005.

Goldstein, Alyosha. *Poverty in Common: The Politics of Community Action during the American Century.* Durham, NC: Duke University Press, 2012.

González, Aníbal. *Journalism and the Development of Spanish American Narrative.* New York: Cambridge University Press, 2006.

Gosse, Van. *Where the Boys Are: Cuba, Cold War America and the Making of a New Left.* New York: Verso, 1993.

Grandin, Greg. "The Liberal Traditions in the Americas: Rights, Sovereignty, and the Origins of Liberal Multilateralism," *American Historical Review* 117, no. 1 (2012): 68–91.

Gray, Albert Zabriski. *Mexico as It Is, Being Notes of a Recent Tour in That Country.* New York: E. P. Dutton & Company, 1878.

Graybill, Andrew R., and Benjamin Johnson, eds. *Bridging National Borders in North America: Transnational and Comparative Histories.* Durham, NC: Duke University Press, 2010.

Greene, Julie. *The Canal Builders: Making America's Empire at the Panama Canal.* New York: Penguin, 2009.

Greenwood, Willard B. *Smoked Yankees and the Struggle for Empire: Letters from Negro Soldiers, 1898–1902.* Champaign: University of Illinois Press, 1971.

Greeson, Jennifer Rae. *Our South: Geographical Fantasy and the Rise of American Literature.* Cambridge, MA: Harvard University Press, 2010.

Griffin, Megan Jenison. "Jane McManus Storm Cazneau, 1807–1878," *Legacy: A Journal of American Women Writers* 27, no. 2 (2010): 416–32.

Gronbeck-Tedesco, John A. *Cuba, the United States, and Cultures of the Transnational Left 1930–1975.* New York: Cambridge University Press, 2015.

Gruesz, Kirsten Silva. "The Mercurial Space of Central America: New Orleans, Honduras, and the Writing of the Banana Republic." In *Hemispheric American Studies,* ed. Caroline Levander and Robert S. Levine. New Brunswick, NJ: Rutgers University Press, 2007.

Guerra y Sanchez, Ramiro. *Manual De Historia De Cuba.* Havana, Cuba: Editorial Pueblo y Educación, 1985.

Guillén, Nicolás. *Cuba Libre: Poems by Nicolás Guillén.* Trans. Langston Hughes and Ben Frederic Carruthers. Los Angeles: The Ward Ritchie Press, 1948.

———. *Man-Making Words: Selected Poems of Nicolás Guillén.* Trans. and ed. Robert Márquez and David Arthur McMurray. Northampton: University of Massachusetts Press, 1972.

———. *Obra Poética.* Vol. I. Havana, Cuba: Editorial de Arte y Literatura, 1974.

———. *Nicolás Guillén: Prosa De Prisa.* Vol. II. Havana, Cuba: Editorial Arte y Literature, 1975.

———. "Son y soneros," *Diario de la Marina,* 15 June 1930.

———. *Sóngoro Sosongo: Poemas Mulatos.* Havana, Cuba: Úcar, García, y Cía, 1931.

——. *Sóngoro Cosongo: Poemas Mulatos*. Mexico City: Presencia Latino-americana SA, 1931.

Guridy, Frank Andre. *Forging Diaspora: Afro-Cubans and African Americans in a World of Empire and Jim Crow*. Chapel Hill: University of North Carolina Press, 2010.

Gurko, Leo. "The Achievement of Ernest Hemingway," *The English Journal* 41, no. 6 (1952): 296.

Guterl, Matthew Pratt. *American Mediterranean: Southern Slaveholders in the Age of Emancipation*. Cambridge, MA: Harvard University Press, 2008.

——. "Comment: The Futures of Transnational History," *American Historical Review* 118 (2013): 130–39.

Hacque, M. Shamsul. *Restructuring Development Theories and Policies: A Critical Study*. Albany: State University of New York Press, 1999.

Hall, Morduant. "A Devil with Women," *The New York Times*, 20 Oct. 1930.

Halstead, Murat. *The Story of Cuba: Her Struggles for Liberty: The Cause, Crisis and Destiny of the Pearl of the Antilles*. Indianapolis, IN: Heeb Publishing Company, 1896.

Hamment, John C. *Cannon and Camera: Sea and Land Battles of the Spanish American War in Cuba, Camp Life, and the Return of the Soldier*. New York: D. Appleton & Company, 1898.

Hancock, H. Irving. *What One Man Saw: Being the Personal Impressions of a War Correspondent in Cuba*. New York: Street and Smith, 1900.

Hardy, Richardson. *The History and Adventures of the Cuban Expedition, from the First Movements Down to the Dispersion of the Army at Key West, and the Arrest of General Lopez. Also: An Account of the Ten Deserters at Isla De Mugueres*. Cincinnati, OH: Lorenzo Stratton, 1850.

Harootunian, Harry. *The Empire's New Clothes: Paradigm Lost, and Regained*. Chicago: Prickly Paradigm Press, 2004.

Harris, Marie, and Kathleen Aguero, eds. *An Ear to the Ground: An Anthology of Contemporary American Poetry*. Athens: University of Georgia Press, 1989.

Harrison, Brady. *Agent of Empire: William Walker and the Imperial Self in American Literature*. Athens: University of Georgia Press, 2004.

Harrison, Lawrence E. *Underdevelopment Is a State of Mind: The Latin American Case*. Lanham, MD: Madison Books, 2000.

Harrison, Louis Reeves. "'Captain Macklin': An Interesting Four-Reel Majestic Gives Vent to the Prevailing Military Spirit—Story by Richard Harding Davis," *The Moving Picture World*, 1 May 1915, 739.

Harrison, Newton. "To Change Earth's Climate and Freeze Out Spain," *New York Sunday World*, 1 July 1898.

Harvey, Bruce. *American Geographies: U.S. National Narratives and the Representation of the Non-European World, 1830–1865*. Stanford, CA: Stanford University Press.

Harvey, David. *Spaces of Capital: Towards a Critical Geography.* New York: Routledge, 2001.

Hazard, Samuel. *Cuba with Pen and Pencil.* London: Sampson Low, 1873.

———. *Santo Domingo, Past and Present: With a Glance at Hayti.* New York: Harper & Bros., 1873.

Hegel, Georg Wilhelm Friedrich. *The Philosophy of History.* Trans. J. Sibree. New York: The Colonial Press, 1900.

Hemingway, Ernest. *To Have and Have Not.* New York: Scribner, 2003.

———. *The Old Man and the Sea.* New York: Scribner, 2003.

Henry, O. *Cabbages and Kings.* New York: McClure, Phillips, & Co., 1904.

Hernandez, Rafael, and Rafael Rojas, eds. *Ensayo Cubano Del Siglo XX.* Mexico City: Fondo de Cultura Económica, 2002.

Hill, Jane. "Language, Race, and Public Space," *American Anthropologist* 100, no. 3 (1998): 680–89.

Hitchman, James H. "Unfinished Business: Public Works in Cuba, 1898–1902," *The Americas* 31, no. 3 (1975): 355–59.

Hoganson, Kristin L. *Consumers' Imperium: The Global Production of American Domesticity, 1865–1920.* Chapel Hill: University of North Carolina Press.

Hollander, Peter. *Political Pilgrims: Western Intellectuals in Search of the Good Society.* New York: Oxford University Press, 1981.

Hooker, Janet. "Beloved Enemies": Race and Official Mestizo Nationalism in Nicaragua," *Latin American Research Review* 40, no. 3 (2005): 20.

Howe, Julia Ward. *A Trip to Cuba.* Boston: Ticknor and Fields, 1860.

Howells, William Dean. *Literature and Life: Studies.* New York: Harper & Brothers Publishers, 1902.

Hsu, Hsuan. *Geography and the Production of Space in Nineteenth-Century American Literature.* New York: Cambridge University Press, 2010.

Hudson, Linda S. *Mistress of Manifest Destiny: A Biography of Jane McManus Storm Cazneau, 1807–1878.* Austin: Texas State Historical Association, 2001.

Huffington, Arianna. *Third World America: How Our Politicians Are Abandoning the Middle Class and Betraying the American Dream.* New York: Broadway, 2010.

Hughes, Langston. *The Collected Poems of Langston Hughes.* Ed. Arnold Rampersad. New York: Vintage Classics, 1994.

———. "A Cuban Sculptor," *Opportunity,* Nov. 1930, 334.

———. *I Wonder as I Wander.* New York: Thunder's Mouth, 1986.

———. "The Negro Artist and the Racial Mountain," *The Nation,* 23 June 1926, 692.

Hulme, Peter. *Cuba's Wild East: A Literary Geography of Oriente.* Liverpool, UK: Liverpool University Press, 2011.

Humboldt, Alexander von. *The Island of Cuba.* Trans. J. S. Thrasher. Princeton, NJ: Markus Wiener Publishers, 2001.

Huntington, Ellsworth. *Civilization and Climate*. New Haven, CT: Yale University Press, 1915.

Hutchinson, William. *Under the Southern Cross: A Guide to the Sanitariums and Other Charming Places in the West Indies and Spanish Main*. Providence, RI: Ryder and Dearth, 1891.

Indych-López, Anna. *Muralism without Walls: Rivera, Orozco, and Siquieros in the United States, 1927–1940*. Pittsburgh, PA: University of Pittsburgh Press, 2009.

Irwin, Robert McKee. *Mexican Masculinities*. Minneapolis: University of Minnesota Press, 2003.

Jackson, Richard. "The Shared Vision of Langston Hughes and Black Hispanic Writers," *Black American Literature Forum* 15, no. 3 (1981): 89–92.

Jacobs, Jane. *The Death and Life of Great American Cities*. New York: Vintage, 1961.

James, C. L. R. *The Black Jacobins: Toussaint L'Ouverture and the San Domingo Revolution*. New York: Vintage, 1963.

Jennings, Eric T. *Curing the Colonizers: Hydrothereapy, Climatology, and French Colonial Spas*. Durham, NC: Duke University Press, 2006.

Johannssen, Robert Walter. *To the Halls of the Montezumas: The Mexican War in the American Imagination*. New York: Oxford University Press, 1985.

Johnson, Benjamin, and Andrew Graybill, eds. *Bridging National Borders in North America: Transnational and Comparative Histories*. Durham, NC: Duke University Press, 2010.

Johnson, James Weldon, ed. *The Book of American Negro Poetry: Chosen and Edited with an Essay on the Negro's Creative Genius*. New York: Harcourt Brace Jovanovich, 1922.

Johnson, Walter. *Soul by Soul: Life Inside the Antebellum Slave Market*. Cambridge, MA: Harvard University Press, 2003.

Jones, Leroi. "Cuba Libre," *Fair Play for Cuba Committee* (1961).

Joseph, Philip, *American Literary Regionalism in a Global Age*. Baton Rouge: Louisiana State University Press, 2007.

Juergens, George. *Joseph Pulitzer and the New York World*. Princeton, NJ: Princeton University Press, 1966.

Kaplan, Amy. *The Anarchy of Empire in the Making of U.S. Culture*. Cambridge, MA: Harvard University Press, 2002.

———. "Left Alone with America: The Absence of Empire in the Study of American Culture." In *Cultures of United States Imperialism*, ed. Kaplan and Pease, 3–21.

Kaplan, Amy, and Donald Pease, eds. *Cultures of United States Imperialism*. Durham, NC: Duke University Press, 1993.

Karem, Jeff. *The Purloined Islands: Caribbean-US Crosscurrents in Literature and Culture, 1880–1959*. Charlottesville: University of Virginia Press, 2011.

Katz, Friedrich. *The Life and Times of Pancho Villa*. Stanford, CA: Stanford University Press, 1998.

Keim, Randolph DeBenneville. *San Domingo: Pen Pictures and Leaves of Travel, Romance and History. From the Portfolio of a Correspondent in the American Tropics.* Philadelphia, PA: Claxton, Remsen & Haffelfinger, 1870.

Kenworthy, E. W. "Castro Leaves Big Question Mark: Worry About Economic Problems Tempers Capital's Enthusiasm," *New York Times,* 19 Apr. 1959.

Kerouac, Jack. *On the Road.* New York: Penguin, 2002.

Kidd, Benjamin. *The Control of the Tropics.* London: Macmillan, 1898.

Kimball, Richard B. *Cuba and the Cubans: Comprising a History of the Island of Cuba, Its Present Social, Political, and Domestic Condition; Also, Its Relation to England and the United States.* New York: Putnam, 1850.

Klein, Kerwin Lee. *Frontiers of Historical Imagination: Narrating the European Conquest of Native America, 1890–1990.* Berkeley: University of California Press, 1999.

Kristof, Nicholas. "Our Banana Republic," *New York Times,* 7 Nov. 2010.

Krugman, Paul. "The Austerity Delusion," *New York Times,* 24 Mar. 2011.

Kutzinski, Vera. *Sugar's Secrets: Race and the Erotics of Cuban Nationalism.* Charlottesville: University of Virginia Press, 1993.

———. *The Worlds of Langston Hughes: Modernism and Translation in the Americas.* Ithaca, NY: Cornell University Press, 2012.

———. "'Yo también soy América': Langston Hughes Translated," *American Literary History* 18, no. 3 (2006): 567.

Kyne, Peter B. *Webster—Man's Man.* New York: Grosset & Dunlap, 1917.

Laclau, Ernesto. "Feudalism and Capitalism in Latin America," *New Left Review* 67 (1971): 19–38.

Landes, David S. *The Wealth and Poverty of Nations: Why Some Are So Rich and Some So Poor.* New York: W. W. Norton, 1999.

LaRose, Michael, and Germán R. Mejía. *The United States Discovers Panama: The Writings of Soldiers, Scholars, Scientists, and Scoundrels, 1850–1905.* Lanham, MD: Rowman and Littlefield Publishers, 2004.

Larrain, Jorge. *Theories of Development: Capitalism, Colonialism and Dependency.* New York: Wiley, 1991.

Larsen, Neil. *Reading North by South: On Latin American Literature, Culture, and Politics.* Minneapolis: University of Minnesota Press, 1995.

Latham, Michael. *The Right Kind of Revolution: Modernization, Development, and U.S. Foreign Policy from the Cold War to the Present.* Ithaca, NY: Cornell University Press, 2011.

Lazo, Rodrigo. "The Invention of America Again: On the Impossibility of an Archive," *American Literary History* 25, no. 4 (2013): 751–71.

———. *Writing to Cuba: Filibustering and Cuban Exiles in the United States.* Chapel Hill: University of North Carolina Press, 2005.

Leary, John Patrick. "American Studies and the Transnational Ideal," *Criticism* 51, no. 3 (2009): 505–12.

Leite Júnior, Jorge. "Where To? Monstrosity, (Dis)Patholigization, Social (In)

Security, and Transgender Indentities," *Estudos Feministas* 20, no. 2 (2012): 559–68. Trans. Micol Siegel, for the Tepoztlán Institute, 2013.

Lekus, Ian. "Queer Harvests: Homosexuality, the US New Left, and the Venceremos Brigades to Cuba," *Radical History Review* 89 (2004): 57–91.

Le Plongeon, Alice Dixon. *Here and There in Yucatan: Miscellanies.* New York: J. W. Lovell, 1889.

———. *Queen Moo's Talisman: The Fall of the Maya Empire.* New York: P. Eckler, 1902.

Le Riverend, Julio, ed. *Orbita De Fernando Ortíz.* Havana, Cuba: UNEAC, 1973.

de Leuchsenring, Emilio Roig. *Cuba no debe su independencia a los Estados Unidos.* Havana, Cuba: Sociedad Cubana de Estudios Históricos Internacionales, 1950.

Levander, Caroline. "Confederate Cuba," *American Literature* 78, no. 4 (2006): 821–45.

Levinson, Sandra, and Carol Brightman, eds. *Venceremos Brigade: Young Americans Sharing the Life and Work of Revolutionary Cuba.* New York: Simon & Schuster, 1971.

Lewis, David, Dennis Rodgers, and Michael Woolcock, eds. *Popular Representations of Development: Insights from Novels, Films, Television and Social Media.* London: Routledge, 2014.

Lindemann, Marilee. *Willa Cather: Queering America.* New York: Columbia University Press, 2013.

Livingstone, David. "Changing Climate, Human Evolution, and the Revival of Environmental Determinism," *Bulletin of the History of Medicine* 86 (2012).

———. "Climate's Moral Economy: Science, Race and Place in Post-Darwinian British and American Geography." In *Geography and Empire,* ed. Godlewska and Smith. London: Blackwell, 1994.

———. *The Geographical Tradition: Episodes in the History of a Contested Enterprise.* New York: Wiley, 1992.

———. "The Moral Discourse of Climate: Historical Considerations on Race, Place, and Virtue," *The Journal of Historical Geography* 17, no. 4 (1991): 413–34.

Llorente, Antonio Gonzalez Ponce de. *Que es la anexion? consideraciones sobre la pretendida union de la isla de Cuba a la republica de los Estados Unidos de América.* Havana, Cuba: n.p., 1850.

Lobe, Guillermo. *Cartas a Mis Hijos Durante Un Viaje a Los Estados Unidos.* New York: Imprenta de Don Juan de la Granja, 1839.

Lockwood, Allison. *Passionate Pilgrims: The American Traveler in Great Britain, 1800–1914.* Rutherford, NJ: Fairleigh Dickinson University Press, 1981.

López, Marissa K. *Chicano Nations: The Hemispheric Origins of Mexican American Literature.* New York: NYU Press, 2011.

Lott, Eric. *Love and Theft: Blackface Minstrelsy and the American Working Class.* New York: Oxford University Press, 1993.

Lowe, Lisa. *The Intimacies of Four Continents*. Durham, NC: Duke University Press, 2015.

Luce, Henry. "The American Century," *Diplomatic History* 23, no. 2 (1999): 171.

Luis-Brown, David. "An 1848 for the Americas: The Black Atlantic, 'El negro mártir,' and Cuban Exile Anticolonialism in New York City," *American Literary History* 21, no. 3 (2009): 431–63.

Lummins, Charles Fletcher. *The Land of Poco Tiempo*. Charles Scribner's Sons: New York, 1897.

Lumsden, Ian. *Machos, Maricones, and Gays: Cuba and Homosexuality*. Philadelphia, PA: Temple University Press, 1996.

Mackie, J. Milton. *From Cape Cod to Dixie and the Tropics*. New York: G. P. Putnam, 1864.

Mailer, Norman. *Advertisements for Myself*. New York: New American Library, 1960.

———. *The Presidential Papers*. New York: Putnam, 1963.

Manthorne, Katherine Emma. *Tropical Renaissance: North American Artists Exploring Latin America, 1839–1879*. Washington, DC: Smithsonian University Press, 1989.

Mañach, Jorge. *La crisis de la alta cultura en Cuba: indagacion del choteo*. Miami: Ediciones Universal, 1991.

Martí, José. *Obras completas. Vol. 11*. Havana, Cuba: Editorial Nacional de Cuba, 1963–73.

———. *José Martí: Selected Writings*. Trans. Esther Allen. New York: Penguin, 2002.

Marvin, George. "Villa," *World's Work* 28 (July 1914).

Marx, Karl. *Grundrisse*. Trans. Martin Nicolaus. New York: Penguin, 1973.

Mast, Gerald, Marshall Cohen, and Leo Braudy, eds. *Film Theory and Criticism: Introductory Readings*. New York: Oxford University Press, 1992.

Matilda, Julia Louisa (W. M. L. Jay). *My Winter in Cuba*. New York: E. P. Dutton & Co., 1871.

Matthiessen, F. O. *The James Family*. New York: Random House, 1980.

Mawsom, Henry. "A Hot Wave Among the Poor," *Harpers Weekly* 36 (20 Aug. 1892).

May, Robert E. *The Southern Dream of a Caribbean Empire*. Baton Rouge: Louisiana State University Press, 1972.

McClelland, David C. *The Achieving Society*. New York: Free Press, 1967.

McGovern, Eileen. "From Varela to Martí: Four Nineteenth-Century Cuban Émigré Newspapers." PhD diss., Temple University, 1990.

McGuinness, Aims. *Path of Empire: Panama and the California Gold Rush*. Ithaca, NY: Cornell University Press, 2008.

McIntosh, Burr. *The Little I Saw of Cuba*. New York: F. Tennyson Neely, 1899.

Meinig, D.W. *The Shaping of America: A Geographical Perspective on 500 Years of History, Vol. 2: Continental America, 1800–1867*. New Haven, CT: Yale University Press, 1995.

Meiselas, Susan. *Nicaragua: June 1978–July 1979*. New York: Aperture, 2008.

Mendible, Maya, ed. *From Bananas to Buttocks: The Latina Body in Popular Film and Culture*. Austin: University of Texas Press, 2007.

Mermann-Jozwiak, Elisabeth. "Writing Mexico: Travel and Intercultural Encounter in Contemporary American Literature," *Symploke* 17, nos. 1–2 (2009): 95–114.

Merril, Dennis. *Negotiating Paradise: U.S. Tourism and Empire in Twentieth-Century Latin America*. Chapel Hill: University of North Carolina Press, 2009.

Michaels, Walter Benn. *Our America: Nativism, Modernism, and Pluralism*. Durham, NC: Duke University Press, 1995.

Miller, Shawn William. *An Environmental History of Latin America*. New York: Cambridge University Press, 2007.

Milton, Joyce. *The Yellow Kid: Foreign Correspondents in the Heyday of Yellow Journalism*. New York: Harper & Row, 1989.

Moore, Joseph Hampton. *With Speaker Cannon through the Tropics: A Descriptive Story of a Voyage to the West Indies, Venezuela and Panama: Containing Views of the Speaker Upon Our Colonial Possessions*. Philadelphia, PA: The Book Print, 1907.

Morejón, Nancy. *Nación y mestizaje en Nicolás Guillén*. Havana, Cuba: Unión de Escritores y Artistas de Cuba, 1982.

Morelet, Arthur. *Travels in Central America: Including Accounts of Some Regions Unexplored Since the Conquest*. Trans. Mrs. M. F. Squier. New York: Leypoldt, Holt, & Williams, 1871.

Morgan, Bill, ed. *The Letters of Allen Ginsberg*. Cambridge, MA: Da Capo Press, 2008.

Mumford, Lewis. *The Brown Decades: A Study of the Arts in America, 1865–1895*. New York: Harcourt, Brace and Company, 1931.

———. "Orozco in New England," *New Republic* (10 Oct. 1934): 231.

Murphy, Gretchen. *Shadowing the White Man's Burden: U.S. Imperialism and the Problem of the Color Line*. New York: NYU Press, 2010.

Myrdal, Gunnar. *Rich Lands and Poor: The Road to World Prosperity*. New York: Harper and Brotthers, 1957.

Neibaur, James L. *The Charley Chase Talkies, 1929–1940*. Lanham, MD: Scarecrow Press, 2013.

Nisbet, Robert. *Social Change and History: Aspects of the Western Theory of Development*. New York: Oxford University Press, 1969.

Nocera, Joe. "Those Banana Republicans," *New York Times*, 30 Sept. 2013.

O'Grady, Maria Anastasia. "Donald Trump's Latin Role Models," *Wall Street Journal*, 6 Mar. 2016.

Okihiro, Gary Y. *Pineapple Culture: A History of the Tropical and Temperate Zones*. Berkeley: University of California Press, 2009.

Oles, James. *South of the Border: Mexico in the American Imagination, 1914–1947*. Washington, DC: Smithsonian Institution Press, 1993.

Olívares, José de. *Our Islands and Their People as Seen with Camera and Pencil*. St. Louis, MO: N. D. Thompson Publishing Co., 1899.

O'Neill, Kimberly. "On the Limits of History and Hemispheric Literary Studies," *American Literary History* 27, no. 1 (2015): 172–85.

Orellana de, Margarita. *Filming Pancho: How Hollywood Shaped the Mexican Revolution.* Trans. John King. New York: Verso, 2009.

Ortíz, Fernando, ed. *Contra La Anexión.* Havana, Cuba: Instituto Cubano del Libro, 1974.

Ott, Mark P. *A Sea of Change: Ernest Hemingway and the Gulf Stream: A Contextual Biography.* Kent, OH: Kent State University Press, 2008.

Panama Canal Zone Health Department. *Mosquito-Borne Diseases: Issued by the Health Department for Use in the Public Schools of the Canal Zone.* Washington, DC: Government Printing Office, 1914.

Paquette, Robert. *Sugar Is Made with Blood: The Conspiracy of La Escalera and the Conflict Between Empires over Slavery in Cuba.* Middletown, CT: Wesleyan University Press, 1988.

Paravisini-Gebert, Lizabeth. "Oriental Imprisonments: Habaneras as Seen by Nineteenth-Century Women Travel Writers." In *Between Anthropology and Literature: Interdisciplinary Discourse,* ed. Rose De Angelis. London: Routledge, 2002.

Park, James William. *Latin American Underdevelopment: A History of Perspectives in the United States, 1870–1965.* Baton Rouge: Louisiana State University Press, 1995.

Park, Stephen M. *The Pan American Imagination: Contested Visions of the Hemisphere in Twentieth-Century Literature.* Charlottesville: University of Virginia Press, 2014.

Parker, Howard. "*El Nuevo Rivera* / The New Rivera." *Mexican Folkways* (Jan.–Mar. 1932).

Parker, Simon. "Hidden in Plain Sight: Baltimore, *The Wire,* and the Politics of Under-development in Urban America." In *Popular Representations of Development,* ed. Lewis, Rodgers, and Woolcock, 92–109.

Paulmier, Hilah, and Robert Haven Schauffler, eds. *Pan-American Day: An Anthology of the Best Prose and Verse on Pan Americanism and the Good Neighbor Policy.* New York: Dodd, Mead & Company, 1943.

Pérez Firmat, Gustavo. *The Havana Habit.* New Haven, CT: Yale University Press, 2010.

Pérez, Louis. *1898: The United States and Cuba in History and Historiography.* Chapel Hill: University of North Carolina Press 1998.

———. *Cuba and the United States: Ties of Singular Intimacy.* Athens: University of Georgia Press, 2003.

———. *Cuba in the American Imagination: Metaphor and the Imperial Ethos.* Chapel Hill: University of North Carolina Press, 2008.

———. "Incurring a Debt of Gratitude: 1898 and the Moral Sources of United States Hegemony in Cuba," *American Historical Review* 104, no. 2 (1999) 356–98.

Pérez-Torres, Rafael. *Movements in Chicano Poetry: Against Myths, Against Margins*. New York: Cambridge University Press, 1995.

Pick, Zuzana M. *Constructing the Image of the Mexican Revolution: Cinema and the Archive*. Austin: University of Texas Press, 2010.

Pike, Frederick B. *FDR's Good Neighbor Policy: Sixty Years of Generally Gentle Chaos*. Austin: University of Texas Press, 1995.

———. *The United States and Latin America: Myths and Stereotypes of Civilization and Nature*. Austin: University of Texas Press, 1992.

Pollard, Edward A. *Black Diamonds Gathered in the Darkey Homes of the South*. New York: Pudney & Russell, 1859.

Pollard, Josephine. *The History of the United States: Told in One-Syllable Words*. New York: McLoughlin Brothers, 1914.

Portell Vilá, Hermino. *Narciso López y su epoca*, vol. I. Havana: Cultural and Compañia Editorial, 1930.

Porter, Robert. *Industrial Cuba: Being a Study of Present Commercial and Industrial Conditions, with Suggestions as to the Opportunities Presented in the Island for American Capital, Enterprise, and Labor*. New York: The Knickerbocker Press, 1899.

Poyo, Gerald. *"With All and for the Good of All": The Emergence of Popular Nationalism in the Cuban Communities of the United States, 1848–1898*. Durham, NC: Duke University Press, 1989.

Prashad, Vijay. *The Darker Nations: A People's History of the Third World*. New York: The New Press, 2008.

Pratt, Mary Louise. *Imperial Eyes: Travel Writing and Transculturation*. New York: Routledge, 1992.

Preston, Peter W. *New Trends in Development Theory: Essays in Development and Social Theory*. London: Routledge & Kegan Paul, 1985.

Quijada, Mónica. "Sobre el origen y difusión del nombre 'América Latina' (o una variacioón heterodoxa en torno al tema de la construcción social de la verdad)," *Revista de Indias* 58, no. 214 (1998): 595–616.

Quijano, Aníbal, and Immanuel Wallerstein. "Americanity as a Concept, or the Americas in the Modern World-System, *International Journal of Social Sciences* 134 (1992): 549–57.

Rambles in Cuba. New York: Carleton, 1870.

Ramos, Julio. *Divergent Modernities: Culture and Politics in Nineteenth-Century Latin America*. Trans. John D. Blanco. Durham, NC: Duke University Press, 2001.

Rampersad, Arnold. *The Life of Langston Hughes, Volume 1: 1902–1941: I, Too, Sing America*. New York: Oxford University Press, 1986.

Rauch, Basil. *American Interest in Cuba: 1848–1855*. New York: Columbia University Press, 1948.

Rector, Charles. *Beautiful Porto Rico: A Graphic Description of the Garden Spot of the World by Pen and Camera*. Chicago: Laird and Lee, 1898.

Redfield, Robert. *Tepoztlan, A Mexican Village: A Study of Folk Life.* Chicago: University of Chicago Press, 1930.

Redmond, Shana. *Anthem: Social Movements and the Sound of Solidarity in the African Diaspora.* New York: NYU Press, 2013.

Reed, John. *Insurgent Mexico.* New York: International Publishers, 1969.

Retman, Sonnet. *Real Folks: Race and Genre in the Great Depression.* Durham, NC: Duke University Press, 2011.

Reyes, Aurelio de los. *Con Villa en México: testimonios sobre camarógrafos norteamericanos en la revolución, 1911–1916.* Mexico City: Universidad Nacional Autónoma de México, 1985.

Riera, Emilio García. *México visto por el cine extranjero, tomo 2: 1906–1950.* Mexico City: Ediciones Era, 1987.

Riis, Jacob. *The Battle with the Slum.* New York: The Macmillan Company, 1902.

———. *How the Other Half Lives.* New York: Penguin, 1997.

———. *The Making of an American.* New York: The Macmillan Company, 1901.

Rifkin, Mark. *Manifesting America: The Imperial Construction of U.S. National Space.* New York: Oxford University Press, 2009.

Ripley, Elizabeth McHatton. *From Flag to Flag: A Woman's Adventures and Experiences in the South During the War, in Mexico, and in Cuba.* New York: D. Appleton, 1889.

Rivera, Diego. "Painting of Pulquerias/Pintura de Pulquerías," *Mexican Folkways* (June–July 1926): 8.

Robertson, Michael. *Stephen Crane, Journalism, and the Making of Modern American Literature.* New York: Columbia University Press, 1997.

Robinson, Albert Gardner. *The Porto Rico of to-Day: Pen Pictures of the People and the Country.* New York: Charles Scribner's Sons, 1899.

Rodney, Walter. *How Europe Underdeveloped Africa.* Washington, DC: Howard University Press, 1981.

Rodó, José Enrique. *Ariel.* Trans. Margaret Sayers Peden. Austin: University of Texas Press, 1988.

Rohy, Valerie. *Anachronism and Its Others: Sexuality, Race, Temporality.* Albany: SUNY Press, 2009.

Roosevelt, Theodore. *The Strenuous Life: Essays and Addresses.* New York: Charles Scribner's Sons, 1906.

Root, Deborah. *Cannibal Culture: Art, Appropriation, and the Commodification of Difference.* Boulder, CO: Westview Press, 1996.

Ross, Kristin. *Fast Cars, Clean Bodies. Decolonization and the Reordering of French Culture.* Cambridge, MA: The MIT Press, 1996.

Rostow, Walt Whitman. *The Stages of Economic Growth: A Non-Communist Manifesto.* New York: Cambridge University Press, 1965.

Rotker, Susana. *The American Chronicles of José Martí: Journalism and Modernity in Spanish America.* Trans. Jennifer French and Katherine Semler. Hanover, NH: University Press of New England, 2000.

Ruiz, Jason. *Americans in the Treasure House: Travel to Porfirian Mexico and the Cultural Politics of Empire.* Austin: University of Texas Press, 2014.

Ryan, John George. *Life and Adventures of Gen. W.A.C. Ryan, the Cuban Martyr.* New York and Chicago: Scully & Company, 1876.

Sachs, Aaron. *The Humboldt Current: Nineteenth-Century Exploration and the Roots of American Environmentalism.* New York: Penguin, 2007.

Said, Edward. *Orientalism.* New York: Vintage, 1979.

———. *The World, the Text, and the Critic* Cambridge, MA: Harvard University Press, 1984.

Saldaña-Portillo, Maria Josefina. *The Revolutionary Imagination in the Americas and the Age of Development.* Durham, NC: Duke University Press, 2003.

Saldívar, José David. *Border Matters: Remapping American Cultural Studies.* Berkeley: University of California Press, 1997.

Salvatore, Ricardo D. "The Enterprise of Knowledge: Representational Machines of Informal Empire." In *Close Encounters of Empire: Writing the Cultural History of U.S.–Latin American Relation,* ed. Gilbert M. Joseph, Catherine C. LeGrand, and Ricardo D. Salvatore. Durham, NC: Duke University Press, 1998.

Samuels, Gertrude. "Peace Corps Trains in New York," *New York Times,* 21 Oct. 1962.

Sanborn, Helen. *A Winter in Central America and Mexico.* Guatemala City: Popul Vuh Museum, Francisco Marroquín University, 1996.

Sandburg, Carl. *Cornhuskers.* New York: Henry Holt, 1918.

Sandino, Augusto. *El pensamiento vivo de Sandino.* Ed. Sergio Ramírez. San Juan, Costa Rica: Editorial Universitaria Centroamericana, 1980.

Schulten, Susan. *The Geographical Imagination in America, 1880–1950.* Chicago: University of Chicago Press, 2001.

Schwartz, Rosalie. "Cuba's Roaring Twenties: Race Consciousness and the Column 'Ideales de una Raza.'" In *Between Race and Empire,* ed. Brock and Castañeda Fuertes, 104–19.

Schwarz, Roberto. *Misplaced Ideas: Essays on Brazilian Culture.* Trans. and ed. John Gledson. New York: Verso, 1992.

Sears, John F. *Sacred Places: American Tourist Attractions in the Nineteenth Century.* New York: Oxford University Press.

Segur, S. Desmond. "On a Venezuelan Coffee Plantation," *Los Angeles Times,* 11 Aug. 1895.

Semple, Ellen Churchill. *Influences of Geographic Environment: On the Basis of Ratzel's System of Anthropo-Geography.* New York: Henry Holt and Company, 1911.

Shepard, Todd. *The Invention of Decolonization: The Algerian War and the Remaking of France.* Ithaca, NY: Cornell University Press, 2006.

Shriber, Mary Suzanne. *Writing Home: American Women Abroad, 1830–1920.* Charlottesville: University of Virginia Press, 1997.

Sinclair, Upton. *The Jungle*. New York: Doubleday, Page, & Co., 1906.

Slobodian, Quinn. "How to See the World Economy: Statistics, Maps, and Schumpeter's Camera in the First Age of Globalization," *Journal of Global History* 10 (2015): 307–32.

Slotkin, Richard. *Gunfighter Nation: The Myth of the Frontier in Twentieth-Century American Culture*. Norman: University of Oklahoma Press, 1998.

Smart, Ian. *Nicolás Guillén, Popular Poet of the Caribbean*. Columbia: University of Missouri Press, 1990.

Smith, F. Hopkinson. *A White Umbrella in Mexico*. Boston: Houghton, Mifflin, and Company, 1889.

Smith, Harold Frederick. *American Travelers Abroad: A Bibliography of Accounts Published Before 1900*. Lanham, MD: The Scarecrow Press, 1999.

Smith, James Morton, ed. *The Republic of Letters: The Correspondence between Thomas Jefferson and James Madison, 1776–1826, Vol. III*. New York: W. W. Norton, 1995.

Smith, Joseph. *The Spanish-American War: Conflict in the Caribbean and the Pacific, 1895–1902*. London: Longman, 1994.

Smith, Neil. *Uneven Development: Nature, Capital, and the Production of Space*. Athens: University of Georgia Press, 2008.

Smith, Robert F. *What Happened in Cuba? A Documentary History*. New York: Twayne Publishers, 1963.

Soto, Hernando de. *The Mystery of Capital: Why Capitalism Triumphs in the West and Fails Everywhere Else*. New York: Basic Books, 2003.

Spellacy, Amy. "Mapping the Metaphor of the Good Neighbor: Geography, Globalism, and Pan-Americanism during the 1940s," *American Studies* 47 (2006): 39–66.

Spratling, William. *Little Mexico*. New York: Jonathan Cape & Harrison Smith, 1932.

Stacy-Judd, Robert. "Wanted: An All-American Architecture with Ancient Mayan Motifs as a Background," *Architect and Engineer* 115, no. 1 (1933): 2–9.

Stallman, R. W. *Stephen Crane: A Biography*. New York: George Braziller, 1968.

Stallman, R. W., and E. R. Hagemann, eds. *The War Dispatches of Stephen Crane*. New York: New York University Press, 1964.

Steele, James. *Cuban Sketches*. New York: G. P. Putnam's Sons, 1881.

Steele, Janet. *The Sun Shines for All: Journalism and Ideology in the Life of Charles A. Dana*. Syracuse, NY: Syracuse University Press, 1993.

Stepan, Nancy Leys. *Picturing Tropical Nature*. Ithaca, NY: Cornell University Press, 2001.

Stephenson, Charles. *The Cuban Martyrs and Other Poems*. Rock Island, IL: The Union Printing Company, 1874.

Streeby, Shelly. *American Sensations: Class, Empire, and the Production of Popular Culture*. Berkeley: University of California Press, 2002.

Streeten, Paul. *First Things First: Meeting Basic Human Needs in the Developing Countries.* New York: Oxford University Press, 1981.

Sublette, Ned. *Cuba and Its Music: From the First Drums to the Mambo.* Chicago: Chicago Review Press, 2004.

Sundquist, Eric. *To Wake the Nations: Race in the Making of American Literature.* Cambridge, MA: Harvard University Press, 1993.

Talmage, Thomas de Witt. *The Masque Torn Off.* Chicago: Fairbanks, Palmer, and Co., 1882.

Taylor, Diana. *The Archive and the Repertoire: Performing Cultural Memory in the Americas.* Durham, NC: Duke University Press, 2003.

———. "In Memory: Augusto Boal 1931–2009," *TDR: The Drama Review* 53, no. 4 (2009): 10–11.

Terry, T. Philip. *Terry's Guide to Mexico: The New Standard Guidebook to the Mexican Republic.* Boston: Houghton Mifflin Company, 1923.

Tietchen, Todd. "The Cubalogues (and After): On the Beat Literary Movement and the Early Cuban Revolution," *Arizona Quarterly: A Journal of American Literature, Culture, and Theory* 63, no. 4 (2007): 119–52.

Tinnemeyer, Andrea. *Identity Politics of the Captivity Narrative after 1848.* Lincoln: University of Nebraska Press, 2006.

Tinsman, Heidi and Sandhya Shukla, "Introduction: Across the Americas." In *Imagining Our Americas: Toward a Transnational Frame,* ed. Sandhya Shukla and Heidi Tinsman. Durham, NC: Duke University Press, 2007.

Tipps, Dean C. "Modernization Theory and the Comparative Study of Societies: A Critical Perspective," *Comparative Studies in Society and History* 15, no. 2 (1973): 199–226.

Toor, Frances. *New Guide to Mexico.* New York: Crown Publishing, 1948.

———. "Notas sobre este Número/Notes on this Number," *Mexican Popular Arts.* Mexico City: Frances Toor Studios, 1939.

Turner, Frederick Jackson. *Rereading Frederick Jackson Turner: "The Significance of the Frontier in American History" and Other Essays.* New Haven, CT: Yale University Press, 1998.

Twain, Mark. *Life on the Mississippi.* New York: Harper & Son, 1917.

Valenčius, Conevery Bolton. *The Health of the Country: How American Settlers Understood Themselves and Their Land.* New York: Basic Books 2003.

Vasconcelos, José. *The Cosmic Race/ La Raza Cósmica.* Baltimore, MD: Johns Hopkins University Press, 1997.

Vasey, Ruth. *The World According to Hollywood, 1918–1939.* Madison: University of Wisconsin Press, 1997.

Verdad, La. *Cuestión negrera de la isla de Cuba por los editores y colaboradores de La Verdad.* New York: La Verdad, 1851.

Villa, Raul H. "Between Nationalism and Women's Standpoint: Lorna Dee Cervantes's Freeway Poems." In *Stunned into Being: Essays on the Poetry of*

Lorna Dee Cervantes, ed. Eliza Rodríguez y Gibson. San Antonio, TX: Wings Press, 2012.

Waligora-Davis, Nicole A. *Sanctuary: African Americans and Empire.* New York: Oxford University Press, 2011.

Walsh, Raoul. *Each Man in His Time: The Life Story of a Director.* New York: Farrar, Straus and Giroux, 1974.

Waring, George E., Jr. *Street-Cleaning and the Disposal of a City's Wastes: Methods and Results and the Effect Upon Public Health, Public Morals, and Municipal Prosperity.* New York: Doubleday and McClure Co., 1898.

Warner, Charles Dudley. *Our Italy.* New York: Harper & Brothers, 1891.

Warren, Kenneth. "Appeals for (Mis)recognition: Theorizing the Diaspora." In *Cultures of United States Imperialism,* ed. Kaplan and Pease, 392–406.

Waxer, Lise. "Of Mambo Kings and Songs of Love: Dance Music in Havana and New York from the 1930s to the 1950s," *Latin American Music Review / Revista de Música Latinoamericana* 15, no. 2 (1994): 139–76.

Weitzer, Edward. "'A Species of Mexican Man': A Three-Reel Romantic Drama. Written and Produced by Romaine Fielding for the Lubin Company," *Moving Picture World,* 4 Sept. 1915, 1666.

Wexler, Laura. *Tender Violence: Domestic Visions in an Age of U.S. Imperialism.* Chapel Hill: University of North Carolina Press, 2000.

Whitehall, Geoffrey and Cedric Johnson. "Making Citizens in Magnaville: Katrina Refugees and the Neoliberal Erasure of Race." In *Neoliberal Deluge: Hurricane Katrina, Late Capitalism, and the Remaking of New Orleans,* ed. Cedric Johnson. Minneapolis: University of Minnesota Press, 2011.

Wilson, Christopher. "Plotting the Border: John Reed, Pancho Villa, and *Insurgent Mexico.*" In *Cultures of United States Imperialism,* ed. Kaplan and Pease, 340–64.

———. "Stephen Crane and the Police," *American Quarterly* 48, no. 2 (1996): 273–315.

Wilson, Harold, "A Bibliography of American Travellers' Books About Cuba Published Before 1900," *The Americas* 22, no. 4 (1966): 404–12.

Winthrop, Theodore. *A Companion to the Heart of the Andes.* New York: D. Appleton and Company, 1859.

Wisan, Joseph E. *The Cuban Crisis as Reflected in the New York Press (1895–1898).* New York: Octagon Books, 1965.

Witherbee, Sidney, ed. *Spanish-American War Songs: A Complete Collection of Newspaper Verse during the Recent War with Spain.* Detroit, MI: Sidney Witherbee, 1898.

Wright, Irene Aloha. *Cuba.* New York: The Macmillan Company, 1910.

Wright, Richard. *The Color Curtain: A Report on the Bandung Conference.* Jackson, MS: Banner Books, 1994.

Wynter, Syvia. "Is 'Development' a Purely Empirical Concept or also Teleological?:

A Perspective from 'We the Underdeveloped.'" In *Prospects for Recovery and Sustainable Development,* ed. Yansansé, 299–16.

Yansansé, Aguibou Y., ed. *Prospects for Recovery and Sustainable Development in Africa.* Westport, CT: Greenwood, 1996.

Zamora, Lois Parkinson. *The Usable Past: The Reimagination of History in Recent Fiction of the Americas.* New York: Cambridge University Press, 1997.

Ziff, Larzer. *The American 1890s: Life and Times of a Lost Generation.* New York: Viking Press, 1966.

Zolov, Eric. "Latin America in the Global Sixties," *The Americas* 30, no. 3 (2014): 350–62.

———. "Showcasing the Mexico of Tomorrow: Mexico and the 1968 Olympics," *Americas* 61, no. 2 (2004): 159–88.

Index